Mastering
iOS 14 Programming

Fourth Edition

Build professional-grade iOS 14 applications with
Swift 5.3 and Xcode 12.4

Mario Eguiluz Alebicto

Chris Barker

Donny Wals

BIRMINGHAM—MUMBAI

Mastering iOS 14 Programming

Fourth Edition

Associate Group Product Manager: Pavan Ramchandani
Publishing Product Manager: Rohit Rajkumar
Senior Editor: Hayden Edwards
Content Development Editor: Aamir Ahmed
Technical Editor: Deepesh Patel
Copy Editor: Safis Editing
Project Coordinator: Manthan Patel
Proofreader: Safis Editing
Indexer: Manju Arasan
Production Designer: Aparna Bhagat

First published: December 2016
Second Edition: October 2017
Third Edition: October 2018
Fourth Edition: March 2021

Production reference: 1170321

Published by Packt Publishing Ltd.
Livery Place
35 Livery Street
Birmingham
B3 2PB, UK.

ISBN 978-1-83882-284-2

www.packt.com

To my mother, Rosa; my sister, Laura; and my lovely Jasmine. Thanks for pushing me to improve every day, thanks for helping me, and thanks for supporting me along the way. Keep making everyone around you shine with your positivity, energy, and inspiration.

– Mario Eguiluz Alebicto

For my partner, Mandy, who is the strongest and bravest woman I have ever met, and to our beautiful daughter, Madeleine – thank you both for your love and support.

– Chris Barker

Contributors

About the authors

Mario Eguiluz Alebicto is a software engineer with over 15 years of experience in development. He started developing software with Java, later switched to Objective-C when the first iPhone delighted the world, and now, he is working with Swift and involved in backend technologies. He loves to code, build exciting projects, and learn new languages and frameworks.

Apart from software development, Mario loves to travel, learn new hobbies, practice sports, and considers himself a hardcore gamer, which he has been since he was a child.

> *I want to thank my mother, my sister, and my girlfriend, for their love and unconditional support. Also, I want to thank Divij, Aamir, and all the team at Packt for their guidance and work on this book. You all are awesome!*

Chris Barker is an iOS developer and tech lead for fashion retailer N Brown (JD Williams, SimplyBe, Jacamo), where he heads up the iOS team. Chris started his career developing .NET applications for online retailer dabs.com (now BT Shop) before he made his move into mobile app development with digital agency Openshadow (now MyStudioFactory Paris). There, he worked on mobile apps for clients such as Louis Vuitton, L'Oréal Paris, and the Paris Metro. Chris often attends and speaks at local iOS developer meetups and conferences such as NSManchester, Malaga Mobile, and CodeMobile.

Donny Wals is a passionate, curious, iOS developer from the Netherlands. With several years of experience in building apps and sharing knowledge under his belt, Donny is a respected member of the iOS development community. Donny enjoys delivering talks on small and large scales to share his knowledge and experiences with his peers. In addition to sharing knowledge, Donny loves learning more about iOS, Apple's frameworks, and development in general. This eagerness to learn has made him a versatile iOS developer with knowledge of a significant number of Apple's frameworks and tools. During WWDC, you will often find Donny binge-watching the talks that Apple engineers deliver to introduce new features and frameworks.

About the reviewers

Juan Catalan is a software developer with more than 10 years of experience, having started learning iOS almost from the beginning. He has worked as a professional iOS developer in many industries, including industrial automation, transportation, document management, fleet tracking, real estate, and financial services. Juan has contributed to more than 30 published apps, some of them with millions of users. He has a passion for software architecture, always looking for ways to write better code and optimize a mobile app.

Gareth Hallberg is an experienced mobile solutions architect with a demonstrated history of working in the information technology and services industry, skilled in mobile applications, iOS and Android development, and social media.

He's been writing software for over 20 years, focusing mostly on iOS and Android apps since the days of iOS 3 and Android Froyo, using Objective-C and Java before embracing Swift and Kotlin. He doesn't miss the days of retain, release, and auto release but likes to get down close to the metal to create apps that work efficiently and elegantly.

Table of Contents

Preface

1

What's New in iOS 14?

Technical requirements	2
Introducing App Clips	2
App Clip user journey	3
App Clips invocation methods	4
App Clips guidelines	5
Introducing WidgetKit	6
Widgets options	7
Widget guidelines	7
Improvements in augmented reality	8
Improvements in machine learning	9
Core ML Model Deployment, collections, and targeted deployments	9
Model encryption	9
Improvements in user privacy	10
Introducing Swift 5.2	11
Key path expressions as functions	11
Callable values of user-defined nominal types	12

Subscripts can now declare default arguments	13
Lazy filtering order is now reversed	14
New and improved diagnostics	15
Introducing Swift 5.3	16
Multi-pattern catch clauses	16
Multiple trailing closures	18
Synthesized comparable conformance for enum types	19
Increase availability of implicit self in escaping closures when reference cycles are unlikely to occur	20
Type-based program entry points – @ main	21
Use where clauses on contextually generic declarations	22
Enum cases as protocol witnesses	23
Refine didSet semantics	23
Float16	24
Summary	24
Further reading	24

2

Working with Dark Mode

Technical requirements	26	Working with the asset catalog for Dark Mode	44
What is Dark Mode?	26		
Understanding why we would need Dark Mode	26	Using custom adaptive colors	44
		Using custom adaptive images	49
Core developer concepts of Dark Mode	28	**Further exploring Dark Mode**	**52**
Dark mode from inside Xcode	29	Using Dark Mode with SwiftUI	52
Working with views in Dark Mode	**33**	Programatically handling changes with trait collection	53
What are adaptive colors?	34	Specifying an appearance for views, ViewControllers, and windows	55
What are semantic colors?	37	Accessibility in Dark Mode	55
Using the programmatic approach	42		
		Summary	**56**
		Further reading	**57**

3

Using Lists and Tables

Technical requirements	60	**Working with UICollectionView**	**79**
Working with UITableView	**60**	Setting up our collection view	80
Setting up the project	60	Implementing layout with UICollectionViewDelegateFlowLayout	85
Fetching contacts data	64		
Prepping UITableView to display our contacts	67	**Exploring UICollectionView further**	**89**
Understanding protocols and delegation	69	Implementing a custom UICollectionViewLayout	90
Conforming to the UITableView protocols	71	Cell selection in collection views	93
Understanding the custom UITableViewCell override and the reuse identifier	74	**Working with lists in SwiftUI**	**93**
		Creating our first SwiftUI project	94
Exploring UITableView further	**76**	Building a list in SwiftUI	96
Further understanding reuse identifiers	76	The equivalent to creating a custom cell in SwiftUI	98
Prefetching in table views	77		
Cell selection in table views	78	**Summary**	**99**
		Further reading	**99**

4
Creating a Detail Page

Technical requirements	102	Passing data between view	
Implementing navigation with		controllers	111
segues	102	Updating the data loading	112
Creating our new details view	103	Passing the model to the details page	112
Implementing and understanding		Updating our outlets	113
segues	104	Best practices – creating a view model	114
Creating a manual segue	106	Summary	115
Creating our layouts with		Further reading	115
UIStackView	107		
Containing labels in a stack view	108		

5
Immersing Your Users with Animation

Technical requirements	118	Adding vibrancy to animations	132
Using UIView.animate and		Adding dynamism with UIKit	
UIViewPropertyAnimator	118	Dynamics	134
Creating our first animation	119	Customizing view controller	
Working with multiple animations	120	transitions	139
Refactoring with		Implementing a custom modal	
UIViewPropertyAnimator	122	presentation transition	139
Understanding and controlling		Summary	147
animation progress	125		
Interactions with a pan gesture			
recognizer	129		

6
Understanding the Swift Type System

Technical requirements	150	Working with value types	153
Understanding available types		Understanding structs	155
in Swift	150	Understanding enums	157
Working with reference types	150		

Understanding differences in types 158

Comparing value types to reference types 158

Differences in usage 159

Deciding which type to use 162

When should I use a reference type? 162

When to use a value type 163

Summary 164

7

Flexible Code with Protocols, Generics, and Extensions

Technical requirements 166

Understanding and implementing protocols 166

Defining your own protocols 166

Checking for traits instead of types 169

Extending your protocols with default behavior 173

Improving your protocols with associated types 176

Adding flexibility with generics 180

Summary 182

8

Adding Core Data to Your App

Technical requirements 184

Understanding the Core Data stack 184

Adding Core Data to an existing application 186

Creating a Core Data model 189

Creating the models 190

Defining relationships 192

Using your entities 193

Persisting data and reacting to data changes 195

Understanding data persistence 195

Persisting your models 196

Refactoring the persistence code 199

Reading data with a simple fetch request 201

Filtering data with predicates 204

Reacting to database changes 206

Understanding the use of multiple instances of NSManagedObjectContext 212

Refactoring the persisting code 214

Summary 216

Further reading 216

9

Fetching and Displaying Data from the Network

Technical requirements 218
Fetching data from the web
with URLSession 218
Understanding the basics of
URLSession 219

Working with JSON in Swift 222

Updating Core Data objects
with fetched data 225
Implementing the fetch logic 227
Updating a movie with a popularity
rating 231
Visualizing multiple threads 233

Summary 237

10

Making Smarter Apps with Core ML

Technical requirements 240
Understanding machine
learning and Core ML 240
Understanding what machine learning
is 240
Understanding Core ML 242

Combining Core ML and
computer vision 247
Understanding the Vision framework 247
Implementing an image classifier 248

Training your own models with
Create ML 252
Training a Natural Language model 252
Training a Vision model 255

Updating models remotely with
Model Deployment 256
Using the Core ML API to retrieve
collections of models 257
Preparing and deploying the model 259

Encrypting Core ML models 265
Summary 269

11

Adding Media to Your App

Technical requirements 272
Playing audio and video 272
Creating a simple video player 273
Creating an audio player 275
Playing media in the background 282

Recording video and taking
pictures 286
Taking and storing a picture 287
Recording and storing video 289

Manipulating photos with Core
Image 294
Summary 298

12

Improving Apps with Location Services

Technical requirements	300	Subscribing to location changes	305
Requesting a user's location	300	Setting up geofences	308
Asking for permission to access location data	300	Summary	310
Obtaining a user's location	303		

13

Working with the Combine Framework

Technical requirements	312	Understanding Subject	323
Understanding the Combine framework	312	Combining Publishers, Subscribers, and Operators	325
Understanding Publisher	312	Using Operators to build error-proof streams	333
Understanding Subscriber	313	Summary	340
Understanding Operators	317		

14

Creating an App Clip for Your App

Technical requirements	342	Sharing resources and code with the App Clip	351
Introducing App Clips	342	Using Active Compilation Conditions	355
App Clip User Journey	343	Configuring, linking, and triggering your App Clip	357
App Clips Invocation Methods	345	Testing your App Clip Experiences	366
Developing your first App Clip	346	Summary	369
Creating the App Clip's Target	348		

15

Recognition with Vision Framework

Technical requirements	372	Recognizing text in images	376
Introduction to the Vision framework	372	Region of interest	378

Recognizing hand landmarks in real time   382

Understanding hand landmarks   382

Implementing hand detection   384

Summary   393

16
Creating Your First Widget

Technical requirements   396

Introducing widgets and WidgetKit   396

Widget options   398
Widget guidelines   398

Developing your first widget   399

Creating a widget extension   401
Implementing multiple-size widgets   410
Providing the widget with data and configuration   416
Refreshing the widget's data   422

Summary   426

17
Using Augmented Reality

Understanding ARKit   428

Understanding how ARKit renders content   428
Understanding how ARKit tracks the physical environment   429

Using ARKit Quick Look   431

Implementing the ARKit Quick Look view controller   432

Exploring SpriteKit   436

Creating a SpriteKit scene   438

Exploring SceneKit   439

Creating a basic SceneKit scene   439

Implementing an Augmented Reality gallery   442

Adding image tracking   443
Preparing images for tracking   443
Building the image tracking experience   445
Placing your own content in 3D space   449

Summary   454

18
Creating a macOS app with Catalyst

Technical requirements   456
Discovering Mac Catalyst   456

Exploring new Mac Catalyst features   457

Building your first Mac Catalyst app   **458**

Exploring the iPad app   458

Scaling your iPad app for Mac   460
Optimizing your iPad app for Mac   462

Summary   **472**

19

Ensuring App Quality with Tests

Testing logic with XCTest   **474**

Understanding what it means to test code   474
Setting up a test suite with XCTest   478

Optimizing code for testability   **480**

Introducing the question loader   482
Mocking API responses   484
Using models for consistency   489

Gaining insights through code coverage   **493**

Testing the user interface with XCUITest   **497**

Making your app accessible to your tests   497
Recording UI tests   500
Passing launch arguments to your app   501
Making sure the UI updates as expected   503

Summary   **508**

20

Submitting Your App to the App Store

Adding your application to App Store Connect   **512**

Packaging and uploading your app for beta testing   **517**

Preparing your app for launch   **520**
Summary   **523**
Why subscribe?   **525**

Other Books You May Enjoy

Packt is searching for authors like you   **528**

Leave a review - let other readers know what you think   **528**

Index

Preface

The iOS development environment has significantly matured, and with Apple users spending more money in the App Store, there are plenty of development opportunities for professional iOS developers. However, the journey to mastering iOS development and the new features of iOS 14 are not straightforward. This book will help you make that transition smoothly and easily. With the help of Swift 5.3, you'll not only learn how to program for iOS 14, but also how to write efficient, readable, and maintainable Swift code that maintains industry best practices.

Mastering iOS 14 Programming will help you build real-world applications and reflect the real-world development flow. You will also find a mix of thorough background information and practical examples, teaching you how to start implementing your newly gained knowledge.

By the end of this book, you will have gotten to grips with building iOS applications that harness advanced techniques and make the best use of the latest and greatest features available in iOS 14.

Who this book is for

If you're a developer with some experience of iOS programming and want to enhance your skills by unlocking the full potential of the latest iOS version with Swift to build great applications, this book is for you. This book assumes you are somewhat familiar with Swift and iOS development

What this book covers

Chapter 1, What's New in iOS 14, explores the latest APIs just released along with some of the current cutting-edge features available in iOS and the new changes in Swift 5.

Chapter 2, Working with Dark Mode, teaches you how a few easy steps from the start can make all the difference when implementing Dark Mode into either your new or existing iOS app.

Chapter 3, Using Lists and Tables, gets you to grips with how to handle Lists and Tables in iOS – while also explaining the finer details behind what makes them work.

Chapter 4, Creating a Detail Page, takes everything we've learned so far a step further by building out a specific details page for data taken from our Lists and Tables.

Chapter 5, Immersing Your Users with Animation, takes a look, with the foundation of our app set up, at what UIKit has to offer in terms of animation in Swift and iOS.

Chapter 6, Understanding the Swift Type System, allows you to get to grips with the theory behind the Swift type system, which plays a massive part in Swift programming languages.

Chapter 7, Flexible Code with Protocols, Generics, and Extensions, allows you to take the structure of an application that little bit further, learning core principles of software development in Swift.

Chapter 8, Adding Core Data to Your App, introduces Apple's CoreData framework as a way to include a database for user data in your app.

Chapter 9, Fetching and Displaying Data from the Network, shows how to make use of web APIs to fetch and display data.

Chapter 10, Making Smarter Apps with CoreML, explains what machine learning is, how it works, how you can use trained machine learning models in your apps, how you can use Apple's Vision framework to analyze images, and you'll see how it integrates with CoreML for powerful image detection. Lastly, you'll learn how to use the new CreateML tool to train your own models.

Chapter 11, Adding Media to Your App, covers playing back audio and video, taking photos, and extracting depth data from photos when available.

Chapter 12, Improving Apps with Location Services, shows several ways that apps can implement location tracking to enhance and improve a user's experience.

Chapter 13, Working with the Combine Framework, covers the Combine framework, allowing you to learn and understand the fundamentals of event-driven programming, including why and how we'd use it in our day-to-day applications.

Chapter 14, Creating an App Clip for Your App, focuses on creating a new App Clip for an existing app, understanding the restrictions, design guidelines, and options available for it.

Chapter 15, Recognition with Vision Framework, explains the Vision framework and how to recognize text in images and hand landmarks in video streams with iOS 14.

Chapter 16, Creating Your First Widget, focuses on creating a new Widget for an existing app, understanding the different options, sizes, and functionality that can bring to users.

Chapter 17, Using Augmented Reality, introduces ARKit and all its available features, including how to use 3D models and Scene Kit in order to build an augmented reality world for your app.

Chapter 18, Creating a macOS App with Catalyst, teaches Mac Catalyst, a way to develop iPadOS apps to run as native macOS apps. It takes an example project and turns it into a fully functioning macOS app that can be distributed to the Mac App Store.

Chapter 19, Ensuring App Quality with Tests, shows you how to set up tests for iOS applications.

Chapter 20, Submitting Your App to the App Store, demonstrates how to distribute apps to beta testers through TestFlight and how to submit an app for review in order to publish it to the App Store.

To get the most out of this book

All sample code in this book was written in Swift 5.3, at the time of writing Swift 5.4 is the latest release and the book is compatible with the new release, with Xcode 12.4 on a Mac running macOS Big Sur. To follow along with all the examples in this book, you must have at least Xcode 12.4 installed on your machine. It is recommended that you also have at least macOS Big Sur installed on your Mac because not all code samples are compatible with older versions of macOS.

This book assumes that you are somewhat familiar with Swift and iOS development. If you have no experience with Swift at all, it is recommended that you skim through Apple's Swift manual and go over the basics of iOS development. You don't have to be an expert on iOS development yet, but a solid foundation won't hurt you since the pacing of the book is aimed at somewhat experienced developers.

Software/Hardware covered in the book	OS Requirements
Xcode 12.4	macOS Big Sur
Swift 5.3	

If you are using the digital version of this book, we advise you to type the code yourself or access the code via the GitHub repository (link available in the next section). Doing so will help you avoid any potential errors related to the copying and pasting of code.

Download the example code files

You can download the example code files for this book from GitHub at `https://github.com/PacktPublishing/Mastering-iOS-14-Programming-4th-Edition`. In case there's an update to the code, it will be updated on the existing GitHub repository.

We also have other code bundles from our rich catalog of books and videos available at `https://github.com/PacktPublishing/`. Check them out!

Download the color images

We also provide a PDF file that has color images of the screenshots/diagrams used in this book. You can download it here: `https://static.packt-cdn.com/downloads/9781838822842_ColorImages.pdf`.

Conventions used

There are a number of text conventions used throughout this book.

`Code in text`: Indicates code words in text, database table names, folder names, filenames, file extensions, pathnames, dummy URLs, user input, and Twitter handles. Here is an example: "Go ahead and open the project named `CryptoWidget_start` from the code bundle of this chapter."

A block of code is set as follows:

```
func doSomething(completionHandler: (Int) -> Void) {
    // perform some actions
    var result = theResultOfSomeAction
    completionHandler(result)
}
```

When we wish to draw your attention to a particular part of a code block, the relevant lines or items are set in bold:

```
func doSomething(completionHandler: (Int) -> Void) {
    // perform some actions
    var result = theResultOfSomeAction
    completionHandler(result)
}
```

Any command-line input or output is written as follows:

```
$ mkdir css
$ cd css
```

Bold: Indicates a new term, an important word, or words that you see onscreen. For example, words in menus or dialog boxes appear in the text like this. Here is an example: "In the project named `CryptoWidget_start`, go to **File** | **New** | **Target** | **Widget Extension**."

> **Tips or important notes**
> Appear like this.

Get in touch

Feedback from our readers is always welcome.

General feedback: If you have questions about any aspect of this book, mention the book title in the subject of your message and email us at customercare@packtpub.com.

Errata: Although we have taken every care to ensure the accuracy of our content, mistakes do happen. If you have found a mistake in this book, we would be grateful if you would report this to us. Please visit www.packtpub.com/support/errata, selecting your book, clicking on the Errata Submission Form link, and entering the details.

Piracy: If you come across any illegal copies of our works in any form on the Internet, we would be grateful if you would provide us with the location address or website name. Please contact us at copyright@packt.com with a link to the material.

If you are interested in becoming an author: If there is a topic that you have expertise in and you are interested in either writing or contributing to a book, please visit authors.packtpub.com.

Reviews

Please leave a review. Once you have read and used this book, why not leave a review on the site that you purchased it from? Potential readers can then see and use your unbiased opinion to make purchase decisions, we at Packt can understand what you think about our products, and our authors can see your feedback on their book. Thank you!

For more information about Packt, please visit packt.com.

1
What's New in iOS 14?

During WWDC 2020, Apple introduced the new features and improvements included in iOS 14. Using the latest features in your apps can make a huge difference for users in terms of engagement, positive reviews, and overall user experience. It can also lead to other benefits, such as being featured by Apple in the App Store, and having an advantage over competitors' apps in the same category.

Apple made Swift 5.2 available for developers on March 24, 2020. Later in the year, Apple released Swift 5.3. These versions focus on quality and performance improvements, new language features, and increased support for Windows platforms and Linux distributions.

There was another big announcement during WWDC 2020: Apple Silicon. Apple introduced its own processors to the world. Developers can start building apps and ship them by the end of 2020, starting a transition that will last two years. This transition will establish a common architecture across all Apple products. With a common architecture, it will be easier to create apps for the entire Apple ecosystem.

In this chapter, you will learn the basics of two of the most significant new features on iOS 14: App Clips and widgets. We will also cover the latest additions to augmented reality, machine learning, and user privacy. At the end of the chapter, you will learn about the new additions to the Swift language with some code examples.

In this chapter, we're going to cover the following main topics of iOS 14, Swift 5.2, and Swift 5.3:

- Introducing App Clips
- Introducing WidgetKit
- Improvements in augmented reality
- Improvements in machine learning
- Improvements in user privacy
- Introducing Swift 5.2
- Introducing Swift 5.3

Technical requirements

The code for this chapter can be found here: `https://github.com/PacktPublishing/Mastering-iOS-14-Programming-4th-Edition/tree/master/Chapter%201%20-%20Whats%20New`.

If you want to try out Swift 5.2 features as you read through the chapter, you need to install Xcode version 11.4 or later: `https://itunes.apple.com/app/xcode/id497799835`.

Introducing App Clips

App Clips allow users to discover your app in a fast and lightweight manner. With App Clips, a user can quickly use a feature of your app even without having the app installed on their phone. Let's see an example of what an App Clip looks like:

Figure 1.1 – App Clip UI

App Clips should be lightweight, brief, and finish a user task in seconds. Let's see some use cases of App Clips:

- An App Clip to order coffee when you pass by the coffee shop door and tap on an NFC tag.

- An App Clip to rent an electric bike parked in the street, just by scanning a QR code on it. Also, you can use Sign in with Apple and Apple Pay to avoid forms and interface complexities, allowing you to rent the bike in seconds.

- An App Clip to pre-order from the menu in a restaurant and save time while you wait to be seated.

- An App Clip that triggers when you tap around NFC spots in an art gallery or a museum and displays augmented reality scenes on your iPhone.

As you can see, the possibilities with App Clips are endless. Now that we have covered what an App Clip is, we are going to explain the user's journey using an App Clip (from the invocation to the end). We will cover the invocation methods (how to trigger an App Clip to appear). Finally, we will explore the recommended guidelines when building an App Clip.

App Clip user journey

Let's now explore the whole process and steps in more detail, starting from when the user discovers your App Clip to when the user finishes the App Clip journey.

Let's imagine that we have an app to rent electric bikes on the street. There are several stages involved in the App Clip process:

Figure 1.2 – App Clip process and steps

The steps of an AppClip are as follows:

1. **Invocation method**: The App Clip invocation method is how the user can trigger and open an App Clip. For our example with the electric bike rental, a user scans a QR code placed in the bike with their device camera, and the App Clip opens on the home screen. The invocation method, in this case, is the QR code. We will explore more of them later in the chapter.

2. **User Journey**: After the invocation, the App Clip presents some options for the user to choose from (for example, 1-hour rental for $2 and 24-hour rental for $5). The user makes the desired selections inside the App Clip.

3. **Accounts and Payment**: In our rental bike example, our App Clip needs to identify which user is renting the bike, and the user needs to pay for the service. Some App Clips will not require a registered user account nor payment to work; this step is optional.

4. **Full app recommendation**: When the rental of the bike is settled and ready, your App Clip can recommend the user to download your complete app, so the next time the user can use it instead of the App Clip. Suggesting the entire app is an optional step, but it is very much recommended.

Now that we have an overview of the high-level steps of an App Clip, let's review some parts in more detail.

App Clips invocation methods

We have seen that in order to display an App Clip, the user needs to invoke it or discover it. We discussed before that it could be invoked by a QR code, an NFC tag, or a link in a message. Here is a summary of the options available:

- App Clip codes: Each App Clip code includes a QR code and an NFC tag so that a user can scan it with their camera or tap on it. It also works with individual NFC tags and QR codes.

- Safari App Banner

- Links in messages

- Place cards in Maps

- The recently used App Clips category in the new App Library on iOS 14

Let's discuss now the recommended guidelines from Apple when designing and developing your App Clip.

App Clips guidelines

In order to make App Clips effective, lightweight, and easy to use for the user, Apple has several guidelines:

- Focus on the essential task of your app: Suppose that you have a coffee shop app with lots of different features, including allowing the user to collect points, order coffee, save user preferences, buy coffee gift cards, and so on. Your app should not display such a big set of functionalities all at once. The App Clip should only provide the most important task (for this example, just the feature to order coffee). If the user needs more features, they can download the full app.

- App Clips should be fast and easy to use from the start to the end of the process. Avoid using complex UIs, too many menus, detailed views, and other elements that can cause the user to spend too much time on it.

- App Clips should be small in size, so fast to download. Include all the assets necessary inside the App Clip but avoid big downloads.

- Avoid complex user account creation processes in your App Clip. Just '**Sign in with Apple**'.

- Avoid requiring the user to enter complex and error-prone credit card forms and details. When necessary, try using Apple Pay.

- When users finish with the App Clip task, they can't go back to it. Your App Clip can suggest the user install the full app to keep users engaged later on. But do it in a non-intrusive, polite way, for example, after the user journey finishes and without making it mandatory.

- App Clips provide the option to send or schedule notifications up to 8 hours after launch in order to fulfil any required tasks. But it is not recommended to use this feature for purely marketing purposes.

In this section, you have learned what an App Clip is, the journey that a user will go through while using it, the different invocation methods, and the recommended guidelines when building an App Clip for your app. In *Chapter 14, Creating an App Clip for Your App*, we will create an App Clip for an existing app to see a practical example.

Now, let's jump into another exciting new feature that comes with iOS 14: WidgetKit.

Introducing WidgetKit

Users and developers have been requesting a particular feature for years: they all wanted to be able to have widgets on their home screen. Widgets allow users to configure, personalize, and consume little pieces of relevant data from their home screen. They also allow developers to offer users glanceable content and create added value for their apps.

Here is a preview of how a **widget** (in this case Calendar and Reminders widgets) looks on the home screen on the iPhone:

Figure 1.3 – iOS Home screen with Widgets

Now it is possible on iOS 14, macOS 11, and later versions. Developers can create widgets across iOS, iPadOS and macOS using **WidgetKit** and the new **widget API** for SwiftUI.

The **Smart Stack** on iOS 14 contains a set of different widgets, including the ones that the user opens frequently. If the user enables **Smart Rotate**, Siri can highlight relevant widgets within custom stacks.

> **Widgets created on iOS 13 and earlier**
>
> Widgets created before iOS 14 can't be placed on the home screen, but they are still available on the Today View and macOS Notification Center.

After this introduction to the new widgets, let's see what options we have when building a widget and look at the design guidelines from Apple.

Widgets options

Users can place widgets on the home screen or the Today View on iOS, or the Today View on iPad and the Notification Center on macOS.

Widgets come in three sizes: small, medium, and large. Each size should have a different purpose. This means that a bigger version of a widget should not be just the same as the small one but with bigger font and images. The idea of having different sizes for a widget is that the bigger the size, the more information it should contain. For example, a weather widget will provide just the current temperature in the small version, but it will also include a weekly forecast in the medium one.

Users can arrange widgets in different parts of their screen, and even create stack widgets to group them.

In order to develop a widget, developers need to create a new extension for their app: a **widget extension**. They can configure the widget with a timeline provider. A timeline provider updates the widget information when needed.

If a widget needs some configuration (for example, selecting a default city in a weather app, or multiple cities to display in a large weather widget), developers should add a custom Siri intent to the widget extension. Doing so automatically provides the widget with a customization interface for the user.

Widget guidelines

When creating a widget for iOS 14 or macOS 11, take into account the following design guidelines:

- Focus your widget on the feature of your app. If your app is about the stock market, your widget can display the total value of the user's portfolio.

- Each widget size should display a different amount of information. If your cycling tracker widget displays the current calories burned today in the small widget, it can also display the calories per day of the week in the medium widget and add extra information such as km/miles traveled in the large widget.

- Prefer dynamic information that changes during the day to fixed information; it will make your widget more appealing to the user.

- Prefer simple widgets with fewer configuration options, compared to complex widgets with more options.

- Widgets offer tap target and detection, letting the user select and tap on them to open detailed information in the app. Small widgets support a single tap target, medium and large widgets support multiple targets. Try to keep it simple.

- Support dark mode. Also, consider using SF Pro as the font and SF Symbols if needed.

In this section, we have had an introduction to the new widgets and WidgetKit. We have covered the different options available and the design guidelines when building a widget. In the next section, we are going to cover the new improvements and additions to augmented reality in iOS 14.

Improvements in augmented reality

In the new ARKit 4 for iOS 14 and iPadOS 14, there are four big new features:

- **Location Anchors** allow developers to place AR scenes at geographic coordinates. Location Anchors enable users to display those AR experiences at specific locations, landmarks, and places around the world.

- **Extended Face** tracking support allows AR experiences accessible via the front camera in devices with the A12 Bionic chip or a later version.

- **RealityKit** will enable developers to add video textures to any part of the AR scene or AR object. Video textures also include spatialized audio.

- **Scene Understanding** has one objective: to make virtual content interact with the real world. Scene Understanding is a new option set into the `ARView – Environment` object. Scene Understanding contains four options: **Occlusion**, where real-world objects occlude virtual objects; **Receives Lighting**, which allows virtual objects to cast shadows on real-world objects; **Physics**, which enables virtual objects to interact with the real world physically; and **Collision**, which enables collisions between virtual objects and real-world objects.

> **Note**
> Activating the **Receives Lighting** option automatically turns on **Occlusion**.
> Activating the **Physics** option automatically turns on **Collision**.

In this section, we have seen the improvements in augmented reality. Let's now review what's new in machine learning.

Improvements in machine learning

Improvements to Core ML presented during WWDC2020 will help developers with the development of their machine learning apps, with improvements that upgrade your app models, secure them, and group them in targeted collections. We are going to cover in this section the new Core ML Model Deployment, the new model collections with targeted deployments, and the new model encryption.

Core ML Model Deployment, collections, and targeted deployments

One of the most significant features introduced in WWDC 2020 for Core ML is **Core ML Model Deployment**. To describe it in simple words, it lets developers update their models on the fly. Developers are no longer required to update the whole app in the AppStore to make changes to their machine learning models. Apps can just download a new `mlmodel` file from the cloud.

Developers will be able to create **machine learning model collections** on the cloud and update them on CloudKit. Apps will download those collections and stay up to date, with no version upgrading process in the middle. However, developers don't control the download process. The app will detect that there is a new model version available and will download it when the system decides it's appropriate (for example, in the background while the phone is locked and charging on a Wi-Fi connection). So, developers should take into account that the model update may or may not be fast or in real time. The operating system will have the last word.

A useful feature of model collections is that they can be targeted to different users (for example, users on devices with varying capabilities, such as iPhones vs iPads). Assigning different models to different users can be done with **targeted deployments** applied to collections. There are six options available to configure and target the model that the device will deploy: language code, device class, operating system, operating system version, region code, and app version.

Model encryption

Starting on iOS 14 and macOS 11, Core ML can automatically encrypt the Core ML models.

Xcode will encrypt the compiled model, `mlmodelc` (not the original `mlmodel`). The decryption happens when the app is instantiated and occurs on the device. Moreover, the decryption result is not stored anywhere; it is just loaded into memory.

More good news on this: Xcode will help you to create an encryption key, associate it with your developer account, and it will be stored in the Apple servers automatically. You can always download a local copy for yourself, but the process is not seamless.

When the encryption key is stored in Apple servers, the file is `.mlmodelkey`. When you want to encrypt your model, you just need to add `--encrypt {YourModel}.mlmodelkey` to the compiler flags. If you prefer using CloudKit, you just need to provide the encryption key when creating the model archive.

The drawback of this process is this: when the app instantiates, it needs to have an internet connection with the Apple servers to download the encryption key and decrypt your model. If for any reason there is no connectivity, you need to implement your fallback process inside the completion errors of the new `{YourModel}.load()` method. The completion handler will throw a `modelKeyFetch` error if the encryption key is not available, and you can act accordingly.

> **Important note**
> You should not include the encryption key in your app bundle. It is not necessary, and it can compromise your data.

In this section, we have discovered how we can upgrade our machine learning models without updating our apps, how we can group models into collections and assign them to a different type of users/devices, and how we can have our models encrypted and keep our machine learning data safe with no effort. In the next section, we are going to cover the additions to user privacy.

Improvements in user privacy

With iOS 14, Apple is giving users more control over their privacy and personal data in different ways:

- The App Store will show the privacy practices of every app, so the user will be able to check them before downloading the app.

- When an app is using the camera or the microphone, an indicator will appear in the top-right corner of the phone indicating it. The Control Center will keep a history of which apps have used them recently.

- Apps can offer users to keep the account they already have but integrate it with **Sign in with Apple**.

- **Approximate Location** is a new option for location services that gives a less accurate location for apps that shouldn't need your exact location.
- Limited Photos library access: users can now grant access to selected photos only instead of to the entire library.

In each new version of iOS, Apple is giving users and developers more and more control over the privacy settings. In this section, we have seen new additions that keep the user location and their photos more private, improvements on letting the user know when an app is using the camera or the microphone, and the addition of extra information about an app's usage of data and privacy on its App Store page. The next section focuses on the changes that Swift 5.2 introduces in the language.

Introducing Swift 5.2

Introduced by Apple (on March 24, 2020), Swift 5.2 has handy features focused on improving the developer experience and providing additional language features. Some of the new language features seem to be oriented toward enhancing the functional programming style. Let's review these new features with some code examples.

Key path expressions as functions

This new feature allows developers to use key path expressions such as \Root.value wherever (Root) -> Value functions are allowed. Let's see it in action.

Let's create a Car struct with two properties, brand and isElectric:

```
struct Car {
    let brand: String
    let isElectric: Bool
}
```

Then, let's instantiate an array of Car structs with two cars, one that's electric and one that's not electric:

```
let aCar = Car(brand: "Ford", isElectric: false)
let anElectricCar = Car(brand: "Tesla", isElectric: true)
let cars = [aCar, anElectricCar]
```

Now, if we want to filter this `cars` array and get only the electric cars in it, we used to do it like this:

```
let onlyElectricCars = cars.filter { $0.isElectric }
```

We could also do it this way:

```
let onlyElectricCarsAgain = cars.filter { $0[keyPath: \Car.
    isElectric] }
```

Now, with Swift 5.2, we are able to do this more briefly:

```
let onlyElectricCarsNewWay = cars.filter(\.isElectric)
```

If you print the results, you will see that the output is the same:

```
print(onlyElectricCars)
print(onlyElectricCarsAgain)
print(onlyElectricCarsNewWay)
```

The output is as follows:

```
[__lldb_expr_5.Car(brand: "Tesla", isElectric: true)]
[__lldb_e xpr_5.Car(brand: "Tesla", isElectric: true)]
[__lldb_expr_5.Car(brand: "Tesla", isElectric: true)]
```

Note that this applies to more cases, such as `map`, `compactMap`, and wherever the `(Root) -> Value` function is allowed.

The **SE-0249** proposal contains all the details behind this change. For additional reference and the motivation behind the proposal, you can check the original document at `https://github.com/apple/swift-evolution/blob/master/proposals/0249-key-path-literal-function-expressions.md`.

Callable values of user-defined nominal types

This new feature allows values that have a method whose base name is `callAsFunction` to be called like a function.

It is easier to explain this concept with a simple example. Let's create a struct called `MyPow` that helps us to calculate the power of a number, given the base number:

```
import Foundation
struct MyPow {
```

```
    let base: Double

    func callAsFunction(_ x: Double) -> Double {
        return pow(base, x)
    }
}
```

Now, we can calculate the `pow` of the `base` just by doing the following:

```
let base2Pow = MyPow(base: 2)
print(base2Pow.callAsFunction(3))
```

This `print` statement will have the following result:

```
8.0
```

Now, with Swift 5.2, we can calculate the `pow` of the `base` but using this method instead:

```
print(base2Pow(3))
```

This results in the same output:

```
8.0
```

The Swift **SE-0253** proposal document contains all the details behind this change. For additional reference and the motivation behind the proposal, you can check the original document at https://github.com/apple/swift-evolution/blob/master/proposals/0253-callable.md.

Subscripts can now declare default arguments

When declaring a subscript, we are now able to assign a default value for an argument.

Let's see it in action with an example. We create a `Building` struct that contains an array of `String` representing floor names. We add a subscript to get the name of a floor with a given index. If the index doesn't exist, we want to get the default value, `Unknown`:

```
struct Building {
    var floors: [String]

    subscript(index: Int, default default: String = "Unknown")
        -> String {
```

```
        if index >= 0 && index < floors.count {
            return floors[index]
        } else {
            return `default`
        }
    }
}

let building = Building(floors: ["Ground Floor", "1st", "2nd",
    "3rd"])
```

We can see in the following output that when we access index 0 with `building[0]`, we return the value `Ground Floor`:

```
print(building[0])
```

The console output is as follows:

```
Ground Floor
```

And in the following scenario, when we access the index 5 with `building[5]`, we return the value `Unknown`:

```
print(building[5])
```

The console output is as follows:

```
Unknown
```

This code example shows how we can make use of default arguments when using subscripts and how it can be helpful to tackle edge cases.

Lazy filtering order is now reversed

When working with a lazy array and filter, there is a new change in the order of the operations applied to the filters chain. Take a look at the following code:

```
let numbers = [1,2,3,4,5]
    .lazy
    .filter { $0 % 2 == 0 }
    .filter { print($0); return true }
_ = numbers.count
```

In Swift 5.2, this code will print the following:

```
2
4
```

This is because the `.filter { $0 % 2 == 0 }` statement is applied before the `.filter { print($0); return true }` statement.

However, if we execute this code in a Swift version prior to 5.2, we will notice that the order will be the opposite. First, we will print all the numbers; then, we will filter and get only the even ones. The `.filter` statements will execute from bottom to top.

This behavior will change again if we remove `.lazy` from the code. Then, regardless of the Swift version, we will see the output as only 2 and 4. The filters will be applied from top to bottom, as expected.

> **Important note**
> This change can break your code and the logic of your app. Make sure you review for any similar scenario when updating your code to Swift 5.2 or later.

New and improved diagnostics

In Swift 5.2, error messages have improved in quality and precision. In the previous version, the compiler tried to guess the exact location of an error by breaking down expressions into smaller pieces. But this method left some errors out there.

Now the compiler, when encountering failures while trying to infer a type, records the location of those elements. These recordings allow the compiler to detect the exact error later on if needed.

Let's see an example compiled in Swift 5.1 versus Swift 5.2 and the output on each version. Look at this code which contains an error:

```
enum Test { case a, b }

func check(t: Test) {
    if t != .c {
        print("okay")
    }
}
```

In Swift 5.2, we get a clear error in the exact location where it happens, and with an accurate reason:

```
error: Chapter 1.5.playground:14:12: error: type 'Test' has no
   member 'c'
   if t != .c {
          ~ ^
```

As you can see, the compiler is telling us that we are trying to use a member of the enum that doesn't exist, c.

If we try to compile the same code in Swift 5.1, we will see a different (and incorrect) error message:

```
error: binary operator '!=' cannot be applied to operands of
   type 'Test' and '_'
   if t != .c {
      ~ ^  ~~~~~~
```

The improvements in the compiler errors make iOS developers' day-to-day debugging much more comfortable.

In this section, you have learned about the latest additions to the language and the improved diagnostics on Swift 5.2 with code examples. Now, let's jump into the features of Swift 5.3.

Introducing Swift 5.3

Introduced by Apple during 2020, the main goal in Swift 5.3 is to enhance quality and performance and to expand the number of platforms on which Swift is available by adding support for Windows and additional Linux distributions.

Now, let's review some of the new language features.

Multi-pattern catch clauses

With this new feature, Swift will allow multiple error-handling blocks inside a do catch clause. Take a look at the following example.

Imagine that we have a `performTask()` function that can throw different types of `TaskError` errors:

```
enum TaskError: Error {
  case someRecoverableError
  case someFailure(msg: String)
  case anotherFailure(msg: String)
}


func performTask() throws -> String {
  throw TaskError.someFailure(msg: "Some Error")
}


func recover() {}
```

Prior to Swift 5.3, if we want to handle different `TaskError` cases inside a `do catch` block, we need to add a `switch` statement inside the `catch` clause, complicating the code, as follows:

```
do {
  try performTask()
} catch let error as TaskError {
  switch error {
  case TaskError.someRecoverableError:
    recover()
  case TaskError.someFailure(let msg),
       TaskError.anotherFailure(let msg):
    print(msg)
  }
}
```

Now Swift 5.3 allows us to define multiple `catch` blocks so we can make our code more readable, as in the following example:

```
do {
  try performTask()
} catch TaskError.someRecoverableError {
  recover()
} catch TaskError.someFailure(let msg),
```

```
        TaskError.anotherFailure(let msg) {
    print(msg)
  }
```

We no longer need the `switch` inside the `catch` block.

Multiple trailing closures

Since the beginning of Swift, it has supported trailing closures syntax. See this classic example when using the `UIView.animate` method:

```
UIView.animate(withDuration: 0.3, animations: {
  self.view.alpha = 0
}, completion: { _ in
  self.view.removeFromSuperview()
})
```

Here, we were able to apply the trailing closure syntax to the `completion` block to make our code shorter and more readable by extracting `completion` from the parentheses and removing its label:

```
UIView.animate(withDuration: 0.3, animations: {
  self.view.alpha = 0
}) { _ in
  self.view.removeFromSuperview()
}
```

This closure syntax has some side-effects too. It can make our code hard to read if a developer is not used to our methods (think about our own API library that is not as well known as UIKit methods). It also makes the code a bit unstructured.

With Swift 5.3, when we have multiple closures in the same method, we can now extract and label all of them after the first unlabeled parameter:

```
UIView.animate(withDuration: 0.3) {
  self.view.alpha = 0
} completion: { _ in
  self.view.removeFromSuperview()
}
```

Notice how now we have both closures outside of the parentheses, `UIView.`
`animate(withDuration: 0.3)`. Also notice how labeling the `completion` method
makes it easier to understand, and how the code now looks more symmetrical in terms of
structure, with all the closures written in the same way.

Synthesized comparable conformance for enum types

Swift 5.3 allow `enum` types with no associated values or with only `Comparable` values
to be eligible for synthetized conformance. Let's see an example. Before Swift 5.3, if we
wanted to compare the values of an `enum`, we needed to conform to `Comparable`, and
we needed to implement < and `minimum` methods (among other ways to achieve this):

```swift
enum Volume: Comparable {
    case low
    case medium
    case high

    private static func minimum(_ lhs: Self, _ rhs: Self) ->
        Self {
        switch (lhs, rhs) {
        case (.low,    _), (_, .low   ):
            return .low
        case (.medium, _), (_, .medium):
            return .medium
        case (.high,   _), (_, .high  ):
            return .high
        }
    }

    static func < (lhs: Self, rhs: Self) -> Bool {
        return (lhs != rhs) && (lhs == Self.minimum(lhs, rhs))
    }
}
```

This code is hard to maintain; as soon as we add more values to the enum, we need to update the methods again and again.

With Swift 5.3, as long as the enum doesn't have an associated value or it only has a Comparable associated value, the implementation is synthesized for us. Check out the following example, in which we define an enum called Size, and we are able to sort an array of Size instances (without any further implementation of Comparable methods):

```
enum Size: Comparable {
  case small(Int)
  case medium
  case large(Int)
}

let sizes: [Size] = [.medium, .small(1), .small(2), .large(0)]
```

If we print the array with print(sizes.sorted()), we will get this in the console:

```
[.small(1), .small(2), .medium, .large(0)]
```

Note how the order of sorting is the same as the order in which we define our cases, assuming it is an increasing order: .small appears before .large when we sort the values. For instances of the same case that contain associated values (such as .small(Int) and .large(Int)) we apply the same principle when ordering: .small(1) appears before .small(2).

Increase availability of implicit self in escaping closures when reference cycles are unlikely to occur

Sometimes the rule that forced all uses of self in escaping closures to be explicit was adding boilerplate code. One example is when we are using closures within a Struct (where the reference cycle is unlikely to occur). With this new change in Swift 5.3, we can omit self, like in this example:

```
struct SomeStruct {
    var x = 0

    func doSomething(_ task: @escaping () -> Void) {
      task()
    }
}
```

```
func test() {
  doSomething {
    x += 1 // note no self.x
  }
}
}
```

There is also a new way to use `self` in the capture list (just by adding `[self] in`) when needed so that we can avoid using `self` again and again inside the closures. See the following example:

```
class SomeClass {
  var x = 0

  func doSomething(_ task: @escaping () -> Void) {
    task()
  }

  func test() {
    doSomething { [self] in
      x += 1 // instead of self.x += 1
      x = x * 5 // instead of self.x = self.x * 5
    }
  }
}
```

This change reduces the use of `self` in many situations and omits it completely when it is not needed.

Type-based program entry points – @main

Up until now, when developing a Swift program (such as a terminal app), we needed to define the program startup point in a `main.swift` file. Now we are able to mark a struct or a base class (in any file) with `@main` and a `static func main()` method on it, and it will be triggered automatically when the program starts:

```
@main
struct TerminalApp {
  static func main() {
```

```
        print("Hello Swift 5.3!")
    }
}
```

> **Important note**
>
> Take into consideration the following about @main: it should not be used if a
> main.swift file already exists, it should be used in a base class (or struct),
> and it should only be defined once.

Use where clauses on contextually generic declarations

We can use where clauses in functions with generic types and extensions. For example,
look at the following code:

```swift
struct Stack<Element> {
    private var array = [Element]()

    mutating func push(_ item: Element) {
        array.append(item)
    }

    mutating func pop() -> Element? {
        array.popLast()
    }
}

extension Stack {
    func sorted() -> [Element] where Element: Comparable {
        array.sorted()
    }
}
```

We constrained the sorted() method on the extension of this Stack struct to elements
that are Comparable.

Enum cases as protocol witnesses

This proposal aims to lift an existing restriction, which is that enum cases cannot participate in protocol witness matching. This was causing problems when conforming enums to protocol requirements. See the following example of a protocol that defines a `maxValue` variable:

```
protocol Maximizable {
    static var maxValue: Self { get }
}
```

We can make `Int` conform to `Maximizable` like this:

```
extension Int: Maximizable {
  static var maxValue: Int { Int.max }
}
```

But if we try the same with an enum, we will have compile issues. Now it is possible to do this:

```
enum Priority: Maximizable {
    case minValue
    case someValue(Int)
    case maxValue
}
```

This code now compiles properly with Swift 5.3.

Refine didSet semantics

This is a very straightforward change, according to the Swift proposal:

- If a `didSet` observer does not reference the `oldValue` in its body, then the call to fetch the `oldValue` will be skipped. We refer to this as a "simple" `didSet`.

- If we have a "simple" `didSet` and no `willSet`, then we could allow modifications to happen in-place.

Float16

Float16 has been added to the standard library. Float16 is a half-precision (16b) floating-point value type. Before Swift 5.3, we had Float32, Float64, and Float80.

In this section, you have learned about the latest additions to the language in Swift 5.3 with code examples. Now, let's finish with the chapter summary.

Summary

In this chapter, we've covered new features on iOS 14, Swift 5.2, and Swift 5.3. We started by introducing App Clips and the fantastic possibilities they bring to iOS and macOS. We listed some real-world examples and we have learned the different ways to invoke them. We looked at the design guidelines and the streamlined process by using Sign in with Apple and Apple Pay. Later, we jumped into widgets with WidgetKit. We have described how you can create widgets of three different sizes and looked at their design guidelines. We have discovered the new features and improvements in augmented reality and machine learning. Privacy also gets some updates, allowing end users to control what they share in more detail. Finally, we also learned about new language features of Swift 5.2 and Swift 5.3.

In our next chapter, we'll take a look at Dark Mode in iOS 14, covering everything you need to know about it and putting it into practice.

Further reading

- Apple Human Interface Guidelines (App Clips): `https://developer.apple.com/design/human-interface-guidelines/app-clips/overview/`

- Apple Human Interface Guidelines (Widgets): `https://developer.apple.com/design/human-interface-guidelines/ios/system-capabilities/widgets/`

2
Working with Dark Mode

We all love it…well most of us do anyway, and those who do have been asking for it for a while now too. Apple first took the plunge into Dark Mode with macOS Mojave back in 2018, not only changing the way users interacted with the OS but also paving the way for developers to build native dark-themed apps for the first time.

Dark mode for iPhone wasn't announced until WWDC 2019, but we all knew it was coming, and with everything that AppKit had offered, we knew we were in for a treat with what UIKit would have to offer.

In this chapter, we'll cover everything you need to know to get up and running with dark mode in iOS and iPadOS; everything from taking an existing app and making the necessary adjustments to support dark mode, to all the little hidden extras that we can add in when building our app to ensure we give the user the best possible experience. We'll also touch on best practices too – taking note of the little things we can do that allow Dark Mode in UIKit to make our lives so much easier from the start.

The following topics will be covered in this chapter:

- What is Dark Mode?

- Working with views in Dark Mode

- Working with assets

- Further exploring Dark Mode

Technical requirements

For this chapter, you'll need to download Xcode version 11.4 or above from Apple's App Store.

You'll also need to be running the latest version of macOS (Catalina or above). Simply search for Xcode in the App Store and select and download the latest version. Launch Xcode and follow any additional installation instructions that your system may prompt you with. Once Xcode has fully launched, you're ready to go.

Download the sample code from the following GitHub link: `https://github.com/PacktPublishing/Mastering-iOS-14-Programming-4th-Edition`.

What is Dark Mode?

In this section, we'll start by taking a look at what exactly Dark Mode is, how we can use it, and what it can do not only for the end user but also for developers. We'll cover everything from enabling it on our devices to using environment overrides in Xcode and developer options in the simulator.

Understanding why we would need Dark Mode

As I covered in the introduction of this chapter, most of us have been craving dark mode in iOS for a very long time now. Us developers got our Xcode fix back in 2018 – but one of the burning questions I've been asked many times (especially in the past 12 months) is…why?

It could be down to something as simple as the time of the day. Satellite navigation systems have been doing it in our cars for years – as soon as the sun goes down, our system switches, and a more relaxing, subtle version of our road home pops up on our screen – so why not do that for our apps?

Well, it turns out that some apps have already been doing that for a while (to a degree), while not necessarily offering an automatic nocturnal mode. The Twitter app for iOS offered a "dark mode" option long before the WWDC 19 announcement.

Let's stop for a moment and think about the logic behind such a control, along with everything you'd need to change to achieve this. I'm sure a company as big as Twitter has written their own internal framework to handle this, but under the hood, it's basically going look a lot like the following:

```swift
var isDarkMode = false
var profileLabel: UILabel? {
    didSet {
        profileLabel?.textColor = isDarkMode ? .white : .black
    }
}
var profileBackground: UILabel? {
    didSet {
        profileBackground?.textColor = isDarkMode ? .black :
            .white
    }
}
```

Everything will have to be taken into consideration, from the text color to the drop shadows that you might have decorating your UIButton or UIViews.

The background is a massive change to consider too. One common pattern that a lot of iOS developers follow is to quite simply develop a brand-new app on top of a white canvas; from here, we don't need to worry about controlling the background color or keeping track of it with an IBOutlet – it's simply the tablecloth for the rest of our app to sit on.

With implementing a dark mode feature, everything needs to be changed – even asset images that sit proudly on one style of background could be lost in another. Let's take a look at some of the developer features that come bundled with Xcode when implementing Dark Mode.

Core developer concepts of Dark Mode

Let's start by taking a look at how we go about developing with Dark Mode by switching to it on our device. If you've not already done this, you can simply toggle it by going to **Settings | Display & Brightness**, and you should be presented with the following screen:

Figure 2.1 – Display and brightness

You'll also notice the **Automatic** toggle option too, giving us the ability to use either **Sunset to Sunrise** or a custom schedule, which will automatically switch between light and dark appearance (just like our sat nav).

Now that we've got that covered, let's take a look at some options given to developers in the iOS simulator. Let's start by taking the following steps:

1. Open up Xcode.

2. Launch the simulator (**Xcode | Open Developer Tool | Simulator**).

   In a slightly different location than the end user's version of iOS, you'll find the dark toggle under the developer settings (**Settings | Developer | Dark Appearance**):

Figure 2.2 – Dark mode developer settings

Rather than a fancy interface like we saw earlier, we're presented with just the standard toggle. Let's take a look now at what we can do as developers with Dark Mode.

Dark mode from inside Xcode

Now that we've taken a look at how iOS handles switching to dark mode, let's have a look at how we, the developer, can do the same in Xcode.

Out of the box, all new projects building against the iOS 13 SDK will automatically support dark mode; however, building against any earlier SDKs won't.

This helps out a little as your existing app may not have all the necessary tweaks to support dark mode yet and you don't want to release an update to find you have broken your app for those now running dark mode.

However, if you update your project to the iOS 13 SDK, then you could potentially run into this problem, but don't worry, we'll cover getting your existing app ready for dark mode later, in the *Migrating existing apps to Dark Mode* section in this chapter.

Let's start by having a look at storyboards – we all love them (or hate them) but the one thing they have done over the years is present themselves on a whiter-than-white canvas.

Let's get started:

1. Launch Xcode and create a new **Single View - Storyboard** project.
2. Call this anything you want (I'll call mine Chapter 2 - Dark Mode).

    You can either follow along throughout this chapter or download the sample code from GitHub.

Once created, click on **Main.Storyboard** and you should be presented with the following:

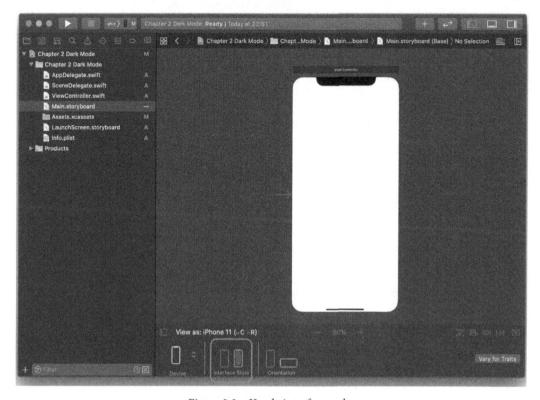

Figure 2.3 – Xcode interface style

I've highlighted in the preceding screenshot our area of interest – here, we have a preview toggle for both light and dark appearances from within the storyboard, so at a quick glance, we can see what the objects we've added to our canvas look like without the need to launch the simulator.

Now, this won't always help us as some of our UILabels or UIButtons could be decorated programmatically. However, it's a great start and will most definitely come in useful during the development cycle of any app.

Let's take a look at our labels in action. Here, we've added a UILabel straight out of the box. **Light Appearance** is selected, and the label looks just how we are used to seeing things at this stage:

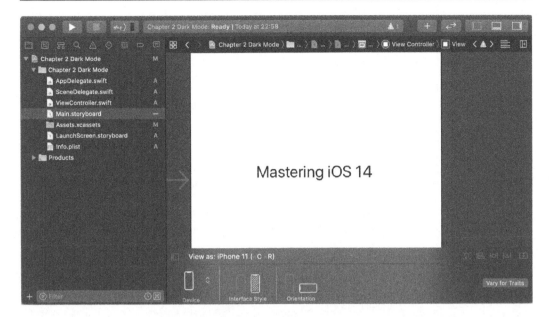

Figure 2.4 – Main storyboard

Now, let's switch the toggle to **Dark Appearance** and see what happens:

Figure 2.5 – Main storyboard – dark mode

As if by magic, our canvas enters dark mode, and the color of our UILabel is automatically adjusted. We can see straight away, without the need to compile or run the app on a device or in the simulator, how it will look with each interface style.

I guess the million-dollar question is *how did iOS know to switch the color of the UILabel's font?* Good question, and we'll cover that in more detail in the *Working with views and Dark Mode* section later in this chapter.

However, as I mentioned earlier, there are going to be occasions where you'll need to test your app in the simulator. Labels and views will not always be static and could be generated dynamically – this is where environment overrides come in.

We'll start by launching our app in the simulator. Once successfully launched, you should see the following highlighted option available in Xcode:

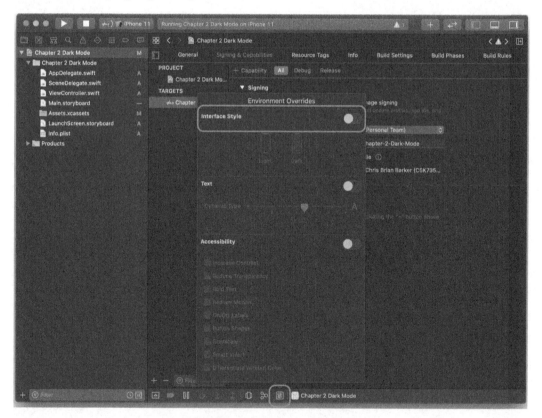

Figure 2.6 – Environment Overrides

Click on this icon and you'll be presented with the **Environment Overrides** popup. Here, you'll have the option to toggle the **Interface Style** overrides, which in turn will allow you to choose between light and dark appearance.

If you flick the toggle and switch between each option, you'll see your app in the simulator automatically update without the need to close your app, change the settings, and re-launch. Very nice indeed – thanks, Xcode!

One last little thing to point out before we move on: we mentioned previously that existing apps built with previous iOS SDKs won't be affected by dark mode, but should you choose to update your app to the iOS 13 SDK, you may run into a couple of issues.

Tight deadlines and urgent bug fixes might not necessarily give you the chance to adopt dark mode in your app, so Xcode gives you the option to force light appearance regardless of the user's preference.

In `Info.plist` (or the **Info** tab under our project settings), add the following key with the value `Light`:

Figure 2.7 – Info.plist – User Interface Style

You'll now see that even with the environment overrides, you won't be able to switch to dark mode.

In this section, we got up and running with Dark Mode in iOS and, more importantly, Xcode, and learned about the little things that Xcode does to get us ready for developing our apps in both light and dark appearance. In the next section, we'll begin to look at how Xcode handles views and introduce ourselves to semantic "dynamic" colors.

Working with views in Dark Mode

So far in this chapter, we've covered not only what dark mode is but also what it has to offer from a development perspective.

In this chapter, we're going to deep dive further into dark mode by looking at how Xcode dynamically handles our UIViews (and objects that are sub-classed from UIViews).

We'll start by understanding the core concept behind adaptive and semantic colors, and by following a simple pattern, Xcode can do so much of the heavy lifting for us.

We'll then dive further and take a look at the various levels of semantic colors available to us, including primary, secondary, and tertiary options, but more importantly, when we would be expected to use them.

What are adaptive colors?

For me, this was a major step in getting developers on board with designing and developing their apps for dark mode and, of course, it was well within Apple's interest to make it as seamless as possible for the developer.

Adaptive colors are a way of defining a single color type or style for a particular appearance. Let's start by diving straight into Xcode and seeing this for ourselves:

1. Head back on over to the project you previously created and highlight the UILabel we added in.

2. Now, take a look at the **Color** property in the **Attributes Inspector** window:

Figure 2.8 – Label properties

You'll notice that the color selected is **Default (Label Color)** – **Label Color** is our adaptive color.

But what does that mean? Actually, it's very simple: it means that for one interface style it's one color, and for the other, it's a different color.

In the case of our previous example, our UILabel was black in light mode and white in dark mode – makes sense, right?

Well, to a degree is does, but surely it depends on what type of background our UILabel sits on – let's take a look.

Back in our storyboard, highlight the background of our view and again head over to the **Attributes Inspector** window:

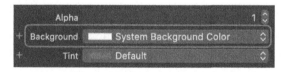

Figure 2.9 – Background color properties

Again, here we have our adaptive color, **System Background Color**. Xcode is doing all the work for us when we need to switch appearances.

The preceding parts in the section are a great example of contrasting between two primary colors (black and white used in our labels), which itself is the stereotypical understanding between what colors should be in light and dark appearance – but we're not always going to be using black or white, are we?

So, Apple has updated all their available system colors to be adaptive. Let's take a look.

Head back over to Xcode and highlight our UILabel, and change **Color** to **System Indigo Color**:

Figure 2.10 – Font color properties

Now, let's switch between light and dark mode using the toggle in Xcode's storyboard. What do we see? The color indigo, just as we expected:

Figure 2.11 – Light mode with Indigo text color

The following screenshot shows the screen with dark mode:

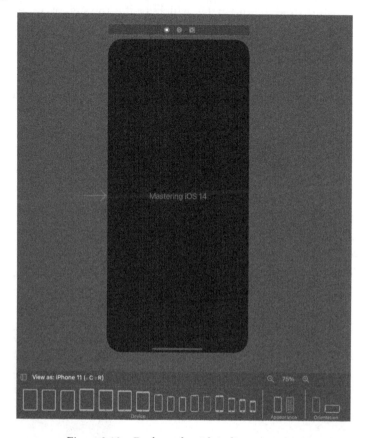

Figure 2.12 – Dark mode with indigo text color

However, each system color has been specifically adapted to each appearance. Let's take a look at the RGB values for each appearance:

- **Dark**: R 94: G 92: B 230
- **Light**: R 88: G 86: B 214

Although there is a subtle difference in each RGB value, it has a massive effect in terms of appearance and allowing it to stand out against other adapted colors defined by Apple (such as our system background color).

Now that we've learned all about adaptive colors, let's take a look at semantic colors and how Apple helps us pre-define not only the colors we want to use but also where a type of color should be used.

What are semantic colors?

To answer the questions of this section requires us to take a quick look back at what we already covered in the *What are adaptive colors?* section, because we've already touched on semantic colors.

Remember **Label Color** from our UILabel and **System Background Color**? These are all semantic colors – not so much by physical color, but more by their definition and intended purpose.

With semantic colors, Apple has created a whole pre-defined range of adaptive colors that are designed specifically for objects such as labels, backgrounds, and grouped content such as table views. Each of these has additional primary, secondary, and tertiary variants.

Let's put this into practice and update our current Xcode project:

Figure 2.13 – UILabel with semantic variants

I've added a couple more UILabels here and just done a little bit of re-arranging (nothing special), but what I have done is set the semantic variant for each **Label** with a corresponding variant – let's take a look:

Figure 2.14 – Color options

If we expand the color options for our UILabel, we can see a list of all the pre-defined adaptive/semantic and system and variant colors available to us. I've highlighted the colors I've chosen for each of the new labels.

Now, let's switch the appearance to dark and see how it looks:

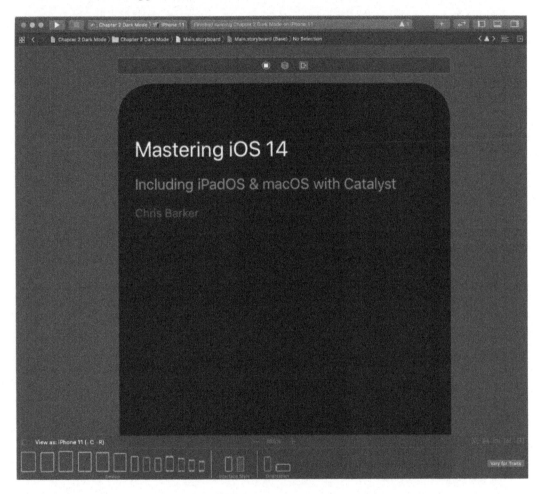

Figure 2.15 – Semantic labels in Dark Mode

Let's go a step further and add some more adaptive content in there. Here, I've dropped in a UIView to act as a separator between content, a UIButton, which will be a URL link, and a UITableView:

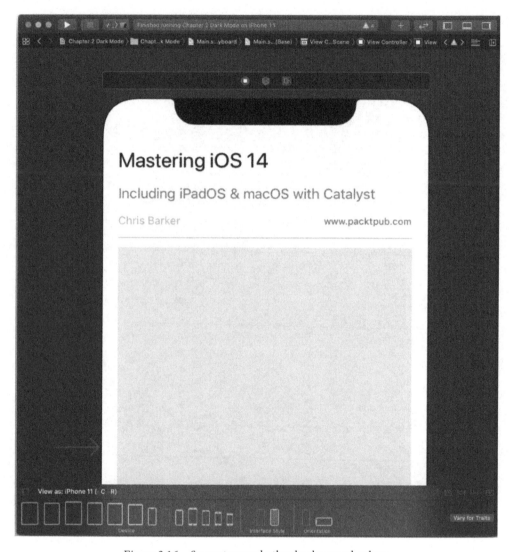

Figure 2.16 – Separators and other background colors

I've assigned the following semantic colors to each of my new views:

- **Separator**: **Separator Color**
- **Button**: **Link Color**
- **Table View**: **Group Table View Background Color**

Let's fire this up in the iOS simulator and see side by side how it looks. You'll notice something interesting:

Figure 2.17 – Table view in light and Dark Mode

In the light appearance, you can clearly see the table view's group background color against the system background color; yet if we take a look at this in the dark appearance, you don't see it as much. That's because with a much darker primary background color, the separation isn't needed as much; the black on black doesn't get lost and looks more natural, whereas white on white does.

This all looks great built into Interface Builder, but now let's take a look at how we would do this programmatically.

Using the programmatic approach

Let's start by creating IBOutlets for each of our objects. If you're unfamiliar with creating an outlet, simply, in `ViewController`, we do the following:

1. Declare all our outlet properties first.

2. Then, from the `IBOutlet` connector (just to the left of your property), press *Command + Primary Cursor Click*.

3. Hold and drag this to the UIView or object you want to connect to.

    Opening both Interface Builder and `ViewController` in separate windows will really help this process too:

Figure 2.18 – Creating an outlet

4. We'll need to create these in our `ViewController.swift` file just inside the class declaration. Copy the following highlighted code into your class:

```swift
class ViewController: UIViewController {

    @IBOutlet weak var headerImageView: UIImageView!
    @IBOutlet weak var primaryLabel: UILabel!
    @IBOutlet weak var secondaryLabel: UILabel!
    @IBOutlet weak var tertiaryLabel: UILabel!

    @IBOutlet weak var linkButton: UIButton!

    @IBOutlet weak var separatorView: UIView!

    @IBOutlet weak var tableView: UITableView!


    override func viewDidLoad() {
        super.viewDidLoad()
    }

}
```

5. Now, we can programmatically assign our colors. Inside the `viewDidLoad()` function, add the following highlighted code:

```swift
override func viewDidLoad() {
    super.viewDidLoad()

    primaryLabel.textColor = UIColor.label
    secondaryLabel.textColor = UIColor.secondaryLabel
    tertiaryLabel.textColor = UIColor.tertiaryLabel

    linkButton.titleLabel?.textColor = UIColor.link

    separatorView.backgroundColor = UIColor.separator
```

```
tableView.backgroundColor = UIColor.
    systemGroupedBackground


    }
```

If you launch the app in the simulator, you'll see that everything should stay the same. If we really want to test our logic, head back on over to Interface Builder and set one of our UILabels to **System Green Color**. Re-run the app and watch the programmatic code take precedence and override Interface Builder.

In this section, we've looked at how working with views for Dark Mode either in Interface Builder or programmatically is possible with the use of adaptive and semantic colors. We also looked at and understood the value behind using color variations and saw the effect they both have in both light and dark appearance. In the next section, we'll take a look at the asset catalog and how we can create custom adaptive colors and images for use in our app.

Working with the asset catalog for Dark Mode

Since the ability to add colors to the asset catalog became available back in Xcode 9, there is now even more reason to take full advantage of one of Xcode's prized assets.

In this section, we'll look at how we can use the asset catalog not only to create our custom colors but also to create our own adaptive colors and images, allowing us to harness the power of Xcode when developing dynamic appearance applications.

Using custom adaptive colors

Sticking with our current project, head on over to the file inspector, and highlight the `Assets.xcassets` folder. With the following layout visible, click on the + button highlighted in the following screenshot and select **New Color Set** from the list of options:

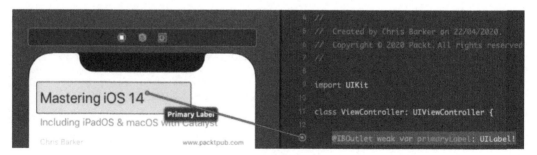

Figure 2.19 – Creating a color set

Add in another three color sets and name them the following:

- `brandLabel`
- `brandSecondaryLabel`
- `brandTertiaryLabel`

Highlight `brandLabel`, and then highlight the option in the central asset preview window. Notice the list of attribute options now made available to us in the **Attributes Inspector** pane:

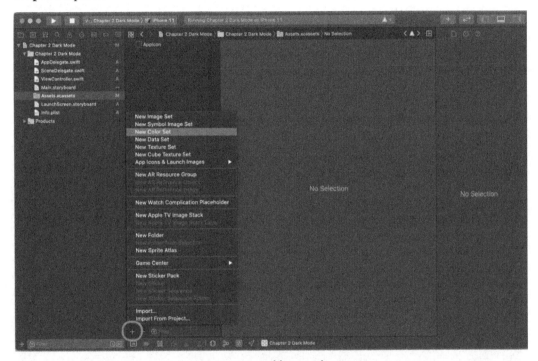

Figure 2.20 – Adding a color set

As you can see, we can now define the `brandLabel` color that we want to use. But first, let's make it adaptive. In the **Attributes Inspector** pane, change **Appearance** from **None** to **Any, Light, Dark**.

You'll have noticed on the dropdown that there was another option of **Any, Dark**, so let's go through what this means:

- **None**: This is a default color and won't be adaptive to your selected appearance.

- **Any, Dark**: In this scenario, **Any** will support legacy versions of your app, along with any other variations that aren't dark (so light, basically). **Dark** will be dark…

- **Any, Light, Dark**: Same as the preceding but will allow you to specifically select a value for legacy and light (along with dark).

So, with that covered, let's add some colors. Now, as mentioned before, this is where you can be really specific with your color choices, either by personal preference or brand guidelines you have to follow. For me, I'm just going to click **Show Color Picker** and pick my favorite colors:

- Tangerine for **Any (Legacy)** and light

- A more subtle **Cantaloupe** for dark:

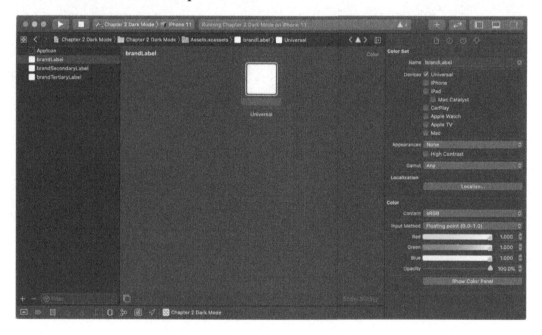

Figure 2.21 – Choosing a color

Do the same for `brandSecondaryLabel` and `brandTertiaryLabel`, remembering to slightly alter the colors based on the semantic purpose you intend to use them for.

Once you've done that, head back on over to Interface Builder and highlight `primaryLabel`, then bring open the options of colors from **Attributes Inspector**. You should see the following:

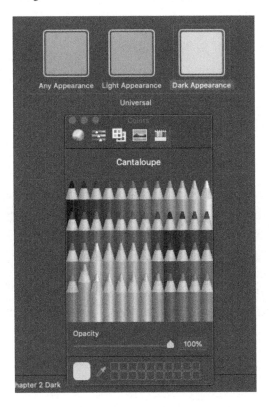

Figure 2.22 – Default label color

All the color sets you created in the asset catalog are available to use right there in Interface Builder. Go ahead and add them in for each label and see how they look by switching appearance in Interface Builder:

Figure 2.23 – Color set, light mode versus dark mode

With that done, you've created your very own adaptive, semantic and dynamic colors for your app – all within the power of Xcode.

If you wanted to use the colors programmatically, you can do that by simply referring to the asset name in a couple of different ways.

First is a direct reference to the name of the assets:

```
primaryLabel.textColor = UIColor(named: "brandLabel")
```

Alternatively, you can select the asset directly from the media library by pressing *Shift + CMD + M* and selecting **show color palette** from the icon options and selecting the color you want.

This will insert the color from the assets catalog as a swatch, directly inside your code:

Figure 2.24 – Assigning a color set programmatically

Or another option, if you really wanted to keep your code clean, would be to create an extension of UIColor allowing you to define your own property:

```
extension UIColor {
    static var brandLabel: UIColor {
        return UIColor(named: "brandLabel") ?? UIColor.label
    }
}
```

This can now be used just like this:

```
primaryLabel.textColor = UIColor.brandLabel
```

This is a nice, clean, and manageable way to look after your custom color sets programmatically, but this really is a personal preference, and each to their own. If you're working with a large alternative color guideline, making the change to a primary color in one extension will roll the change out to your entire app without the worry of missing a label or two.

Next, let's take a look at the same approach but for images.

Using custom adaptive images

We've learned a lot about how the asset catalog works with adaptive images from the previous section, *Custom adaptive colors*, and luckily, we can take full advantage of that in creating adaptive images for our project.

In the same way that we created a new color set, let's follow these steps:

1. Head on back over to **Assets.xcassets**.

2. Create a new image set:

Figure 2.25 – New image set

3. Name your new image **header**, highlight it, and change the appearance in the **Attributes Inspector** window to **Any, Dark**. You should now see the following:

Figure 2.26 – Add new image set

When adding an image to the image catalog, you'll be given the option for adding **1x**, **2x**, or **3x** images – these are different image scales you can set for various screen sizes. For further information, see the following from Apple's documentation.

For this example, we are going to add in two different images to the **2x** option: one for **Any** and the other for **Dark**. You can grab the images I've used from the sample project found in GitHub or choose your own – it's up to you. From the Finder, simply drag and drop the images into the **2x** placeholder inside Xcode. You should see the following once done:

Figure 2.27 – New image set variants

Now, head back on over to your storyboard and add in a UIImageView to your project. Add this to the top of `ViewController` to act as a header.

Once in place, head on over to the **Attributes Inspector** pane and select the dropdown for the **Image** option – there, you should see your newly created asset, **header**:

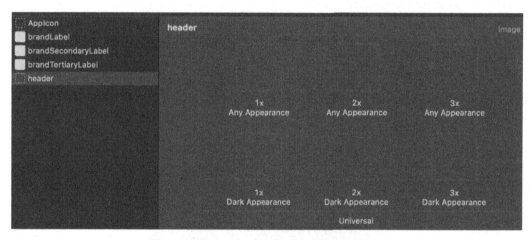

Figure 2.28 – Setting header from the image set

Select this and take a look (depending on the size of the image you chose, you may need to set **Content Mode** to **Aspect Fill** – these options can also be found in **Attributes Inspector**).

Run the simulator and have a look at everything you've achieved so far in this chapter, remembering to switch from light to dark appearance by using the environment override in Xcode... looks pretty good, right?

Figure 2.29 – Header light mode versus dark mode

Just like we did with color sets, we can of course handle this programmatically, should we wish. Let's add another extension to our app to handle this for us:

```
extension UIImage {
    static var header: UIImage {
        return UIImage(named: "header") ?? UIImage()
    }
}
```

We can again use this in just the same way as before:

```
headerImageView.image = UIImage.header
```

We do this by assigning our header image directly onto our UIImageView.

In this section, we harnessed the power of the asset catalog to allow us to create custom adaptive and dynamic colors and images for our app. In the next section, we'll take a look at how best to update a legacy app to support dark mode with everything we've learned so far, and also how best to identify the little things we can do to futureproof our apps for various appearances.

Further exploring Dark Mode

In the previous sections, we gave you a lot to think about when either creating or migrating existing apps to Dark Mode under specific circumstances. In this section, we'll take a look at a couple of little "nice to knows" that should always be in the back of your mind when approaching Dark Mode.

Using Dark Mode with SwiftUI

With the announcement of SwiftUI back in June 2019, a massive shift in focus on UI-based development took place. Released at the same time as Dark Mode, and as expected, SwiftUI takes full advantage of switching appearances.

Let's start by taking a look at how we could detect dark mode programmatically in SwiftUI:

1. First, we'll create an environment variable that allows us to access the current state of the appearance of the device:

    ```
    @Environment(\.colorScheme) var appearance
    ```

2. Next, let's use a simple ternary operator to display some text based on the current appearance:

    ```
    Text(appearance == .dark ? "Dark Appearance" : "Light
        Appearance")
    ```

It really is that simple.

Now, let's have a look at the options available to us in the automatic preview window. SwiftUI uses `PreviewProvider`, which allows us to display dynamically what we are designing/developing.

To enable Dark Mode in `PreviewProvider`, simply add the following highlighted code and hot refresh:

```
struct ContentView_Previews: PreviewProvider {
    static var previews: some View {
        ContentView()
            .environment(\.colorScheme, .dark)
    }
}
```

Here, we've added a modifier to set the `.colorScheme` environment variable to `.dark`. If we want to preview both `.light` and `.dark` side by side, we can simply do the following:

```
struct ContentView_Previews: PreviewProvider {
    static var previews: some View {
        Group {
            ContentView().environment(\.colorScheme, .light)
            ContentView().environment(\.colorScheme, .dark)
        }
    }
}
```

> **Tip**
>
> To learn more about SwiftUI, take a look at *Learn SwiftUI*, available from Packt Publishing: `https://www.packtpub.com/business-other/learn-swiftui`.

Programatically handling changes with trait collection

During the development of your new app, there could be a couple of occasions where you might need to handle a specific scenario based on the current appearance. However, we'll need to take a slightly different approach to this than what we did with the SwiftUI example previously.

The interface style is part of the `UITraitCollection` class (which, in turn, is part of UIKit). We can do a conditional check against a value using the following anywhere in our `ViewController`:

```
traitCollection.userInterfaceStyle == .dark
```

Unlike SwiftUI, we can't just use a simple ternary operator as there are more than two values for `userInterfaceStyle`:

```
public enum UIUserInterfaceStyle : Int {
    case unspecified
    case light
    case dark
}
```

Unspecified is an option too (think **Any**, back in our asset catalog), so it's best to use another approach when detecting changes to our interface style.

Let's start by heading back into our `ViewController.swift` file and adding in the following `override` function:

```
override func traitCollectionDidChange(_
    previousTraitCollection: UITraitCollection?) {

    super.traitCollectionDidChange(previousTraitCollection)

    // Logic here

}
```

This override is called whenever a change is made to a trait (such as appearance). From this, we now action any changes we would like to make, but the problem we have is traits are used for more than just appearances, and this override could be called for a variety of reasons.

So, if we are looking particularly for changes in our appearance, we can use the `previousTrait` property passed into our delegate function and compare against the current system trait – if there is a difference, we know the appearance has changed. Let's take a look at how we'd do this:

```
override func traitCollectionDidChange(_
    previousTraitCollection: UITraitCollection?) {

    super.traitCollectionDidChange(previousTraitCollection)


    let interfaceAppearanceChanged = previousTraitCollection?.
        hasDifferentColorAppearance(comparedTo: traitCollection)


}
```

By using the `hasDifferentColorAppearance` method, we can now easily compare the previous trains against the current one to see whether there have been any changes – the resulting method returns a Boolean, so we can use this at our convenience.

Specifying an appearance for views, ViewControllers, and windows

You may, in some circumstances, wish to specify an appearance based on a particular area of your app or if you are migrating to dark mode (but need a little more time for a certain feature). Simply drop in the following appropriate code to meet your desire.

Views

Here, we'll create and instantiate a basic UIView:

```
let view = UIView()
view.overrideUserInterfaceStyle = .dark // .light
```

We assign either a light or dark value.

ViewController

If we wanted to do this in a UIViewController, we would simply just do the following:

```
overrideUserInterfaceStyle = .dark
```

Again, we assign either a light or dark value (usually within `viewDidLoad()`).

Window

If we need to access the current window, we could do so as follows:

```
for window in UIApplication.shared.windows {
    window.overrideUserInterfaceStyle = .dark
}
```

(This is not a recommended approach and you would be hard-pressed to find any real reason to want to do this...)

Accessibility in Dark Mode

Ask around and someone will joke about how **Dark Mode** has existed in iOS for years, either as the **Classic Invert** or **Smart Invert** accessibility feature. I even had it on one of my slides at a conference about 2 months prior to Dark Mode being officially announced.

But with this in mind, a lot of things started to be said about accessibility in iOS – some comments referring to Dark Mode as "Apple finally supporting accessibility," which I have to be honest makes me very sad.

Accessibility has always played a massive part in iOS regardless of the appearance – but, even with the introduction of Dark Mode, this still goes unchanged as Dark Mode supports all accessibility features.

If you refer back to an earlier section in this chapter, *Core development concepts in Dark Mode*, you'll remember that we mentioned the option to schedule our light and dark appearances – much like you could with Nightshift that was introduced in iOS 9, again another element with a focus on accessibility.

In this section, we went a little outside of the box with regard to Dark Mode and stepped away from the basic implementation, allowing us to look at the wider options available to use and things to think about when implementing Dark Mode in our apps.

Summary

In this chapter, we've covered a lot about Dark Mode – not only from a programmatic perspective but also the theory behind the appearances and purpose of colors used within our apps.

We started by taking a look at how Xcode and iOS are set up for Dark Mode, learning about the environment overrides used in Xcode, and how we can even switch appearances in our storyboard while developing.

Next, we covered adaptive and semantic colors, and learned not only how these are used with Apple's default system colors but also how we can create dynamic and adaptive color sets ourselves.

Following on from what we learned about color sets, we applied this to images and harnesses the power of the assets catalog.

Finally, we covered some "great to know" topics, such as Dark Mode in SwiftUI, programmatically hailing appearances, and accessibility.

In the next chapter, we'll take a look at lists in iOS 14, covering everything you need to know about UITableViews and UICollectionViews.

Further reading

- **Apple human interface guidelines (dark mode)**: `https://developer.apple.com/design/human-interface-guidelines/ios/visual-design/dark-mode/`

- **Apple human interface guidelines (color)**: `https://developer.apple.com/design/human-interface-guidelines/ios/visual-design/color/`

- **Asset catalog reference**: `https://developer.apple.com/library/archive/documentation/Xcode/Reference/xcode_ref-Asset_Catalog_Format/index.html`

3
Using Lists and Tables

There's a good chance that you have built a simple app before, or maybe you have tried but didn't quite succeed. If this is the case, you have likely used `UITableView` or `UICollectionView`, as both are core components of many iOS applications.

If an app shows a list of items, it was likely built using `UITableView`. This chapter will ensure that you are up to speed with the ins and outs of `UITableView` and `UICollectionView`. In addition to covering the basics, such as how we use the delegation pattern, you'll also learn how to access users' data – in this case, their contacts – which will be rendered in a `UITableView` and `UICollectionView` object.

We'll finish this chapter by taking a look at lists in SwiftUI, Apple's new UI framework announced back in 2019. We'll touch on the fundamental differences between what SwiftUI and UIKit have to offer.

The following topics will be covered in this chapter:

- Working with `UITableView`
- Exploring table views further
- Working with `UICollectionView`
- Exploring collection views further
- Working with lists in SwiftUI

Technical requirements

For this chapter, you'll need to download Xcode version 11.4 or above from Apple's App Store.

You'll also need to be running the latest version of macOS (Catalina or above). Simply search for Xcode in the App Store, and select and download the latest version. Launch Xcode and follow any additional installation instructions that your system may prompt you with. Once Xcode has fully launched, you're ready to go.

Download the sample code from the following GitHub link:

```
https://github.com/PacktPublishing/Mastering-iOS-14-
Programming-4th-Edition
```

Working with UITableView

In this section, we'll start by taking a look at `UITableView`, one of the most – if not *the* most – common ways of displaying data in a list in iOS.

Setting up the project

Every time you start a new project in Xcode, you have the option to pick a template for your app. Every template contains a small amount of code or some boilerplate code to get you started. In most cases, a basic layout will even be set up for you. Throughout this book, you should default to using the **Single View App** template. Don't be fooled by its name; you can add as many views to your app as you would like. This template just provides you with one view to start with.

In this chapter, you will create an app that is called My Contacts. This app displays your user's contacts list in a `UITableView` component that you will set up. Let's create a project for this app right now.

In the menu bar, do the following:

1. Select **File | New | Project**.

2. Select **Single View App**.

3. Name your project `Contacts List` or anything you like.

4. Make sure your programming language is set to **Swift** and the user interface is set to **Storyboard** – it should resemble something like the following:

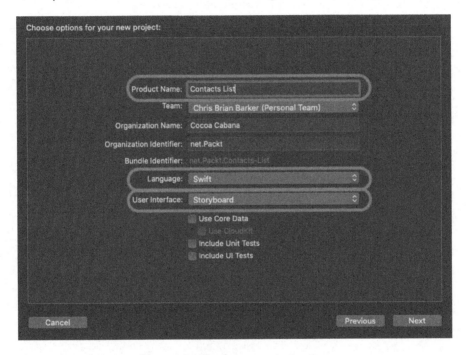

Figure 3.1 – Xcode new project options

5. From here, click **Next** and then **Create**.

6. Once your project has loaded, open the file named `Main.storyboard` found in the navigation tree to the left-hand side.

The storyboard file is used to lay out all of your application's views and to connect them to the code you write. The editor you use to manipulate your storyboard is called Interface Builder.

If you have used `UITableView` in the past, you may have used `UITableViewController`. The `UITableViewController` class is a subclass of a regular `UIViewController` class.

The difference is that `UITableViewController` contains a lot of setup that you would otherwise have to perform on your own, either in Interface Builder or programmatically. To fully understand how `UITableView` is configured and set up, we won't use `UITableViewController` in this example.

Back in Xcode, you'll notice a button at the top right that has a plus symbol on it. Click on this to bring up the object explorer. Once opened, search for `Table View`. If you begin typing the name of a potential component, you should see a list of suggested options become available – just like in the following screenshot:

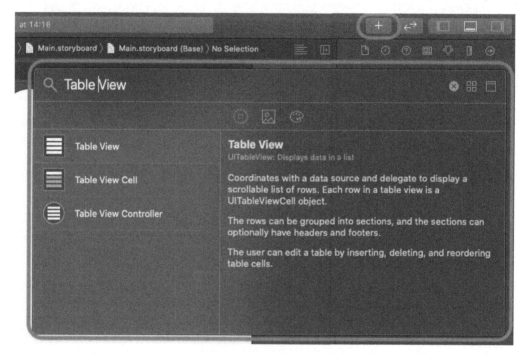

Figure 3.2 – Adding an object

Once you find **Table View**, drag it straight onto your canvas in Interface Builder. Don't worry about it being placed awkwardly, we're going to fix that now by using Auto Layout to add some constraints.

Inside our canvas, highlight the `UITableView` object we just added and click on the icon highlighted in the following screenshot. Add in top, leading, trailing, and bottom constraints of `0`:

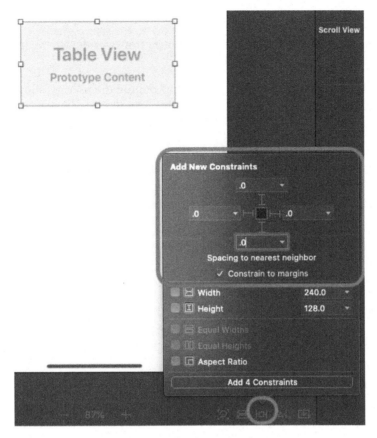

Figure 3.3 – Setting constraints

Once done, click **Add 4 Constraints** – you'll see straight away in the canvas that your `UITableView` object is now pinned perfectly to each edge of your screen. Regardless of what size device this is displayed on, those constraints will also be adhered to.

Auto Layout enables you to create layouts that automatically adapt to any screen size that exists. Your layout currently uses fixed coordinates and dimensions to lay out the table view. For instance, your table view is set up to be positioned at 0, with a size of (375, 667). This size is perfect for devices such as the iPhone 8 and SE, but it wouldn't fit nicely with the iPhone 11 or iPad Pro. This combination of a view's position and size is called the frame.

Auto Layout uses constraints to define a layout instead of a frame. For instance, to make the table view fit the entire screen, you would add constraints that pin every edge of the table view to the corresponding edge of its superview. Doing so would make the table view match its superview's size at all times.

Fetching contacts data

In order for us to be able to fetch the user's contacts from our device, we first need to be granted access via the `Contacts` framework.

Apple are really heavy on privacy, so in turn, they require the user to "allow" access whenever an app first tries to read from the Address Book. This doesn't just stop at the Address Book, too; this can be found for camera access, location services, photos, and more.

As in our case, when you need to access privacy-sensitive information, you are required to specify a reason as to why you would like to access the information. Nothing too detailed – but enough to give the user peace of mind as to why you would like to access their data.

This is done by adding an entry to the `Info.plist` file in your project. Whenever you need access to privacy-sensitive information, you are required to specify this in your app's `Info.plist` file.

In order to add this information to `Info.plist`, take the following steps:

1. Open it from the list of files in the Project navigator on the left.

2. Once opened, hover over the words `Information Property List` at the top of the file.

3. A plus icon should appear. Clicking it adds a new empty item with a search field to the list.

4. When you begin typing `Privacy - contacts`, Xcode will filter out options for you until there is only one left for you to pick.

5. This option is called **Privacy – Contacts Usage Description** and is the key we are looking for.

The value for this newly added key should describe the reason that you need access to the specified piece of information. In this case, "reads contacts and shows them in a list" should be a sufficient explanation. When the user is asked for permission to access their contacts, the reason you specified here will be shown, so make sure you add an informative message.

> **Tip**
> Make sure you do choose an informative message that is relevant to your app.
> If Apple review this and don't find it to be acceptable, they could question you, or even worse, reject the submission of your app.

Now, let's get down to writing some code. Before you can read contacts, you must make sure that the user has given the appropriate permissions for you to access the contacts data. To do this, the code must first read the current permission status. Once done, the user must either be prompted for permission to access their contacts, or the contacts must be fetched.

Add the following highlighted code to `ViewController.swift`; we'll cover the details a section at a time – but don't worry, it will all make sense in the end:

```swift
import UIKit
import Contacts


class ViewController: UIViewController {


    override func viewDidLoad() {
        requestContacts()
    }
}
```

To start, we've imported `Contacts` into our `ViewController` class; by doing this, we're allowing the `Contacts` framework API to not just be inside our project, but specifically in our `ViewController` class.

Next, we've added a call to a function named `requestContacts` in `viewDidLoad()` – we'll now need to create this function:

```swift
private func requestContacts() {

    let store = CNContactStore()
    let authorizationStatus = CNContactStore.
        authorizationStatus(for: .contacts)


    if authorizationStatus == .notDetermined {
        store.requestAccess(for: .contacts) { [weak self]
            didAuthorize, error in
            if didAuthorize {
                self?.retrieveContacts(from: store)
            }
        }
    } else if authorizationStatus == .authorized {
        retrieveContacts(from: store)
```

```
    }


}
```

Basically, without going into too many details, this forces iOS (if not already) to request permission for your app to access the contacts data. If the current status is unknown (or `notDetermined`), then permission will be requested. If this is not the case and the framework responds with `didAuthorize == true`, then we can now attempt to access the contacts information. We've also added an extra condition in there too to check whether we have already previously been authorized. You'll notice that `store.requestAccess` looks a little different from a regular function call; this is because it uses a completion handler.

In asynchronous programming, completion handlers are used often. They allow your app to perform some work in the background and then call the completion handler when the work is completed. You will find completion handlers throughout many frameworks. If you implement a very simple function of your own that takes a callback, it might look as follows:

```
func doSomething(completionHandler: (Int) -> Void) {
    // perform some actions
    var result = theResultOfSomeAction
    completionHandler(result)
}
```

Calling a completion-handler looks just like calling a function. The reason for this is that a completion handler is a block of code, called a closure. Closures are a lot like functions because they both contain a potentially reusable block of code that is expected to be executed when called.

Now, let's add our final piece of the puzzle by adding in our function to retrieve the contacts:

```
func retrieveContacts(from store: CNContactStore) {

    let containerId = store.defaultContainerIdentifier()
    let predicate = CNContact.predicateForContactsInContainer(
      withIdentifier: containerId)
    let keysToFetch = [CNContactGivenNameKey as
      CNKeyDescriptor,
```

```
CNContactFamilyNameKey as CNKeyDescriptor,
    CNContactImageDataAvailableKey as CNKeyDescriptor,
CNContactImageDataKey as CNKeyDescriptor]


    let contacts = try! store.unifiedContacts(matching:
        predicate, keysToFetch: keysToFetch)


}
```

A brief explanation of the preceding code: we pass an instance of CNContactStore (which we've previously been given permission to access), and then we set up a request for specific information we would like with the array of CNKeyDescriptor.

Finally, the call is made and will fetch this information, which is returned to us in a CNContact object.

Prepping UITableView to display our contacts

With all that ready, let's head on back to Interface Builder and add in a table view cell:

1. Highlight the UITableView object we added to the canvas.

2. Click on the + button to add another object. This time, search for Table View Cell.

3. Now, drag this object onto UITableView.

You'll notice something a little different this time: the UITableViewCell object that we dragged automatically snapped into position on our UITableView object – don't worry, that's fine, this is because UITableViewCell's position is controlled by the configuration of its UITableView object. Next, we are going to create an IBOutlet for our code. In the same way that we did in *Chapter 2, Working with Dark Mode*, create an outlet programmatically in your ViewController.swift file, and then connect these using Interface Builder.

Here is an example of the outlet you are going to create:

```
@IBOutlet weak var tableView: UITableView!
```

Now, we need to create a class for UITableViewCell – by doing this, we can add custom properties to UITableViewCell, such as a name, contact information, or even an image.

Back inside our `ViewController.swift` file (but outside of the `ViewController` class declaration), add the following code:

```
class ContactCell: UITableViewCell {
    @IBOutlet weak var nameLabel: UILabel!
    @IBOutlet weak var contactImageView: UIImageView!
}
```

Here, we've created our custom cell, which is a subclass of `UITableViewCell` and will carry all the traits of a table view cell that we need. I've also added a couple of `IBOutlet` components for the data that we are going to display.

Now, let's go hook this up. Head on back to Interface Builder and select the `UITableViewCell` object that we added.

Once highlighted, click on the Identity inspector in the right-hand tool window and add `ContactCell` as the **Class** name:

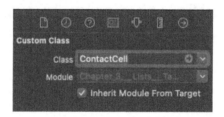

Figure 3.4 – Table view class

Then, click on the Attributes Inspector and type in `contactCell` for **Identifier**:

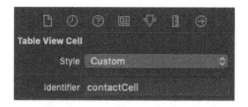

Figure 3.5 – Table view cell identifier

Overriding `UITableViewCell`'s class to our custom class will allow us to use Interface Builder to connect objects to the `IBOutlet` components that we just created. We'll touch on the identifier later on in this chapter, but it's always good to get these bits out of the way at the start.

Now, let's add a couple of objects to `UITableViewCell`. We'll start with `UILabel`, and then `UIImageView` (add these in the same way you did the table view and cell – have the image to the left of the cell).

Once added, have a play with the Autolayout constraints we learned about earlier. The best way to master Auto Layout is trial and error - if you get stuck, just refer to the sample project for this chapter to guide you along.

Once you are done, your cell will look something like this:

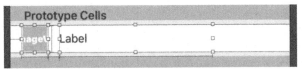

Figure 3.6 – Label with constraints

Now, let's hook each one of these up to the IBOutlet components we created – all going well, Interface Builder should pick up on the associated class (ContactCell) and will allow the outlets to be attached without any problems.

Awesome, we're making great progress, and believe it or not, we're not a million miles away from displaying the data in our app – but first, we need to cover some important fundamentals of UITableView and, more importantly, the delegation pattern that iOS used so heavily.

Understanding protocols and delegation

Throughout the iOS SDK and the Foundation framework, a design pattern named delegation is used. Delegation allows an object to have another object to perform work on its behalf.

When implemented correctly, it's a great way to separate concerns and decouple code within your app.

The table view uses the help of two objects to function correctly. One is the delegate, and the other is the data source. Any time you use a table view, you must configure these two objects yourself. When the time comes for the table view to render its contents, it asks data source for information about the data to display. The delegate comes into play when a user interacts with the items in the table view.

If you look at the documentation for UITableView, you can find the delegate property. The type for delegate is UITableViewDelegate?. This tells you two things about delegate. First of all, UITableViewDelegate is a protocol. This means that any object can act as a delegate for a table view, as long as it implements the UITableViewDelegate protocol. Second, the question mark at the end of the type name tells you that the delegate is an optional property. An optional property either has a value of the specified type, or it is nil. The table view's delegate property is optional because you do not have to set it to create a functioning table view.

A protocol, such as `UITableViewDelegate`, defines a set of properties and methods that must be implemented by any type that wants to conform to the protocol. Not all methods must be explicitly implemented by conforming objects. Sometimes, a protocol extension provides a reasonable default implementation.

In addition to delegate, `UITableView` has a data source property. data source's type is `UITableViewDataSource?`, and just like `UITableViewDelegate`, `UITableViewDataSource` is a protocol. However, `UITableViewDelegate` only has optional methods, meaning you don't need to implement any methods to conform to `UITableViewDelegate`. `UITableViewDataSource` does have required methods: the methods that need to be implemented are used to provide the table view with just enough information to be able to display the correct number of cells with the right content in them.

If this is the first time you're learning about protocols and delegation, you might feel a little bit lost right now. That's OK; you'll get the hang of it soon. Throughout this book, your understanding of topics such as these will improve bit by bit. You will even learn about a concept called protocol-oriented programming!

For now, you must understand that a table view asks for a different object for the data it needs to show and that it also uses a different object to handle certain user interactions.

We can break the flow of displaying content in a table view down into a couple of steps; when the table view needs to reload the data, it does the following:

1. The table view checks whether `dataSource` is set, and asks it for the number of sections it should render.

2. Once the number of sections is passed back to the table view, `dataSource` is asked for the number of items for each section.

3. With knowledge about the number of sections and items that need to be shown, the table view asks `dataSource` for the cells it should display.

4. After receiving all of the configured cells, the table view can finally render these cells to the screen.

These steps should give you a little bit more insight into how a table view uses another object to figure out the contents it should render. This pattern is compelling because it makes the table view an extremely flexible component. Let's put some of this newfound knowledge to use!

Conforming to the UITableView protocols

To make `ViewController` both the delegate and the data source for its table view, it will have to conform to both protocols. It is a best practice to create an extension whenever you make an object conform to a protocol. Ideally, you make one extension for each protocol you want to implement. Doing this helps to keep your code clean and maintainable.

Add the following extension to `ViewController.swift`:

```
extension ViewController: UITableViewDelegate,
  UITableViewDataSource {

}
```

After doing this, your code contains an error. That's because none of the required methods from `UITableViewDataSource` have been implemented yet.

There are two methods you need to implement to conform to `UITableViewDataSource`. These methods are the following:

- `tableView(_:numberOfRowsInSection:)`
- `tableView(_:cellForRowAt:)`

Let's go ahead and fix the error Xcode is showing by adjusting the code a little bit. We'll also need to make a couple of small changes to display our contacts within our table view.

We'll start by adding a global variable to our `ViewController` class. Add in the following just after the class declaration:

```
var contacts = [CNContact]()
```

Here, we've instantiated an array of `CNContact`, which is what we get back in our `retrieveContacts` function when `store.unifiedContacts` is called.

Now, make the following modification to our `retrieveContacts` function:

```
contacts = try! store.unifiedContacts(matching: predicate,
  keysToFetch: keysToFetch)
```

Perfect – now fill in the blanks with those delegates:

```
func tableView(_ tableView: UITableView, numberOfRowsInSection
  section: Int) -> Int {
    return contacts.count
}
```

Our first delegate method, `tableView(_:numberOfRowsInSection:)`, requires us to return the number of cells we want to display. As we want to display all of our contacts, we simply pass back the number of contacts in our array, as highlighted in the preceding code.

Next, let's implement the `tableView(_:cellForRowAt:)` delegate. Copy in the following code and we'll go through it one step at a time:

```
func tableView(_ tableView: UITableView, cellForRowAt
  indexPath: IndexPath) -> UITableViewCell {
    let contact = contacts[indexPath.row]


    let cell = UITableViewCell()
    cell.textLabel?.text = contact.familyName


    return cell
}
```

Basically, this delegate method is called for every cell that is going to be generated in our table view, so if `contacts.count == 5`, then this will be called 5 times. A way for us to identify which cell is currently being called is to inspect the `indexPath.row` value that is being passed in with each call.

If you take a look at the first line of code with the preceding delegate, you'll see that we have accessed the specific contact by querying our array of `CNContact` with the `indexPath.row` value. From this, we simply just create an instance of `UITableViewCell`, assign a property of `CNContact` to `.textLabel`, and return the instance.

We're almost ready to see our changes in action; just a couple more things to add in.

Head on back to our `viewDidLoad()` function and add the following highlighted lines:

```
override func viewDidLoad() {
    tableView.delegate = self
    tableView.dataSource = self


    requestContacts()
}
```

Here, we are telling our `UITableView` instance that our current `ViewController` class is the delegate base for all `UITableView` protocol operations. In a nutshell – the delegates we just added will get called when we try to perform any actions on our table view.

Finally, add the following highlighted code to the end of our `retrieveContacts` functions:

```
contacts = try! store.unifiedContacts(matching: predicate,
  keysToFetch: keysToFetch)
DispatchQueue.main.async {
self.tableView.reloadData()
}
```

The reason we do this is again down to asynchronous programming. By design, our table view will try and display data as soon as `ViewController` is loaded. At this point, our contacts may not be available, we may have not been given suitable permission, or simply, the function's callback may not have returned all the data in time.

So, if that's the case, once we know that all the data is ready to be displayed, we simply ask the table view to reload. Go ahead and run your app in the simulator – all going well, you will be prompted by the `Contacts` framework to allow permission to access your contacts, shortly followed by a list of contact details:

Figure 3.7 – User consent and user list

In this part, we learned about how important protocols and delegates are in iOS development, and by hooking up a couple of simple functions, we were able to easily yet effectively display data in UITableView. Now, let's take a look at how we can customize each cell some more, with the UITableViewCell override we created earlier.

Understanding the custom UITableViewCell override and the reuse identifier

Back in a previous section, *Prepping UITableView to display our contacts*, you'll remember that we created our custom UITableViewCell override called ContactCell, but in the end we never really used it.

We did this on purpose, firstly to introduce you to the fact that UITableViewCell does have a minimal default offering where textLabel is given for you to add your required text. This can come in handy as a really lightweight way of generating a UITableView object and displaying some simple data – a no-fuss approach for quick wins or a situation where one line is good enough. However, if you want to be creative with your cells, then this is where the custom option comes into play.

Let's head back to tableView(_:cellForRowAt:) and see how we'd make the change:

```
let contact = contacts[indexPath.row]


guard let cell = tableView.dequeueReusableCell(withIdentifier:
   "contactCell", for: indexPath) as? ContactCell else {
          return UITableViewCell()
}


cell.nameLabel.text = contact.givenName
if let imageData = contact.imageData {
    cell.conatctImageView.image = UIImage(data: imageData)
} else {
    cell.conatctImageView.image = UIImage(systemName: "person.
       circle")
}
```

Now, to start with, let's take a look at the first part:

```
tableView.dequeueReusableCell(withIdentifier: "contactCell",
   for: indexPath) as? ContactCell
```

Here, we are instantiating the use of a reusable UITableViewCell with the identifier of contactCell, which is of the ContactCell class.

Sounds confusing? Maybe a little, but think of it this way – we created a custom cell class that we assigned to our `UITableViewCell` object back in Interface Builder. We then gave this an identifier of `contactCell` – here, we simply called upon that cell to be used so that we can access its properties (remember the `nameLabel` and `contactImageView` properties we added).

Once we have access to an instance of that cell, we can then simply assign each property accordingly with data taken from our contact instance. Notice that we're doing a check against the image data in the contacts due to the possibility of no image yet being associated with a contact – here, we've added a little fallback to display a system image (using SF Symbols).

If you want you add an image, simply fire up the Contacts app in the simulator and drag an image from your Mac over - You should now be able to select this and assign this from the Contacts app.

Go ahead and make those changes, and then run the app again:

Figure 3.8 – Contact list with image

Perfect, but what is this `dequeueReusableCell` all about? Don't worry, we'll cover that in a later section, *Advances in UITableView and UICollectionView*.

In this section, we learned how to implement `UITableView` and a custom `UITableViewCell`, pulling data obtained by accessing our contacts via the `Contacts` framework and displaying it within our app. Now, let's spend some time digging a little deeper into the art of table views and how they work.

Exploring UITableView further

In this section, we'll touch on some extra little bits that will allow you to make the most out of `UITableView`. We'll also cover in more detail some areas previously explored, such as the reuse identifier.

Further understanding reuse identifiers

Earlier in this chapter, you learned about cell-reuse in table views. We assigned a reuse identifier to a table view cell so that the table view would know which cell it should use to display contacts in. Cell-reuse is a concept that is applied to a table view so that it can reuse cells that it has already created.

This means that the only cells that are in memory are either on the screen or barely off the screen. The alternative would be to keep all cells in memory, which could potentially mean that hundreds of thousands of cells are held in memory at any given time.

For a visualization of what cell reuse looks like, have a look at the following diagram:

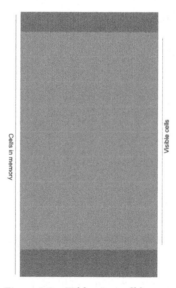

Figure 3.9 – Table view cell layout

As you can see, there are just a few cells in the diagram that are not on the visible screen. This roughly equals the number of cells that a table view might keep in memory. This means that regardless of the total amount of rows you want to show, the table view has roughly constant pressure on your app's memory usage.

A cell is first created when `dequeueReusableCell(withIdentifier:)` is called on the table view and it does not have an unused cell available. Once the cell is either reused or created, `prepareForReuse()` is called on the cell. This is a great spot to reset your cells to their default state by removing any images or setting labels back to their default values.

Next, `tableView(_:willDisplay:forRowAt:)` is called on the table view's delegate. This happens right before the cell is shown. You can perform some last-minute configuration here, but the majority of the work should already be done in `tableView(_:cellForRowAtIndexPath:)`.

When the cell scrolls off screen, `tableView(_:didEndDisplaying:forRowAt:)` is called on the delegate. This signals that a previously visible cell has just scrolled out of the view's bounds.

With all this cell life cycle information in mind, the best way to fix the image reuse bug is by implementing `prepareForReuse()` on `ContactCell`. Add the following implementation to remove any images that have previously been set:

```
override func prepareForReuse() {
    super.prepareForReuse()
    conatctImageView.image = nil
}
```

Now, let's take a look at some other enhancements that we can make in our app by using prefetching.

Prefetching in table views

In addition to `UITableViewDelegate` and `UITableViewDataSource`, a third protocol exists that you can implement to improve your table view's performance.

It's called `UITableViewDataSourcePrefetching`, and you can use it to enhance your data source. If your data source performs some complex task, such as retrieving and decoding an image, it could slow down the performance of your table view if this task is performed at the moment that the table view wants to retrieve a cell. Performing this operation a little bit sooner than that can positively impact your app, in those cases.

So, how would we implement this? Simple, we first just conform `ViewController` to the new delegate:

```
extension ViewController: UITableViewDataSourcePrefetching {
    func tableView(_ tableView: UITableView, prefetchRowsAt
      indexPaths: [IndexPath]) {


    }
}
```

You'll notice that a fundamental difference here is within the `indexPath` parameter being passed in. This time, we have an array of `IndexPath`, as opposed to a single index, in turn, allowing us to perform batch processing on a set of cells that our table view would like us to display.

This would be ideal if data from your cell has to be obtained asynchronously – such as an image or real-time data. You could really work hard here to perform and calculate the right way to display your data to get the optimum performance.

Cell selection in table views

Since a table view will call methods on its delegate whenever they are implemented, you don't need to tell the table view that you want to respond to cell selection. This automatically works if the table view has a delegate, and if the delegate implements `tableView(_:didSelectRowAt:)`.

The implementation you'll add to our app, for now, is a very simple one. When the user taps a cell, the app displays an alert.

Add the following code to the extension in `ViewController.swift`:

```
func tableView(_ tableView: UITableView, didSelectRowAt
 indexPath: IndexPath) {

    let contact = contacts[indexPath.row]
    let alertController = UIAlertController(title: "Contact
      Details", message: "Hey \(contact.givenName)!!",
        preferredStyle: .alert)
    let dismissAction = UIAlertAction(title: "Done", style:
      .default, handler: { action in
```

```
        tableView.deselectRow(at: indexPath, animated: true)
    })


    alertController.addAction(dismissAction);
    present(alertController, animated: true, completion: nil)


}
```

The `tableView(_:didSelectRowAt:)` method receives two arguments: the first is the table view that called this delegate method. The second argument is the index path at which the selection occurred.

The implementation you wrote for this method uses the index path to retrieve the contact that corresponds with the tapped cell, so the contact name can be shown in an alert.

You could also retrieve the contact's name from the tapped cell. However, this is not considered good practice because your cells and the underlying data should be as loosely coupled as possible.

When the user taps the **Done** button in the alert, the table view is told to deselect the selected row.

If you don't deselect the selected row, the last tapped cell will always remain highlighted. Note that the alert is displayed by calling `present(_:animated:completion:)` on the view controller. Any time you want to make a view controller display another view controller, such as an alert controller, you use this method.

In this section, you learned a lot about what makes a table view tick, including a good understanding of how the reuse identifier works. Next, we'll take a look at `UICollectionView`, the `UITableView` class's bigger (or younger, really) brother, comparing similarities to each class and also key differences, too.

Working with UICollectionView

In the previous section, we took on the mighty `UITableView` – learning all about the delegate pattern and how to build our unique lists with custom cells. In this section, we'll take a look at `UICollectionView`, mainly looking at how we are comparing one class to another.

From the outset, when asked what the fundamental differences are between them both, most people will initially say the same thing: "Collection views allow horizontal scrolling" – which is very true, but what it's doing is harnessing the power of UITableView with the ability to manipulate and override a layout that would allow a grid layout, for example.

If you need to go deeper into a complex custom layout, this again is where UICollectionView comes into play, with the support of the UICollectionViewDelegateFlowLayout protocol, allowing you as a developer to manipulate custom layouts.

Setting up our collection view

Let's start by creating a new project in the exact same way as we did for a table view:

1. This time, search for Collection View in the object window (*you won't need to add in a* CollectionView *cell as the collection view already does this for you*).

2. Add in your constraints too so that it scales to the full size of the device.

Back to ViewController, we'll need to create and hook up our IBOutlet components just like we did with the table view (but call your property something like collectionView).

Once you've done that, we'll need to create another extension, but this time, our protocols will be slightly different:

```
extension ViewController: UICollectionViewDelegate,
  UICollectionViewDataSource {

    func collectionView(_ collectionView: UICollectionView,
      numberOfItemsInSection section: Int) -> Int {
        contacts.count
    }

    func collectionView(_ collectionView: UICollectionView,
      cellForItemAt indexPath: IndexPath) ->
      UICollectionViewCell {
        let contact = contacts[indexPath.item]

        guard let cell = collectionView.
          dequeueReusableCell(withReuseIdentifier:
          "contactCell", for: indexPath) as? ContactCell else {
            return UICollectionViewCell()
        }
```

```
        cell.setup(contact: contact)

        return cell
    }

}
```

Our two delegate methods in the preceding example are as follows:

- `collectionView(_:numberOfItemsInSection:)`
- `collectionView(_:cellForItemAt:)`

Both offer the same as their `UITableView` counterparts; only one difference you'll notice is the reference to the term `Item` rather than `Row`. This is because in `UITableView`, the layout is purely linear, so each cell is treated as a row. With `UICollectionView`, this is not the case – so, each cell is referred to as an item.

Next, we want to create another custom cell. Copy and paste the one we made for our table view and make the following highlighted changes:

```
class ContactCell: UICollectionViewCell {

    @IBOutlet weak var familyNameLabel: UILabel!
    @IBOutlet weak var givenNameLabel: UILabel!
    @IBOutlet weak var contactImageView: UIImageView!


    func setup(contact: CNContact) {
        givenNameLabel.text = contact.givenName
        familyNameLabel.text = contact.familyName

        if let imageData = contact.imageData {
            conatctImageView.image = UIImage(data: imageData)
        } else {
            conatctImageView.image = UIImage(systemName:
                "person.circle")
        }

    }

}
```

The differences in the preceding code are subtle, but one of them is very important: our subclass is now of the `UICollectionViewCell` type (as opposed to `UITableViewCell`), and we've also added in a couple of extra outlets, as we'll be adding a touch more data.

For something different, we are going to create a scrolling horizontal list of our contacts and a grid layout. Let's head on over back to the interface builder and modify our canvas a little.

We'll start by adding another text field. Notice from the following figure how I can adjust the size of my cell too:

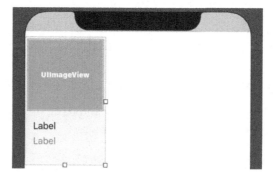

Figure 3.10 – Collection view cell

We can do this in a couple of places. If we highlight **Collection View** and select the Size Inspector, we can do it in there:

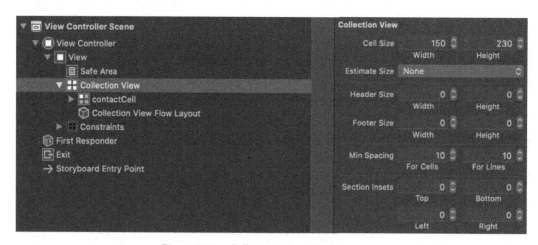

Figure 3.11 – Collection View Size Inspector

Alternatively, we can do this directly on the cell itself, as shown in the following screenshot, again by selecting the Size Inspector:

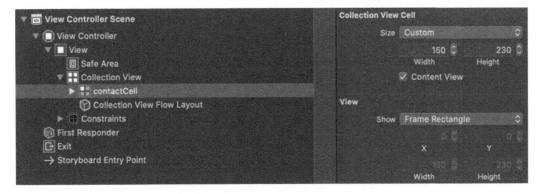

Figure 3.12 – Collection View Cell Size Inspector

This is great for two reasons. First, you can set the size of your cell visually, which is always a nice and convenient way to do things. Secondly, even if you are going to override your cell size programmatically (due to you requiring a more dynamic approach), it allows you to visualize and set your constraints so that you know what you have to play with. I'm just going to set mine to 150 width x 230 height, for now, which should give us enough to play with.

So, let's carry on with setting up our interface. Again, we'll need to override **Class** with our custom class:

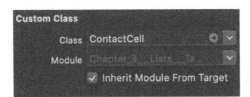

Figure 3.13 – Collection View class

Then, we need to assign our cell identifier:

Figure 3.14 – Collection View cell identifier

Then, we set **Estimated Height** to **None**. This stops our cell from dynamically resizing itself based on the size of the content within the cell (for example, a label with a really long name or address):

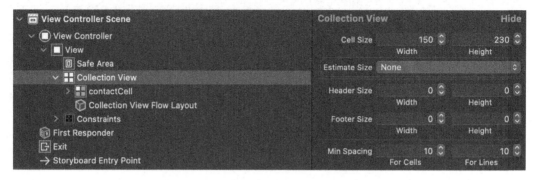

Figure 3.15 – Collection View estimated cell size

We're almost done – just a few more little things we need to add in. Notice anything missing from our `viewDidLoad()` function that we had in the `UITabelView` example?

Yep, we've yet to set our delegate method to our `ViewController` object, but for this example, I'm going to show you another way that we can do that via Interface Builder, as opposed to doing this programmatically.

Highlight your `CollectionView` object, press and hold *Ctrl* on your keyboard, then primary click and hold your cursor – if you start to drag your cursor, you'll see a line (just like when we connect `IBOutlet`). Drag the line to the `ViewController` object and release. You'll then be presented with the following options:

Figure 3.16 – Collection View delegate outlet

Select **dataSource**, and then repeat the process and select **delegate**.

That's it – other than a few minor changes here and there, we've successfully set up `UICollectionView` in pretty much the same way as we did for our `UITableView`. Let's go ahead now and run the project to see how it all looks:

Figure 3.17 – Collection View layout

That looks great – I mean, apart from the cells looking a little out of place – but don't worry, we're going to take a look at our options on how we can change that in the next part, by being introduced to the UICollectionViewDelegateFlowLayout protocol.

Implementing layout with UICollectionViewDelegateFlowLayout

In the last section, we created our very first UICollectionView project based on everything we had learned from creating a UITableView project previously. One thing we did learn that was fundamentally different from a table view was that our cells can be laid out differently.

So, how do we go about manipulating our cells to get them to do exactly what we want them to do? For that, we need to implement the UICollectionViewDelegateFlowLayout protocol – but what does this have to offer? Let's start by taking a look at one of the most commonly used delegate methods in this protocol and how easily it can transform our app.

Over in our extension, add in the following highlighted protocol alongside the existing ones:

```
extension ViewController: UICollectionViewDelegate,
UICollectionViewDataSource, UICollectionViewDelegateFlowLayout
```

Now, in good practice, you can separate each one of these protocols into its own extension – but as we are only dealing with a few delegates for each, we'll be fine to keep them in one place for now.

> **Tip**
>
> If your ViewController object starts to get a little large, you can move your extensions out into a separate file – this makes working on them easier and keeps your files nice and clean.

Now, we're going to add in the following delegate method:

```
func collectionView(_ collectionView: UICollectionView, layout
    collectionViewLayout: UICollectionViewLayout, sizeForItemAt
    indexPath: IndexPath) -> CGSize { }
```

The sizeForItem delegate simply allows us to programmatically set a size of our cell, so let's have a play with that and see what we can come up with. Add the following code to the preceding function:

```
let width = (collectionView.bounds.size.width / 2) - 10
return CGSize(width: width, height: 180)
```

So, here, we're performing a nice simple calculation: we're taking the width of the current screen, dividing it by 2, and then subtracting 10 (for a little padding), and having that as our cell width. Finally, we'll add a nice static value for our height. Go ahead and run your app and see what it gives us:

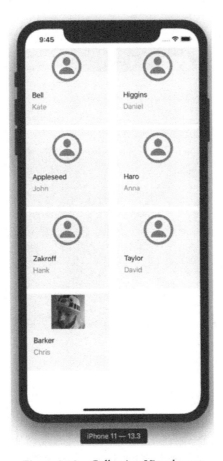

Figure 3.18 – Collection View layout

Nice, let's look at what else we could do. How about simply returning the full size of the screen?

```
return collectionView.bounds.size
```

Next, let's change the direction of the scroll direction; we can do this via Interface Builder by selecting **Collection View**. Change the value to **Horizontal**:

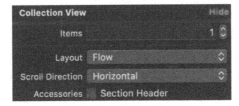

Figure 3.19 – Collection View Scroll Direction

Go ahead and run the app again – how does it look?

Figure 3.20 – Collection View Scroll Direction layout

Perfect – with only a small change, we've managed to make a massive difference to our app, clearly highlighting the power of `UICollectionView` compared to `UITableView`.

Before we wrap up this section on `UICollectionView`, let's take a quick look at the other delegate methods offered to us by `UICollectionViewDelegateFlowLayout`.

Size of an item (cell)

When you need to manipulate the bounds or frame of an item, use `collectionView(_:layout:sizeForItemAt:`, which asks the delegate for the size of the specified item's cell.

Section and spacing

The following are options to programmatically adjust the spacing between cell items and sections (excluding headers and footers):

- `collectionView(_:layout:insetForSectionAt:)`: Asks the delegate for the margins to apply to content in the specified section

- `collectionView(_:layout:minimumLineSpacingForSectionAt:)`: Asks the delegate for the spacing between successive rows or columns of a section

- `collectionView(_:layout:minimumInteritemSpacing ForSectionAt:)`: Asks the delegate for the spacing between successive items in the rows or columns of a section

Footer and header sizing

The following are options to programmatically adjust the spacing between cell items specifically for headers and footers:

- `collectionView(_:layout:referenceSizeForHeaderInSection:)`: Asks the delegate for the size of the header view in the specified section

- `collectionView(_:layout:referenceSizeForFooterInSection:)`: Asks the delegate for the size of the footer view in the specified section

In this section, we learned all about `UICollectionView` components – how to set them up in Xcode and the differences between them and `UITableView` components – and were able to see the benefits they give us along with the `UICollectionViewDelegateFlowLayout` protocol in order customize our apps more visually. In the next section, we're going to take a look a little deeper into some of the advancements in `UITableView`.

Exploring UICollectionView further

In this section, we'll again touch on some extra little bits that, just like with our table views, will allow us to really harness the power of a collection view – specifically when it comes to calculating the size of your layout. We'll start by taking a look at some overrides that we can make use of to achieve this.

Implementing a custom UICollectionViewLayout

Implementing a large and complex feature such as a custom collection view layout might seem like a huge challenge for most people.

Creating your layout involves calculating the position for every cell that your collection view will display. You must ensure that these calculations are performed as quickly and as efficiently as possible because your layout calculations directly influence the performance of your collection view. A poor layout implementation will lead to slow scrolling and a lousy user experience eventually.

Luckily, the documentation that has been provided for creating a collection view layout is pretty good as a reference to figure out whether you're on the right track.

If you take a look at Apple's documentation on UICollectionViewLayout, you can read about its role in a collection view. The available information shows that a custom layout requires you to handle the layout for cells, supplementary views, and decoration views. Supplementary views are also known as headers and footers.

Let's take a look at how we could begin to implement that. We'll start by creating our own class to do the job:

```swift
class ContactsCollectionViewLayout: UICollectionViewLayout {

    override var collectionViewContentSize: CGSize {
        return .zero
    }

    override func prepare() {

    }

    override func shouldInvalidateLayout(forBoundsChange
        newBounds: CGRect) -> Bool {
        return false
    }

    override func layoutAttributesForElements(in rect: CGRect)
        -> [UICollectionViewLayoutAttributes]? {
        return nil
    }
```

```
override func layoutAttributesForItem(at indexPath:
    IndexPath) -> UICollectionViewLayoutAttributes? {
        return nil
    }

}
```

As you can see from the preceding code, here we've implemented a subclass of UICollectionViewLayout and have a variety of overridden functions that we can use – let's go through these now.

Implementing collectionViewContentSize

A collection view uses the collectionViewContentSize property from its layout to figure out the size of its contents. This property is especially important because it is used to configure and display the scrolling indicators for the collection view.

It also provides the collection view with information about the direction in which scrolling should be enabled.

Implementing this property uses the number of rows and columns in the collection view. It also takes the item size and item spacing into account to come up with the size of all of its contents together.

Implementing layoutAttributesForElements(in:)

More complex than collectionViewContentSize is layoutAttributesForElements(in:). This method is responsible for providing a collection view with the layout attributes for several elements at once.

The collection view always provides a rectangle, for which it needs layout attributes. The layout is responsible for providing these attributes to the collection view as fast as possible. The implementation of this method must be as efficient as you can get it to be. Your scroll performance depends on it.

Even though there is only a small number of cells visible at a time, the collection view has a lot more content outside of its current viewport. Sometimes it is asked to jump to a particular cell, or the user scrolls extremely fast.

There are many cases where the collection view will ask for all layout attributes for several cells at once. When this happens, the layout object can help the cell determine which cells should be visible for a particular rectangle. This is possible because the layout attributes not only contain the rectangle in which a cell should be rendered but they also know the IndexPath object that corresponds with that specific cell.

This is a pretty complicated matter, and it's okay if you find this to be a little bit confusing. As long as you understand that a collection view can ask its layout which cells are present in a certain CGRect instance and how they should be rendered, you understand what layoutAttributesForElements(in:) does.

Implementing layoutAttributesForItem(at:)

Another way that a collection view can request layout attributes for its layout is by requesting the attributes for a single item. Because the collection view does so by supplying an index path, this method is quite simple to implement.

The layout you implemented assumes that only a single section exists in the collection view and the layout attributes array is sorted by index path because that's the order in which all items were inserted into the array.

Implementing shouldInvalidateLayout(forBoundsChange:)

Getting the implementation for shouldInvalidateLayout(forBoundsChange:) is crucial to having a great collection view layout that has amazing performance.

If you implement this method incorrectly, you could constantly be invalidating the layout, meaning you will need to recalculate all the time.

It's also possible that the collection view will never update its layout at all, even when it should. The collection view will call this method any time its size changes. For instance, when the user rotates their device or when your app runs on an iPad, the user opens another app in multitasking mode.

Assigning a custom layout to your collection view

The final step to using your custom layout is telling your collection view to use your layout. You have already seen that you can assign a custom class to the layout for a collection view in Interface Builder.

However, this only works when your layout inherits from UICollectionViewFlowLayout, which your layout does not inherit from. Luckily, you can also set your collection view's layout in code. Update your viewDidLoad method in ViewController.swift by adding the following line to it:

```
collectionView.collectionViewLayout =
  ContactsCollectionViewLayout()
```

This line sets your new layout as the current layout. You can now remove the `UICollectionViewDelegateFlowLayout` extension from `ViewController.swift` as it is not needed anymore.

Now that we've looked at layouts in more detail, let's take a look at how we handle user interaction with cell selection.

Cell selection in collection views

Although almost identical to its `UITableView` counterpart, I thought it was worth calling this function out:

```
func collectionView(_ collectionView: UICollectionView,
    didSelectItemAt indexPath: IndexPath)
```

With again the only real difference being that `Row` is replaced with `Item`, this delegate method performs in the exact same way.

We can make use of the reuse identifier and work with our cell directly should we need to manipulate it in any way (see *Chapter 5, Immersing Your Users with Animation*, for some exciting things we can do here).

In this section, we delved into the inner workings of the `UICollectionView` layout options and explored further how we can use `UICollectionViewLayout` to subclass our own layout, allowing us, the developer, to utilize specific and complex calculations should we need too. In our next and final section, we'll take a look at how Apple's new powerful UI framework, SwiftUI, handles lists.

Working with lists in SwiftUI

Back at WWDC 2019, Apple unveiled to the world a brand-new UI framework called SwiftUI. Built from the ground up, SwiftUI is a powerful alternative to UIKit and AppKit, offering developers the ability to write code using declarative syntax.

In this section, we are going to cover what SwiftUI has to offer in terms of generating lists and what we may need to do going forward should we require the use of anything that isn't available to use just yet.

Creating our first SwiftUI project

For this, we're going to need to create a new single view app, the same as before, but only this time we'll need to select **SwiftUI** for our user interface, as highlighted in the following screenshot:

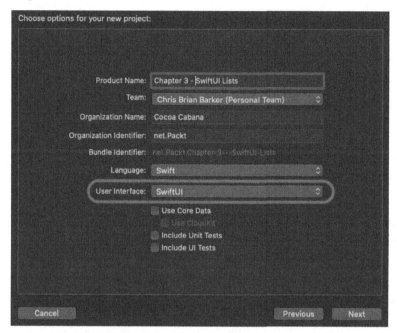

Figure 3.21 – New SwiftUI project

If you're unfamiliar with SwiftUI, you'll notice a couple of differences. You'll no longer have a `ViewController.swift` file – this has been replaced with `ContentView.swift`.

Highlight the file to take a look at the contents; you should see the following boilerplate code:

```
import SwiftUI
struct ContentView: View {
    var body: some View {
        Text("Hello, World!")
    }
}


struct ContentView_Previews: PreviewProvider {
    static var previews: some View {
        ContentView()
```

```
        }
    }
}
```

First, let's take a look at the `ContentView` struct – this is the first step of how SwiftUI builds up its declarative interface. Inside the `ContentView` struct is the body. Notice how these conform to either `View` or `some View` – that's because the concept of `ViewController` components in SwiftUI is no longer used; everything is a view being returned to the window.

But without getting too involved in the workings of SwiftUI, all we care about now is the contents of the body declaration. So, in the case of the preceding example, all we care about is the following:

```
Text("Hello, World!")
```

`Text` is SwiftUI's equivalent to `UILabel` – pretty neat, right, how a simple one line of code can construct, instantiate, and accept a value to display? Oh, and no need to add it to the view either – the fact that this line of code is present is enough.

Another benefit to using SwiftUI is the ability to preview code changes on the fly. If you take a look in Xcode to the right of our opened `ContentView.swift` file, you'll see the preview assistant. Click **Resume** at the top left and we should see a preview of our app appear:

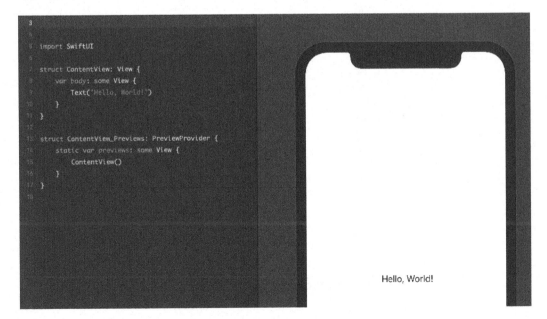

Figure 3.22 – SwiftUI "Hello, World!"

Now, let's take a look at how we would add in a list of items.

Building a list in SwiftUI

We'll start simple, by just adding our already-existing label to a list. Make the following highlighted code change, and if required, press resume in the preview assistant window:

```
var body: some View {
    List {
        Text("Hello, World!")
    }
}
```

That's right, it really is as simple as that. Go on and add a couple more Text views and see how it looks – even try running this in your simulator to see how it looks:

Figure 3.23 – SwiftUI list

Nice and simple, but much like we did with our `UITableView` components and `UICollectionView` components, let's see how we could go about adding in some external data.

Make the following highlighted change to our code in `ContentView.swift`:

```swift
@State var contacts: [String] = [String]()


var body: some View {
    List {
    ForEach(contacts, id: \.self) { contact in
        Text(contact)
        }
    }
}
```

Here, we've added in a `ForEach` function to our list; this is going to iterate around our array of contacts that we created just outside our body.

But if we press resume, you'll see that we get no data…let's fix this. Take a look just below the `ContentView` struct and you'll see the following code:

```swift
struct ContentView_Previews: PreviewProvider {
    static var previews: some View {
        ContentView()
    }
}
```

This struct is how our preview assistance can display our app – our own little internal testing/playground while we develop our SwiftUI view – without even needing to run the simulator.

Let's add some code in then to inject a little mock data into our preview. Make the following highlighted changes:

```swift
struct ContentView_Previews: PreviewProvider {
    static var previews: some View {
        let mockData = ["Chris", "Andy", "Harry", "Nathan",
            "Sam"]
        return ContentView(contacts: mockData)
    }
}
```

We simply just create some mock data that we can inject straight into our view, if not already updated. Click **Resume** on the preview assistant and see your code in action – however, if you run this in the simulator, you won't see anything, as the preview is no longer in effect and the app you see is your actual app (which we haven't added any data to yet).

The equivalent to creating a custom cell in SwiftUI

It's hard trying not to make a direct comparison to UIKit objects when developing with SwiftUI – but we'll all do it and it's okay, because usually there is a way to perform a similar action or a new way to learn.

Going back to the beginning of this section, I mentioned that SwiftUI is all about views, and that's no different when implementing a custom "cell" for a list in SwiftUI. We'll start by creating a new view (we'll do this inside of your ContentView.swift file, but outside of the initial class declaration):

```
struct RowView: View {

    @State var name: String

    var body: some View {
        Text(name)
    }

}
```

Just like ContentView, our new RowView is a simple view being created that can be used anywhere within SwiftUI. The structs can accept a name: String variable and will display this within a Text view – just like we did inside ContentView.

Now, let's amend our code to make use of this. Make the following highlighted changes:

```
List {
    ForEach(contacts, id: \.self) { contact in
        RowView(name: contact)
    }
}
```

It really is a simple as that; we can now treat RowView as we did collection view or table view cells and decorate them or work on them independently to their parent lists.

You can even create your own preview provider just for `RowView` so that you can again inject mock data whilst developing.

In this section, we were introduced to SwiftUI as a framework and took a look at the basic building blocks needed to create a project. From this, we learned about how lists are used and how we can use the preview assistant to our advantage when developing SwiftUI interfaces.

Summary

In this chapter, we looked at everything to do with lists. We started by learning how to create a `UITableView` object – pulling in contacts from our device and displaying them in the way we want. We then moved on to `UICollectionView`, comparing it against our previous implementation and looking at some of the subtle and larger differences it had to offer – such as cell layout and manipulation.

We then delved a little deeper into each of these, specifically looking at layouts with `UICollectionView` components, which is one of its most powerful features.

We then finished off by taking a look at the SwiftUI framework and how Apple has made it so easy not only to develop but also to display data in different ways that we have been used to previously with the ease of the declarative syntax and the use of the preview assistant.

In the next chapter, we'll be looking at taking our lists a step further and creating a details page for them to navigate to with the use of the cell interaction that we covered in this chapter.

Further reading

- Apple Developer documentation on table views:

  `https://developer.apple.com/documentation/uikit/views_and_ controls/table_views`

- Apple Developer documentation on collection views:

  `https://developer.apple.com/documentation/uikit/views_and_ controls/collection_views`

- *Learn SwiftUI* (Packt Publishing):

  `https://www.packtpub.com/business-other/learn-swiftui`

4
Creating a Detail Page

So far, you have managed to build an app that shows a set of contacts on a custom grid in a collection view. This is pretty impressive but not very useful. Typically, a user will expect to be able to see more information when tapping on an item in an overview.

In this case, they would likely expect to see more details about the tapped contact, for instance, their email address and phone number. In this chapter, you will see how to do just that.

We'll also be introduced to UIStackView for the first time too, a comprehensive and powerful way to lay out a display without the need for over-complex autolayout solutions.

Finally, we'll touch on the best practices when it comes to passing data from one view controller to another.

The following topics will be covered in this chapter:

- Implementing navigation with segues
- Creating our layout with UIStackView
- Passing data between view controllers

Technical requirements

For this chapter, you'll need to download Xcode version 11.4 or above from Apple's App Store.

You'll also need to be running the latest version of macOS (Catalina or above). Simply search for Xcode in the App Store and select and download the latest version. Launch Xcode and follow any additional installation instructions that your system may prompt you with. Once Xcode has fully launched, you're ready to go.

Download the sample code from the following GitHub link: `https://github.com/PacktPublishing/Mastering-iOS-14-Programming-4th-Edition`

Implementing navigation with segues

Most good applications have more than a single screen. I bet that most app ideas you have in your head involve at least a couple of different screens. Maybe you would like to display a table view or a collection view that links to a detail page. Or perhaps you want your user to drill down into your app's contents in a different way. Maybe you don't have any detail views but you would like to display a couple of modal screens for data input instead.

Every time your user moves from one screen in your app to another, they are navigating. Navigation is an essential aspect of building an app, and you must understand the possibilities and patterns for building good navigation on the iOS platform. The easiest way to gain insight into navigation is by using a storyboard to explore the available options.

Up until now, and with the exception of SwiftUI you have used your storyboard to create the layout for a single screen.

However, the name storyboard implies that you can do a lot more than laying out a single screen. The purpose of using a storyboard is the ability to lay out all screens of your application in a single place so you can easily see how screens and sections of your app are related and how users navigate between them.

In this section, we'll cover the following:

- Creating our new details view
- Implementing and understanding segues
- Creating a manual segue

Let's get started.

Creating our new details view

In this section, you will add a second view controller to your storyboard that functions as a detail page when a user taps on a contact – we'll continue working on our collection view project from *Chapter 3, Using Lists and Tables*.

Let's start by doing the following:

1. Open the `Main.storyboard` file.

2. Search and drag out a view controller from the **Object Library** (just like we did with our collection view objects).

3. Drop it next to the existing view controller.

4. Look for a label in the **Object Library** and add it to the new view controller you just added to the storyboard.

All going well, it should look something like the following figure:

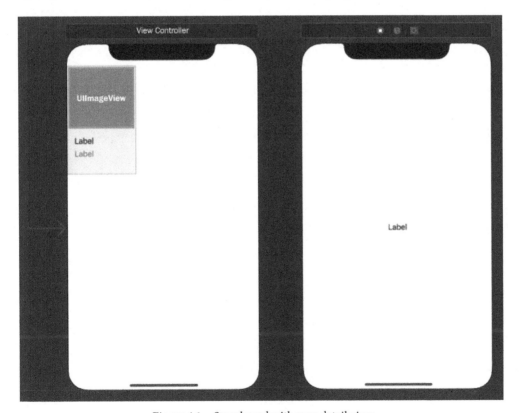

Figure 4.1 – Storyboard with new detail view

Before you add all the content for the contact detail page to the second view controller, it's a good idea to configure the navigation from the overview page to the detail page. To do this, you're going to create a selection segue.

Implementing and understanding segues

A **segue** is a transition from one screen to the next. Not all segues are animated; sometimes you might need to present the next screen without performing a smooth animation. Both animated and static transitions can be set up with segues.

Any time you connect one screen to the next to perform navigation, you are creating a segue. Some segues are performed when the user taps a button; these are called **action segues**. Segues that are only triggered through code are called **manual segues**.

The selection segue you're going to use in this sample is a segue that is set up by connecting a table view cell or collection view cell to the next screen. The segue is performed when the user taps on a cell.

To set up your selection segue, follow these steps:

1. Select the prototype collection view cell you have created for the contacts overview page.

2. Next, press and hold the *Ctrl* key while you drag from the cell to the second view controller.

When you release the mouse over the second view controller, a list of options is shown:

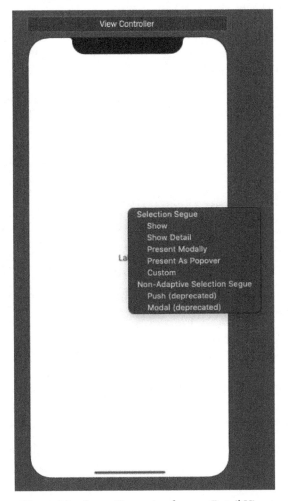

Figure 4.2 – Segue Connector for new Detail View

This list of possibilities describes how the detail view will be presented to the user.

For example, select the modal presentation style from the generated list. This will display the detail page with an upward animation from the bottom of the screen (a model), this is not quite the route we are going to take. However, if you now launch the iOS simulator and select one of the cells, you'll see the effect it has.

A better way to show the contact is by adding it to the navigation stack. Doing this will make a back button appear in the navigation bar, and the user will immediately understand that they are looking at a detail page due to the animation that moves the new view controller in from the right-hand side of the screen.

To set this up, you need to select the **Show** segue – highlight the previously created segue and hit *Delete* on your keyboard.

This segue pushes the newly presented view controller onto the existing navigation controller's navigation stack, but until we tell our app that we require navigation in this way, it will still be treated as a model.

To fix this, add a new object via the Object Library called **Navigation Controller**, and drag this into your storyboard. You'll notice this will have brought across what appears to be two view controllers.

The first is the navigation view controller itself (the one we care about) and the other is a template or a pre-defined `rootViewController`, which is already hooked into the navigation view controller.

In order to modify this, do the following:

1. Simply delete this `rootViewController`, leaving the navigation controller where it is.

2. Then, press *Ctrl* and primary click from the navigation controller and drag to our exiting `ViewController`.

3. When released, you'll be offered the option to make this the `rootViewController`. Select this option.

One final change to make is you'll notice an arrow going into the side of our existing **View Controller**; drag this from here to the **Navigation Controller** – all this is doing is setting this as our **Initial View Controller** so when the app is launched, it knows where to start.

Go ahead now and run the app. You should be able to successfully navigate back and forth whilst clicking on cells. Let's take a look now at how we would create a manual segue.

Creating a manual segue

We'll start by deleting the segue we just created. Now drag from the yellow circle at the top of the first view controller window to the second view controller – you've now just created a manual segue.

When the dialog to determine how the segue is performed appears, select **show** again because you don't want to use a different animation.

Click on the connecting line to inspect the segue and set the value for the **Identifier** field to `detailViewSegue` in **Attributes Inspector**. Similar to how you set a reuse identifier on table view cells and collection view cells, segues also use a string as their identifier.

To trigger the segue after the animation, you must manually do so from your code. Open `ViewController.swift` and update the contents of `collectionView(_:didSelectItemAt:)` as shown in the following snippet:

```
func collectionView(_ collectionView: UICollectionView,
    didSelectItemAt indexPath: IndexPath) {
        self.performSegue(withIdentifier: "detailViewSegue",
        sender: self)
}
```

With one line of code, we can hook into our segue via its identifier and away we go. Run the app now and see how easy that was.

In this section, we've started to create and build our very own details view page, learning all about how we can configure and control segues to push from one View Controller to the next.

In the next section, we'll take a look at creating adaptive layouts without the need for `Autolayout`.

Creating our layouts with UIStackView

Now we've got the foundations all set up, let's look at how we are going to build our details page.

We have several options. One way is **Autolayout**, which is exceptionally powerful and will certainly give us what we need. However, there is a much simpler way we can achieve this, by using a powerful component called `UIStackView`.

Stack views can lay out views that are added next to each other or on top of each other all by itself. This saves you adding constraints for the vertical spacing between labels like we did for the contact detail information.

Since stack views can also lay out objects that are next to each other and stack views can be nested, it could also take care of the two-column layout that you implemented for screens with a regular width size class. And to top it all off, you can swap the direction in which a stack view lays out its items at runtime, meaning you can change it from horizontal to vertical depending on the available space.

This will simplify a lot of the work that needs to be done and it makes your layout a lot more maintainable as well. To use a stack view, all you need to do is add one to your new view controller in Interface Builder via **Object Library** (simply search for `Stack View`).

Containing labels in a stack view

Let's start to create our page layout:

1. Adding in six UILabel's, three will be titles, and the others will be variable data (make sure you set your colors correctly: see *Chapter 2, Working with Dark Mode*). Something like this will work nicely:

Figure 4.3 – Updated storyboard with labels

2. Now, select the six labels in the contact info view and embed them in a stack view by using the **Embed In** menu as shown in the following screenshot:

Figure 4.4 – Embed In Stack View

3. Add in two other elements, such as image view or contact name, and group those together (separately from the labels you've just embedded).

4. Now, for the clever part, highlight both stack views and click on **Embed In** to embed them into a single Stack View.

Looking good. Well, almost – we'll still need to make a few minor tweaks. First, we'll add an `Autolayout` constraint to our main stack view of `0,16,16,0` (basically, hugging this to our bounds apart from the trailing and leading).

Next, you'll need to set a height in **Autolayout** for each label (and image) inside your stack view:

1. Set your constraint values to `250` and all labels to `25`.

2. Once done, select the parent stack view and within **Attributes Inspector**, make sure that **Alignment** is set to **Fill** and **Distribution** is set to **Fill Proportionally**.

These settings make sure that items are positioned a certain way within the stack view. In this case, **Leading** makes the items stick to the left side of the stack view. Setting this value to **Center** would align them in the middle, and **Fill** ensures that the stack's children are all stretched out to fill the entire width.

Once you've done that, you should have something that looks like the following:

Figure 4.5 – Detail View in Stack View

Now our detail view is all ready for some data, so let's see how we go about doing that in the next part, but first, we'll need to create a new **View Controller** file.

In the navigation tree, highlight the root level group (folder) and do the following:

1. Secondary-click to bring up the menu.

2. Click on **New File**.

3. Select **Cocoa Touch Class** from the list of options (click **Next**).

4. Name the new file `DetailsViewController` with a subclass of `UIViewController`.

5. Click **Next** and then **Create**.

Once you've done this, add in all the required outlets and hook them up. But before Interface Builder will let you hook these up, you'll need to set the class of your **Details Storyboard** to be `DetailsViewController` – just as we did with the custom cells back in *Chapter 3, Using Lists and Tables*.

We'll also need to add in the following variable, as we'll be passing this model across to our new View Controller very soon:

```
var contact = CNContact()
```

With all that done, we can now look to update our `retrieveContacts()` logic to fetch the new data we require.

Passing data between view controllers

So, the next part of our app is to pass some data over to our new details view but to do this, we need to create a new View Controller and hook up our labels and images to some outlets.

The code that fetches contact information also needs to be updated too, so a contact's phone number, email address, and postal address are fetched.

Finally, the contact data needs to be passed from the overview to the details page so the details page can display the data. The steps involved in this process are the following:

1. Updating the data loading

2. Passing the model to the details page

3. Updating our outlets

4. Best practices (creating a view model)

Let's now go through each step.

Updating the data loading

Currently, the code in `ViewController.swift` specifies that just the given name, family name, image data, and image availability for a contact should be fetched.

This needs to be expanded so the email address, postal address, and phone number are fetched as well.

Update the `retrieveContacts(store:)` method with the following code for `keysToFetch`:

```
let keysToFetch = [CNContactGivenNameKey as CNKeyDescriptor,
  CNContactFamilyNameKey as CNKeyDescriptor,
    CNContactImageDataAvailableKey as CNKeyDescriptor,
      CNContactImageDataKey as CNKeyDescriptor,
        CNContactEmailAddressesKey as CNKeyDescriptor,
          CNContactPhoneNumbersKey as CNKeyDescriptor,
            CNContactPostalAddressesKey as CNKeyDescriptor]
```

Here, we are just explicitly setting the desired data we would like to retrieve from our contacts. Once we've done this, we're ready to pass the data across to our details view controller.

Passing the model to the details page

The transition from the overview page to the details page is implemented with a segue. The segue is triggered when the user taps a contact, putting the details page on the screen.

Because this transition uses a segue, there is a special method that can be implemented to pass data from the first view controller to the second view controller. This special method is called `prepare(for:sender:)`.

This method is called on the source view controller right before a segue is performed and it provides access to the destination view controller.

The segue's destination is used to configure data on the view controller that is about to be presented. Let's implement this right now so you can pass the selected contact to the details page.

Add the following extension to `ViewController.swift`:

```
extension ViewController {
    override func prepare(for segue: UIStoryboardSegue, sender:
      Any?) {
```

```
if let contactDetailVC = segue.destination as?
    DetailsViewController,
    segue.identifier == "detailViewSegue",
    let selectedIndex = collectionView.
        indexPathsForSelectedItems?.first {


    contactDetailVC.contact = contacts[selectedIndex.
        row]



    }

  }

}
```

A quick overview of the preceding code is the segue is checked to see if its identifier is `"detailViewSegue"` (as all segues will pass through this function). If this condition is satisfied, it checks the destination (which is of type `UIViewController`) is that of the `DetailsViewController` we are looking for.

If all is well, we can assign our contact to a property on that View Controller and it will get passed across. Let's hook up our outlets now so we can start to bind some data.

Updating our outlets

We're all set to go; we just need to hook up our data to our outlets. To do this, make the following changes in your `viewDidLoad()` in `DetailsViewController`:

```
contactImageView.image = UIImage(data: contact.imageData ??
    Data())

contactName.text = "\(contact.givenName) \(contact.familyName)"

contactPhoneNumber.text = contact.phoneNumbers.first?.value.
    stringValue

contactEmailAddress.text = contact.emailAddresses.first?.value
    as String?

contactAddress.text = contact.postalAddresses.first?.value.
    street
```

Go ahead and run your app. Lo and behold, if you tap on your contacts, you'll be navigated straight to your new view controller, where you'll be able to see all the details of that particular contact.

However, taking another look at the code we've just added in, it looks a little messy. We're concatenating `givenName` and `familyName` inside our **View Controller**, and also randomly grabbing the street value from the first persisted address that our contact has.

All this logic should not sit in our view controller – this is what we call View model logic, and by that I mean we should create our own contact model that takes everything we need along with all the logic to get it straight from our `CNContent` object. Let's take a look at how we'd do that.

Best practices – creating a view model

In our example, our `CNContact` has multiple properties, some of which we've not even requested yet from `Contacts.framework`. As we saw with the logic in the previous section, making logic decisions based on what the view requires and what the model has should not be performed at this level.

So how can we fix that? Easy. To start with, let's create our custom model. Copy the following to a new file and call it `ContactModel.swift`:

```swift
struct ContactModel {

    var fullName: String?
    var primaryPhoneNumber: String?
    var primaryEmailAddress: String?
    var addressLine1: String?
    var contactImage: UIImage?

    init(_ contact: CNContact) {
        fullName = "\(contact.givenName) \(contact.familyName)"
        primaryPhoneNumber = contact.phoneNumbers.first?.value.
            stringValue
        primaryEmailAddress = contact.emailAddresses.first?.
            value as String?
        addressLine1 = contact.postalAddresses.first?.value.
            street
        contactImage = UIImage(data: contact.imageData ??
            Data()) ?? UIImage(systemName: "person.circle")
    }

}
```

Here, we've simply created a struct and added properties based on exactly what we're going to display. We'll then create a custom initializer, which accepts a parameter of CNContact. From here, we strip out all the logic that we originally had in our View Controller and put it in here – one central location for this view model logic.

All we need to do now is a couple of tweaks. Update our class variable in DetailsViewController to the following:

```
var contact: ContactModel?
```

And adjust our prepare() override in ViewController to the following:

```
contactDetailVC.contact = ContactModel(contacts[selectedIndex.
  row])
```

With that done, run the app again. You'll see that nothing really changed, but you can walk away now knowing that you've taken some great steps into writing and managing good, maintainable code.

In this section, we stitched everything together by using the prepare for segue function to transfer our model over to our DetailViewController.

Summary

In this section, we started by creating a brand-new View Controller dedicated to displaying selected user information. We learned about the different types of segues, including navigation-based segues and model-based segues. We were also introduced to creating segues both programmatically and via Interface Builder.

Once we had our connectors all set up, we then started to build our new Detail View Controller, populating it with a contact's information and using the power of UIStackView to lay out our labels and image views.

We finished off by wiring everything together. We performed some best practices and created a custom view model that we can now pass over to our new **Detail View Controller** via the prepare() override.

In the next chapter, we'll go deep into the use of animations and transitions in iOS as we start to get creative!

Further reading

- **Apple Documentation**: https://developer.apple.com/library/
  archive/featuredarticles/ViewControllerPGforiPhoneOS/
  UsingSegues.html

5
Immersing Your Users with Animation

Your app is starting to look really good now, and we've certainly covered a lot of ground already in this first few chapters, but UIKit has a lot of amazing features we're yet to explore – one of them being animations.

In this chapter, you are going to learn some advanced techniques with UIKit, Apple's animation framework built right into UIKit. We'll start off with the basics of how the little things can make such a massive difference, and then move forward on to some more advanced techniques with `UIViewPropertyAnimator` and how it provides more control over your animations than the animations you implemented in previous chapters. You'll also learn about UIKit Dynamics. UIKit Dynamics can be used to make objects react to their surroundings by applying physics.

Finally, you'll learn how to implement a custom transition when moving from one view controller to the next.

The following topics will be covered in this chapter:

- Using `UIView.animate` and `UIViewPropertyAnimator`
- Vibrant animations using springs in UIKit Dynamics
- Customizing view controller transitions

Technical requirements

For this chapter, you'll need to download Xcode version 11.4 or above from Apple's AppStore.

You'll also need to be running the latest version of macOS (Catalina or above). Simply search for `Xcode` in the App Store and select and download the latest version. Launch Xcode and follow any additional installation instructions that your system may prompt you with. Once Xcode has fully launched, you're ready to go.

Download the sample code from the following GitHub link:

```
https://github.com/PacktPublishing/Mastering-iOS-14-
Programming-4th-Edition
```

Using UIView.animate and UIViewPropertyAnimator

As I said in the intro, we've come a long way so far with our app, but often, it's the little things that we can do that make a massive difference; you just need to take another look at *Chapter 2*, *Working with Dark Mode*, to appreciate that.

In this section, we are going to start by adding some basic animations to our app using the standard practice to achieve a simple yet effective result.

Once we've done that, we'll look at how we can take this much further by refactoring and improving the maintainability of our code base. So, let's get started as we add our first animation to our app.

Creating our first animation

In their most basic form, animations are simple and easy to use. Here is an example of a typical animation that could be performed:

```
UIView.animate(withDuration: 0.8) {
    self.cell.familyNameLabel.alpha = 1.0
}
```

So, what does this mean exactly? Well, the `UIView.animate` function (which itself is a closure) is setting the alpha of our cell property to `1.0`. If we assume that the alpha for this property was set to `0.0`, our `animate` function would, over the duration of `0.8` seconds, change the alpha from `0.0` to `1.0` – thus giving us a simple yet extremely effective fade-in effect!

Let's put this into action, continuing with our project from the previous chapter. Head on over to our `DetailsViewController.swift` file.

First, let's set our contact image to have an alpha of `0.0`. We can achieve this by extending our outlet property to include a `didSet`. Make the following highlighted changes in the view controller:

```
@IBOutlet weak var contactImageView: UIImageView! {
    didSet {
        contactImageView.alpha = 0
    }
}
```

Here, we've simply added a setter and set an additional property on our `UIImageView` – in this case, we've set the alpha to be `0`.

Now, back into the body of our view controller. Add the following to your `viewWillAppear()` function:

```
UIView.animate(withDuration: 0.8) {
    self.contactImageView.alpha = 1
}
```

Just as we saw in the earlier example, we're simply setting a duration for the animation, and inside the closure, we set the alpha value of our property.

Go on and run your code in the simulator; you'll see that when
`DetailsViewController` now loads, you'll get a nice little fade-in animation.
With just a slight tweak to a property and couple of lines of code, your app has
made a massive jump forward!

Working with multiple animations

Let's take this another step further now and add a bounce effect to
`UICollectionViewCell` when it's tapped.

Head on over to our view controller and locate the `didSelectItemAt:` function.
Remember back in *Chapter 3, Using Lists and Tables*, when we identified how we could
grab an instance of the currently selected cell, should we want to do anything with it?
Well, here's our chance.

Add the following code to the start of the `didSelectItemAt:` cell:

```
guard let cell = collectionView.cellForItem(at: indexPath) as?
  ContactCell else {
    return
}
```

Unlike `cellForItem:`, where we make use of the `re-us` identifier in order to recycle
the use of our cells, here we care only about the selected instance – this is the cell we want
to use and do something with.

Next, we're going to add a big chunk of "initially" potentially confusing code, so we'll break
it down first one step at a time. Just underneath the preceding code, add the following:

```
UIView.animate(withDuration: 0.1, delay: 0, options:
  [.curveEaseOut], animations: {
    cell.conatctImageView.transform = CGAffineTransform(scaleX:
      0.9, y: 0.9)
})
```

Here, we're extending the `.animate` function we saw earlier, but this time you see we've
got a parameter for a delay, which we've set to 0 as we want the animation to start straight
away (but I guess it's nice to know that we could delay it if we wanted to).

Next, we've now got an `options` parameter, where we can pass in an array of animation
options available to use through UIKit. Here, we're going to pass in `curveEaseOut`
(don't worry, we'll cover the different types of animation options later in this chapter).

Finally, we set the transform of our image view by setting `CGAffineTransform` to a specific *x* and *y* scale. By setting a transform on the image, we are effectively scaling the original size based on a new *x* and *y* value.

Go ahead, launch the app – what do you see? Hopefully not a great deal – and you'll be wondering why not too. That's because we still have our `performSegue` call in there that is being called (and performed) before our animation can complete. Comment that out for the moment and try again. With any luck, when you tap on the cell, you should see the contact image shrink in size (or give a de-pressed appearance).

So, before we worry about bringing back our `performSegue` call, let's get the animation looking right first. Our new animation block has another trick up its sleeve. Within the closure, we can add a completion handler that will get called as soon as the animation has finished (I know what you're thinking, but let's finish the animation first).

Update the code with the following highlighted lines:

```
UIView.animate(withDuration: 0.1, delay: 0, options:
    [.curveEaseOut], animations: {
        cell.conatctImageView.transform = CGAffineTransform(scaleX:
            0.9, y: 0.9)
}, completion: { finished in
        UIView.animate(withDuration: 0.1, delay: 0, options:
            [.curveEaseOut], animations: {
                cell.conatctImageView.transform = CGAffineTransform.
                    identity
        })
})
```

So, all we've done here is extend our completion handler for our initial animate function by adding `completion: { finished in` and added in another animation function.

Back inside that closure, we reset the transform on our image view by setting it to `CGAffineTransform.identity` (a nice easy way to quickly revert any transform to its original state).

Run the app now in the simulator and all is going well; you should be presented with a really nice bounce effect. Let's add the last piece of the puzzle back in now by again extending our second animate function to have a completion handler, where we will add back in `performSegue`:

```
UIView.animate(withDuration: 0.1, delay:          0, options:
    [.curveEaseOut], animations: {
```

```
    cell.conatctImageView.transform = CGAffineTransform(scaleX:
        0.9, y: 0.9)
}, completion: { finished in
    UIView.animate(withDuration: 0.1, delay: 0, options:
        [.curveEaseIn], animations: {
        cell.conatctImageView.transform = CGAffineTransform.
            identity
    }, completion: { [weak self] finished in
        self?.performSegue(withIdentifier: "detailViewSegue",
            sender:self)
    })
})
```

Run your app again to see your beautiful animation in full bloom, followed by an immediate segue to DetailViewController – where you will be presented with a subtle yet effective fade-in animation of your contact image. Well done, you've done great!

In this section, we've learned how to tackle a basic animation in UIKit – we advanced a little, looking at how our basic animation could be extended to perform a little more complex task.

In the next section, we'll look at how we can simplify this with the use of UIViewPropertyAnimator.

Refactoring with UIViewPropertyAnimator

So, with some basic animation under your belt, we can now dive a little deeper into what iOS has to offer. While our previous code was powerful and not that many lines of code, it was in turn quite ugly, with completion handlers inside completion handlers – spaghetti code like that can become a real nightmare to maintain, especially if you need to build out the animation into anything more complex.

One reason to favor UIViewPropertyAnimator over the implementation you just saw is readability. Let's see what the same bounce animation looks like when it's refactored to use UIViewPropertyAnimator:

```
let downAnimator = UIViewPropertyAnimator(duration: 0.1, curve:
    .easeOut) {
    cell.conatctImageView.transform = CGAffineTransform(scaleX:
        0.9, y: 0.9)
}
```

```
let upAnimator = UIViewPropertyAnimator(duration: 0.1, curve:
    .easeIn) {
        cell.conatctImageView.transform = CGAffineTransform.
            identity
}


downAnimator.addCompletion { _ in
        upAnimator.startAnimation()
}


upAnimator.addCompletion { [weak self] _ in
        self?.performSegue(withIdentifier: "detailViewSegue",
            sender: self)
}


downAnimator.startAnimation()
```

Now, at first glance, you'll see that there appear to be a lot more lines of code here than previously, and you're not wrong, but it sure does make for better reading and maintainability.

With the use of UIViewPropertyAnimator, it does exactly as its name describes: it allows you to assign your animation to a property that you can then execute independently within your function.

The preceding code is no different than a simplified version of the original implementation that we broke down.

Go ahead and add this to your code and run your app. You'll notice no difference at all to the previous version.

The example code uses a version of UIViewPropertyAnimator that accepts a timing function to make the final bounce animation livelier. If you look at the sample code, the first argument passed to the UIViewPropertyAnimator initializer is the duration of the animation in seconds.

The second argument controls the timing function. A timing function describes how an animation should progress over time. For instance, the easeIn option describes how an animation starts off at a slow pace and speeds up over time.

The following diagram describes some of the most commonly used timing functions:

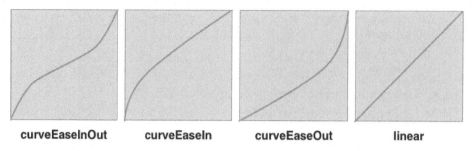

curveEaseInOut   **curveEaseIn**   **curveEaseOut**   **linear**

Figure 5.1 – Curve timing function scales

In these graphs, the *horizontal* axis represents the animation's progress. For each graph, the animation timeline is described from left to right on the *x* axis. The animation's progress is visualized on the *y* axis from bottom to top. At the bottom-left point, the animation hasn't started yet. At the right of the graph, the animation is completely done. The vertical axis represents time.

The final argument that is passed to the `UIViewPropertyAnimator` initializer is an optional argument for the animation that you wish to execute. This is quite similar to the `UIView.animate` way of doing things; the most significant difference is that you can add more animations after creating the animator, meaning that `nil` can be passed as the argument for the animations and you can add animations you wish to execute at a later time. This is quite powerful because you're even allowed to add new animations to `UIViewPropertyAnimator` while an animation is running!

The second section in the sample code you saw earlier adds completion closures to the animators. The completion closures both receive a single argument. The received argument describes at what point in the animation the completion closure was called. This property will usually have a value of `.end`, which indicates that the animation ended at the end position.

However, this isn't always true, because you can finish animations halfway through the animation if you desire. You could also reverse an animation, meaning that the completion position would be `.start`.

Once the completion closure is added, and the property animators are fully configured, the final step is to start the animation by calling `startAnimation()` on an animator object. Once the `startAnimation()` method is called, the animation begins executing immediately. If needed, you can make the animation start with a delay by calling `startAnimation(afterDelay:)`.

Now you've got a better understanding of how `UIViewPropertyAnimator` works, why don't you try and change over our fade that we added in `DetailViewController`? For such a simple piece of code like this, `UIViewPropertyAnimator` is probably a little overkill, but it might be good just for fun.

In the sample project, I'll include both scenarios and comment the other out for reference if you get stuck.

In this section, we took a massive leap into the world of animation in iOS development, learning the basic way to just drop in an animation and how to build out more complex animation with `UIViewPropertyAnimator` for improved code maintainability.

In the next section, we'll take a look at how to control an animation.

Understanding and controlling animation progress

One of the best features of `UIViewPropertyAnimator` is that you can use it to create animations that can be interrupted, reversed, or interacted with. Many of the animations you see in iOS are interactive animations – for instance, swiping on a page to go back to the previous page is an interactive transition.

Swiping between pages on the home screen, opening the control center, or pulling down the notification center are all examples of animations that you manipulate by interacting with them.

While the concept of interactive animations might sound complicated, `UIViewPropertyAnimator` makes it quite simple to implement them.

As an example, you'll see how to implement a drawer on the contact detail page in our app. First, you'll prepare the view, so the drawer is partially visible in the app. Once the view is all set up, you will write the code to perform an interactive show-and-hide animation for the drawer.

Let's start by heading back over to `Main.storyboard` and doing the following:

1. Add a UIView to our canvas via the object library (make sure this sits on top of the parent UIStackView, not inside it).

2. Set up Auto Layout constraints to make sure that the drawer view's width is equal to the main view's width (trialing and leading both set to 0).

3. Make the view `350pt` in height.

4. Then, set the bottom constraint to `-305`.

This should leave the view just visible enough to cover the safe area at the bottom of the screen. Next, we need to add a button to our new view:

1. Add the button via the object library.

2. Set the top constraint to be 8pt from the top of the new view (its parent view).

3. Set the leading and trailing to be around 16pts.

4. Set the label of the button to Toggle.

5. Also, set the background to **System Secondary Background Color**.

All going well, you should have something like this:

Figure 5.2 – Detail view with image view

Now that we've got the layout sorted, let's hook up the code we need. Our drawer functionality should implement the following features:

1. Toggle the drawer by tapping on the **Toggle** button.

2. Toggle the drawer interactively when swiping on the drawer.

3. Allow the user to tap on the **Toggle** button and then swipe the drawer to manipulate or reverse the animation.

Behavior such as this is not straightforward; without UIViewPropertyAnimator, you would have to write a lot of complex code, and you'd still be pretty far from your desired results. Let's see what UIViewPropertyAnimator does to make implementing this effect manageable.

To prepare for the implementation of the drawer, add the following properties to DetailsViewController:

```
@IBOutlet var drawer: UIView!
var isDrawerOpen = false
var drawerPanStart: CGFloat = 0
var animator: UIViewPropertyAnimator?
```

Also, add an extension to DetailsViewController that holds an @IBAction for the tap action. @IBAction is similar to @IBOutlet, but it is used to call a particular method in response to a specific user action. An extension is used, so it's easy to group the animation code nicely:

```
extension DetailsViewController {
    @IBAction func toggleDrawerTapped() {
    }
}
```

Now, let's connect our outlets:

1. Connect our UIView to the IBOutlet we just added in.

2. Connect your UIButton to the IBAction we just created in the extension.

When you drag from the action to the button, a menu appears from which you can select the action for which @IBAction should trigger. To respond to a button tap, choose **Touch Up Inside** from this menu.

Finally, add the following lines to the end of `viewDidLoad()`:

```
let panRecognizer = UIPanGestureRecognizer(target: self,
    action:#selector(didPanOnDrawer(recognizer:)))
drawer.addGestureRecognizer(panRecognizer)
```

Also, add the following method to the extension you created earlier for `@IBAction`. This is the method that is called when the user performs a pan gesture on the drawer:

```
@objc func didPanOnDrawer(recognizer: UIPanGestureRecognizer) {
}
```

Now that all of the placeholders are implemented, let's create a simple first version of the open drawer animation.

When the user taps on the toggle button, the drawer should open or close depending on the drawer's current state. The following snippet implements such an animation:

```
animator = UIViewPropertyAnimator(duration: 1, curve: .easeOut)
    { [unowned self] in

    if self.isDrawerOpen {
        self.drawer.transform = CGAffineTransform.identity
    } else {
        self.drawer.transform = CGAffineTransform(translationX:
            0, y: -305)
    }

}

animator?.addCompletion { [unowned self] _ in
    self.animator = nil
    self.isDrawerOpen = !(self.drawer.transform ==
        CGAffineTransform.identity)
}

animator?.startAnimation()
```

The animation that is passed to the property animator uses the value of `isDrawerOpen` to determine whether the animation should open or close the drawer. When the drawer is currently open, it should close, and vice versa.

Once the animation finishes, the `isDrawerOpen` variable is updated to reflect the new state of the drawer. To determine the current state, the application reads the drawer's current transformation. If the drawer is not transformed, its transformation will equal `CGAffineTransform.identity` and the drawer is considered closed. Otherwise, the drawer is considered open.

Go ahead and build and run your app now to see it in action. You'll see just how well it works.

Interactions with a pan gesture recognizer

To allow the user to interrupt or start the animation by dragging their finger on the screen, the code must check whether an existing property animator is performing an animation.

If no animator exists or if the current animator is not running any animations, a new instance of the animator should be created. In all other circumstances, it's possible to make use of the existing animator.

Let's refactor the animator creation code from `toggleDrawerTapped()` so that it reuses the animator if possible and creates a new animator if needed.

Add the following new function, `setUpAnimation()`, to our extension:

```swift
private func setUpAnimation() {

    guard animator == nil || animator?.isRunning == false else
        { return }

        animator = UIViewPropertyAnimator(duration: 1, curve:
            .easeOut) { [unowned self] in
        if self.isDrawerOpen {
            self.drawer.transform = CGAffineTransform.identity
        } else {
            self.drawer.transform =
                CGAffineTransform(translationX: 0, y: -305)
        }
    }

    animator?.addCompletion { [unowned self] _ in
        self.animator = nil
        self.isDrawerOpen = !(self.drawer.transform ==
```

```
                CGAffineTransform.identity)
    }


}
```

You'll notice how we've just lifted the majority of the code from `IBAction` – now we'll need to update `IBAction` to call this new function:

```
@IBAction func toggleDrawerTapped() {
    setUpAnimation()
    animator?.startAnimation()
}
```

Now, add the following implementation for `didPanOnDrawer(recognizer: UIPanGestureRecognizer)`:

```
switch recognizer.state {
case .began:
    setUpAnimation()
    animator?.pauseAnimation()
    drawerPanStart = animator?.fractionComplete ?? 0
case .changed:
    if self.isDrawerOpen {
        animator?.fractionComplete = (recognizer.
            translation(in: drawer).y / 305) + drawerPanStart
    } else {
        animator?.fractionComplete = (recognizer.
            translation(in: drawer).y / -305) + drawerPanStart
    }
default:
    drawerPanStart = 0
    let timing = UICubicTimingParameters(animationCurve:
        .easeOut)
    animator?.continueAnimation(withTimingParameters: timing,
        durationFactor: 0)

    let isSwipingDown = recognizer.velocity(in: drawer).y > 0
    if isSwipingDown == !isDrawerOpen {
        animator?.isReversed = true
```

```
        }
    }
```

This method is called for any change that occurs in the pan gesture recognizer. When the pan gesture first starts, the animation is configured, and then pauseAnimation() is called on the animator object.

This allows us to change the animation progress based on the user's pan behavior. Because the user might begin panning in the middle of the animation – for instance, after tapping the toggle button first – the current fractionComplete value is stored in the drawerPanStart variable.

The value of fractionComplete is a value between 0 and 1 and it's decoupled from the time that your animation takes to run. So, imagine that you are using an ease-in and ease-out timing parameter to animate a square from an *x* value of 0 to an *x* value of 100. The *x* value of 10 is not at 10% of the time the animation takes to complete.

However, fractionComplete will be 0.1, which corresponds to the animation being 10% complete. This is because UIViewPropertyAnimator converts the timescale for your animation to linear once you pause it.

Usually, this is the best behavior for an interactive animation. However, you can change this behavior by setting the scrubsLinearly property on your animator to false. If you do this, fractionComplete will take any timing parameters you've applied into account.

You can try playing around with this to see what it feels like for the drawer animation. Once the initial animation is configured and paused, the user can move their finger around.

When this happens, the fractionComplete property is calculated and set on the animator by taking the distance traveled by the user's finger and dividing it by the total distance required. Next, the progress made by the animation before being interrupted is added to this new value.

Finally, if the gesture ends, it gets canceled, or anything else, the start position is reset. Also, a timing parameter to use for the rest of the animation is configured and the animation is set up to continue. Bypassing a durationFactor value of 0, the animator knows to use whatever time is left for the animation while taking into account its new timing function.

If the user tapped the toggle button to close the drawer, yet they catch it mid-animation and swipe upward, the animation should finish in the upward direction. The last couple of lines take care of this logic.

There is no right or wrong way of creating your perfect animation. Have a play around with the various values that feel right for you and your app. In this section, we took everything we learned about animations a step further by looking at how we can control animations via either an event action such as a UIButton toggle or via a user gesture interaction.

In the next section, we'll start to add some real vibrancy to our animation by looking at how we can add some spring and bounce to our app!

Adding vibrancy to animations

A lot of animations on iOS look bouncy and feel natural. For instance, when an object starts moving in the real world, it rarely does so smoothly. Often, something moves because something else applied an initial force to it, causing it to have a certain momentum. Spring animations help you to apply this sort of real-world momentum to your animations.

Spring animations are usually configured with an initial speed. This speed is the momentum an object should have when it begins moving. All spring animations require damping to be set on them.

The value of this property specifies how much an object can overflow its target value. A smaller damping value will make your animation feel bouncier because it will float around its end value more drastically.

The easiest way to explore spring animations is by slightly refactoring the animation you just created for the drawer.

Instead of using an `easeOut` animation when a user taps the **Toggle Drawer** button, you can use a spring animation instead. The following code shows the changes you need to make to `setUpAnimation()`:

```
guard animator == nil || animator?.isRunning == false else {
    return
}


let spring: UISpringTimingParameters
if self.isDrawerOpen {
    spring = UISpringTimingParameters(dampingRatio: 0.8,
```

```
                initialVelocity: CGVector(dx: 0, dy: 10))
} else {
    spring = UISpringTimingParameters(dampingRatio: 0.8,
        initialVelocity: CGVector(dx: 0, dy: -10))
}


animator = UIViewPropertyAnimator(duration: 1,
    timingParameters: spring)


animator?.addAnimations { [unowned self] in
    if self.isDrawerOpen {
        self.drawer.transform = CGAffineTransform.identity
    } else {
        self.drawer.transform = CGAffineTransform(translationX:
            0, y: -305)
    }
}
animator?.addCompletion { [unowned self] _ in self.animator =
    nil
    self.isDrawerOpen = !(self.drawer.transform ==
        CGAffineTransform.identity)
}
```

When you implement a spring animation, you use a special initializer for UIViewPropertyAnimator. Since you can't pass animations to this initializer, you must add them by calling addAnimations(_:). Adding spring animations did not require a considerable code change, but try running the app and tapping on the toggle button. The drawer will now feel more realistic because its animation curve is not as static as it was before.

Play around with the values for the spring damping and the velocity. If you use some extreme values, you'll get interesting results. Keep in mind that the damping should be a value between 0 and 1 and that a value closer to 1 will make your animation bounce less.

The animation that is executed by the pan recognizer doesn't feel great at this point. It's very static and doesn't take into account how fast a user is panning on the drawer.

When the user ends their pan gesture, you can set the sprint timing's `initialVelocity` value based on the actual pan velocity. This will make the animation feel even more realistic because it will now use the actual pan speed as the initial speed for animation.

Update the default case statement with the following code:

```
drawerPanStart = 0
let currentVelocity = recognizer.velocity(in: drawer)
let spring = UISpringTimingParameters(dampingRatio: 0.8,
initialVelocity: CGVector(dx: 0, dy: currentVelocity.y))

animator?.continueAnimation(withTimingParameters: spring,
    durationFactor: 0)
let isSwipingDown = currentVelocity.y > 0
if isSwipingDown == !isDrawerOpen {
    animator?.isReversed = true
}
```

As you've just seen, the use of spring animations can benefit your animations and they are not very hard to add to your apps. While they might not always be the best solution, their ease of implementation makes spring animations a worthy candidate to experiment with to determine whether your animation needs a spring.

While the animation you have just implemented is pretty lifelike and realistic, your animations might need even more realism. The next section covers UIKit Dynamics, which is a special method of animating objects that uses a physics engine and can detect collisions between objects.

Adding dynamism with UIKit Dynamics

Most apps implement simple animations, such as the ones you've seen so far in this chapter. However, some animations might need a little more realism – this is what UIKit Dynamics is for.

With UIKit Dynamics, you can place one or more views in a scene that uses a physics engine to apply certain forces to the views it contains. For instance, you can apply gravity to a particular object, causing it to fall off the screen. You can even have objects bumping into each other, and if you assign a mass to your views, this mass is taken into account when two objects crash into each other.

When you apply a certain force to an object with very little mass, it will be displaced more than an object with a lot of mass, just like you would expect in the real world.

For this, we're going to create another little project away from our current app, so we can perform some physics experiments.

So, let's get started by creating a new project in Xcode:

1. Create a new project and call it Dynamics.

2. In Main.Storyboard, configure the preview to **Landscape**.

3. Add three UIViews around 100 x 100 in size (don't worry about constraints for this project).

4. Give each UIView a background color (think systems colors from *Chapter 3, Using Lists and Tables*).

All going well, it should look something like this:

Figure 5.3 – Main storyboard with views

Next, add instances of @IBOutlet in ViewController.swift for the views you just added and connect them to the storyboard in the same way you did before. You can name the outlets anything you like, but I'll name mine ball1, ball2, and ball3 (more on that later).

The simplest thing you can implement at this point is to set up a scene that contains the three squares and apply some gravity to them. This will cause the squares to fall off the screen because they'll start falling once gravity is applied, and there is no floor to stop the squares from dropping off the screen.

To set up a scene like the one described here, add the following highlighted code to your `ViewController.swift` file:

```swift
var animator: UIDynamicAnimator?

override func viewDidLoad() {
    super.viewDidLoad()

    let balls: [UIDynamicItem] = [ball1, ball2, ball3]
    animator = UIDynamicAnimator(referenceView: view)

    let gravity = UIGravityBehavior(items: balls)
    animator?.addBehavior(gravity)

}
```

If you test your app now, you'll notice that your views start falling immediately. Setting up a simple scene such as this is easy with UIKit Dynamics.

The downside of this simple example is that it's not particularly interesting to look at. Before you add features to make this sample more interesting, let's see what the preceding four lines of code do.

The views in a dynamic scene must be of the `UIDynamicItem` type. A UIView can be used as `UIDynamicItem`, so by adding them to a list that has `[UIDynamicItem]` works automatically.

Then, we create an instance of `UIDynamicAnimator` and you tell it the view to which it will apply its physics engine. The last step is to configure and apply a behavior. This example uses `UIGravityBehavior` but there are several other behaviors you can use in your scenes.

For instance, you can create `UIAttachmentBehavior` to attach an item to another item or to some point on the screen.

The following code implements an attachment behavior for every square on the screen and attaches it to the top of the screen. This will cause the squares to fall for a moment, and then they will bounce and swing a little until they eventually come to a standstill. You can add the following code to `viewDidLoad()` to implement this:

```
var nextAnchorX = 250


for ball in balls {
    let anchorPoint = CGPoint(x: nextAnchorX, y: 0)
    nextAnchorX -= 30
    let attachment = UIAttachmentBehavior(item: ball,
        attachedToAnchor: anchorPoint)
    attachment.damping = 0.7
    animator?.addBehavior(attachment)
}
```

Every square is set up with a slightly different attachment point in this example. Note that the attachment behavior has a `damping` property.

This damping is similar to the damping that is used in spring animations. Try experimenting with the value for `attachment.damping` to see what it does.

If you run the app now, you'll notice that every square is attached to an invisible point on the screen that keeps it from falling. Some things are still missing though.

The squares can now simply cross over each other – how cool would it be if they bumped into each other instead?

To do this, add the following line of code to `viewDidLoad()`:

```
let collisions = UICollisionBehavior(items: balls)
animator?.addBehavior(collisions)
```

Are you convinced that UIKit Dynamics is cool yet? I thought so; it's amazing how much you can do with just a little bit of code. Let's add some mass to the squares and make them more elastic to see whether this has any effect on how the squares collide.

Update your `for` loop with the following code:

```
let dynamicBehavior = UIDynamicItemBehavior()
dynamicBehavior.addItem(ball)
dynamicBehavior.density = CGFloat(arc4random_uniform(3) + 1)
dynamicBehavior.elasticity = 0.8
animator?.addBehavior(dynamicBehavior)
```

The preceding code should augment what you already have in the loop; it shouldn't replace the existing logic.

By setting `density` on `UIDynamicItemBehavior`, the engine can derive the mass of an item. This will change how the physics engine treats the item when it collides with another item.

Again, this is a perfect time for you to go away and have a play with the behaviors and physics engine that Apple has provided. Now, a swinging square game might not be of interest to anyone – but update each of your ball properties to the following and run again…a lot more fun now, right?

```
@IBOutlet weak var ball1: UIView! {
    didSet {

    // Make a ball
    ball1.layer.cornerRadius = ball1.frame.size.width/2
    ball1.clipsToBounds = true

    // Cool gradient effect!
    let gradient = CAGradientLayer()
    gradient.frame = ball1.bounds
    gradient.colors = [UIColor.systemBlue.cgColor, UIColor.
        systemTeal.cgColor]

    ball1.layer.insertSublayer(gradient, at: 0)

    }
}
```

In the final section, we will learn everything we need to know about view controller transitions, again another way to really make a difference when moving away from the default behavior of our app.

Customizing view controller transitions

Implementing a custom view controller transition is one of those things that can take a little while to get used to. Implementing custom transitions involves implementing several objects, and it's not always easy to make sense of how this works. This section aims to explain exactly how custom view controller transitions work so that you can add one more powerful tool to your developer toolbox.

A nicely implemented custom view controller transition will entertain and amaze your users. Making your transitions interactive could even ensure that your users spend some extra time playing around with your app, which is exactly what you want.

We'll continue by working on our Contacts app we started earlier on. Firstly, you'll learn how you can implement a custom modal transition. Once you've implemented that, you will learn about custom transitions for `UINavigationController` so that you can show and hide the contact details page with a custom transition. The dismissal of both the modal view controller and the contact detail page will be interactive, so users can swipe to go back to where they came from.

In this section, you will work through the following steps:

1. Implement a custom modal presentation transition.

2. Make the transition interactive.

3. Implement a custom `UINavigationController` transition.

Implementing a custom modal presentation transition

A lot of applications implement modally presented view controllers. A modally presented view controller is typically a view controller that is presented on top of the current screen as an overlay. By default, modally presented view controllers animate upward from the bottom of the screen and are often used to present forms or other temporary content to the user. In this section, you'll take a look at the default modal presentation transition and how to customize it to suit your own needs.

Let's start by creating a brand new View Controller. For this, we'll head back to our Contacts app project where we can add this in here (or feel free to start a brand-new project):

1. Create a new **Cocoa Touch** class and name it `TransitionViewController` (with a subclass of `UIViewController`).

2. Add a new View Controller to `Main.Storyboard`.

3. Set the object class for that new View Controller to be `TransitionViewController`.

   Once you've done that, we'll add a bar button item to our existing navigation so that we can present our modal.

4. Add `BarButtonItem` from our object library to our navigation bar in `rootViewContoller` (basically our first view controller).

5. Set the button's text to be `Show Modal` (or whatever you want).

6. Now, press *Ctrl* and drag the bar button item's connector to the new view controller we just created.

7. When presented with options, choose **Present Modally**.

All going well, it should look like the following:

Figure 5.4 – Modal action segue

Finally, give our new view controller a system orange background color, so it will be easier to see the transition later.

If you run your app now, you can click on the **Show Modal** button and you'll see an empty view controller pop up from the bottom.

Until iOS 13, you had to create an interface in order for the user to dismiss a modal. Now, unless implicitly set, you can just swipe down to dismiss a modal, which is worth bearing in mind when developing apps that go further back than iOS 13.

Custom view controller transitions use several objects to facilitate the animation. The first object you will look at is `transitioningDelegate` for `UIViewController`. The `transitioningDelegate` property is responsible for providing an animation controller that provides the custom transition.

The animation controller uses a transitioning context object that provides information about the view controllers that are involved in the transition. Typically, these view controllers will be the current view controller and the view controller that is about to be presented.

A transitioning flow can be described in the following steps:

1. A transition begins. The target view controller is asked for `transitioningDelegate`.

2. `transitioningDelegate` is asked for an animation controller.

3. The animation controller is asked for the animation duration.

4. The animation controller is told to perform the animation.

When the animation is complete, the animation controller calls `completeTransition(_:)` on the transitioning context to mark the animation as completed.

If *step 1* or *step 2* return `nil`, or aren't implemented at all, the default animation for the transition is used. The objects involved in a custom transition are displayed in the following diagram:

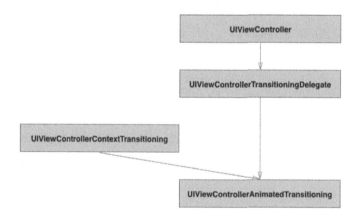

Figure 5.5 – Animation transition flow

Creating a separate object to control the animation is often a good idea because it allows you to reuse a transition and it keeps your code nice and clean. The animation controller should be an object that conforms to UIViewControllerAnimatedTransitioning. This object will take care of animating the presented view onto the screen.

Let's create the animation controller object next:

1. Create a new **Cocoa Touch** class and name it CustomAnimator (using NSObject as a subclass).

2. Add the following extension in order to make the class conform to UIViewControllerAnimatedTransitioning:

    ```
    extension CustomAnimator:
    UIViewControllerAnimatedTransitioning {

    }
    ```

    This makes the new class conform to the protocol that's required to be an animation controller. Xcode will show a build error because you haven't implemented all the methods to conform to UIViewControllerAnimatedTransitioning yet.

Let's go over the methods one by one so that you end up with a full implementation for the animation controller.

The first method that must be implemented for the animation controller is transitionDuration(using:). The implementation of this method is shown here:

```
func transitionDuration(using transitionContext:
  UIViewControllerContextTransitioning?) -> TimeInterval {
    return 0.6
}
```

This method is used to determine the total transition duration in seconds. In this case, the implementation is simple – the animation should last *0.6* seconds.

The second method that needs to be implemented is animateTransition(using:). Its purpose is to take care of the actual animation for the custom transition.

This implementation will take the target view controller and its view will be animated from the top of the screen downward to its final position. It will also do a little bit of scaling, and the opacity of the view will be animated; to do this, UIViewPropertyAnimator will be used.

Add the following implementation to the animator:

```
func animateTransition(using transitionContext:
  UIViewControllerContextTransitioning) {

    // 1
    guard let toViewController = transitionContext.
      viewController(forKey:
        UITransitionContextViewControllerKey.to) else {
          return
    }

    // 2
    let transitionContainer = transitionContext.containerView

    // 3
    var transform = CGAffineTransform.identity
    transform = transform.
      concatenating(CGAffineTransform(scaleX: 0.6, y: 0.6))
    transform = transform.concatenating
      (CGAffineTransform(translationX: 0, y: -200))

    toViewController.view.transform = transform
    toViewController.view.alpha = 0

    // 4
    transitionContainer.addSubview(toViewController.view)

    // 5
    let animationTiming =
      UISpringTimingParameters(dampingRatio: 0.5,

 initialVelocity: CGVector(dx: 1, dy: 0))

    let animator = UIViewPropertyAnimator(duration:
      transitionDuration(using: transitionContext),
        timingParameters: animationTiming)
```

```
animator.addAnimations {
    toViewController.view.transform = CGAffineTransform.
        identity
    toViewController.view.alpha = 1
}


// 6
animator.addCompletion { finished in
    transitionContext.completeTransition(!transition
        Context.transitionWasCancelled)
}


// 7
animator.startAnimation()


}
```

A lot is going on in the preceding code snippet. Let's go through the code step by step to see what's happening:

1. The target view controller is extracted from the transition context. This allows you to use the view controller's view in the animation that you're about to perform.

2. Obtain the animation's container view. The container view is a regular UIView and it is intended to contain all the animated views.

3. Prepare the target view controller's view for the animation. The view is transformed, so it's off the screen, and transparency is set to make the view completely transparent.

4. Once the view is prepared, it is added to the container view.

5. The animations are set up and added to a property animator.

6. The completion handler for the property animator is configured, so `completeTransition(_:)` is called on the context. The `transitionWasCancelled` variable is used to determine whether the animation completed normally.

7. Start the property animator so that the animations begin.

Now that the animation controller is complete, the
`UIViewControllerTransitioningDelegate` protocol should be
implemented on `TransitionViewController` so that it can act as its own
`transitioningDelegate`.

Open the file and add the following code:

```
extension TransitionViewController:
  UIViewControllerTransitioningDelegate {
    func animationController(forPresented presented:
      UIViewController, presenting: UIViewController, source:
      UIViewController) ->
      UIViewControllerAnimatedTransitioning? {
        return CustomAnimator()
    }


    func animationController(forDismissed dismissed:
    UIViewController) ->
      UIViewControllerAnimatedTransitioning? {
        return nil
    }
}
```

Now, add the following code to `TransitionViewController`:

```
public required init?(coder aDecoder: NSCoder) {
    super.init(coder: aDecoder)
    transitioningDelegate = self
}
```

This code adds conformance to the `UIViewControllerTransitioningDelegate`
protocol and assigns the view controller as its own transitioning delegate. The
`animationController(forPresented:presenting:source:)`
method returns the animation controller you created before. The
`animationController(forDismissed:)` method returns `nil` for now.

Go ahead and test your custom transition! This is all the code required to create a custom
display transition.

In this chapter, we learned loads about how to fine-tune and polish off our app. Visual
effects play such a big part in any application – so learning about animations transitions
is an absolute must for any iOS developer.

Summary

In this chapter, we took the solid core of our Contacts app and decorated it with animations and vibrancy. We started by learning the basics of animation and how a couple of lines of code could make a massive difference. We then took this a step further and refactored more complex code to make it not only maintainable but also easier to understand.

UIKit offers much more than just fancy animations. Looking at dynamics, we saw how we could apply physics to even a UIView to give us an app with a truly awesome experience.

Finally, we looked at transitions, something that is very powerful in iOS development, yet something we take so easily for granted. We created a custom class that allowed us to create our very own modal transition.

In the next chapter, we're going to delve a little deeper into the Swift programming language and learn all about Swift's type system.

6
Understanding the Swift Type System

The previous chapters have left you with a solid foundation that you can use to build great, adaptive apps on. At this point, it is a good idea to take a step back and look at the code you have written to gain a deeper understanding of Swift and how it works. This section focuses on teaching you more about Swift as a language, regardless of what you intend to build.

In this chapter, you will learn about Swift's fantastic type system. Swift's type system is one of its most powerful features because it allows developers to express complex and flexible principles safely and predictably.

The following topics will be covered in this chapter:

- Understanding available types in Swift
- Understanding differences in types
- Deciding which type to use

Technical requirements

For this chapter, you'll need to download Xcode version 11.4 or above from Apple's App Store.

You'll also need to be running the latest version of macOS (Catalina or above). Simply search for Xcode in the App Store and select and download the latest version. Launch Xcode and follow any additional installation instructions that your system may prompt you with. Once Xcode has fully launched, you're ready to go.

Download the sample code from the following GitHub link:

```
https://github.com/PacktPublishing/Mastering-iOS-14-
Programming-4th-Edition
```

Understanding available types in Swift

To write great code, you need to learn what tools are available in your toolbox. This applies to building apps and understanding the features UIKit has to offer, but it also applies to the language you use to write software in. Different languages come with various features, best practices, pros, and cons. The deeper your understanding of the language you work with is, the better the decisions you can make about the code you write. As mentioned before, Swift's type system is one of the features that make Swift such an excellent language for both experts and beginners to develop in.

Before you dive into the details of Swift's types and how they compare to each other, it's essential that you know what types Swift has to offer. On a high level, you can argue that Swift has two types:

- Reference types
- Value types

Let's have a closer look at each type to see what they mean, how they work, and how you can use them.

Working with reference types

The types you have seen so far in this book were mostly, if not all, reference types. Two types of objects are classified as reference types:

- Classes
- Closures

You have seen both of these object types in this book already. For instance, all the UIViewController subclasses you have created are reference types. All the closures that you used as callbacks or to perform animations are also reference types.

So, what does it mean if something is a reference type, and why should it matter to you? Well, reference types come with behavior that can be both convenient and very frustrating depending on what you are trying to achieve in your code.

One feature that is unique to reference types and classes is the ability to subclass. The only type that can inherit functionality from another object is a class. This will be covered in more depth when you learn about the differences between types, but it's good to be aware of this information already. Let's examine reference types up close by writing some code in a playground.

Create a new playground project in Xcode and give it any name you like. Then, add the following code:

```
class Pet {
    var name: String

    init(name: String) {
        self.name = name
    }
}
func printName(for pet: Pet) {
    print(pet.name)
}
let cat = Pet(name: "Jesse")
printName(for: cat)
```

Likely, you're not too excited about this little snippet of code. All it does is define a new Pet class, make an instance of it, and then pass that instance into printName(for:). However, this code is extremely well-suited to illustrating what a reference type is.

When you call printName(for: cat), you pass a *reference* to your cat instance to printName(for:). This means that it is possible for anybody who gets ahold of this reference to make changes to the object that is referenced. If this sounds confusing, that's okay.

Add the following code to the playground you have created, and then run it:

```
func printName2(for pet: Pet) {
    print(pet.name)
    pet.name = "Pugwash"
}


let dog = Pet(name: "Astro")
printName2(for: dog)
print(dog.name)
```

What do you notice in the console after running this?

If you noticed that the dog's name changes from `Astro` to `Pugwash`, you have just observed what it means to pass a reference to something around.

Since `printName2(for:)` received a reference to your `Pet` instance, it was able to change its name. If you have programmed in other languages, this might be obvious to you. If not, this might be very surprising.

One more thing you should note is that `dog` was declared as a constant. Regardless, you were able to change the name of your instance from `Astro` to `Pugwash`.

If you think this is obvious, add the following code to your playground and run it:

```
let point = CGPoint(x: 10, y: 10)
point.x = 10
```

This code is very similar to what you did with the `Pet` instance. You make a constant instance of a thing, and then you change one of its properties. This time, however, when you try to run your playground, you should see the following error:

```
Cannot assign to property: 'point' is a 'let' constant
```

Even though the code you implemented so far is pretty short, it does a great job of demonstrating reference types. You have currently seen two properties of a reference type in action:

- Anybody that receives an instance of a reference type can mutate it.
- You can change properties on a reference type, even if the property that holds onto the reference type is declared as a constant.

These two characteristics are typical of reference types. The reason reference types work like this is that a variable or constant that is assigned a reference type *does not contain or own* the object. The constant or variable only points to an address in memory where the instance is stored.

Any time you create an instance of a reference type, it is written to RAM, where it will exist at a particular address. RAM is a special type of memory that is used by computers, such as an iPhone, to temporarily store data that is used by a certain program.

When you assign an instance of a reference type to a property, the property will have a **pointer** to the memory address for this instance. Let's have another look at the following line of code:

```
let dog = Pet(name: "Astro")
```

The dog constant now points to a particular address in memory where the Pet instance is stored. You are allowed to change properties on the Pet instance as long as the underlying memory address isn't changed.

In fact, you could theoretically put something entirely different at that memory address, and let dog won't care because it still points to the same address.

For this same reason, it is possible for printName2(for:) to change a pet's name. Instead of passing it an instance of Pet, you pass it the memory address at which the instance is expected to exist. It's okay for printName2(for:) to make changes to the Pet instance because it doesn't change the underlying address in memory.

If you tried to assign a new instance to dog by typing the following, you would get an error:

```
dog = Pet(name: "Iro")
```

The reason this would cause an error is that you can't change the memory address dog points to since it's a constant.

Now that you know what a reference type is and how it works, you might have already concluded that CGPoint that you saw in the preceding example must be a value type. Next, let's see what value types are all about.

Working with value types

In the examples for references types, you saw the following snippet of code:

```
let point = CGPoint(x: 10, y: 10)
point.x = 10
```

At first sight, you might expect a value type to be a special kind of class because it looks like this snippet creates an instance of a class called CGPoint. You would be right in your observation, but your conclusion is wrong. CGPoint is not a class at all.

Classes are inherently reference types, and they can't ever be something else. So, what are value types, then?

There are two types of objects that are considered to be value types:

- Stucts

- Enums

These two types are both very different, so let's make sure that you understand the basics of value types first, and then you'll learn what each of these two types is.

Let's have a look at the Pet example again, but use a struct instead of a class.

Create a new playground page in Xcode, again naming this anything you like.

Once created, add the following code:

```
struct Pet {
    var name: String
}


func printName(for pet: Pet) {
    print(pet.name)
    pet.name = "Jesse"
}


let dog = Pet(name: "Astro")
printName(for: dog)
print(dog.name)
```

You will immediately notice that Xcode complains.

The error you should see in the console tells you that `pet` is a `let` constant and you are not allowed to change its name. You can turn `pet` into a variable by updating `printName`, as follows:

```
func printName(for pet: Pet) {
    var pet = pet
    print(pet.name)
    pet.name = "Jesse"
}
```

If you run your playground now, make sure to look at the console closely. You'll notice that the pet's name remains unchanged in the second print.

This demonstrates one of the key features of a value type. Instead of passing a reference to an address in memory around, a copy of the object is passed around. This explains why you aren't allowed to change properties on a value type that is assigned to a constant.

Changing that property would change the value type's value, and it would, therefore, change the value of the constant. This also means that when you pass `dog` to `printName`, you pass a copy of the `Pet` instance to `printName`, meaning that any changes made to the instance are local to the `printName` function and won't be applied to `dog`, in this case.

This behavior makes using value types extremely safe because it's tough for other objects or functions to make unwanted changes to a value type. Also, if you define something as a constant, it truly is a constant. Another characteristic of value types is that they're typically very fast and lightweight because they can exist on the stack, while reference types exist on the heap. You'll learn more about this later when we compare reference types and value types.

Now that you have a basic understanding of value types, let's have a look at the specific value types.

Understanding structs

Structs are similar to classes in the way you define them. If you look at the `Pet` class you defined earlier, it might be easy to miss the fact that it's a struct. If you pay close attention, you will notice one big difference, though: you didn't have to write an initializer for the struct! Swift can automatically generate initializers for structs. This is extremely convenient and can save you a lot of typing for larger structs.

Structs also can't inherit functionality from other objects. This means that structs always have a very flat and transparent set of properties and methods. This allows the compiler to make optimizations to your code that make structs extremely lightweight and fast.

A struct can, however, conform to protocols. The Swift standard library is full of protocols that define features for many of the built-in types, such as `Array`, `Dictionary`, and `Collection`. Most of these built-in types are implemented as structs that adopt one or more protocols.

One last thing you need to understand about structs is that they are very strict about whether they can be modified. Consider a struct that looks as follows:

```
struct Car {
    var fuelRemaining: Double

    func fillFuelTank() {
        fuelRemaining = 1
    }
}
```

This struct will cause the compiler to throw an error.

A struct itself is immutable by default, which means you cannot change any of its values. It's up to you to make it explicit to the compiler when a method can mutate or change a struct. You do this by adding the `mutating` keyword to a function, as follows:

```
mutating func fillFuelTank() {
    fuelRemaining = 1
}
```

When you create a constant instance of `Car` and call `fillFuelTank()` on it, the compiler will error again. If you call a mutating function on a `let` instance, you mutate the instance, meaning the value of the property would change. Because of this, you can only call mutating functions on variable properties.

Understanding enums

An enum is a type that holds a finite set of predefined values. Enums are often used to represent a particular state or result of an operation. The best way to learn what this means is to look at an example of an enum that represents the state of a traffic light:

```
struct TrafficLight {
    var state: TrafficLightState
}


enum TrafficLightState {
    case green
    case yellow
    case red
}
```

This sample shows a `TrafficLight` struct that has a `state` property. The type of this property is `TrafficLightState`, which is an enum.

`TrafficLightState` defines three possible states for a traffic light. This is very convenient because an enum such as this eliminates the possibility of a bad state because the compiler can now enforce that you never end up with an invalid value.

Enums can also contain properties and methods, just like structs can. However, an enum can also have an *associated value*. This means that each possible case can have a representation in a different type, such as a string.

If you modify `TrafficLightState`, as shown here, it will have `String` for `rawValue`:

```
enum TrafficLightState: String {
    case green
    case yellow
    case red
}
```

If Swift can infer the raw value, you don't have to do anything more than add the type of the raw value to the enum's type declaration. In this sample, the raw value for the `green` enum case will be the `green` string. This can be convenient if you need to map your enum to a different type – for instance, to set it as a label's text.

Just like structs, enums cannot inherit functionality from other objects, but they can conform to protocols. You make an enum conform to a protocol with an extension, just like you would do for classes and structs.

This wraps up the exploration of value types. Now that you know what value types and reference types are, let's explore some of their differences!

Understanding differences in types

Being aware of the available types in Swift – knowing their similarities and, more importantly, their differences – will help you make better decisions about the way you write your code. The preceding segments have listed several properties of value types and reference types. More specifically, you learned a lot about classes, structs, and enums. Closures are also a reference type because they get passed around by their location in memory, rather than their value, but there isn't much else to say about them in this context.

The most obvious comparison you can make is probably between structs and classes. They look very similar, but they have very different characteristics, as you have already seen. Enums are a special type altogether; they represent a value from a fixed number of possible values but are very similar to structs otherwise.

The most important difference you need to understand is the general difference between value types and reference types, and the difference between structs and classes specifically. Let's have a look at value types and reference types first, so you have the general picture. Then, you'll learn about the specific differences between structs and classes.

Comparing value types to reference types

When comparing value types to reference types, it is essential to distinguish between the differences you can see as a developer and the differences that are internal to Swift and the way your app will end up working. Knowing these details will ensure that you can make a well-informed decision that considers all the implications instead of only focusing on memory usage or developer convenience.

Let's examine the more obvious and visible differences first. Afterward, you will learn about the memory implications for each type.

Differences in usage

Create a new playground, once again naming it anything you like, and add the following code:

```
protocol PetProtocol {
    var name: String { get }
    var ownerName: String { get set }


}

class Animal {
    let name: String
    init(name: String) {
        self.name = name
    }
}

class Pet: Animal, PetProtocol {
    var ownerName: String

    init(name: String, ownerName: String) {
        self.ownerName = ownerName
        super.init(name: name)
    }
}
```

This code defines a PetProtocol that requires two properties to exist on all objects that conform to this protocol. The name property is defined as a constant since it only needs it to be gettable, and ownerName is a variable since it requires both get and set. The code also defines an Animal and Pet class. Pet is a subclass of Animal, and it conforms to PetProtocol because Animal satisfies the name constant requirement and Pet itself satisfies the ownerName variable.

Try changing the `class` declarations to `struct`. Your playground will not compile now because structs cannot inherit from other objects as classes can. This is a limitation that is sometimes frustrating because you can end up with a lot of code duplication. Imagine that, in addition to `Pet`, you would like to create more types of animals, such as a `WildAnimal` or `SeaCreature`. This would be easy to achieve with classes because you can inherit from `Animal`. This is not possible with structs, so you would implement all these types as structs they would need to duplicate their `Animal` logic.

Another difference between value types and reference types is how they act when they are passed around. Add the following code to your playground:

```swift
class ImageInformation {
    var name: String
    var width: Int
    var height: Int

    init(name: String, width: Int, height: Int) {
        self.name = name
        self.width = width
        self.height = height
    }
}

struct ImageLocation {
    let location: String
    let isRemote: Bool
    var isLoaded: Bool
}

let info = ImageInformation(name: "ImageName", width: 100,
    height: 100)
let location = ImageLocation(location: "ImageLocation",
    isRemote: false, isLoaded: false)
```

The declarations for `info` and `location` look very similar, but their underlying types are entirely different. Try writing a function that takes both `ImageLocation` and `ImageInformation` as an argument. Then, try updating the `isLoaded` property of `location` and changing the `name` property of `info`. The compiler will complain when you try to set `isLoaded` because the argument for `ImageLocation` is `let constant`. The reason for this was described earlier in the discussion on value types.

Value types are passed around by value, meaning that changing the property of the argument will change the value altogether. Arguments for a function are always constants. This might not be obvious when you use a reference type, though, because it is perfectly fine to change the `name` property on `ImageInformation` inside of a function. This is because you don't pass the entire value around when you pass a reference type to a function; you pass the reference to the memory address around. This means that instead of the value being a constant, the underlying memory address is a constant. This, in turn, means that you can change whatever is in memory as much as you like; you just can't change the address that a constant points to.

Imagine that you need to drive to somebody's house and they send you the address where they live. This is what it's like to pass around a reference type. Rather than sending you their entire house, they send you the address for their house. While you are driving to their house, the house can change in many ways. The owner could paint it, or replace the windows or doors, anything. In the end, you will still find the house because you received the address for this house, and, as long as the owner doesn't move to a different address, you will find the correct house.

If you change this analogy to use value types, the person whose house you're looking for will simply send you a full copy of their house. So, rather than you driving toward their house based on the address, they won't give you an address; they will just send you their whole house. If the owner makes changes to their copy of the house, you won't be able to see them reflected on your copy of the house unless they send you a new copy. This is also true for any modifications you make to your copy of the house.

You can imagine that in some cases, it can be very efficient to send somebody a copy of something rather than the address. The example of a house might be a bit extreme, but I'm pretty sure that if you order a parcel, you would much rather receive the parcel itself than receiving an address to fetch the parcel. This sort of efficiency is what you will learn about next by comparing how value types and reference types behave in terms of memory allocation.

Deciding which type to use

Choosing the wrong type of object to use in your application can have bad implications for your app on several levels. For instance, your app could suffer from unwanted side effects when a reference type is modified in some unexpected place. Or, you could end up with a lot of duplicated logic if you use a struct instead of a class in certain places. Your app could even suffer in terms of performance when you choose a slow reference type where a value type would have been a better choice.

You should always evaluate what type of object is best suited for your current use case to make sure your code strikes a balanced trade-off between maintainability and performance.

When should I use a reference type?

A great time to use a reference type is when you are subclassing a built-in class, such as `UIViewController`. In these cases, there is no point in fighting the system because that would definitely do more harm than good. Another time to use a reference type is when you are creating your own delegate protocols.

Delegates are best implemented as weak reference types. This means that the object that acts as a delegate is referenced weakly by an object to avoid memory leaks.

Because value types are passed around by making copies, it does not make sense to have a weak reference to them. In this case, your only choice is to use a reference type.

You also need a reference type if it doesn't make sense to pass around copies of something. If you think back to the example of driving to somebody's house, it makes a lot more sense to pass around the address of a house than to give everybody full copies of the house. You might consider the house as having an identity.

This means that each house is *unique*; there is only one house with that exact address, and making copies of it makes no sense. If you are working with an object where copying it makes no sense, you likely want to implement it as a reference type, so everybody that receives an instance of that type is looking at the same instance.

One last reason to choose a reference type is if it can save you a lot of typing by subclassing. A lot of people consider subclassing bad, and you can often avoid it, but sometimes it just makes a lot more sense to work with a class hierarchy.

The downside is that a lot of subclasses can lead to muddy classes that contain functionality to save typing on a couple of subclasses even though the functionality is not relevant to all subclasses. But just like many tools, subclassing can be quite convenient when used correctly; it's not inherently bad to use it.

When to use a value type

It is often said that you should always start with a struct and change to a different type when needed. This is great advice for a lot of cases because structs are often fine for most cases. However, structs aren't the only value type, and it's always good to not default to using certain things blindly.

If you need an object that represents a finite set of possible states or results, such as a network connection state, a traffic light state, or a limited set of valid configuration options for your app, you will likely need an enum.

Regardless of the value semantics that make value types great, an enum is a great way to avoid typos and represent a state. It's often pretty clear when you should use an enum due to its nature.

Structs are used for objects that do not have an identity. In other words, it makes sense to pass copies of it around. A good example of this is when you create a struct that can communicate with the network or a database. This struct would have no identity because it's mostly a collection of properties and methods that aren't associated with a single version of the struct.

A good example of a struct is the `CGPoint` struct that you read about at the beginning of this section. `CGPoint` represents a location in a two-dimensional grid. It has no identity, and passing copies of it around makes sense. It only contains two properties, so it doesn't require any inheritance. These features make it a great candidate to be implemented as a value type.

If you follow the advice of always starting with a struct, try to figure out reasons for your new object to *not* be a struct. If you find a good reason to not use a struct, then make it a class. Often, you won't be able to find a good reason to use a class instead of a struct. If this is the case, make your new object a struct; you can always switch to using a class later. It's usually harder to switch from a class to a struct due to the stricter rules regarding mutability and the lack of subclassing for structs.

Summary

You learned a lot about value types and reference types in this chapter. You learned what each type is and how you can use them. You learned that you can use classes, closures, structs, and enums in Swift and that each of these object types has its own pros and cons.

After learning about all types, you saw how value types and reference types compare to each other, which has shed some light on the sometimes subtle and sometimes obvious use cases for each type. You learned that structs can't be subclasses, while classes can. You also learned that passing around value types passes around copies of each instance, and passing around reference types does not copy each instance but rather passes around a pointer to the addresses in memory. Then, you learned how each type is held in memory and what this means for the performance of the objects you create.

Lastly, you read about how to choose between value types and reference types by using several rules of thumb that should make choosing between structs, classes, and enums fairly straightforward without blindly picking one. The next chapter will take your Swift knowledge one step further by showing you how to write ultra-flexible code with Swift's generics.

7
Flexible Code with Protocols, Generics, and Extensions

Seasoned programmers will (or should) know the core concepts of **object-oriented programming (OOP)**. It's been around for a while, and it has shaped the way many of us develop and think about software. But a relatively new paradigm on the scene comes in the form of protocols with **protocol-oriented programming (POP)**. Not intended as a replacement for OOP, POP has gained a lot of traction over the years, especially with the Swift community.

In this chapter, we'll learn everything we need to know about POP, from standard implementation to associated types and then onto generics. By the end of this chapter, you'll be extremely confident with not only implementing POP in your app, but also understanding what it has to offer.

The following topics will be covered in this chapter:

- Understanding and implementing protocols
- Getting the best out of extensions
- Adding flexibility with generics

Technical requirements

For this chapter, you'll need to download Xcode version 11.4 or above from Apple's App Store.

You'll also need to be running the latest version of macOS (Catalina or above). Simply search for Xcode in the App Store and select and download the latest version. Launch Xcode and follow any additional installation instructions that your system may prompt you with. Once Xcode has fully launched, you're ready to go.

Download the sample code from the following GitHub link: `https://github.com/PacktPublishing/Mastering-iOS-14-Programming-4th-Edition/tree/master/Chapter%207%20-%20Playground/Protocols.playground`

Understanding and implementing protocols

Swift and `UIKit` have protocols at the core of their design. You might have noticed this when you were implementing custom `UIViewController` transitions, or when you worked on a table view or collection view. When you implement these features, you create objects that function as delegates for the transitions, table views, and collection views and conform them to specific protocols. When you worked on view controller transitions in *Chapter 5, Immersing Your Users with Animation*, we also implemented an `NSObject` subclass that conformed to `UIViewControllerAnimatedTransitioning`.

With that said, let's take a deeper look at how we would handle creating and designing our own protocols to use in our Swift app.

Defining your own protocols

Protocols are not confined to delegate behavior only. Defining a protocol is very similar to defining a class, struct, or enum. The main difference is that a protocol does not implement or store any values on its own. It acts as a contract between whoever calls an object that conforms to a protocol and the object that claims to conform to the protocol.

Let's take a look at this by writing some code, we'll create a new playground in order to do this.

Let's implement a simple protocol that defines the expectations for any object that claims to be a pet. The protocol will be called the `PetType` protocol. Protocols defined in UIKit and the Swift standard library use either `Type`, `Ing`, or `Able` as a suffix to indicate that the protocol defines a behavior rather than a concrete type. You should try to follow this convention as much as possible because it makes your code easier to understand for other developers:

```swift
protocol PetType {

    var name: String { get }
    var age: Int { get set }
    static var latinName: String { get }

    func sleep()

}
```

The definition for `PetType` states that any object that claims to be `PetType` must have a get-only variable (a constant) called `name`, an `age` that can be changed because it specifies both `get` and `set`, a `sleep()` method that makes the pet rest, and finally, a static variable that describes the Latin name of `PetType`.

Whenever you define that a protocol requires a certain variable to exist, you must also specify whether the variable should be gettable, settable, or both. If you specify that a certain method must be implemented, you write the method just as you usually would, but you stop at the first curly bracket. You only write down the method signature.

A protocol can also require that the implementer has a static variable or method. This is convenient in the case of `PetType` because the Latin name of a pet does not necessarily belong to a specific pet, but to the entire species that the pet belongs to, so implementing this as a property of the type rather than the instance makes a lot of sense.

To demonstrate how powerful a small protocol such as `PetType` can be, you will implement two pets: a cat and a dog. You'll also write a function that takes any pet and then makes them take a nap by calling the `sleep()` method.

An OOP approach to this protocol could be to create a class called `Pet`, and then create two subclasses, `Cat` and `Dog`. A `sleep()` method would take an instance of `Pet`, and it would look a bit like this:

```
func sleep(pet: Pet) {
    pet.sleep()
}
```

Don't get me wrong, the preceding object-oriented approach works and on such a small scale, no real problems will occur.

However, when the inheritance hierarchy grows, you typically end up with base classes that contain methods that are only relevant to a couple of subclasses. Alternatively, you will find yourself unable to add certain functionalities to a certain class because the inheritance hierarchy gets in the way after a while.

Let's see what it looks like when you use the `PetType` protocol to solve this challenge without using inheritance at all:

```
struct Cat: PetType {

    let name: String
    var age: Int
    static let latinName: String = 'Felis catus'

    func sleep() {
        print('Cat: Zzzz')
    }

}

struct Dog: PetType {
    let name: String
    var age: Int
    static let latinName: String = 'Canis familiaris'

    func sleep() {
        print('Dog: Zzzz')
    }
```

```
}

func nap(pet: PetType) {
    pet.sleep()
}
```

We just managed to implement a single method that can take both the `Cat` and `Dog` objects and makes them take a nap.

Instead of checking for a type, the code checks that the pet that is passed in conforms to the `PetType` protocol, and if it does, its `sleep()` method can be called because the protocol dictates that any `PetType` instance must implement a `sleep()` method. This brings us to the next topic of this chapter: checking for traits instead of types.

Checking for traits instead of types

In classic OOP, you often create superclasses and subclasses to group together objects with similar capabilities. If you roughly model a group of felines in the animal kingdom with classes, you end up with a diagram that looks like this:

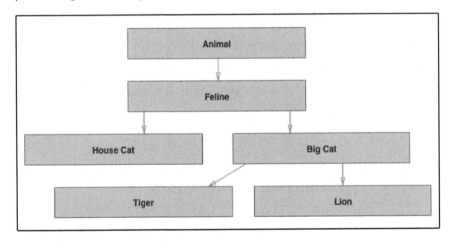

Figure 7.1 – Object-orientated flow

If you try to model more animals, you will find that it's a complex task because some animals share a whole bunch of traits, although they are quite far apart from each other in the class diagram.

One example would be that both cats and dogs are typically kept as pets. This means that they should optionally have an owner and maybe a home. But cats and dogs aren't the only animals kept as pets because fish, guinea pigs, rabbits, and even snakes are kept as pets.

It would be tough to figure out a sensible way to restructure your class hierarchy in such a way that you don't have to redundantly add owners and homes to every pet in the hierarchy because it would be impossible to add these properties to the right classes selectively.

This problem gets even worse when you write a function or method that prints a pet's home. You would either have to make that function accept any animal or write a separate implementation of the same function for each type that has the properties you're looking for. Neither of these approaches makes sense because you don't want to write the same function over and over again with just a different class for the parameter. Even if you choose to do this and you end up with a method that prints an animal's home address that accepts a `Fish` instance, passing an instance of `GreatWhiteShark` to a function called `printHomeAddress()` doesn't make a lot of sense either, because sharks typically don't have home addresses. Of course, the solution to this problem is to use protocols.

In the situation described in the previous section, objects were mostly defined by what they are, not by what they do. We care about the fact that an animal is part of a particular family or type, not about whether it lives on land. You can't differentiate between animals that can fly and animals that can't because not all birds can fly.

Inheritance isn't compatible with this way of thinking. Imagine a definition for a `Pigeon` struct that looks like this:

```
struct Pigeon: Bird, FlyingType, OmnivoreType, Domesticatable
```

Since `Pigeon` is a struct, you know that `Bird` isn't a struct or class—it's a protocol that defines a couple of requirements about what it means to be a bird.

The `Pigeon` struct also conforms to the `FlyingType`, `OmnivoreType`, and `Domesticatable` protocols. Each of these protocols tells you something about `Pigeon` regarding its capabilities or traits. The definition explains what a pigeon is and does instead of merely communicating that it inherits from a certain type of bird.

For example, almost all birds can fly, but there are some exceptions to the rule. You could model this with classes, but this approach is tedious and might be inflexible, depending on your needs and how your code evolves.

Setting the `Pigeon` struct up with protocols is powerful; you can now write a `printHomeAddress()` function and set it up so that it accepts any object that conforms to `Domesticatable`:

```
protocol Domesticatable {
    var homeAddress: String? { get }
}
```

```
func printHomeAddress(animal: Domesticatable) {
    if let address = animal.homeAddress {
        print(address)
    }
}
```

The `Domesticatable` protocol requires an optional `homeAddress` property. Not every animal that can be domesticated actually is.

For example, think about the pigeon; some pigeons are kept as pets, but most aren't. This also applies to cats and dogs, because not every cat or dog has a home.

This approach is powerful, but shifting your mind from an object-oriented mindset, where you think of an inheritance hierarchy, to a protocol-oriented mindset, where you focus on traits instead of inheritance, isn't easy.

Let's expand the example code a bit more by defining `OmnivoreType`, `HerbivoreType`, and `CarnivoreType`. These types will represent the three main types of eaters in the animal kingdom. You can make use of inheritance inside of these protocols because `OmnivoreType` is both `HerbivoreType` and `CarnivoreType`, so you can make `OmnivoreType` inherit from both of these protocols:

```
protocol Domesticatable {
    var homeAddress: String? { get }
}
```

```
protocol HerbivoreType {
    var favoritePlant: String { get }
}
```

```
protocol CarnivoreType {
    var favoriteMeat: String { get }
```

```
}
```

```
protocol OmnivoreType: HerbivoreType, CarnivoreType { }
```

Composing two protocols into one like you did in the preceding example is powerful, but be careful when you do this.

You don't want to create a crazy inheritance graph like you would when you do OOP; you just learned that inheritance could be wildly complex and inflexible.

Imagine writing two new functions, one to print a carnivore's favorite meat and one to print a herbivore's favorite plant. Those functions would look like this:

```
func printFavoriteMeat(forAnimal animal: CarnivoreType) {
    print(animal.favoriteMeat)
}
```

```
func printFavoritePlant(forAnimal animal: HerbivoreType) {
    print(animal.favoritePlant)
}
```

The preceding code might be exactly what you would write yourself. However, neither of these methods accepts OmnivoreType. This is perfectly fine because OmnivoreType inherits from HerbivoreType and CarnivoreType.

This works in the same way that you're used to in classical OOP, with the main exception being that OmnivoreType inherits from multiple protocols instead of just one.

This means that the printFavoritePlant() function accepts a Pigeon instance as its argument because Pigeon conforms to OmnivoreType, which inherits from HerbivoreType.

Using protocols to compose your objects like this can drastically simplify your code. Instead of thinking about complex inheritance structures, you can compose your objects with protocols that define certain traits. The beauty of this is that it makes defining new objects relatively easy.

Imagine that a new type of animal is discovered, one that can fly, swim, and lives on land. This weird new species would be really hard to add to an inheritance-based architecture since it doesn't fit in with other animals.

When using protocols, you could add conformance to the `FlyingType`, `LandType`, and `SwimmingType` protocols and you'd be all set. Any methods or functions that take a `LandType` animal as an argument will happily accept your new animal since it conforms to the `LandType` protocol.

Getting the hang of this way of thinking isn't simple, and it will require some practice. But any time you're getting ready to create a superclass or subclass, ask yourself why. If you're trying to encapsulate a certain trait in that class, try using a protocol.

This will train you to think differently about your objects, and before you know it, your code will be cleaner, more readable, and more flexible, using protocols and checking for traits instead of taking action based on what an object is.

As you've seen, a protocol doesn't need to have a lot of requirements; sometimes one or two are enough to convey the right meaning. Don't hesitate to create protocols with just a single property or method; as your projects grow over time and your requirements change, you will thank yourself for doing so.

Extending your protocols with default behavior

The previous examples have mainly used variables as the requirements for protocols. One slight downside of protocols is that they can result in a bit of code duplication.

For example, every object that is `HerbivoreType` has a `favoriteMeat` variable. This means that you have to duplicate this variable in every object that conforms to `HerbivoreType`. Usually, you want as little code repetition as possible, and repeating a variable over and over again might seem like a step backward.

Even though it's nice if you don't have to declare the same property over and over again, there's a certain danger in not doing this. If your app grows to a large size, you won't remember every class, subclass, and superclass all of the time. This means that changing or removing a specific property can have undesired side-effects in other classes.

Declaring the same properties on every object that conforms to a certain protocol isn't that big a deal; it usually takes just a few lines of code to do this. However, protocols can also require certain methods to be present on objects that conform to them.

Declaring them over and over again can be cumbersome, especially if the implementation is the same for most objects. Luckily, you can make use of protocol extensions to implement a certain degree of default functionality.

To explore protocol extensions, let's move the `printHomeAddress()` function into the `Domesticatable` protocol so all `Domesticatable` objects can print their own home addresses. The first approach you can take is to immediately define the method on a protocol extension without adding it to the protocol's requirements:

```
extension Domesticatable {
    func printHomeAddress() {
        if let address = homeAddress {
            print(address)
        }
    }
}
```

By defining the `printHomeAddress()` method in the protocol extension, every object that conforms to `Domesticatable` has the following method available without having to implement it with the object itself:

```
let pidgeon = Pigeon(favoriteMeat: 'Insects',
                     favoritePlant: 'Seeds',
                     homeAddress: 'Greater Manchester,
                     England')
pidgeon.printHomeAddress()
```

This technique is very convenient if you want to implement default behavior that's associated with a protocol.

You didn't even have to add the `printHomeAddress()` method as a requirement to the protocol. However, this approach will give you some strange results if you're not careful. The following snippet shows an example of such odd results by adding a custom implementation of `printHomeAddress()` to the `Pigeon` struct:

```
struct Pigeon: Bird, FlyingType, OmnivoreType, Domesticatable {
    let favoriteMeat: String
    let favoritePlant: String
    let homeAddress: String?

    func printHomeAddress() {
        if let address = homeAddress {
            print('address: \(address.uppercased())')
        }
```

```
        }
    }
```

When you call `myPigeon.printHomeAddress()`, the custom implementation is used to print the address. However, if you define a function, such as `printAddress(animal:)`, that takes a `Domesticatable` object as its parameter, the default implementation provided by the protocol is used.

This happens because `printHomeAddress()` isn't a requirement of the protocol. Therefore, if you call `printHomeAddress()` on a `Domesticatable` object, the implementation from the protocol extension is used. If you use the same snippet as in the preceding section, but change the `Domesticatable` protocol as shown in the following code, both calls to `printHomeAddress()` print the same thing, that is, the custom implementation in the `Pigeon` struct:

```
protocol Domesticatable {
    var homeAddress: String? { get }
    func printHomeAddress()
}
```

This behavior is likely to be unexpected in most cases, so it's usually a good idea to define all methods you use in the protocol requirements unless you're absolutely sure you want the behavior you just saw.

Protocol extensions can't hold stored properties. This means that you can't add your variables to the protocol to provide a default implementation for them. Even though extensions can't hold stored properties, there are situations where you can still add a computed property to a protocol extension to avoid duplicating the same variable in multiple places. Let's take a look at an example:

```
protocol Domesticatable {
    var homeAddress: String? { get }
    var hasHomeAddress: Bool { get }
    func printHomeAddress()
}
extension Domesticatable {
    var hasHomeAddress: Bool {
        return homeAddress != nil
    }

    func printHomeAddress() {
```

```
        if let address = homeAddress {
            print(address)
        }
    }
}
```

If you want to be able to check whether a `Domesticatable` has a home address, you can add a requirement for a Bool value, `hasHomeAddress`. If the `homeAddress` property is set, `hasHomeAddress` should be true. Otherwise, it should be false.

This property is computed in the protocol extension, so you don't have to add this property to all `Domesticatable` objects. In this case, it makes a lot of sense to use a computed property because the way its value is computed should most likely be the same across all `Domesticatable` objects.

Implementing default behaviors in protocol extensions makes the protocol-oriented approach we've seen before even more powerful; you can essentially mimic a feature called multiple inheritance without all the downsides of subclassing.

Simply adding conformance to a protocol can add all kinds of functionality to your objects, and if the protocol extensions allow it, you won't need to add anything else to your code. Let's see how you can make protocols and extensions even more powerful with associated types.

Improving your protocols with associated types

One more awesome aspect of protocol-oriented programming is the use of associated types. An associated type is a generic, non-existing type that can be used in your protocol like any type that does exist.

The real type of this generic is determined by the compiler based on the context it's used in. This description is abstract, and you might not immediately understand why or how an associated type can benefit your protocols. After all, aren't protocols themselves a very flexible way to make several unrelated objects fit certain criteria based on the protocols they conform to?

To illustrate and discover the use of associated types, you will expand your animal kingdom a bit. What you should do is give the herbivores an `eat` method and an array to keep track of the plants they've eaten, as follows:

```
protocol HerbivoreType {
    var plantsEaten: [PlantType] { get set }
    mutating func eat(plant: PlantType)
```

```
}
```

```
extension HerbivoreType {
    mutating func eat(plant: PlantType) {
        plantsEaten.append(plant)
    }
}
```

This code looks fine at first sight. An herbivore eats plants, and this is established by this protocol. The `PlantType` protocol is defined as follows:

```
protocol PlantType {
    var latinName: String { get }
}
```

Let's define two different plant types and an animal that will be used to demonstrate the problem with the preceding code:

```
struct Grass: PlantType{ var latinName = 'Poaceae'
}
```

```
struct Pine: PlantType{ var latinName = 'Pinus'
}
```

```
struct Cow: HerbivoreType {
    var plantsEaten = [PlantType]()
}
```

There shouldn't be a big surprise here. Let's continue with creating a `Cow` instance and feed it `Pine`:

```
var cow = Cow()
let pine = Pine()
cow.eat(plant: pine)
```

This doesn't really make sense. Cows don't eat pines; they eat grass! We need some way to limit this cow's food intake because this approach isn't going to work.

Currently, you can feed `HerbivoreType` animals anything that's considered a plant. You need some way to limit the types of food your cows are given. In this case, you should restrict `FoodType` to `Grass` only, without having to define the `eat(plant:)` method for every plant type you might want to feed a `HerbivoreType`.

The problem you're facing now is that all `HerbivoreType` animals mainly eat one plant type, and not all plant types are a good fit for all herbivores. This is where associated types are a great solution. An associated type for the `HerbivoreType` protocol can constrain the `PlantType` that a certain herbivore can eat to a single type that is defined by `HerbivoreType`. Let's see what this looks like:

```
protocol HerbivoreType {
    associatedtype Plant: PlantType
    var plantsEaten: [Plant] { get set }
    mutating func eat(plant: Plant)
}

extension HerbivoreType {
    mutating func eat(plant: Plant) {
        print('eating a \(plant.latinName)')
        plantsEaten.append(plant)
    }
}
```

The first highlighted line associates the generic `Plant` type, which doesn't exist as a real type, with the protocol. A constraint has been added to `Plant` to ensure that it's a `PlantType`.

The second highlighted line demonstrates how the `Plant` associated type is used as a `PlantType`. The plant type itself is merely an alias for any type that conforms to `PlantType` and is used as the type of object we use for `plantsEaten` and the `eat` methods. Let's redefine the `Cow` struct to see this associated type in action:

```
struct Cow: HerbivoreType {
    var plantsEaten = [Grass]()
}
```

Instead of making `plantsEaten` a `PlantType` array, it's now defined as an array of `Grass`. In the protocol and the definition, the type of plant is now `Grass`.

The compiler understands this because the `plantsEaten` array is defined as `[Grass]`.

Let's define a second `HerbivoreType` that eats a different type of `PlantType`:

```
struct Carrot: PlantType {
    let latinName = 'Daucus carota'
}


struct Rabbit: HerbivoreType {
    var plantsEaten = [Carrot]()
}
```

If you try to feed a cow some carrots, or if you attempt to feed the rabbit a pine, the compiler will throw errors. The reason for this is that the associated type constraint allows you to define the type of `Plant` in each struct separately.

One side note about associated types is that it's not always possible for the compiler to correctly infer the real type for an associated type. In our current example, this would happen if we didn't have the `plantsEaten` array in the protocol.

The solution would be to define a `typealias` on types that conform to `HerbivoreType` so that the compiler understands which type `Plant` represents:

```
protocol HerbivoreType {
    associatedtype Plant: PlantType
    var plantsEaten: [Plant] { get set }
    mutating func eat(plant: Plant)
}
```

Associated types can be really powerful when used correctly, but sometimes using them can also cause you a lot of headaches because of the amount of inferring the compiler has to do.

If you forget a few tiny steps, the compiler can quickly lose track of what you're trying to do, and the error messages aren't always the most unambiguous messages.

Keep this in mind when you're using associated types, and try to make sure that you're as explicit as possible about the type you're looking to be associated with.

Sometimes, adding a type alias to give the compiler a helping hand is better than trying to get the compiler to infer everything on its own correctly.

This type of flexibility is not limited to protocols. You can also add generic properties to functions, classes, structs, and enums. Let's see how this works and how it can make your code extremely flexible.

Adding flexibility with generics

Programming with generics is not always easy, but it does make your code extremely flexible. When you use something such as generics, you are always making a trade-off between the simplicity of your program and the flexibility of your code. Sometimes it's worth it to introduce a little bit of complexity to allow your code to be written in otherwise impossible ways.

For instance, consider the Cow struct you saw before. To specify the generic associated type on the HerbivoreType protocol, a type alias was added to the Cow struct. Now imagine that not all cows like to eat grass. Maybe some cows prefer flowers, corn, or something else. You would not be able to express this using the type alias.

To represent a case where you might want to use a different PlantType for every cow instance, you can add a generic to the Cow itself. The following snippet shows how you can do this:

```
struct Cow<Plant: PlantType>: HerbivoreType {
    var plantsEaten = [Plant]()
}
```

Between < and >, the generic type name is specified as Plant. This generic is constrained to the PlantType type.

This means that any type that will act as Plant has to conform to PlantType. The protocol will see that Cow has a generic Plant type now, so there is no need to add a type alias. When you create an instance of Cow, you can now pass every instance its own PlantType:

```
let grassCow = Cow<Grass>()
let flowerCow = Cow<Flower>()
```

Applying generics to instances like this is more common than you might think. An Array instance uses generics to determine what kind of elements it contains. The following two lines of code are identical in functionality:

```
let strings = [String]()
let strings = Array<String>()
```

The first line uses a convenient syntax to create an array of strings. The second line uses the Array initializer and explicitly specifies the type of element it will contain.

Sometimes, you might find yourself writing a function or method that can benefit from a generic argument or return type. An excellent example of a generic function is map. With map, you can transform an array of items into an array of different items. You can define your own simple version of map as follows:

```
func simpleMap<T, U>(_ input: [T], transform: (T) -> U) -> [U]
{

    var output = [U]()
    for item in input {
        output.append(transform(item))
    }

    return output
}
```

Here, simpleMap(_:transform:) has two generic types, T and U. These names are common placeholders for generics, so they make it clear to anybody reading this code that they are about to deal with generics.

In this sample, the function expects an input of [T], which you can read as an array of something. It also expects a closure that takes an argument, T, and returns U.

You can interpret this as the closure taking an element out of that array of something, and it transforms it into something else.

The function finally returns an array of [U], or in other words, an array of something else.

You would use simpleMap(_:transform:) as follows:

```
let result = simpleMap([1, 2, 3]) { item in
    return item * 2
}

print(result) // [2, 4, 6]
```

Generics are not always easy to understand, and it's okay if they take you a little while to get used to it. They are a powerful and complex topic that we could write many more pages about.

The best way to get into them is to use them, practice with them, and read as much as you can about them. For now, you should have more than enough to think about and play with.

Note that generics are not limited to structs and functions. You can also add generics to your enums and classes in the same way you add them to a struct.

Summary

In this chapter, you saw how you can leverage the power of protocols to work with an object's traits or capabilities, rather than just using its class as the only way of measuring its capabilities. Then, you saw how protocols can be extended to implement a default functionality. This enables you to compose powerful types by merely adding protocol conformance, instead of creating a subclass.

You also saw how protocol extensions behave depending on your protocol requirements, and that it's wise to have anything that's in the protocol extension defined as a protocol requirement. This makes the protocol behavior more predictable.

Finally, you learned how associated types work and how they can take your protocols to the next level by adding generic types to your protocols that can be tweaked for every type that conforms to your protocol. You even saw how you can apply generics to other objects, such as functions and structs.

The concepts shown in this chapter are pretty advanced, sophisticated, and powerful. To truly master their use, you'll need to train yourself to think regarding traits instead of an inheritance hierarchy.

Once you've mastered this, you can experiment with protocol extensions and generic types. It's okay if you don't fully understand these topics right off the bat; they're completely different and new ways of thinking for most programmers with OOP experience.

Now that we've explored some of the theory behind protocols and value types, in the next chapter, you will learn how you can put this new knowledge to use by shortly revisiting the Contacts app from our previous chapters to improve the code you wrote there.

8

Adding Core Data to Your App

Core Data is Apple's data persistence framework. You can use this framework whenever your application needs to store data. Simple data can often be stored in `UserDefaults`, but when you're handling data that is more complex, has relationships, or needs some form of efficient searching, Core Data is much better suited to your needs.

You don't need to build a very complex app or have vast amounts of data to make Core Data worth your while. Regardless of your app's size, even if it's tiny with only a couple of records, or if you're holding onto thousands of records, Core Data has your back.

In this chapter, you'll learn how to add Core Data to an existing app. The app you will build keeps track of a list of favorite movies for all members of a family. The main interface is a table view that shows a list of family members. If you tap on a family member's name, you'll see their favorite movies. Adding family members can be done through the overview screen and adding movies can be done through the detail screen.

In this chapter, the following topics are covered:

- Understanding the Core Data stack
- Adding Core Data to an existing application
- Creating a Core Data model

- Persisting data and reacting to data changes
- Understanding the use of multiple instances of `NSManagedObjectContext`

Technical requirements

You won't build the screens in this app from scratch. The code bundle for this chapter includes a starter project called `MustC`. The starter project contains all of the screens, so you don't have to set up the user interface before you get around to implementing Core Data.

Download the sample code from the following GitHub link:

```
https://github.com/PacktPublishing/Mastering-iOS-14-
Programming-4th-Edition
```

Understanding the Core Data stack

Before you dive right into the project and add Core Data to it, let's take a look at how Core Data works, what it is, and what it isn't. In order to make efficient use of Core Data, you must know what you're working with.

When you work with Core Data, you're utilizing a stack of layers that starts with managed objects and ends with a data store. This data store is often a SQLite database, but there are different storage options you can use with Core Data, depending on your application's needs. Let's take a quick look at the layers involved with Core Data and discuss their roles in an application briefly:

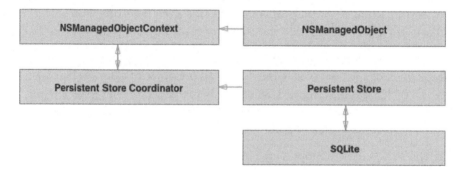

Figure 8.1 – A Core Data stack

At the top right of this diagram is the `NSManagedObject` class. When you use Core Data, this is the class you'll interact with most often since it's the base class for all the Core Data models that your app contains. For instance, in the app that you will build in this chapter, the family member and movie models are subclasses of `NSManagedObject`.

Each managed object belongs to an instance of `NSManagedObjectContext`. The managed object context is responsible for communicating with the **persistent store coordinator**. Often, you'll only need a single managed object context and a single persistent store coordinator. However, it is possible to use multiple persistent store coordinators and multiple managed object contexts. It's even possible to have multiple managed object contexts for the same persistent store coordinator.

A setup with multiple managed object contexts can be particularly useful if you're performing costly operations on your managed objects; for example, if you're importing or synchronizing large amounts of data. Usually, you will stick to using a single managed object context and a single persistent store coordinator because most apps don't need more than one.

The persistent store coordinator is responsible for communicating with the **persistent store**. In most scenarios, the persistent store uses SQLite as its underlying storage database. However, you can also use other types of storage, such as an in-memory database. An in-memory database is especially useful if you're writing unit tests or if your app does not need long-term storage.

If you've worked with MySQL, SQLite, or any other relational database, it is tempting to think of Core Data as a layer on top of a relational database. Although this isn't entirely false since Core Data can use SQLite as its underlying storage, Core Data does not work the same as using SQLite directly; it's an abstraction on top of it.

One example of a difference between SQLite and Core Data is the concept of primary keys. Core Data doesn't allow you to specify your own primary keys. Also, when you define relationships, you don't use foreign keys. Instead, you simply define the relationship and Core Data will figure out how to store this relationship in the underlying database. You will learn more about this later. It's important to know that you should not directly translate your SQL experiences to Core Data. If you do, you will run into issues, simply because Core Data is not SQL. It just so happens that SQLite is one of the ways that data can be stored, but the similarities end right there.

To recap, all Core Data apps have a **persistent store**. This store is backed by an in-memory database or a SQLite database. A **persistent store coordinator** is responsible for communicating with the **persistent store**. The object communicating with the **persistent store coordinator** is the **managed object context**. An application can have multiple **managed object context** instances talking to the same **persistent store coordinator**. The objects that a **managed object context** retrieves from the **persistent store coordinator** are **managed objects**.

Now that you have an overview of the Core Data stack and where all the parts involved with its usage belong, let's add the Core Data stack to the **MustC** application.

Adding Core Data to an existing application

When you create a new project in Xcode, Xcode asks whether you want to add Core Data to your application. If you check this checkbox, Xcode will automatically generate some boilerplate code that sets up the Core Data stack. For practicing purposes, MustC was set up without Core Data, so you'll have to add this to the project yourself.

Start by opening AppDelegate.swift and add the following import statement:

```
import CoreData
```

Next, add the following lazy variable to the implementation of AppDelegate:

```
private lazy var persistentContainer: NSPersistentContainer = {
  let container = NSPersistentContainer(name: "MustC")
  container.loadPersistentStores(completionHandler: {
      (storeDescription, error) in
    if let error = error {
      fatalError("Unresolved error (error), (error.userInfo)")
    }
  })
  return container
} ()
```

> **Tip**
>
> If you declare a variable as lazy, it won't be initialized until it is accessed. This is particularly useful for variables that are expensive to initialize, rely on other objects, or are not always accessed. The fact that the variable is initialized just in time comes with a performance penalty since the variable needs to be set up the first time you access it. In some instances, this is fine, but in other cases, it might negatively impact the user experience. When used correctly, lazy variables can offer significant benefits.

The preceding code snippet creates an instance of `NSPersistentContainer`. The persistent container is a container for the persistent store coordinator, persistent store, and managed object context. This single object manages different parts of the Core Data stack, and it ensures that everything is set up and managed correctly.

If you let Xcode generate the Core Data code for your app, it adds a similar property to create `NSPersistentContainer`. Xcode also adds a method called `saveContext()` to `AppDelegate`. This method is used in `applicationWillTerminate(_:)` to perform a last-minute save of any changes and updates when the application is about to terminate. Since you're setting up Core Data manually, this behavior isn't added by Xcode, so it must be added by you manually.

Instead of placing the `saveContext()` method in `AppDelegate`, you will add this method as an extension to `NSPersistentContainer`. This makes it easier for other parts of your code to use this method, without having to rely on `AppDelegate`.

Next, create a new folder in the Project Navigator and name it `Extensions`. Also, create a new Swift file and name it `NSPersistentContainer.swift`. Add the following implementation to this file:

```
import CoreData


extension NSPersistentContainer {
  func saveContextIfNeeded() {
    if viewContext.hasChanges {
      do {
        try viewContext.save()
      } catch {
        let nserror = error as NSError
        fatalError("Unresolved error \(nserror), \(nserror.
          userInfo)")
```

```
        }
      }
    }
  }
```

This code adds a new method to `NSPersistentContainer` instances by extending it. This is convenient because it decouples the save method from `AppDelegate` entirely. This is much nicer than the default save mechanism provided for Core Data apps by Xcode.

Add the following implementation of `applicationWillTerminate(_:)` to `AppDelegate` to save the context right before the app terminates:

```
func applicationWillTerminate(_ application: UIApplication) {
    persistentContainer.saveContextIfNeeded()
}
```

Now, whenever the application terminates, the persistent store will check whether there are any changes to the managed object context that the `viewContext` property points to. If there are any changes, an attempt to save them is made. If this attempt fails, the app will crash with `fatalError`. When creating your own app, you might want to handle this scenario a bit more gracefully. It could very well be that failing to save data before the app terminates might not be a reason that crashes your app. You can modify the error-handling implementation of `saveContextIfNeeded()` if you think a different behavior is more appropriate for your app. You can, for example, upload the error to your analytics or reporting tool to analyze it later, or avoid `fatalError` and just log the error without crashing the app.

Now that you have the Core Data stack set up, you need a way to provide this stack to the view controllers in the app. A common technique to achieve this is called **dependency injection**. In this case, dependency injection means that `AppDelegate` will pass the persistent container to `FamilyMemberViewController`, which is the first view controller in the app. It then becomes the job of `FamilyMemberViewController` to pass the persistent container to the next view controller that depends on it, and so forth.

In order to inject the persistent container, you need to add a property to `FamilyMembersViewController` that holds the persistent container. Don't forget to add `import CoreData` at the top of the file and add the following code:

```
var persistentContainer: NSPersistentContainer!
```

Now, in `AppDelegate`, modify the `application(_:didFinishLaunchingWith`
`Options:)` method, as follows:

```
func application(_ application: UIApplication,
   didFinishLaunchingWithOptions launchOptions: [UIApplication.
   LaunchOptionsKey: Any]?) -> Bool {
   if let navVC = window?.rootViewController as?
     UINavigationController,
      let initialVC = navVC.viewControllers[0] as?
        FamilyMembersViewController {
      initialVC.persistentContainer = persistentContainer
   }
   return true
}
```

This code is using dependency injection to inject `persistentContainer` into
`FamilyMemberViewController`. But you can still make one major improvement:
you know that there might be more view controllers that depend on a persistent container,
so you will need a `persistentContainer` property in each of them. This will cause a
lot of repeated code. We can improve our code if we define a protocol that we can reuse
in order to reduce the duplicated code in each `UIViewController` instance that
needs `persistentContainer`. As an exercise, attempt to improve the code by adding
a protocol called `PersistentContainerRequiring`. This protocol should add a
requirement for an implicitly unwrapped `persistentContainer` property. Make
sure that `FamilyMembersViewController` conforms to this protocol, and fix the
implementation of `application(_:didFinishLaunchingWithOptions:)`
as well so that it uses your new protocol.

You have just put down the foundation that is required to use Core Data in your app.
Before you can use Core Data and store data in it, you must define what data you would
like to save by creating your data model. Let's go over how to do this next.

Creating a Core Data model

So far, you have worked on the persistence layer of your app. The next step is to
create your models so that you can actually store and retrieve data from your Core
Data database. All models in an application that uses Core Data are represented
by `NSManagedObject` subclasses. When you retrieve data from your database,
`NSManagedObjectContext` is responsible for creating instances of your managed
objects and populating them with the relevant fetched data.

The **MustC** application requires two models: a family-member model and a movie model. When you define models, you can also define relationships. For the models in **MustC**, you should define a relationship that links multiple movies to a single family member.

Creating the models

In order for Core Data to understand which models your application uses, you must define them in Xcode's model editor. Let's create a new model file so that you can add your own models to the **MustC** application. Create a new file, and from the file template selection screen, pick **Data Model**. First, you will set up the basic models, and then see how you can define a relationship between family members and their favorite movies:

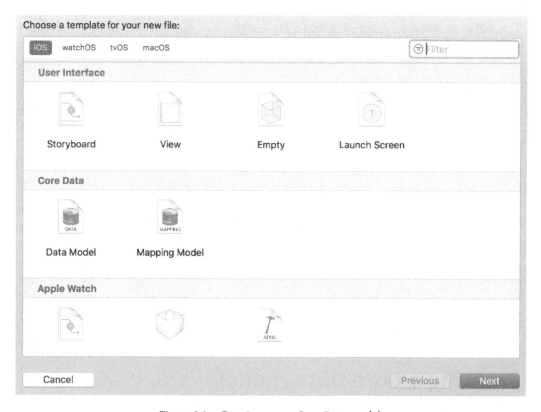

Figure 8.2 – Creating a new Core Data model

Name your model file MustC. Your project now contains a file called MustC. xcdatamodeld. Open this file to go to the model editor. In the bottom-left corner of the editor, you'll find a button labeled **Add Entity**. Click this button to add a new entity, and name it FamilyMember.

When you select an entity by clicking it, you can see all of its attributes, relationships, and fetched properties. Let's add a name property to the family member. Click on the plus (+) icon at the bottom of the empty attributes list and add a new attribute called name. Make sure that you select **String** as the type for this attribute:

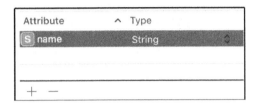

Figure 8.3 – Adding an attribute to a Core Data entity

Click on this new property to select it. In the sidebar on the right, select the fourth tab to open the Data Model inspector. This is where you can see more detailed information on this attribute. For instance, you can configure a property to be indexed for faster lookups. You can also choose whether you want the attribute to be optional. For now, you shouldn't care too much about indexing since you're not performing lookups by family members' names, and, even if you were, a family doesn't tend to have hundreds or thousands of members. By default, the **Optional** checkbox is checked. Make sure that you uncheck this box because you don't want to store family members without a name.

Some other options you have for attributes are adding validation, adding a default value, and enabling indexing in Spotlight. For now, leave all those options at their default settings:

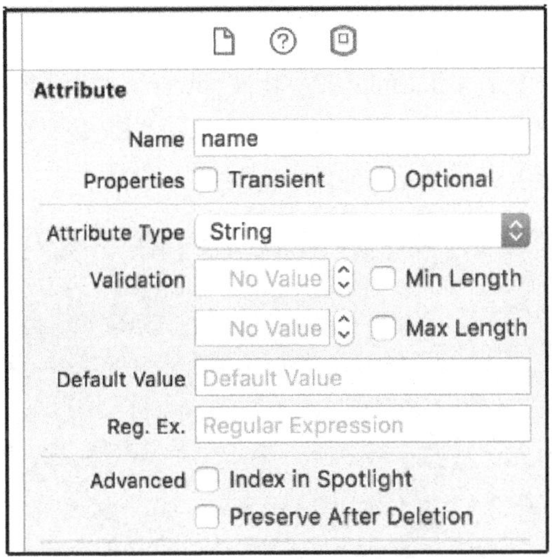

Figure 8.4 – Attribute properties

In addition to a `FamilyMember` entity, **MustC** also needs a `Movie` entity. Create this entity using the same steps as before and give it a single property: `title`. This property should be a string and it shouldn't be optional. Once you've added this property, you can set up a relationship between family members and their favorite movies.

Defining relationships

A relationship in Core Data adds a reference as a property onto an entity. In this case, you want to define a relationship between `FamilyMember` and `Movie`. The best way to describe this relationship is a one-to-many relationship. This means that every movie will have only one family member associated with it and every family member can have multiple favorite movies.

> **Tip**
>
> Configuring your data model with a one-to-many relationship from `Movie` to `FamilyMember` is not the most efficient way to define this relationship. A many-to-many relationship is likely a better fit because that would allow multiple family members to add the same movie instance as their favorite. A one-to-many relationship is used in this example to keep the setup simple and make it easy to follow along with the example.

Select the **FamilyMember** entity and click on the plus icon at the bottom of the **Relationships** list. Name the relationship **movies** and select `Movie` as the destination. Don't select an **Inverse** relationship yet because the other end of this relationship is not defined yet. The **Inverse** relationship will tell the model that `Movie` has a property that points back to `FamilyMember`. Make sure that you select **To Many** as the relationship type in the Data Model inspector panel for the `movies` property.

Also, select **Cascade** as the value for **Delete Rule**:

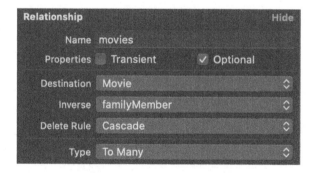

Figure 8.5 – Relationship properties

Delete Rule is a very important property to be set correctly. Not paying attention to this property could result in a lot of orphaned, and even corrupted, data in your database. For instance, setting this property to **nullify** simply sets the inverse of the relationship to `nil`. This is the correct behavior when deleting a movie because deleting a movie shouldn't delete the entire family member who added this movie as their favorite. It should simply be removed from the list of favorites.

However, if a family member is deleted and the relationship is `nullified`, you would end up with a bunch of movies that don't have a family member associated with them. In this application, these movies are worthless; they won't be used anymore because every movie only belongs to a single family member. For this app, it's desirable that when a family member gets deleted, Core Data also deletes their favorite movies. This is precisely what the **Cascade** option does; it cascades the deletion over to the relationship's inverse.

After setting **Delete Rule** to **Cascade**, select the **Movie** entity and define a relationship called `familyMember`. The destination should be `FamilyMember` and the inverse for this relationship is `favoriteMovies`. After adding this relationship, the inverse will be automatically set on the `FamilyMember` entity:

Figure 8.6 – Movie relationship with FamilyMember

Now that we have learned how to create and establish relationships between entities in our model, let's start using the entities to store data in our app.

Using your entities

As mentioned before, every model or entity in your Core Data database is represented by `NSManagedObject`. There are a couple of ways to create or generate `NSManagedObject` subclasses. In the simplest of setups, an `NSManagedObject` subclass contains just the properties for a certain managed object and nothing else. If this is the case, you can let Xcode generate your model classes for you.

This is actually what Xcode does by default. If you build your project now and add the following code to `viewDidLoad()` in `FamilyMembersViewController`, your project should compile just fine:

```
let fam = FamilyMember(entity: FamilyMember.entity(),
    insertInto: persistentContainer.viewContext)
```

This works automatically; you don't have to write any code for your models yourself. Don't worry about what the preceding code does just yet; we'll get into that very soon. The point is that you see that a `FamilyMember` class exists in your project even though you didn't have to create one yourself.

If the default behavior doesn't suit the approach you want in your app – for instance, if you want to prevent your code from modifying your models by defining your variables as `private(set)` – you may want to create a custom subclass instead of making Xcode generate the classes for you. A custom `NSManagedObject` subclass for `FamilyMember` could look like this:

```
class FamilyMember: NSManagedObject {
    @NSManaged private(set) var name: String
    @NSManaged private(set) var favoriteMovies: [Movie]?
}
```

This custom `FamilyMember` subclass makes sure that any external code can't modify the instances by making the setters on `FamilyMember` private. Depending on your application, it might be a good idea to implement this since it will ensure that your models can't accidentally change.

One final option you have is to let Xcode generate the properties for `NSManagedObject` as an extension on a class you define. This is particularly useful if you have some custom stored properties that you'd like to define on your model or if you have a customized `NSManagedObject` subclass that you can use as the base for all of your models.

> **Tip**
> All code that Xcode generates for your Core Data models is added to the `Build` folder in Xcode's Derived Data. You shouldn't modify it or access it directly. These files will be automatically regenerated by Xcode whenever you perform a build, so any functionality you add inside the generated files will be overwritten.

For the **MustC** app, it's okay if Xcode generates the model definition classes since there are no custom properties that you need to add. In the model editor, select each entity and make sure that the **Codegen** field is set to **Class Definition**; you can find this field in the Data Model inspector panel.

At this point, you are all set up to store your first piece of data in the Core Data database:

Figure 8.7 – The Codegen attribute for entities

In the next section, we are going to persist data with the model and relationship that we just created.

Persisting data and reacting to data changes

The first step to implement data persistence for your app is to make sure that you can store data in the database. You have defined the models that you want to store in your database, so the next step is to actually store your models. Once you have implemented a rough version of your data persistence, you will refine the code to make it more reusable. The final step will be to read data from Core Data and dynamically respond to changes in the database.

Understanding data persistence

Whenever you want to persist a model with Core Data, you must insert a new NSManagedObject into NSManagedObjectContext. Doing this does not immediately persist the model. It merely stages the object for persistence in the current NSManagedObjectContext. If you don't properly manage your managed objects and contexts, this is a potential source of bugs. For example, not persisting your managed objects results in the loss of your data once you refresh the context. Even though this might sound obvious, it could lead to several hours of frustration if you aren't aware of this and have bugs in managing your managed object context.

If you want to save managed objects correctly, you must tell the managed object context to persist its changes to the persistent store coordinator. The persistent store coordinator will take care of persisting the data in the underlying SQLite database.

Extra care is required when you use multiple managed object contexts. If you insert an object in one managed object context and persist it, you will manually need to synchronize the changes into the other managed object contexts. Also, managed objects are not thread-safe. This means that you must make sure that you create, access, and store a managed object on a single thread at all times. The managed object context has a helper method called `perform(_:)` to help you with this.

Inserting new objects, updating them, or adding relationships between objects should always be done using the `perform(_:)` method. The reason is that the helper method makes sure that all the code in the closure you want to perform is executed on the same thread that the managed object context is on.

Now that you're aware of how data persistence works in Core Data, it's time to start implementing the code to store family members and their favorite movies. You will implement the family member persistence first. Then, you'll expand the app so that you can safely add movies to family members.

Persisting your models

The first model you will persist is the family member model. The app is already set up with a form that asks for a family member name and a delegate protocol that informs `FamilyMembersViewController` whenever the user wants to store a new family member.

Note that none of the input data is validated; usually, you'd want to add some checks that make sure that the user is not trying to insert an empty family member name, for instance. For now, we'll skip that because this type of validation isn't Core Data-specific.

The code to persist new family members should be added to the `saveFamilyMember(withName:)` method. Add the following implementation to `FamilyMembersViewController`; we'll go over it line by line after adding the code:

```
func saveFamilyMember(withName name: String) {
  // 1
  let moc = persistentContainer.viewContext

  // 2
  moc.perform {
    // 3
    let familyMember = FamilyMember(context: moc)
    familyMember.name = name
```

```
// 4
  do {
    try moc.save()
  } catch {
    moc.rollback()
  }
 }
}
```

The first comment in this code marks where the managed object context is extracted from `persistentContainer`. All `NSPersistentContainer` objects have a `viewContext` property. This property is used to obtain a managed object context that exists on the main thread.

The second comment marks the call to `perform(_:)`. This ensures that the new `FamilyMember` instance is created and stored on the correct thread.

The third comment marks where we create a `familyMember` instance inside our managed object context (`moc`) and we update its name. When you create an instance of a managed object, you must provide the managed object context where the instance will be temporarily stored.

Lastly, saving the managed object context can fail, so you must wrap the `to save()` call in a `do {} catch {}` block, so it correctly handles potential errors. If the managed object context can't be saved, all unsaved changes are rolled back.

This code is all you need to persist family members. Before you implement the required code to read existing family members and respond to the insertion of new family members, let's set up `MoviesViewController` so that it can store movies for a family member.

The code to store movies for a family member is very similar to the code you wrote previously. Before you implement the following snippets, make sure that in the `MoviesViewController` file, you add `import CoreData`. Also, add a `persistentContainer` property to `MoviesViewController`, as follows:

```
var persistentContainer: NSPersistentContainer!
```

In order to connect a new movie to a family member, you also need a variable to hold the family member in `MoviesViewController`. Add the following declaration to `MoviesViewController`:

```
var familyMember: FamilyMember?
```

After doing this, add the following implementation for `saveMovie(withName:)`:

```swift
func saveMovie(withName name: String) {

  guard let familyMember = self.familyMember else { return }

  let moc = persistentContainer.viewContext
  moc.perform {
    let movie = Movie(context: moc)
    movie.title = name

    // 1
    let newFavorites: Set<AnyHashable> = familyMember.movies?.
        adding(movie) ?? [movie]

    // 2
    familyMember.movies = NSSet(set: newFavorites)

    do {
      try moc.save()
    } catch {
      moc.rollback()
    }
  }
}
```

The most important differences between adding the movie and the family member are highlighted with comments. Note that the `movies` property on a family member is `NSSet`. This is an immutable object, so you need to create a copy and add the movie to that copy. If no copy could be made because there is no set created yet, you can create a new set with the new movie in it. Next, this new, updated set is converted back to an `NSSet` instance so that it can be the new value for movies.

As you can see, both save methods share about half of the implementation. You can make some clever use of extensions and generics in Swift to avoid writing this duplicated code. Let's refactor the app a bit.

Important Note

Notice how we have used `viewContext` for persisting data (in both the `saveFamilyMember` and `saveMovie` methods). For this example, it will work perfectly fine, because we are not doing any heavy tasks. But `viewContext` is associated with the main queue of the application, so it is not good practice to do any work with it that can block the UI (such as persisting a large amount of data). In the last section of this chapter, we will refactor this code by creating a private context that works in a background thread. We will persist data in the background and read changes from `viewContext` in the main thread. By using two different contexts, one in the background and one in the main thread, we will follow best practices and ensure we don't block the UI while persisting data.

Refactoring the persistence code

Many iOS developers dislike the amount of boilerplate code that is involved with using Core Data. Simply persisting an object requires you to repeat several lines of code, which can become quite a pain to write and maintain over time. The approach to refactoring the persistence code presented in the following examples is heavily inspired by the approach taken in the *Core Data* book written by *Florian Kugler* and *Daniel Eggert*.

Tip

If you're interested in learning more about Core Data outside of what this book covers, and if you'd like to see more clever ways to reduce the amount of boilerplate code, you should pick up *Core Data* by *Kugler* and *Eggert*..

After creating the code blocks to save `familyMember` and `familyMember.movies` instances into Core Data, use the following pattern:

```
moc.perform {
    // create managed object
    do {
        try moc.save()
    } catch {
        moc.rollback()
    }
}
```

Now, it would be great if you could write the following code to persist data instead, reducing the duplicated code every time you save an object:

```
moc.persist {
    // create managed object
}
```

This can be achieved by writing an extension for NSManagedObjectContext. Add a file called NSManagedObjectContext to the extensions folder, and add the following implementation:

```
extension NSManagedObjectContext {
    func persist(block: @escaping () -> Void) {
        perform {

            block()

            do {
                try self.save()
            } catch {
                self.rollback()
            }
        }
    }
}
```

The preceding code allows you to reduce the amount of boilerplate code, which is something that you should always try to achieve. Reducing boilerplate code greatly improves your code's readability and maintainability. Update both the family overview and the movie list view controllers to make use of this new persistence method.

After optimizing our code to save entities in Core Data with the preceding trick, now let's see how to read data, making use of NSFetchRequest, which allows us to query data in a simple and effective way.

Reading data with a simple fetch request

The simplest way to fetch data from your database is to use a fetch request. The managed object context forwards fetch requests to the persistent store coordinator. The persistent store coordinator will then forward the request to the persistent store, which will then convert the request into a SQLite query. Once the results are fetched, they are passed back up this chain and converted into NSManagedObject instances.

By default, these objects are called faults. When an object is a fault, it means that the actual properties and values for the object are not fetched yet, but they will be fetched once you access them. This is an example of a good implementation of lazy variables because fetching the values is a pretty fast operation, and fetching everything upfront would greatly increase your app's memory footprint because all values would have to be loaded into the app's memory right away.

Let's take a look at an example of a simple fetch request that retrieves all FamilyMember instances that were saved to the database:

```
let request: NSFetchRequest<FamilyMember> = FamilyMember.
    fetchRequest()
let moc = persistentContainer.viewContext
guard let results = try? moc.fetch(request) else { return }
```

As you can see, it's not particularly hard to fetch all of your family members. Every NSManagedObject instance has a class method that configures a basic fetch request that can be used to retrieve data. If you have large amounts of data, you probably don't want to fetch all of the persisted objects at once. You can configure your fetch request to fetch data in batches by setting the fetchBatchSize property. It's recommended that you use this property whenever you want to use fetched data in a table view or collection view. You should set the fetchBatchSize property to a value that is just a bit higher than the number of cells you expect to display at a time. This makes sure that Core Data fetches plenty of items to display while avoiding loading everything at once.

Now that you know how to fetch data, let's display some data in the family members table view. Add a new variable called familyMembers to FamilyMembersViewController. Give this property an initial value of [FamilyMember]() so that you start off with an empty array of family members. Also, add the example fetch request you saw earlier to viewDidLoad(). Next, assign the result of the fetch request to familyMembers, as follows:

```
familyMembers = results
```

Finally, update the table view delegate methods so that
`tableView(_:numberOfRowsInSection:)` returns the number of items in the
`familyMembers` array:

```
func tableView(_ tableView: UITableView, numberOfRowsInSection
    section: Int) -> Int {
    return familyMembers.count
}
```

Also, update the `tableView(_:cellForRowAtIndexPath:)` method by adding the
following two highlighted lines before returning the cell:

```
func tableView(_ tableView: UITableView, cellForRowAt
    indexPath: IndexPath) -> UITableViewCell {
    guard let cell = tableView.
        dequeueReusableCell(withIdentifier: "FamilyMemberCell")
        else { fatalError("Wrong cell identifier requested") }

    let familyMember = familyMembers[indexPath.row]
    cell.textLabel?.text = familyMember.name
    return cell
}
```

If you build and run your app now, you should see the family members you already saved.
New family members won't show up right away. However, when you quit the app and run
it again, new members will show up.

You could manually reload the table view right after you insert a new family member so
that it's always up to date, but this isn't the best approach. You will see a better way to
react to the insertion of new data soon. Let's finish the family member detail view first
so that it shows a family member's favorite movies. Add the following code to the end of
the `prepare(for:sender:)` method in the `FamilyMembersViewController`
view controller:

```
if let moviesVC = segue.destination as? MoviesViewController {
    moviesVC.persistentContainer = persistentContainer
    moviesVC.familyMember = familyMembers[selectedIndex.row]
}
```

The method should look like this:

```
override func prepare(for segue: UIStoryboardSegue, sender:
  Any?) {
  if let navVC = segue.destination as? UINavigationController,
    let addFamilyMemberVC = navVC.viewControllers[0] as?
      AddFamilyMemberViewController {
    addFamilyMemberVC.delegate = self
  }


  guard let selectedIndex = tableView.indexPathForSelectedRow
    else { return }

  if let moviesVC = segue.destination as? MoviesViewController
{

    moviesVC.persistentContainer = persistentContainer
    moviesVC.familyMember = familyMembers[selectedIndex.row]
  }


  tableView.deselectRow(at: selectedIndex, animated: true)
}
```

The preceding lines of code pass the selected family member and the persistent container to MoviesViewController so that it can display and store the current family member's favorite movies.

All you need to do to show the correct movies for a family member is to use the family member's favorite movies in the MovieViewController table view data source methods, as follows:

```
func tableView(_ tableView: UITableView, numberOfRowsInSection
  section: Int) ->Int {
  return familyMember?.movies?.count ?? 0
}


func tableView(_ tableView: UITableView, cellForRowAt
  indexPath: IndexPath) -> UITableViewCell {
  guard let cell = tableView.
    dequeueReusableCell(withIdentifier: "MovieCell"), let
      movies = familyMember?.movies
```

```
    else { fatalError("Wrong cell identifier requested or
        missing family member") }


    let moviesArray = Array(movies as! Set<Movie>)
    let movie = moviesArray[indexPath.row]
    cell.textLabel?.text = movie.title


    return cell
}
```

You don't need to use a fetch request here because you can simply traverse the `movies` relationship on the family member to get their favorite movies. This isn't just convenient for you as a developer, it's also good for your app's performance. Every time you use a fetch request, you force a query to the database. If you traverse a relationship, Core Data will attempt to fetch the object from memory instead of asking the database.

Again, adding new data won't immediately trigger the table view to update its contents. We'll get to that after we take a look at how to filter data. If you want to check whether your code works, build and rerun the app so that all the latest data is fetched from the database. Now that we know how to query from Core Data, let's perform smarter queries by filtering the retrieved data, with the help of the `NSPredicate` class.

Filtering data with predicates

A typical operation you'll want to perform on your database is filtering. In Core Data, you use predicates to do this. A **predicate** describes a set of rules that any object that gets fetched has to match.

When you model your data in the model editor, it's wise to think about the types of filtering you need to do. For instance, you may be building a birthday calendar where you'll often sort or filter by date. If this is the case, you should make sure that you have a Core Data index for this property. You can enable indexing with the checkbox you saw earlier in the model editor. If you ask Core Data to index a property, it will significantly improve performance when filtering and selecting data in large datasets.

Writing predicates can be confusing, especially if you try to think of them as the WHERE clause from SQL. Predicates are very similar, but they're not quite the same. A simple predicate looks as follows:

```
NSPredicate(format: "name CONTAINS[n] %@", "Gu")
```

A predicate has a format; this format always starts with a key. This key represents the property you want to match with. In this example, it would be the name of a family member. Then, you specify the condition – for instance, `==`, `>`, `<`, or `CONTAINS [n]`.

There are more conditions available, but the ones listed are some examples of conditions you'll commonly use. Finally, you will specify a placeholder that is substituted with the true value. This placeholder is `%@` in the preceding example. If you have written any Objective-C before you picked up this book, the `%@` placeholder might look familiar to you because it's used as a placeholder in format strings there.

The example predicate is very simple and bare; it could be the template for a search feature you're building. Usually, a simple search doesn't have to be much more complicated than this as long as there's an index added to the properties you search for.

If you have multiple predicates you want to match on, you can combine them using `NSCompoundPredicate`. This class combines different predicates using either an `and`, `or`, or `not` clause. A typical use case for this approach is when you build a complex filter in your app where the predicate is hard to express in a single statement.

To use a predicate in a fetch request, you assign it to the `predicate` property of a fetch request. Every fetch request has a `predicate` property that you can set. It can handle both a single predicate and a compound predicate. If you set this property before executing the fetch request, the predicate is applied to the request, and you will receive a filtered dataset instead of the full dataset.

Predicates are powerful, and they have many options available.

> **Tip**
> If you're interested in an in-depth overview of predicates and all of the ways in which you can make use of format strings, I recommend that you read *Apple's Predicate Programming Guide* at `http://apple. co/2fF3qHc`. It provides a well-documented overview of predicates and their applications.

Next up, you will learn how to respond to changes in the managed object context – for instance, when you add new family members and movies.

Reacting to database changes

In its current state, the **MustC** app doesn't update its list when a new managed object is persisted. One possible solution for this is to manually reload the table right after a new family member is inserted. Although this might work well for some time, it's not the best solution to this problem. If the app grows, you might add functionality that imports new family members from the network. Manually refreshing the table view would be problematic because the networking logic should not be aware of the table view. Luckily, there is a better solution to react to changes in your data.

One way to respond to database changes is by using `NSFetchedResultsController`. This class is perfect for listening to the insertion of new family members. You will implement this approach in `FamilyMembersViewController`. A second way to respond to updates is through notifications. You will implement this approach in `MoviesViewController`.

Implementing NSFetchedResultsController

`NSFetchedResultsController` is a helper class that specializes in fetching data and managing this data. It listens to changes in its managed object context and notifies a delegate whenever the data it has fetched changes. This is incredibly helpful because it allows you to respond to specific changes in the dataset rather than reloading the table view entirely.

Being a delegate for the fetched results controller involves the following important methods:

- `controllerWillChangeContent(_:)` is called right before the controller passes updates to the delegate. If you're using a table view with a fetched-results controller, this is the perfect method to begin updating the table view.

- `controller(_:didChange:at:for:newIndexPath:)` and `controller(_:didChange:atSectionIndex:for:)` are called to inform the delegate about updates to the fetched items and sections, respectively. This is where you should handle updates in the fetched data. For instance, you could insert new rows in a table view if new items were inserted in the dataset.

- `controllerDidChangeContent(_:)` is called. This is the point where you should let the table view know that you've finished processing the updates so that all the updates can be applied to the table view's interface.

For `MustC`, it doesn't make sense to implement all four methods because the table view that shows family members only has a single section. This means `controller(_:didChange:atSectionIndex:for:)` does not have to be implemented.

To use a fetched-results controller to fetch the stored family members, you need to create an instance of NSFetchedResultsController and assign FamilyMembersViewController as its delegate so that it can respond to changes in the underlying data. You can then implement the delegate methods so that you can respond to changes in the fetched-results dataset. Remove the familyMembers array from the variable declarations in FamilyMembersViewController and add the following fetchedResultsController property:

```
var fetchedResultsController:
  NSFetchedResultsController<FamilyMember>?
```

The viewDidLoad method should be adjusted as follows:

```
override func viewDidLoad() {
  super.viewDidLoad()
  let moc = persistentContainer.viewContext
  let request = NSFetchRequest<FamilyMember>(entityName:
    "FamilyMember")

  request.sortDescriptors = [NSSortDescriptor(key: "name",
    ascending: true)]
  fetchedResultsController =
    NSFetchedResultsController(fetchRequest: request,
    managedObjectContext: moc, sectionNameKeyPath: nil,
    cacheName: nil)
  fetchedResultsController?.delegate = self
  do {
    try fetchedResultsController?.performFetch()
  } catch {
    print("fetch request failed")
  }
}
```

This implementation initializes NSFetchedResultsController, assigns its delegate, and tells it to execute the fetch request. Note that the sortDescriptors property of the fetch request is set to an array that contains NSSortDescriptor. A fetched-request controller requires this property to be set, and for the list of family members, it makes sense to order family members by name.

Now that you have a fetched-results controller, you should implement the delegate methods on `FamilyMembersViewController` and make it conform to `NSFetchedResultsControllerDelegate`. Add the following extension to `FamilyMembersViewController.swift`:

```
extension FamilyMembersViewController:
  NSFetchedResultsControllerDelegate {

  func controllerWillChangeContent(_ controller:
    NSFetchedResultsController<NSFetchRequestResult>) {

    tableView.beginUpdates()
  }


  func controllerDidChangeContent(_ controller:
    NSFetchedResultsController<NSFetchRequestResult>) {

    tableView.endUpdates()
  }
}
```

The implementation of this extension is fairly straightforward. The table view gets notified when the fetched-result controller is about to process changes to its data and when the fetched-results controller is done processing changes. The bulk of the work needs to be done in `controller(_:didChange:at:for:newIndexPath)`. This method is called when an update has been processed by the fetched-result controller. In MustC, the goal is to update a table view, but you could also update a collection view or store all of the updates in a list and do something else with them.

Let's take a look at how you can process changes to fetched data in the following method. Add it to the extension on `FamilyMembersViewController.swift`:

```
func controller(_ controller:
  NSFetchedResultsController<NSFetchRequestResult>,
   didChange anObject: Any, at indexPath: IndexPath?, for type:
  NSFetchedResultsChangeType, newIndexPath: IndexPath?) {

  switch type {

  case .insert:

    guard let insertIndex = newIndexPath else { return }

    tableView.insertRows(at: [insertIndex], with: .automatic)

  case .delete:

    guard let deleteIndex = indexPath else { return }
```

```
        tableView.deleteRows(at: [deleteIndex], with: .automatic)
    case .move:
        guard let fromIndex = indexPath, let toIndex = newIndexPath
            else { return }
        tableView.moveRow(at: fromIndex, to: toIndex)
    case .update:
        guard let updateIndex = indexPath else { return }
        tableView.reloadRows(at: [updateIndex], with: .automatic)
    @unknown default:
        fatalError("Unhandled case")
    }
}
```

This method contains quite a lot of code, but it's actually not that complex. The preceding method receives a type parameter. This parameter is an instance of NSFetchedResultsChangeType, which contains information about the kind of update that was received. The following are the four types of updates that can occur:

- Insert
- Delete
- Move
- Update

Each of these change types corresponds to a database action. If an object was inserted, you will receive an insert change type. The proper way to handle these updates for MustC is to simply pass them on to the table view. Once all the updates are received, the table view will apply all of these updates at once.

If you had implemented controller(_:didChange:atSectionIndex:for:) as well, it would also have received a change type; however, the sections only deal with the following two types of changes:

- Insert
- Delete

Sections don't update or move, so if you implement this method, you don't have to account for all cases because you won't encounter any, other than the two listed types of changes.

If you take a close look at the implementation for
controller(_:didChange:at:for:newIndexPath), you'll notice that it receives
two index paths. One is named indexPath, and the other is named newIndexPath.
They're both optional, so you will need to make sure that you safely unwrap them if you
use them. For new objects, only the newIndexPath property will be present. For delete
and update, the indexPath property will be set. When an object is moved from one
place in the dataset to another, both newIndexPath and indexPath will have a value.

The last thing you need to do is update the code in FamilyMembersViewController
so that it uses the fetched results controller instead of the familyMembers array that it
used earlier. First, update the prepare(for:sender:) method, as follows:

```
if let moviesVC = segue.destination as? MoviesViewController,
    let familyMember = fetchedResultsController?.object(at:
      selectedIndex) {
  moviesVC.persistentContainer = persistentContainer
  moviesVC.familyMember = familyMember
}
```

This makes sure that a valid family member is passed to the movies view controller.
Update the table view data source methods, as shown in the following code. A fetched-
results controller can retrieve objects based on an index path. This makes it a great fit to
use in combination with table views and collection views:

```
func tableView(_ tableView: UITableView, numberOfRowsInSection
    section: Int) -> Int {
  return fetchedResultsController?.fetchedObjects?.count ?? 0
}


func tableView(_ tableView: UITableView, cellForRowAt
    indexPath: IndexPath) -> UITableViewCell {
  guard let cell = tableView.
    dequeueReusableCell(withIdentifier: "FamilyMemberCell"),
      let familyMember = fetchedResultsController?.object(at:
        indexPath) else { fatalError("Wrong cell identifier
        requested") }

  cell.textLabel?.text = familyMember.name
  return cell
}
```

If you run your app now, the interface updates automatically when you add a new family member to the database. However, the list of favorite movies doesn't update yet. That page does not use a fetched-results controller, so it must listen to changes to the dataset directly.

The reason `MoviesViewController` doesn't use a fetched-results controller for the movie list is that fetched-result controllers will always need to drop down all the way to your persistent store (SQLite in this app). As mentioned before, querying the database has a significant memory overhead compared to traversing the relationship between family members and their movies; it's much faster to read the `movies` property than fetching them from the database.

Whenever a managed object context changes, a notification is posted to the default `NotificationCenter`. `NotificationCenter` is used to send events inside of an app so that other parts of the code can react to those events.

Information

It can be very tempting to use notifications instead of delegates, especially if you're coming from a background that makes heavy use of events, such as JavaScript. Don't do this; delegation is better suited to most cases, and it will make your code much more maintainable. Only use notifications if you don't care who's listening to your notifications or if setting up a delegate relationship between objects would mean you'd create very complex relationships between unrelated objects just to set up the delegation.

Let's subscribe `MoviesViewController` to changes in the managed object context so that it can respond to data changes if needed. Before you implement this, add the following method, which should be called when changes in the managed object context occur:

```swift
extension MoviesViewController {
  @objc func managedObjectContextDidChange(notification:
    NSNotification) {
    guard let userInfo = notification.userInfo, let
      updatedObjects = userInfo[NSUpdatedObjectsKey] as?
        Set<FamilyMember>, let familyMember = self.familyMember
        else { return }
    if updatedObjects.contains(familyMember) {
      tableView.reloadData()
    }
  }
}
```

This method reads the notification's `userInfo` dictionary to access the information that's relevant to the current list. You're interested in changes to the current `familyMember` object because when this object changes, you can be pretty sure that a new movie was just inserted. The `userInfo` dictionary contains keys for the inserted, deleted, and updated objects. In this case, you should look for the updated objects because users can't delete or insert new family members in this view. If the family member was updated, the table view is reloaded so that it shows the new data.

The following code subscribes `MoviesViewController` to changes in the persistent container's managed object context:

```swift
override func viewDidLoad() {
  super.viewDidLoad()
  NotificationCenter.default.addObserver(self, selector:
    #selector(self.managedObjectContextDidChange
    (notification:)), name:
    .NSManagedObjectContextObjectsDidChange, object: nil)
}
```

When the view loads, the current `MoviesViewController` instance is added as an observer to the `.NSManagedObjectContextObjectsDidChange` notification. Go ahead and build your app; you should now see the user interface update whenever you add new data to your database.

In this section, we learned how to respond to database changes using two different methods: `NSFetchedResultsController` and notifications. In the next section, we are going to learn how to manage multiple instances of `NSManagedObjectContext` in order to improve the user interface response when dealing with heavy tasks.

Understanding the use of multiple instances of NSManagedObjectContext

It has been mentioned several times in this chapter that you can use multiple managed object contexts. In many cases, you will only need a single managed object context. Using a single managed object context means that all of the code related to the managed object context is executed on the main thread. If you're performing small operations, that's fine. However, imagine importing large amounts of data. An operation such as that could take a while. Executing code that runs for a while on the main thread will cause the user interface to become unresponsive. This is not good, because the user will think your app has crashed. So, how do you work around this? The answer is using multiple managed object contexts.

In the past, using several managed object contexts was not easy to manage; you had to create instances of NSManagedObjectContext using the correct queues yourself. Luckily, NSPersistentContainer helps to make complex setups a lot more manageable. If you want to import data on a background task, you can obtain a managed object context by calling newBackgroundContext() on the persistent container. Alternatively, you can call performBackgroundTask on the persistent container and pass it a closure with the processing you want to do in the background.

One important thing to understand about Core Data, background tasks, and multithreading is that you must always use a managed object context on the same thread it was created on. Consider the following example:

```
let backgroundQueue = DispatchQueue(label: "backgroundQueue")
let backgroundContext = persistentContainer.
  newBackgroundContext()
backgroundQueue.async {
  let results = try? backgroundContext.fetch(someRequest)
  for result in results {
    // use result
  }
}
```

The behavior of this code can cause you a couple of headaches. The background context was created in a different queue than the one it's used it in. It's always best to make sure to use a managed object context in the same queue it was created in by using the perform(_:) method of NSManagedObject. More importantly, you must also make sure to use the managed objects you retrieve on the same queue that the managed object context belongs to.

Often, you'll find that it's best to fetch data on the main queue using the viewContext persistent containers. Storing data can be delegated to background contexts if needed. If you do this, you must make sure that the background context is a child context of the main context. When this relationship is defined between the two contexts, your main context will automatically receive updates when the background context is persisted. This is quite convenient because it removes a lot of manual maintenance, which keeps your contexts in sync. Luckily, the persistent container takes care of this for you.

When you find that your app requires a setup with multiple managed object contexts, it's essential to keep the rules mentioned in this section in mind. Bugs related to using managed objects or managed object contexts in the wrong places are often tedious to debug and hard to discover. When implemented carefully, complex setups with multiple managed object contexts can increase your application's performance and flexibility.

In our project **MustC**, the `saveFamily(...)` method inside the `FamilyMembersViewController` file was using the `viewContext` to persist data. Let's refactor this code to use different managed object contexts and improve the performance of the app.

Refactoring the persisting code

In the **MustC** project, we have been persisting data using `viewContext` (you can see this in the `FamilyMembersViewController` file, inside the `saveFamily` method). Remember that we said before that `viewContext` is associated with the main queue of the application. Therefore, we can block the UI if we do any heavy work with it (usually, persisting data can incur heavy work!). So, it is a good idea to use `viewContext` just to read changes in Core Data and use a different managed object context (in a background queue) to persist them. In this way, we will not block the UI while we persist large amounts of data. Let's do this refactor.

In the code bundle of the chapter, open the project named `MustC_refactor_start`. Open the `FamilyMembersViewController` file and replace `saveFamilyMember(...)` with the following implementation:

```
func saveFamilyMember(withName name: String) {
  // 1
  persistentContainer.performBackgroundTask({ (moc) in

    // 2
    let familyMember = FamilyMember(context: moc)
    familyMember.name = name

    // 3
    do {
      try moc.save()
    } catch {
      moc.rollback()
    }
  })
}
```

Let's go through the comments (notice that we have the old method by the name of `saveFamilyMemberOld` for reference; you can compare both to see the differences):

1. First, we make use of the `performBackgroundTask` persistent container method. Each time this method is invoked, the persistent container creates a new `NSManagedObjectContext` with `concurrencyType` set to `.privateQueueConcurrencyType`. The persistent container then executes the passed-in block against that newly created context on the context's private queue. We can use this new `moc` object to persist data in a background queue, without the risk of blocking the user interface. Note how in our previous method (`saveFamilyMemberOld`), we were using the `viewContext` managed object context, which can block the user interface if the data to persist is large.

2. Second, we create a `familyMember` instance inside our managed object context (`moc`) and we update its name. When you create an instance of a managed object, you must provide the managed object context where the instance will be temporarily stored.

3. Last, in the third comment, we save. Saving the managed object context can fail, so you must wrap the `save()` call in a `do {} catch {}` block so that it correctly handles potential errors. If the managed object context can't be saved, all unsaved changes are rolled back.

Now, let's run the app and add a family member. Oops! Nothing. You will see that when you add the member, the table that displays the existing members doesn't update. However, if you stop and relaunch the app, the new member is there. So, what is happening? Looks like we are saving the data, but the user interface doesn't know about it (until we relaunch and it is reloaded). Why is that? We are persisting the data with a private managed object context, and `viewContext` doesn't know about it. Let's fix this.

In the `viewDidLoad` method, add this line, just after `let moc = persistentContainer.viewContext`:

```
moc.automaticallyMergesChangesFromParent = true
```

Setting `automaticallyMergesChangesFromParent` to `true` basically makes `viewContext` aware of any changes that other contexts are performing in the persisting store. If you execute the app now and add a family member, you will see how the table reflects the changes immediately.

Now, as practice, you can do the same in the `MoviesViewController` file, modifying the `saveMovie` method and setting the `automaticallyMergesChangesFromParent` property of `viewContext` to `true`. Give it a try!

In this section, we have learned how to use multiple managed object contexts to improve the performance of your Core Data code. Let's wrap up the chapter now with a summary.

Summary

This chapter showed you how to implement a relatively simple Core Data database that stores family members and their favorite movies. You used the Core Data model editor in Xcode to configure the models you wanted to store and define the relationship between these models. Once the models were set up, you implemented code that created instances of your models so that they could be stored in the database and retrieved later.

Next, you retrieved the data from the database and saw that your table views don't automatically update when the underlying data changes. You used an `NSFetchedResult` controller to fetch family members and listen to changes on the list of family members. You saw that this setup is very powerful because you can respond to changes in your data quite easily.

Finally, you improved the Core Data code by using different managed object contexts, using the background object context to persist data, and the main queue object context to react to the changes and refresh the user interface.

In the next chapter, you will learn how to enrich the data your users add to the database by fetching and storing data from the web.

Further reading

- The *Core Data* book, by Florian Kugler and Daniel Eggert

- Apple's Predicate Programming Guide: `http://apple.co/2fF3qHc`

9
Fetching and Displaying Data from the Network

Most modern applications communicate with a web service. Some apps rely on them heavily, acting as a layer that merely reads data from the web and displays it in app form. Other apps use the web to retrieve and sync data to make it locally available, and others only use the web as backup storage. Of course, there are a lot more reasons to use data from the internet than the ones mentioned.

In this chapter, you will expand the **MustC** application, so it uses a web service to retrieve popularity ratings for the movies that family members have added as their favorites. These popularity ratings will be stored in the Core Data database and displayed together with the names of the movies.

In this chapter, you'll learn about the following topics:

- Fetching data from the web with `URLSession`
- Working with JSON in Swift
- Updating Core Data objects with fetched data

Technical requirements

The code bundle for this chapter includes a starter project called **MustC**. It also includes a playground file named URLSession.playground.

You will also need to generate an API key from https://www.themoviedb.org/. Create an account on their website and request an API key on your account page. Setting this up should only take a couple of minutes, and if you want to follow along with this chapter, you will need to have your own API key.

After you have created and validated your account on themoviedb.org, you can visit the following link to request an API key: https://www.themoviedb.org/settings/api/request.

The code for this chapter can be found here: https://github.com/PacktPublishing/Mastering-iOS-14-Programming-4th-Edition/tree/master/Chapter%209%20-%20Fetching%20from%20Network.

Fetching data from the web with URLSession

Retrieving data from the web is something that you will often do as an iOS professional. You won't just fetch data from a web service; you'll also send data back to it. For example, you might have to make an HTTP POST request as part of a login flow or to update a user's profile information. Over time, iOS has evolved quite a bit in the web requests department, making it easier to use web services in apps.

> **Important Note**
> HTTP (or HTTPS) is a protocol that almost all web traffic uses for communication between a client, such as an app, and a server. The HTTP protocol supports several methods that signal the request's intent. GET is used to retrieve information from a server. A POST request indicates the intention to push new content to a server, such as, for instance, when submitting a form.

When you want to perform a web request in iOS, you will typically use the URLSession class. The URLSession class makes asynchronous web requests on your behalf. This means that iOS loads data from the web on a background thread, ensuring that the user interface remains responsive throughout the entire request. If a web request is performed synchronously, the user interface is unresponsive for the duration of the network request because a thread can only do one thing at a time, so if it's waiting for a response from the network, it can't respond to touches or any other user input.

If your user has a slow internet connection, a request could take several seconds. You don't want the interface to freeze for several seconds. Even a couple of milliseconds will create a noticeable drop in its responsiveness and frame rate. This can be easily avoided by using URLSession to perform asynchronous network requests.

First, you will experiment with basic network requests in a playground. You can create a new playground or use the one provided in this book's code bundle. After you've seen the basics of URLSession, you'll implement a way to fetch movies from an open source movie database and put this implementation to use in the MustC app.

Understanding the basics of URLSession

Making network calls is one of the fundamental tasks of every app that needs to fetch, post, or modify remote data. It is one of the most common tasks that a developer faces every day. For this task, Apple provides developers with the URLSession class. The URLSession class helps developers to work with remote data easily and by coordinating a group of related network data-transfer tasks.

The following code snippet shows a sample network request that loads the https://apple.com home page:

```
import Foundation
let url = URL(string: 'https://apple.com')!
let task = URLSession.shared.dataTask(with: url) {
  data, response, error in
  if let data = data {
    print(data)
  }
  if let response = response {
    print(response)
  }
  if let error = error {
    print(error)
  }
}

task.resume()
```

This is an elementary example: a URL is created, and then the shared URLSession instance is used to create a new dataTask. This dataTask is an instance of URLSessionDataTask and allows you to load data from a remote server.

Alternatively, you could use a download task if you're downloading a file, or an upload task if you're uploading files to a web server. After creating the task, you must call resume on the task, because new tasks are always created in a suspended state.

If you run this sample in an empty playground, you'll find that the example doesn't work. Because the network request is made asynchronously, the playground finishes its execution before the network request is complete. To fix this, you should make sure that the playground runs indefinitely. Doing so will allow the network request to finish. Add the following lines to the top of the playground source file to enable this behavior:

```
import PlaygroundSupport
PlaygroundPage.current.needsIndefiniteExecution = true
```

Now that the playground runs indefinitely, you'll find that there isn't a lot of useful data printed to the console. In this case, you're not interested in the raw data, HTTP headers, or the fact that the error is nil. When you load data from a URL, you're often most interested in the response's body. The body of a response usually contains the string representation of the data you requested. In the case of the preceding example, the body is the HTML that makes up Apple's home page. Let's see how you can extract this HTML from the response. Replace the data task's completion callback with the following:

```
{ data, response, error in
    guard let data = data, error == nil
        else { return }

    let responseString = String(data: data, encoding: .utf8)
    print(responseString as Any)
}
```

The preceding callback closure makes sure that there are no errors returned by the web service and that there is data present. Then, the raw data is converted to a string, and that string is printed to the console. If you use this callback instead of the old one, you'll see the HTML for the Apple home page printed. Simple requests to a web server like the one you just saw are relatively simple to implement with URLSession.

If you need to customize your network request (for example, to add custom headers) rather than using the simple `dataTask` function with a URL, you need to create your own `URLRequest` instance, instead of letting `URLSession` do it. The example you saw is one where you let `URLSession` create the `URLRequest` on your behalf. This is fine if you want to perform a simple HTTP GET request with no custom headers, but if you're going to post data or include specific headers, you will need to have more control over the request that's used.

Let's take a look at what a GET request with some parameters and a custom header looks like. The following code uses an API key from `https://www.themoviedb.org/`. If you want to try this code example, create an account on their website and request an API key on your account page. Setting this up should only take a couple of minutes, and if you want to follow along with this chapter, you will need to have your own API key. After you have created and validated your account on `themoviedb.org`, you can visit the following link to request an API key: `https://www.themoviedb.org/settings/api/request`:

```swift
let api_key = 'YOUR_API_KEY_HERE'
var urlString = 'https://api.themoviedb.org/3/search/movie/'
urlString = urlString.appending('?api_key=\(api_key)')
urlString = urlString.appending('&query=Swift')


let movieURL = URL(string: urlString)!


var urlRequest = URLRequest(url: movieURL)
urlRequest.httpMethod = 'GET'
urlRequest.setValue('application/json', forHTTPHeaderField:
  'Accept')


let movieTask = URLSession.shared.dataTask(with: urlRequest) {
  data, response, error in
  print(response as Any)
}


movieTask.resume()
```

The preceding code is a bit more complicated than the example you saw before. In this example, a more complex URL request is configured that includes some HTTP GET parameters. The `httpMethod` value for `URLRequest` is specified, and a custom header is provided to inform the receiver of this request about the type of response it would like to receive.

The flow for executing this URL request is the same as the one you saw earlier. However, the URL that is loaded responds with a JSON string instead of an HTML document. JSON is used by many APIs as the preferred format to pass data around on the web. In order to use this response, the raw data must be converted to a useful data structure. In this case, a dictionary will do. If you haven't seen or worked with JSON before, it's a good idea to take a step back and read up on the JSON data format because this chapter will continue under the assumption that you are at least somewhat familiar with JSON.

Working with JSON in Swift

The following snippet shows how you can convert raw data to a JSON dictionary. Working with JSON in Swift can be a little tedious at times, but overall, it's a generally good experience. Let's look at the following example:

```
guard let data = data, let json = try? JSONSerialization.
    jsonObject(with: data, options: []) else { return }
print(json)
```

The preceding snippet converts the raw data that is returned by a URL request to a JSON object. The `print` statement prints a readable version of the response data, but it's not quite ready to be used. Let's see how you gain access to the first available movie in the response.

If you look at the type of object returned by the `jsonObject(with:options:)` method, you'll see that it returns `Any`. This means that you must typecast the returned object to something you can work with, such as an array or a dictionary. When you inspect the JSON response that the API returned, for instance by using `print` to make it appear in the console as you did with Apple's home page HTML, you'll notice that there's a dictionary that has a key called `results`. The `results` object is an array of movies. In other words, it's an array of `[String: Any]`, because every movie is a dictionary, where strings are the keys and the value can be a couple of different things, such as Strings, Int, or Booleans. With this information, you can access the first movie's title in the JSON response, as shown in the following code:

```
guard let data = data,
    let json = try? JSONSerialization.jsonObject(with: data,
    options: []),
```

```
let jsonDict = json as? [String: AnyObject],
  let resultsArray = jsonDict['results'] as? [[String: Any]]
  else { return }
```

```
let firstMovie = resultsArray[0]
let movieTitle = firstMovie['title'] as! String
print(movieTitle)
```

Working with dictionaries to handle JSON isn't the best experience. Since the JSON object is of the `AnyObject` type and you need to typecast every element in the dictionary you want to access, there's a lot of boilerplate code you need to add.

Luckily, Swift has better ways to create instances of objects from the JSON data. The following example shows how you can quickly create an instance of a `Movie` struct without having to cast all the keys in the JSON dictionary to the correct types for the `Movie` struct.

First, let's define two structs, one for the `Movie` itself, and one for the response that contains the array of `Movie` instances:

```
struct MoviesResponse: Codable {
  let results: [Movie]
}
```

```
struct Movie: Codable {
  let id: Int
  let title: String
  let popularity: Float
}
```

Next, you can use the following snippet to quickly convert the raw data from a URL request to an instance of `MoviesResponse`, where all movies are converted to instances of the `Movie` struct:

```
let decoder = JSONDecoder()
guard let data = data,
  let movies = try? decoder.decode(MoviesResponse.self, from:
    data) else { return }
```

```
print(movies.results[0].title)
```

You might notice that both `MoviesResponse` and `Movie` conform to the `Codable` protocol. The `Codable` protocol was introduced in Swift 4, and it allows you to easily encode and decode data objects. The only requirement is that all properties of a `Codable` object conform to the `Codable` protocol. A lot of built-in types, such as `Array`, `String`, `Int`, `Float`, and `Dictionary`, conform to `Codable`. Because of this, you can easily convert an encoded JSON object into a `MoviesResponse` instance that holds `Movie` instances.

By default, each property name should correspond to the key of the JSON response it is mapped to. However, sometimes you might want to customize this mapping. For instance, the `poster_path` property in the response we've been working with so far would be best mapped to a `posterPath` property on the `Movie` struct, according to the general Swift guidelines for property naming. The following example shows how you would tackle these circumstances:

```
struct Movie: Codable {
    enum CodingKeys: String, CodingKey {
        case id, title, popularity
        case posterPath = 'poster_path'
    }

    let id: Int
    let title: String
    let popularity: Float
    let posterPath: String?
}
```

By specifying a `CodingKeys` enum, you can override how the keys in the JSON response should be mapped to your `Codable` object. You must cover all keys that are mapped, including the ones you don't want to change. As you've seen, the `Codable` protocol provides powerful tools for working with data from the network. Custom key mapping makes this protocol even more powerful because it allows you to shape your objects exactly how you want them, instead of having the URL responses dictate the structure to you.

If the only conversion you need to apply in the coding keys is converting from snake case (poster_path) to camel case (posterPath), you don't have to specify the coding keys yourself. The JSONDecoder object can automatically apply this type of conversion when decoding data if you set its keyDecodingStrategy to .convertFromSnakeCase, as shown in the following code:

```
let decoder = JSONDecoder()
decoder.keyDecodingStrategy = .convertFromSnakeCase
```

By applying these lines of code, the decoder will automatically translate property names such as poster_path into the posterPath syntax. Try implementing this in your playground and remove CodingKeys from the Movie object to ensure your JSON decoding still works.

In this section, we have learned how to work with JSON data and how to decode it into our own entities. Now let's move on to storing the fetched data in the Core Data database.

Updating Core Data objects with fetched data

So far, the only thing you have stored in Core Data is movie names. You will expand this functionality by performing a lookup for a certain movie name through the movie database API. The fetched information will be used to display and store a popularity rating for the movies in the Core Data database.

A task such as this seems straightforward at first; you could come up with a flow such as the one shown in the following steps:

1. The user indicates their favorite movie.

2. The movie's popularity rating is fetched.

3. The movie and its rating are stored in the database.

The user interface updates with the new movie. At first glance, this is a fine strategy; insert the data when you have it. However, it's important to consider that API calls are typically done asynchronously so the user interface stays responsive. More importantly, API calls can be really slow if your user doesn't have a good internet connection. This means that you would be updating the interface with some very noticeable lag if the preceding steps are executed one by one.

The following would be a much better approach to implement the feature at hand:

1. The user indicates their favorite movie.

2. The user stores the movie.

3. Update the user interface with the new movie.

4. Begin popularity fetching.

5. Update the movie in the database.

6. Update the user interface with the popularity.

This approach is somewhat more complex, but it will give the user a responsive experience. The user interface responds to new movies immediately by showing them, and then automatically updates as soon as new data is retrieved. Before you can fetch the data and update the models, the Core Data model must be modified in order to store the given movie's popularity rating.

Open the **MustC** project for this chapter (you can find it in the GitHub repository of the book). Then, open the **Core Data** model editor and select the **Movie** entity. All you have to do is to add a new property and name it popularity. Select the Double type for this property because popularity is stored as a decimal value. You have to make sure that this property is optional since you won't be able to provide a value for it straight away:

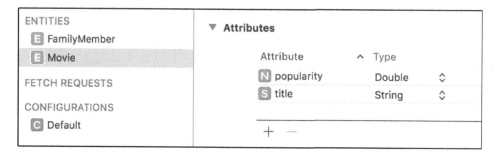

Figure 9.1 – Add the popularity attribute to the Movie entity

If you've worked with Core Data prior to when iOS 10 was released, this is the part where you expect to read about migrations and how you can orchestrate them.

However, for simple changes like this, we don't need to manually manage migrations. All you need to do is simply build and run your application to regenerate your model definitions, and for a simple change, such as the one we performed just now, Core Data will automatically manage the migration for us.

> **Important Note**
>
> If you want to support iOS versions earlier than 10, make sure you read up on Core Data migrations. Whenever you update your models, you have to make sure that your database can properly migrate from one model version to another. During development, this isn't extremely important: you just reinstall the app whenever your models change. However, app updates will crash on launch if the Core Data model isn't compatible with the previous model.

Now that the Core Data model is updated, let's figure out how to implement the flow that was described earlier.

Implementing the fetch logic

The asynchronous nature of network requests makes certain tasks, such as the one you're about to implement, quite complex. Usually, when you write code, its execution is very predictable. Your app typically runs line by line, sequentially, so any line that comes after the previous one can assume that the line before it has finished executing. This isn't the case with asynchronous code. Asynchronous code is taken off the main thread and runs separately from the rest of your code. This means that your asynchronous code might run in parallel with other code. In the case of a network request, the asynchronous code might execute seconds after the function that initiated the request.

This means that you need to figure out a way to update and save movies that were added as soon as the rating was retrieved. However, it's important that you're aware of the fact that it's not as straightforward as it may seem at first.

It's also important that you're aware of the fact that the code you're about to look at is executed on multiple threads. This means that even though all pieces of the code are defined in the same place, they are not executed sequentially. The callback for the network request is executed on a different thread than the code that initiated the network request. You have already learned that Core Data is not thread-safe. This means that you can't safely access a Core Data object on a different thread than the thread it was created on.

If this confuses you, that's okay. You're supposed to be a bit confused right now. Asynchronous programming is not easy and fooling you into thinking it is will cause frustration once you run into concurrency-related troubles (and you will). Whenever you work with callbacks, closures, and multiple threads, you should be aware that you're doing complex work that isn't straightforward.

Now that you understand that asynchronous code is hard, let's take a closer look at the feature you're about to implement. It's time to start implementing the network request that fetches popularity ratings for movies. You will abstract the fetching logic into a helper named `MovieDBHelper`. Go ahead and create a new `Helper` folder in Xcode and add a new Swift file called `MovieDBHelper.swift` to it.

Abstracting this logic into a helper has multiple advantages. One of them is simplicity; it will keep our view controller code nice and clean. Another advantage is flexibility. Let's say that you want to combine multiple rating websites, or a different API, or compute the popularity of movies based on the number of family members who added this same title to their list; it will be easier to implement since all the logic for ratings is in a single place.

Add the following skeleton implementation to the `MovieDBHelper` file:

```swift
struct MovieDBHelper {
  typealias MovieDBCallback = (Double?) -> Void
  let apiKey = 'YOUR_API_KEY_HERE'

  func fetchRating(forMovie movie: String, callback: @escaping
  MovieDBCallback) {

  }

  private func url(forMovie movie: String) -> URL? {
    guard let query =
      movie.addingPercentEncoding(withAllowedCharacters:
        .urlHostAllowed) else { return nil }

    var urlString =
    'https://api.themoviedb.org/3/search/movie/'
    urlString = urlString.appending('?api_key=\(apiKey)')
    urlString = urlString.appending('&query=\(query)')

    return URL(string: urlString)
  }
}
```

The preceding code starts off with an interesting line:

```
typealias MovieDBCallback = (Double?) -> Void
```

This line specifies the type that's used for the callback closure that's called when the rating is fetched. This callback will receive an optional `Double` as its argument. If the network request fails for any reason, the `Double` will be nil. Otherwise, it contains the rating for the movie that the request was created for.

The snippet also contains a `fetchRating` dummy method that performs the fetch; you will implement this method soon. Finally, there's a `url(forMovie movie: String)` method that builds a URL. This method is private because it's only supposed to be used inside of the helper struct. Note that the movie is converted to a percent-encoded string. This is required because if your user were to add a movie with spaces in it, you would end up with an invalid URL if the spaces aren't properly encoded.

Before you implement `fetchRating(forMovie:callback)`, add a new file named `MovieDBResponse.swift` to the `Helper` folder. This file will be used to define a struct that represents the response we expect to receive from `api.themoviedb.org`. Add the following implementation to this file:

```
struct MovieDBLookupResponse: Codable {
  struct MovieDBMovie: Codable {
    let popularity: Double?
  }
  let results: [MovieDBMovie]
}
```

The preceding code uses a nested struct to represent the movie objects that are part of the response. This is similar to what you saw in the playground example in the *Fetching data from the web with URLSession* section at the beginning of this chapter. Structuring the response this way makes the intent of this helper very obvious, which usually makes code easier to reason about. With this struct in place, replace the implementation of `fetchRating(forMovie:callback)` inside `MovieDBHelper` with the following:

```
func fetchRating(forMovie movie: String, callback: @escaping
  MovieDBCallback) {
  guard let searchUrl = url(forMovie: movie) else {
    callback(nil)
    return
  }
```

```
let task = URLSession.shared.dataTask(with: searchUrl) {
  data, response, error in
  var rating: Double? = nil
  defer {
    callback(rating)
  }


  let decoder = JSONDecoder()

  guard error == nil,
        let data = data,
        let lookupResponse = try?
        decoder.decode(MovieDBLookupResponse.self, from:
        data),
        let popularity =
        lookupResponse.results.first?.popularity
  else { return }

  rating = popularity
}


  task.resume()
}
```

This implementation looks very similar to what you experimented with earlier in the playground. The URL-building method is used to create a valid URL. If this fails, it makes no sense to attempt requesting the movie's rating, so the callback is called with a `nil` argument. This will inform the caller of this method that the execution is completed, and no result was retrieved.

Next, a new data task is created and `resume()` is called on this task to kick it off. There is an interesting aspect to how the callback for this data task is called, though. Let's take a look at the following lines of code:

```
var rating: Double? = nil
defer {
  callback(rating)
}
```

A rating optional Double is created here, and it is given an initial value of nil. Then there's a defer block. The code inside of the defer block is called right before exiting the scope. In other words, it's executed right before the code returns from a function or closure.

Since this defer block is defined inside the callback for the data task, the callback for the fetchRating(forMovie:callback:) method is always called just before the data task callback is exited. This is convenient because all you must do is set the value for the rating to double, and you don't have to manually invoke the callback for each possible way the scope can be exited. This also applies when you return because of unmet requirements. For instance, if there is an error while calling the API, you don't need to invoke the callback. You can simply return from the closure, and the callback is called automatically. This strategy can also be applied if you instantiate or configure objects temporarily and you want to perform some clean-up when the method, function, or closure is done.

The rest of the code should be fairly straightforward since most of it is nearly identical to the code used in the playground. Now that you have the networking logic down, let's take a look at how to actually update the movie object with a popularity rating.

Updating a movie with a popularity rating

To update the movie object, you will implement the final step of the approach that was outlined earlier. You need to asynchronously fetch a rating from the movie database and then use that rating to update the movie. The following code should be added to MoviesViewController.swift, inside the saveMovie(withName name: String) method right after the familyMember.movies = NSSet(set: newFavorites line:

```swift
let helper = MovieDBHelper()
helper.fetchRating(forMovie: name) { rating in
  guard let rating = rating else { return }
  moc.persist {
    movie.popularity = rating
  }
}
```

You can see that the helper abstraction provides a nice interface for the view controller. You can simply use the helper and provide it a movie to fetch the rating for with a callback and you're all set. Abstracting code like this can make maintaining your code a lot more fun in the long run.

The most surprising thing in the preceding snippet is that moc.persist is called again inside of the helper callback. This must be done because this callback is actually executed long after the initial persist has finished. Actually, this callback isn't even executed on the same thread as the code it's surrounded by.

To see how your code fails if you don't properly persist your model, try replacing the moc.persist block in the rating retrieval callback with the following code:

```
movie.popularity = rating
do {
    try moc.save()
} catch {
    moc.rollback()
}
```

If you add a new movie now, the rating will still be fetched. However, you will suddenly run into issues when reloading your table view. This is because the managed object context was saved on a background thread. This means that the notification that informs the table view about updates is also sent on a background thread. You could resolve the issue by pushing the reloadData() call onto the main thread as you've done before, but in this case, doing so would only make the problem worse. Your app might work fine for a while, but once your app grows in complexity, using the same managed object context in multiple threads will most certainly cause crashes. Therefore, it's important to always make sure that you access managed objects and their contexts on the correct thread by using a construct, such as the persist method we implemented for this app.

Now that you have looked at all the code involved, let's see what all this threading talk means in a more visual way.

Visualizing multiple threads

The following diagram will help you understand multiple threads:

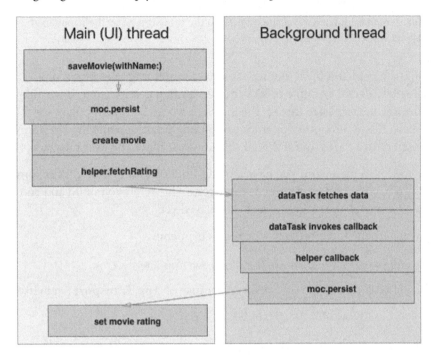

Figure 9.2 – Threads diagram

When `saveMovie(withName:)` is called, the execution is still on the main thread. The persistence block is opened, the movie is created, its name is set, a helper is created, and then `fetchRating(forMovie:callback:)` is called on the helper. This call itself is still on the main thread. However, the fetching of data is pushed to a background thread. This was discussed earlier when you experimented with fetching data in a playground.

The callback that's invoked by `dataTask` is called on the same background thread that the task itself is on. The code will do its thing with the JSON and finally, the callback that was passed to `fetchRating(forMovie:callback:)` is called. The code inside of this callback is executed on the background thread as well.

You can see that the set movie-rating step in the update flow is somehow pushed back to the main thread. This is because of the `persist` method that you added as an extension to the managed object context. The context uses the `perform` method internally to ensure that any code we execute inside of the `persist` block is executed on the thread the managed object context is on. Also, since the managed object context was created on the main thread, the movie rating will be set on the main thread.

> **Important Note**
>
> If you didn't set the movie rating on the same thread that the managed object belongs to, you would get errors and undefined behavior. Always make sure that you manipulate Core Data objects on the same thread as their managed object context.

Threading is a complex subject, but it's essential for building responsive applications. Network logic is a great example of why multithreading is important. If we didn't perform the networking on a separate thread, the interface would be unresponsive for the duration of the request. If you have other operations that might take a while in your app, consider moving them onto a background thread so they don't block the user interface.

All of the code is in place, and you have a better understanding of multithreading and how callbacks can be used in a multithreaded environment. Yet, if you build and run your app and add a new movie, the rating won't be displayed yet.

The following are the three reasons why this is happening:

- The table view cell that shows the movie isn't updated yet.
- The network request doesn't succeed because of **App Transport Security**.
- Updates to movie objects aren't observed yet.

Let's solve these issues in order, starting with the table view cell.

Adding the rating to the movie cell

Currently, the movie table view displays cells that have a title. `UITableViewCell` has a built-in option to display a title and a subtitle for a cell.

Open `Main.storyboard` and select the prototype cell for the movies. In the **Attributes Inspector** field, change the cell's style from basic to subtitle. This will allow you to use `detailTextLabel` on the table view cell. This is where we'll display the movie rating.

In `MoviesViewController`, add the following line to `tableView(_:cellForRow:atIndexPath:)`, right after you set the cell's title:

```
cell.detailTextLabel?.text = 'Rating: \(movie.popularity)'
```

This line will put the movie's popularity rating in a string and assign it as the text for the detail text label.

If you build and run your app now, all movies should have a popularity of 0.0. Let's fix this by resolving the networking issue.

Understanding App Transport Security

With iOS 9, Apple introduced **App Transport Security (ATS)**. ATS makes applications safer and more secure by prohibiting the use of non-HTTPS resources. This is a great security feature, as it protects your users from a wide range of attacks that can be executed on regular HTTP connections.

If you paid close attention to the URL that's used to fetch movies, you may have noticed that the URL should be an HTTPS resource, so it should be fine to load this URL. However, the network requests are still blocked by ATS. Why is this?

Well, Apple has strict requirements. At the time of writing this book, the movie database uses the SHA-1 signing of certificates, whereas Apple requires SHA-2. Because of this, you will need to circumvent ATS for now. Your users should be safe regardless, since the movie database supports HTTPS, just not the version Apple considers to be secure enough.

To do this, open the `Info.plist` file and add a new dictionary key named **App Transport Security Settings**. In this dictionary, you will need an **Exception Domains** dictionary. Add a new dictionary key named `themoviedb.org` to this dictionary and add two Booleans to this dictionary. Both should have **YES** as their values, and they should be named **NSIncludesSubdomains** and **NSTemporaryExceptionAllowsInsecureHTTPLoads**. Refer to the following screenshot to make sure that you've set this up correctly:

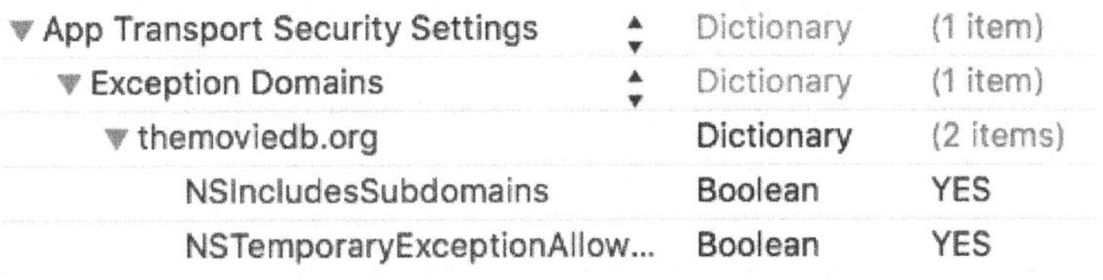

▼ App Transport Security Settings		Dictionary	(1 item)
▼ Exception Domains		Dictionary	(1 item)
▼ themoviedb.org		Dictionary	(2 items)
NSIncludesSubdomains		Boolean	YES
NSTemporaryExceptionAllow...		Boolean	YES

Figure 9.3 – App Transport Security Settings

If you add a new movie to a family member now, nothing updates yet. However, if you go back to the family overview and then back to the family member, you'll see that the rating for the most recent movie is updated (make sure you choose a movie whose title is present on `themoviedb.org`). Great! Now, all you need to do is make sure that we observe the managed object context for updates to the movies, so they are reloaded if their rating changes.

Observing changes to movie ratings

You're already observing the managed object context for changes, but they are only processed if the family member that is shown on the current page has updated. This logic should be replaced so that it will reload the table view if either the family member or their favorite movies change. Update the `managedObjectContextDidChange(_:)` method in `MoviesViewController.swift` as follows:

```swift
@objc func managedObjectContextDidChange(notification:
  NSNotification) {

  guard let userInfo = notification.userInfo else { return }

  if let updatedObjects = userInfo[NSUpdatedObjectsKey] as?
    Set<FamilyMember>,
    let familyMember = self.familyMember,
    updatedObjects.contains(familyMember) {
    tableView.reloadData()
  }

  if let updatedObjects = userInfo[NSUpdatedObjectsKey] as?
  Set<Movie> {
    for object in updatedObjects {
      if object.familyMember == familyMember {
        tableView.reloadData()
        break
      }
    }
  }
}
```

> **Important Note**
>
> The logic for observing the family member hasn't changed; its conditions simply moved from the `guard` statement to an `if` statement. An extra `if` statement was added for the movies. If the updated object set is a list of movies, we loop through the movies and check whether one of the movies has the current family member as its family member. If so, the table is refreshed immediately, and the loop is exited.

It's important that the loop in the second `if` statement is set up like this because you might have just added a movie for family member A and then switched to family member B while the new movie for family member A was still loading its rating. Also, breaking out of the loop early ensures that you don't loop over any more objects than needed. All you want to do is refresh the table view if one of the current family members' favorite movies is updated.

Okay, now build and run your app to take it for a spin! You'll notice that everything works as you'd want it to right now. Adding new movies triggers a network request; as soon as it finishes, the UI is updated with the new rating. Sometimes, this update will be done in an instant, but it could take a short while if you have a slow internet connection. Great! That's it for this feature.

Summary

This chapter was all about adding a small, simple feature to an existing app. We added the ability to load real data from an API. You saw that networking is made pretty straightforward by Apple with `URLSession` and data tasks. You also learned that this class abstracts away some very complex behavior regarding multithreading, so your apps remain responsive while data is loaded from the network. Next, you implemented a `helper` struct for networking and updated the Core Data model to store ratings for movies. Once all this was done, you could finally see how multithreading worked in the context of this app. This wasn't everything we needed to do, though. You learned about ATS and how it keeps your users secure. You also learned that you sometimes need to circumvent ATS, and we covered how you can achieve this.

Even though the feature itself wasn't very complex, the concepts and theory involved could have been quite overwhelming. You suddenly had to deal with code that would be executed asynchronously in the future. And not just that. The code even used multiple threads to make sure that its performance was optimal. The concepts of multithreading and asynchronous programming are arguably two of the more complex aspects of programming. Practice them a lot and try to remember that any time you're passing around a closure, you could be writing some asynchronous code that gets executed on a different thread.

Now that the list of movies is updated with data from the web, let's take it one step further in the next chapter. You will learn how to make your app smarter by using CoreML and Vision Framework features.

10
Making Smarter Apps with Core ML

Over the past few years, machine learning has gained in popularity. However, it has never been easy to implement in mobile applications—that is, until Apple released the **Core ML** framework as part of iOS 11. Core ML is Apple's solution to all of the problems that developers at the company have run into themselves while implementing machine learning for iOS. As a result, Core ML should have the fastest, most efficient implementations for working with sophisticated machine learning models, through an interface that is as simple and flexible as possible.

In this chapter, you will learn what machine learning is, how it works, and how you can use trained machine learning models in your apps. You will also learn how you can use Apple's **Vision framework** to analyze images, and you'll see how it integrates with Core ML for powerful image detection. Lastly, you'll learn how to use the new **Create ML** tool to train your models, how to deploy your models to the cloud, and how to encrypt them for security. You will learn about these topics in the following sections:

- Understanding machine learning and Core ML
- Combining Core ML and computer vision

- Training your own models with Create ML
- Updating models remotely with Model Deployment
- Encrypting Core ML models

By the end of this chapter, you will be able to train and use your Core ML models to make the apps you build more intelligent and compelling.

Technical requirements

The code bundle for this chapter includes three starter projects called `TextAnalyzer`, `ImageAnalyzer`, and `TextAnalyzerCloud`. It also includes a playground file named `Create ML.playground`.

The code for this chapter can be found here: `https://github.com/ PacktPublishing/Mastering-iOS-14-Programming-4th-Edition/tree/ master/Chapter%2010%20-%20Core%20ML`.

Understanding machine learning and Core ML

Machine learning and Core ML go hand in hand, but they're not quite the same. Machine learning is all about teaching a machine how it can recognize, analyze, or apply certain things. The result of all this teaching is a trained model that can be used by Core ML to analyze specific inputs and produce an output based on the rules that were established during the training phase.

Before you learn about Core ML, it's good to obtain some knowledge about machine learning to make sure you're familiar with some of the terms that are used, and so you know what machine learning is.

Understanding what machine learning is

A lot of developers will hear about machine learning, deep learning, or neural networks at some point in their careers. You may have already heard about these topics. If you have, you know that machine learning is a complex field that requires particular domain knowledge. However, machine learning is becoming more prominent and popular by the day, and it is used to improve many different types of applications.

For instance, machine learning can be used to predict what type of content a particular user might like to see in a music app based on the music that they already have in their library, or to automatically tag faces in photos to connect them to people in the user's contact list. It can even be used to predict costs for specific products or services based on past data. While this might sound like magic, the flow for creating machine learning experiences like these can be split roughly into two phases:

1. Training a model

2. Using inference to obtain a result from the model

Large amounts of high-quality data must be collected to perform the first step. If you're going to train a model that should recognize cats, you will need a large number of pictures of cats. You must also collect images that do not contain cats. Each image must then be appropriately tagged to indicate whether the image includes a cat or not.

If your dataset only contains images of cats that face towards the camera, the chances are that your model will not be able to recognize cats from a sideways point of view. If your dataset does contain cats from many different sides, but you only collected images for a single breed or with a solid white background, your model might still have a tough time recognizing all cats. Obtaining quality training data is not easy, yet it's essential.

During the training phase of a model, you must provide a set of inputs that are of the highest quality possible. The smallest mistake could render your entire dataset worthless. Collecting big amounts of high-quality data to train a model is a tedious task. It also takes a lot of time. Certain complex models could take a couple of hours to crunch all the data and train themselves.

A trained model comes in several types. Each type of model is suitable for a different kind of task. For instance, if you are working on a model that can classify specific email messages as spam, your model might be a so-called **support vector machine**. If you're training a model that recognizes cats in pictures, you are likely training a **neural network**.

Each model comes with its pros and cons, and each model is created and used differently. Understanding all these different models, their implications, and how to train them is extremely hard, and you could likely write a book on each kind of model.

In part, this is why Core ML is so great. Core ML enables you to make use of pre-trained models in your own apps. On top of this, Core ML standardizes the interface that you use in your own code. This means that you can use complex models without even realizing it. Let's learn more about Core ML, shall we?

Understanding Core ML

Due to the complex nature of machine learning and using trained models, Apple has built Core ML to make incorporating a trained model as straightforward as possible. On top of this, another goal was to ensure that whenever you implement machine learning using Core ML, your implementation is as fast and energy-efficient as possible. Since Apple has been enhancing iOS with machine learning for a couple of years now, they have loads of experience of implementing complex models in apps.

If you have ever researched machine learning, you might have come across cloud-based solutions. Typically, you send a bunch of data to a cloud-based solution, and the result is passed back as a response to your request. Core ML is very different, since the trained model lives on the device, instead of in the cloud. This means that your user's data never has to leave the device, which is very good for your user's privacy. Also, having your trained model on the device means that no internet connection is required to use Core ML, which saves both time and precious data. And since there is no potential bottleneck regarding response latency, Core ML is capable of calculating results in real time.

In the previous section, you learned that there are several types of trained models. Each type of model is used slightly differently, so if you were to implement machine learning in your app manually, you would have to write different wrappers around each of the different models your app uses. Core ML makes sure that you can use each type of model without even being aware of this in your app; they all share the same programming interface. A Core ML model is domain-agnostic.

To be domain-agnostic, all trained models that you use with Core ML must be in a particular format. Since machine learning already has a vibrant community with several popular formats, Apple has made sure that the most popular models can be easily converted to Apple's own `.mlmodel` format. Let's see how to obtain `.mlmodel` files for you to use in your own apps.

Obtaining Core ML models

There are two ways to obtain a model for you to use in your apps. The simplest way is to find an existing `.mlmodel` file. You can find several ready-to-use `.mlmodel` files on Apple's machine learning website, at `https://developer.apple.com/machine-learning/`. This website contains several of the most popular models. At the time of writing, most of these models are focused on recognizing the dominant objects in an image, and chances are that you have different needs for your app.

If you're looking for something that hasn't already been converted by Apple, you can try to look in several places online for a pre-converted `.mlmodel` file, or you can convert an existing model you have found online. Apple has created converters for several popular machine learning formats, such as **Caffe**. The conversion tools for converting an existing model to a `.mlmodel` file are written in Python, and they ship as part of Xcode. If your needs do not fit the converters that Apple provides, you can extend the **toolchain**, since the conversion tools are open source. This means that everybody can add their own converters or tweak existing converters.

Converting Core ML models using Apple's tools can usually be done with a couple of lines of Python. Writing a good conversion script does typically involve a little bit of domain knowledge in the area of machine learning, because you'll need to make sure that the converted model works just as well as the original model.

Once you have obtained a Core ML model for your app, either by converting one or finding an existing one, you're ready to add it to your project and begin using it. Let's see how to do this next.

Using a Core ML model

Applications can utilize Core ML for many different purposes. One of these purposes is text analysis. You can use a trained model to detect whether a particular piece of text has a positive or negative sentiment. To implement a feature like this, you can use a trained and converted Core ML model.

The code bundle for this chapter includes a project named **TextAnalyzer**. If you open the starter version of this project, you'll find a project that has an implementation of a simple layout along with a button that is hooked up to an `@IBAction`, named `analyze()`. The project folder also contains a file called `SentimentPolarity.mlmodel`. This file is a trained Core ML model that analyzes the sentiment associated with a certain text. Drag this file into Xcode to add the Core ML model to your project.

After adding the model to your project, you can click it in the **Project Navigator** to see more information about the model, as illustrated in the following screenshot:

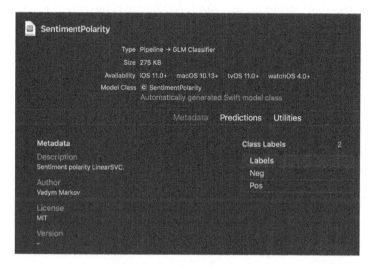

Figure 10.1 – Model metadata

You can see that this model was provided by **Vadym Markov** under the **MIT** license. If you click the **Predictions** tab (see the preceding screenshot), you can find out which **Input** and **Output** you can expect this model to work with:

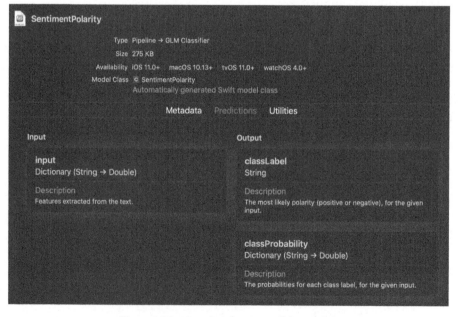

Figure 10.2 – Input and output of the model

You can see in this case; the **Input** is a dictionary of the [String: Double] type. This means that we should feed this model a dictionary of word counts. If you add this model to Xcode, the center section that lists the **Model Class** might notify you that the model is not part of any targets yet. If this is the case, fix it as you have done previously, by adding this model to your app target in the **Utilities** sidebar on the right side of the window.

Now that your model has been implemented, it's time to take it for a spin. First, implement a method that extracts the word count from any given string. You can implement this using the NLTokenizer object from the new NaturalLanguage framework.

NLTokenizer is a text analysis class that is used to split a string into words, sentences, paragraphs, or even whole documents. In this example, the tokenizer is set up to detect individual words. Implement the word count method as follows.

Add an import to the ViewController.swift file as follows:

```
import NaturalLanguage
```

Now add the following method to the same file:

```
func getWordCounts(from string: String) -> [String: Double] {
    let tokenizer = NLTokenizer(unit: .word)
    tokenizer.string = string
    var wordCount = [String: Double]()

    tokenizer.enumerateTokens(in:
        string.startIndex..<string.endIndex) { range, attributes in
        let word = String(string[range])
        wordCount[word] = (wordCount[word] ?? 0) + 1
        return true
    }

    return wordCount
}
```

The previous code iterates over all the words that the tokenizer has recognized and stores it in a dictionary of the [String: Double] type. You might wonder why a Double type is used for the word count, rather than an Int type, since the word counts won't have to deal with decimals. This is true, but the SentimentPolarity model requires its input to be a dictionary of the [String: Double] type, so you must prepare the data accordingly.

Now that you have the code to prepare the input data for the `SentimentPolarity` model, let's see how you can use this model to analyze the user's input. Add the following implementation for the `analyze()` method:

```
@IBAction func analyze() {
    let wordCount = getWordCounts(from: textView.text)
    let model = try? SentimentPolarity(configuration: .init())

    guard let prediction = try? model?.prediction(input:
      wordCount) else { return }

    let alert = UIAlertController(title: nil, message: "Your
      text is rated: \(prediction.classLabel)", preferredStyle:
        .alert)
    let okayAction = UIAlertAction(title: "Okay", style:
      .default, handler: nil)
    alert.addAction(okayAction)
    present(alert, animated: true, completion: nil)
}
```

You might be surprised that this method is so short, but that's how simple Core ML is! First, we retrieve the `wordCount` using the method we implemented earlier. Then, an instance of the Core ML model is created. When you added the `SentimentPolarity` model to the app target, Xcode generated a class interface that abstracted away all complexities involving the model. Because the model is now a simple class, you can obtain a prediction for the sentiment of the text by calling `prediction(input:)` on the model instance.

The `prediction` method returns an object that contains the processed prediction in the `classLabel` property, as well as an overview of all available predictions and how certain the model is about each option in the `classProbability` property. You can use this property if you want to be a bit more transparent to the user about the different options that the model suggested and how certain it was about these options.

Let's see a couple of examples to demonstrate how it works. First, launch the app. Now write `I love rainbows` in the text area and press **Analyze Text**. You will get a popup saying **Your text is rated: Pos**. This means that what you typed has a positive sentiment (according to our model). Now do the same but with this sentence instead: `I am sad on cloudy days`. The result now is **Your text is rated: Neg**. This time, the sentiment of your sentence is negative! You can try out your own ideas to see how the model behaves in different scenarios.

In the last section of this chapter, you will learn how you can use `Create ML` to train your own natural language model to analyze texts that use domain-specific language relevant to your own app.

Using Core ML to perform text analysis was quite simple. Now let's see how you can use computer vision together with Core ML to determine the type of object that exists in a particular picture.

Combining Core ML and computer vision

When you're developing an app that works with photos or live camera footage, there are several things you might like to do using computer vision. For instance, it could be desirable to detect faces in an image. Or, maybe you would want to identify certain rectangular areas of photographs, such as traffic signs. You could also be looking for something more sophisticated, such as detecting the dominant object in a picture.

To work with computer vision in your apps, Apple has created the **Vision** framework. You can combine Vision and Core ML to perform some pretty sophisticated image recognition. Before you implement a sample app that uses dominant object recognition, let's take a quick look at the Vision framework, so you have an idea of what it's capable of and when you might like to use it.

Understanding the Vision framework

The Vision framework is capable of many different tasks that revolve around computer vision. It is built upon several powerful deep learning techniques that enable state-of-the-art facial recognition, text recognition, barcode detection, and more.

When you use Vision for facial recognition, you get much more information than just the location of a face in an image. The framework can recognize several facial landmarks, such as eyes, noses, or mouths. All of this is possible due to the extensive use of deep learning behind the scenes at Apple.

For most tasks, using Vision consists of the following three stages:

1. You create a request that specifies what you want; for instance, a `VNDetectFaceLandmarksRequest` request to detect facial features.

2. You set up a handler that can analyze the images.

3. The resulting observation contains the information you need.

The following code sample illustrates how you might find facial landmarks in an image:

```
let handler = VNImageRequestHandler(cgImage: image, options:
  [:])
let request = VNDetectFaceLandmarksRequest(completionHandler: {
  request, error in
  guard let results = request.results as? [VNFaceObservation]
  else { return }

  for result in results where result.landmarks != nil {
    let landmarks = result.landmarks!

    if let faceContour = landmarks.faceContour {
      print(faceContour.normalizedPoints)
    }
    if let leftEye = landmarks.leftEye {
      print(leftEye.normalizedPoints)
    }

    // etc
  }}
)
try? handler.perform([request])
```

For something as complex as detecting the contour of a face or the exact location of an eye, the code is quite simple. You set up a `handler` and a `request`. Next, the `handler` is asked to `perform` one or more requests. This means that you can run several requests on a single image.

In addition to enabling computer vision tasks like this, the Vision framework also tightly integrates with Core ML. Let's see just how tight this integration is, by adding an image classifier to the augmented-reality gallery app you have been working on!

Implementing an image classifier

The code bundle for this section contains an app called **ImageAnalyzer**. This app uses an image picker to allow a user to select an image from their photo library to use it as an input for the image classifier you will implement. Open the project and explore it for a little bit to see what it does and how it works. Use the starter project if you want to follow along with the rest of this section.

To add an image classifier, you need to have a Core ML model that can classify images. On Apple's machine learning website (`https://developer.apple.com/machine-learning/build-run-models/`), there are several models available that can do image classification. An excellent lightweight model you can use is the **MobileNetV2** model; go ahead and download it from the machine learning page. Once you have downloaded the model, drag the model into Xcode to add it to the **ImageAnalyzer** project. Make sure to add it to your app target so that Xcode can generate the class interface for the model.

After adding the model to Xcode, you can open it to examine the **Model Predictions** tab. The parameters tell you the different types of inputs and outputs the model will expect and provide. In the case of **MobileNetV2**, the input should be an image that is **224** points wide and **224** points high, as shown in the following screenshot:

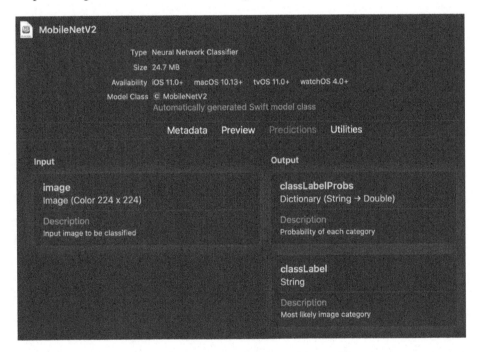

Figure 10.3 – Input and output of the model

After generating the model, the code to use the model is very similar to the code used to detect facial features with Vision earlier. The most significant difference is that the type of request that is used is a special `VNCore MLRequest`. This type of request takes the Core ML model you want to use, in addition to a completion handler.

When combining Core ML and Vision, Vision will take care of image scaling and converting the image to a type that is compatible with the Core ML model. You should make sure that the input image has the correct orientation. If your image is rotated in an unexpected orientation, Core ML might not be able to analyze it correctly.

First, let's import the `Vision` framework. Add this statement at the top of the `ViewController` class in the **ImageAnalyzer** project:

```
import Vision
```

Now, add the following implementation for `analyzeImage(_:)` to the `ViewController` class:

```swift
func analyzeImage(_ image: UIImage) {

  guard
    let cgImage = image.cgImage,
    let classifier = try? VNCore MLModel(for:
    MobileNetV2().model)
  else { return }

  let request = VNCore MLRequest(model: classifier,
  completionHandler: { [weak self] request, error in
    guard
      let classifications = request.results as?
      [VNClassificationObservation],
      let prediction = classifications.first
    else { return }

    DispatchQueue.main.async {
      self?.objectDescription.text = "\(prediction.identifier)
      (\(round(prediction.confidence * 100))% confidence)"
    }
  })

  let handler = VNImageRequestHandler(cgImage: cgImage,
    options: [:])

  try? handler.perform([request])
}
```

The previous method takes a UIImage and converts it to a CGImage. Also, a VNCore MLModel is created, based on the MobileNetV2 model. This particular model class wraps the Core ML model, so it works seamlessly with Vision. The request is very similar to the request you have seen before. In the completionHandler, the results array and first prediction of the image classifications are extracted and shown to the user. Every prediction made by the classifier will have a label that is stored in the identifier and a confidence rating with a value between 0 and 1 stored in the confidence property. Note that the value of the description label is set on the main thread to avoid crashes.

You have already implemented two different types of Core ML models that were trained for general purposes. Sometimes, these models won't be specific enough for your purposes. For instance, take a look at the following screenshot, where a machine learning model labels a certain landscape with only 32% confidence:

Figure 10.4 – Photo analysis result

In the next section, you will learn how to train models for purposes that are specific to you and your apps by using Create ML.

Training your own models with Create ML

As part of Xcode 10 and Apple's version of macOS, **Mojave**, they have shipped a tool that you can use to train your own machine learning models by adding specializations to existing models. This means that you can train your own natural language model that places certain texts in categories that you define. Or, you can train a model that recognizes certain product names or terms in a text that are specific to your application's domain.

If you're building a news app, you might want to train a Core ML model that can automatically categorize the articles in the app. You can then use this model to keep track of the articles your users read, and present articles that are most likely to fit their interests on a dedicated page in your app.

In this segment, you will learn how to train natural language models and how you can train an image recognition model based on the Vision framework. In doing so, you will find that creating a large and optimized training set is crucial when you want to train a machine learning model.

In the code bundle for this chapter, you will find a Playground called **Create ML**. This playground contains all the resources used for training natural language models.

Training a Natural Language model

The Natural Language framework has excellent features to analyze text with. Bundled with the power of machine learning models, you can perform some powerful operations on text. Apple has spent a lot of time training several models with vast amounts of data to ensure that the Natural Language framework can detect names, places, and more.

However, sometimes you might want to add your own analysis tools. To facilitate this, the Natural Language framework works well with Core ML and Apple's new **Create ML** framework. With **Create ML**, you can easily and quickly create your own machine learning models that you can use in your apps straight away.

You can use several different types of training for a Natural Language model. In this section, you will learn about two different models:

- A text classifier
- A word tagger

The **text classifier** will classify a particular piece of text with a label. This is similar to the sentiment analysis you have implemented in the **TextAnalyzer** sample app. An example of an entry in your training data would look as follows:

```
{
    "text": "We took an exclusive ride in a flying car",
    "label": "Tech"
}
```

This is a sample of a news article headline that belongs in a category labeled `Tech`. When you feed a large number of samples like this to your model, you could end up with a classifier that can apply labels to news articles based on their headlines. Of course, this assumes that the headlines are specific enough and contain enough information to train the classifier properly. In reality, you will find that short sentences like these will not make the best models. The sample Playground contains a JSON file with training data that attempts to separate news articles into the two categories of politics and tech. Let's see how the model can be trained so you can then see for yourself how accurate the model is.

The following code trains and stores the custom Core ML model. In the playground file, open the **Project Navigator** (just press *command + 1*). Click on the file named `Labeller`. Check the code:

```
import Create ML
import Foundation

let trainingData = try! MLDataTable(contentsOf: Bundle.main.
    url(forResource: "texts", withExtension: "json")!)
let model = try! MLTextClassifier(trainingData: trainingData,
    textColumn: "text", labelColumn: "label")
try! model.write(to: URL(fileURLWithPath: "/Users/marioeguiluz/
    Desktop/TextClassifier.mlmodel"))

let techHeadline = try! model.prediction(from: "Snap users drop
    for first time, but revenue climbs")
let politicsHeadline = try! model.prediction(from: "President
    Donald Trump is approving a new law")
```

Training the entire model requires only a couple of lines of code. All you need to do is obtain your training data, create the classifier, and save it somewhere on your machine. You can even do some quick testing to see whether your model works well, from right inside the playground.

Note that the preceding code uses a `try!` statement. This is done to keep the code sample brief and simple. In your own apps, you should always strive for proper error handling to avoid surprising crashes.

The string passed to the `URL(fileURLWithPath:)` initializer represents the location where your model will be stored. Make sure to specify the full path here, so, for instance, use `/Users/yourUser/Desktop/TextClassifier.mlmodel`, and not `~/Desktop/TextClassifier.mlmodel`. Make sure to substitute `yourUser` with your own username or folder.

The following lines of code test two different headlines to see if the model correctly labels them:

```
let techHeadline = try! model.prediction(from: "Snap users drop
    for first time, but revenue climbs")
let politicsHeadline = try! model.prediction(from: "President
    Donald Trump is approving a new law")
```

If you're happy with the results of your model, you can grab the trained model from the place where you saved it, and immediately add it to your Xcode project. From there, you can use the model like you would use any other model.

Let's see another example of a model from the Natural Language framework. In this case, the model should label every word in a text to classify it as a certain type of word. For instance, you could train the model to recognize certain brand names, product names, or other words that have special meanings to your app. An example of some training data that you could use to train a model like this is the following:

```
{
    "tokens": ["Apple", "announced", "iOS 12", "and", "Xcode
        10", "at", "WWDC 2018"],
    "labels": ["COMPANY", "NONE", "OPERATING_SYSTEM", "NONE",
        "SOFTWARE", "NONE", "EVENT"]
}
```

By collecting many samples that include the words that you want to label, your model will be able to not only match tags based on the word itself, but even on the surrounding words. Essentially, the model would be aware of the context in which each word is used to then determine the correct tag. Once you have collected enough sample data, you can train the model in a similar way as the classifier:

```
let labelTrainingData = try! MLDataTable(contentsOf: Bundle.
    main.url(forResource: "labels", withExtension: "json")!)
let model = try! MLWordTagger(trainingData: labelTrainingData,
```

```
    tokenColumn: "tokens", labelColumn: "labels")
try! model.write(to: URL(fileURLWithPath: "/Users/marioeguiluz/
    Desktop/TextTagger.mlmodel"))
```

The amount of code to train the model hasn't changed. The only difference is that the previous model was based on the `MLTextClassifier` class, and the current model is based on `MLWordTagger`. Again, you can immediately use the trained model to make some predictions that you can then use to validate whether the model was trained properly. Providing good data and testing often are the keys to building a great Core ML model.

In addition to text analysis models, Create ML can also help you to train your own image recognition models. Let's see how this works next.

Training a Vision model

In the **ImageAnalyzer** sample app, you saw that picking an image of a certain car would be classified as a sports car with a pretty low confidence score. You can train your own vision model that specializes in recognizing certain cars.

Collecting good training data for image classifiers is tough, because you have to make sure that you gather many pictures of your subjects from all sides and in many different environments. For instance, if all your car images feature cars that are next to trees, or on the road, the model might end up classifying anything with trees or a road next to it as a car. The only way to obtain a perfect training set is to experiment, tweak, and test.

Training a Vision model works slightly differently from training a Natural Language model. You can't use a JSON file to feed your test data to the classifier. So, instead, you should create folders that contain your images where the folder name is the label you want to apply to each image inside that folder. The following screenshot is an example of a training set that contains two kinds of labels:

Figure 10.5 – Training set of images

Once you have collected your set of training data, you can store it anywhere on your computer—for instance, on the desktop. You will then pass the path for your training data to your model training code as follows:

```
import Create ML
import Foundation


let dataUrl = URL(fileURLWithPath: "/path/to/trainingdata")
let source = MLImageClassifier.DataSource.
  labeledDirectories(at: dataUrl)
let classifier = try! MLImageClassifier(trainingData: source)
  try! classifier.write(toFile: "/Users/marioeguiluz/Desktop/
  CarClassifier.mlmodel")
```

Again, you only need a couple of lines of code to train a model. That's how powerful Create ML is. If you want, you can quickly test your image classifier by dropping the .mlmodel file in the **ImageAnalyzer** project, and using that instead of the MobileNetV2 classifier that you used before.

Apart from the simple ways of training models, there are certain parameters that you can pass to the different Create ML classifiers. If you have trouble training your models properly, you could tweak some of the parameters that are used by Create ML. For instance, you could apply more iterations to your training set, so the model gains a deeper understanding of the training data.

As mentioned before in this chapter, machine learning is a subject that could span several books on its own, and even though Create ML makes training models straightforward and simple, it's not easy to train a robust model without any prior machine learning experience.

Now that you have learned how to use your own trained data, in the next section, we are going to learn how to update your models from the cloud, without the need to update the app itself.

Updating models remotely with Model Deployment

One of the new features of iOS 14 for machine learning is the ability to keep collections of your models in the cloud, giving you the power to update them at any time without the need to update the app itself.

We are going to use a project, available in the code bundle of this book, in order to demonstrate this new feature. The project's name is **TextAnalyzerCloud**. It is the same project that we used before, but this time, the model will be on the cloud (with a local copy as a fallback).

There are two steps involved in order to use Model Deployment in our apps:

1. Use the Core ML API to retrieve collections of models.

2. Prepare and deploy the model.

Let's implement these steps in the next subsections.

Using the Core ML API to retrieve collections of models

Let's start by learning how to retrieve models that are stored in the cloud into your app. Open the **TextAnalyzerCloud** project in the code bundle of this chapter and let's examine the ViewController class. At this point, the class just contains an analyze method that counts the words inside a textView and makes a prediction if a model exists. The class also contains some methods to display error and success messages to the user. Note that we have also defined the following property: var model: SentimentPolarity?.

In the analyze method, we are going to download a model from the cloud, and in case of failure, we will use a local modal as a fallback. Let's modify the method to achieve this. Update the implementation of the analyze method, and add the following code where it says //add code:

```
//1
_ = MLModelCollection.beginAccessing(identifier:
  "SentimentPolarityCollection") { [self] result in


//2
var modelURL: URL?
switch result {
case .success(let collection):
  modelURL =
    collection.entries["SentimentPolarity"]?.modelURL
case .failure(let error):
  handleCollectionError(error)
}
```

```
//3
let result = loadSentimentClassifier(url: modelURL)


//4
switch result {
case .success(let sentimentModel):
  model = sentimentModel
  guard let prediction = try? model?.prediction(input:
    wordCount) else { return }
  showResult(prediction: prediction)
case .failure(let error):
  handleModelLoadError(error)
}
}
```

Let's review the preceding code blocks (the following numbers refer to the comments in the preceding code):

- First, in //1, we are accessing the new Core ML API to retrieve a collection of models from our account on the Apple servers. We do that by using the MLModelCollection.beginAccessing method with an identifier for the collection (that has to match the one in the cloud) – in our case, we used SentimentPolarityCollection.

- Next, in //2, we are checking the result of beginAccessing. If it is successful and we get a collection of models, we search for a specific model with an identifier of SentimentPolarity and we extract the modelURL from it. If we get any errors (such as there being no network connection), we call the handleCollectionError method to handle it properly (in our case, we inform the user with a modal).

- Now that we have a model URL, in //3, we try to load it. We haven't implemented the loadSentimentClassifier method yet, but we will do it shortly. Just take into account that this method will try to load a model with a given remote URL, and it will wrap it in a Result<SentimentPolarity, Error> enum (to handle errors properly).

- In the last part, under comment //4, we inspect the Result from //3. If we obtained a model, we store it in the model property variable. We store it so we don't need to download the model over and over again. After storing the model, we use it to analyze the text. On the other hand, if we obtained an error, we display a message to the user to inform them about it.

Now let's add the `loadSentimentClassifier` method so the class compiles. Add the following method to the `ViewController`:

```
private func loadSentimentClassifier(url: URL?) ->
    Result<SentimentPolarity, Error> {
  if let modelUrl = url {
    return Result { try SentimentPolarity(contentsOf:
    modelUrl) }
  } else {
    return Result { try SentimentPolarity(configuration:
    .init()) }
  }
}
```

This method receives an optional model URL as a param; that is, the URL of our model stored in Apple Servers. It is an optional value because when we try to fetch it, it can fail (for example, if the user doesn't have an internet connection). Inside the method, we handle two possibilities:

- If the URL is not nil, we use it to initialize the model with `SentimentPolarity(contentsOf:)` and return it inside a `Result`.

- If the URL is nil, we try to initialize the model with a local version and the default configuration with `SentimentPolarity(configuration: .init())`. Again, we return it inside `Result`.

With this method implemented, we have all the code necessary to load a model from the network and use it in our app. However, we still need to perform two important steps to complete the process: Prepare the model to be uploaded to the Apple servers in the proper format, and deploy the model to the cloud.

Preparing and deploying the model

In the previous section, we created the methods to retrieve a model from the Apple servers and into our app. Now, we are going to prepare our local model to be deployed into the cloud.

In the project explorer, click on the file named SentimentPolarity.mlmodel. Now, go to the **Utilities** tab. You will see the following:

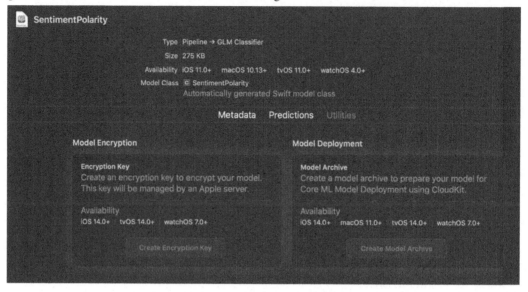

Figure 10.6 – Model Utilities tab

Click on **Create Model Archive**. This new option in iOS 14 will help us to deploy our model onto the Apple servers in the cloud. When you click it, this popup will appear:

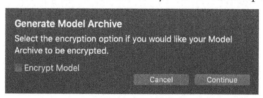

Figure 10.7 – Generate Model Archive

For now, leave the **Encrypt Model** checkbox unchecked and click **Continue** (we will explore this option later in the chapter). After clicking **Continue**, Xcode will generate an archive of the model and will display this modal:

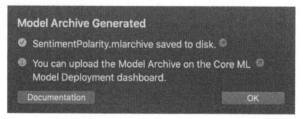

Figure 10.8 – The Model Archive Generated dialog

You can click on the blue arrow to the right of the first option in the preceding screenshot and it will take you to the exact location where the archive of your model is located. You will need to remember this location to upload the archive to the Apple servers. You will see a file with the `.mlarchive` extension, as in the following screenshot:

Figure 10.9 – Location of the archived model

Now click on the blue arrow next to the second option that reads **You can upload the Model Archive on the Core ML Model Deployment dashboard**. It will open your web browser at the following page:

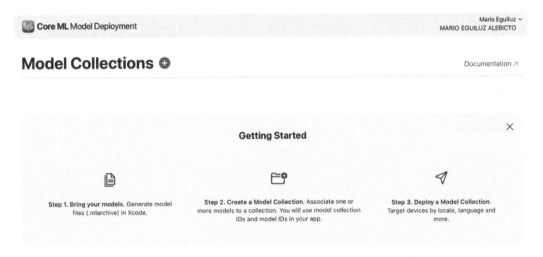

Figure 10.10 – Core ML Model Collections page

This is your dashboard for managing your model collections on the Apple servers. What we need to do now is to create a new collection with a reference to our model inside, and upload the model archive we just created. Let's do this; click on the blue plus (+) icon next to **Model Collections**, and fill in the form that appears with the following information:

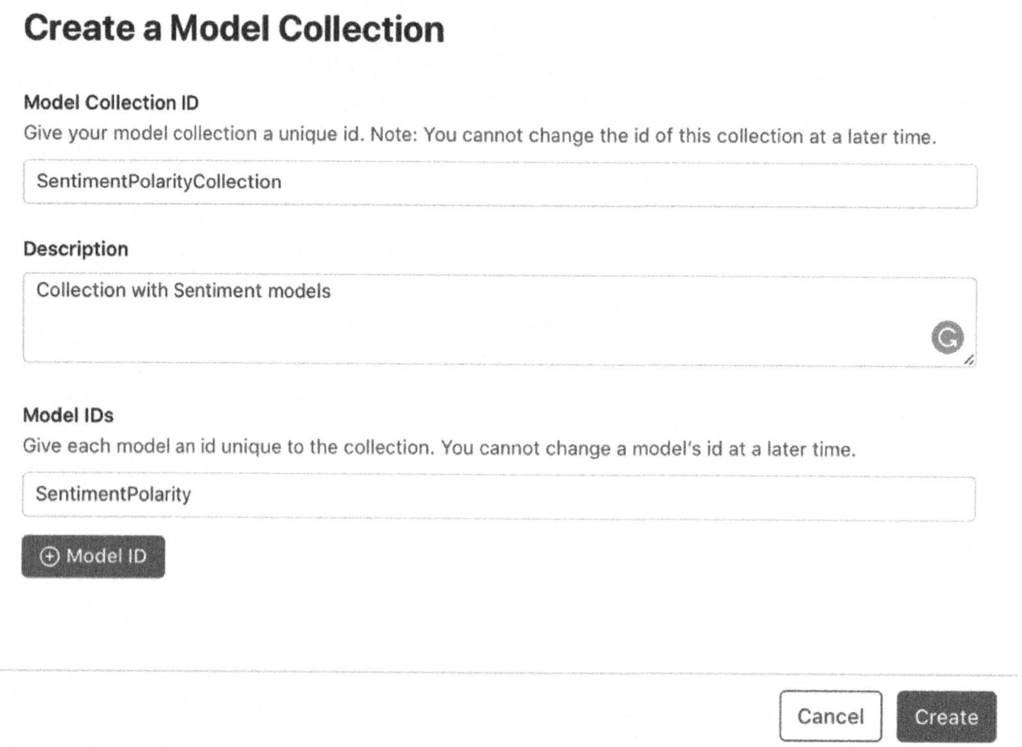

Create a Model Collection

Model Collection ID

Give your model collection a unique id. Note: You cannot change the id of this collection at a later time.

> SentimentPolarityCollection

Description

Collection with Sentiment models

Model IDs

Give each model an id unique to the collection. You cannot change a model's id at a later time.

> SentimentPolarity

⊕ Model ID

Cancel   Create

Figure 10.11 – Create a Model Collection

Let's review the input fields:

- **Model Collection ID**: This is the identifier you are going to use to download the collection into your app later. Remember that in our preceding code (under comment `//1: MLModelCollection.beginAccessing(identifier: "SentimentPolarityCollection")`), we used the identifier `SentimentPolarityCollection`. Use the same one here (otherwise, you will not be able to download the collection).

- **Description**: Use this field to create a description that will help you to recognize this collection later on. Take into account that if you work in a team, it will need to be useful to the other developers too.

- **Model IDs**: In this field, specify the identifier for the model itself. In our code, we used the identifier `SentimentPolarity` (under comment `//2: modelURL = collection.entries["SentimentPolarity"]`). Again, these identifiers have to match each other. You have the possibility to add more model identifiers by pressing the **Model ID** blue button, but in our case, we have just one model inside our collection.

Finally, you can click the blue **Create** button, and you will land on the following model collection page:

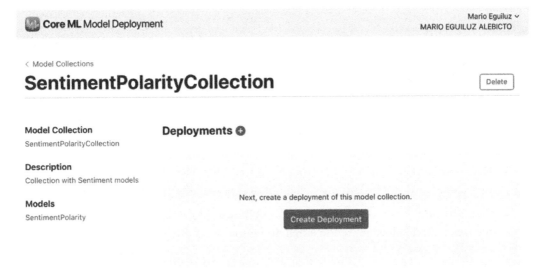

Figure 10.12 – Model collection page

From this page, you can finally deploy or archive the model into its reference on the cloud. Click on the blue plus (+) button next to **Deployments**, and fill in the fields as shown here:

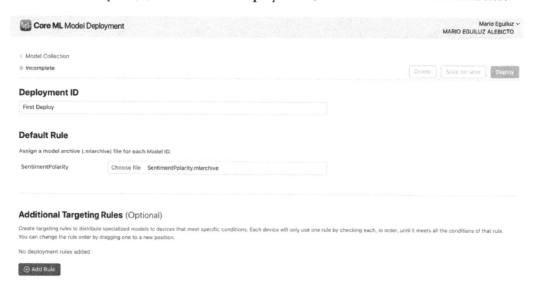

Figure 10.13 – Model deployment properties

Let's review the fields:

- **Deployment ID**: You can specify any text here that describes why you are deploying this model. It is just a descriptive field; it doesn't need to match anything.

- **Default Rule**: Here, you need to click on **Choose file** and upload the `.mlarchive` file we created before in Xcode when archiving the model.

Notice in the bottom part of the form that we can add **Additional Targeting Rules**. This is another new feature of iOS 14 that allows us to target our models based on device characteristics. For example, we can download certain models only to iPads, or for specific OS versions. To keep this example simple, we are not going to add any rules, but you should try it out in your apps!

After you upload the `.mlarchive` file, it should display as follows:

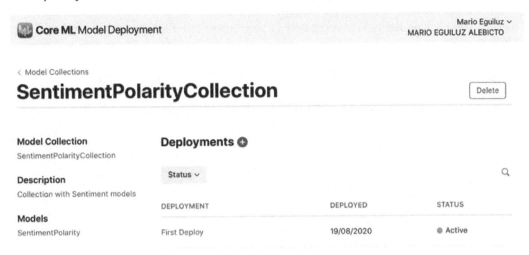

Figure 10.14 – Our first model deployed

When the status is **Active**, you can go to your app and launch it. At first, it may not work; the reason is that iOS will decide when the best moment is to update the app models from the cloud (try to be on Wi-Fi). When you launch in the simulator, try launching a couple of times, giving it some time for the system to download the models in the background. You will see that eventually your model is ready in the device and the `analyze` method will give you a verdict.

In this section, you have learned how to consume the Core ML API to fetch models from the cloud to keep your app models up to date. You also learned how to prepare your models and how to deploy them to the Apple servers. Now you are going to learn how to encrypt those models with a new iOS 14 feature to keep your model's data safe on users' devices.

Encrypting Core ML models

One of the new features of iOS 14 Core ML is the ability to encrypt your machine learning models on users' devices. Xcode 12 has a new tool that will help you to create a private key that you will deploy to the Apple servers. Your app will download that key and store it securely on the users' devices, and will use the key to decrypt the local (encrypted) model, load that decrypted version into memory (so it is not stored insecurely), and have it ready for use in your app.

The steps to create the key and deploy it to the Apple servers are very straightforward. First, you select your model in the project explorer; in our case, open the **TextAnalyzerCloud** project, and click on the `SentimentPolarity.mlmodel` file. Then, click on the **Utilities** tab:

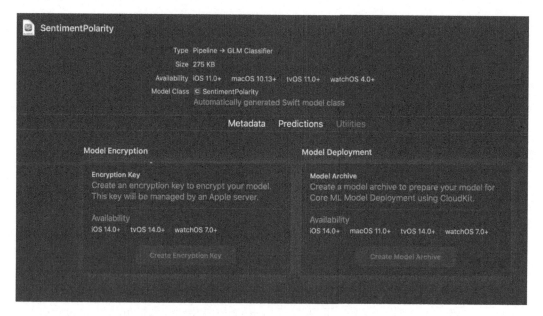

Figure 10.15 – Model encryption

Now, click on **Create Encryption Key**. In the popup that appears, select the proper development account for your app:

Figure 10.16 – Selecting the development team for the encryption key

This will generate a key and `.mlmodelkey` in your folder:

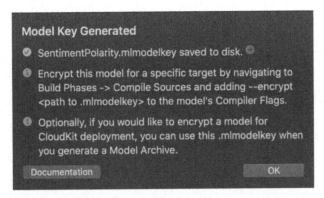

Figure 10.17 – Generating an encryption key

Clicking the blue arrow will take you to the specific folder where this key is stored. You will need to remember the location if you want to deploy this key to the Apple servers later so your team can use it too. Click **OK** and close the popup.

Now if you click on **Create Model Archive**, you will notice that the **Encrypt Model** checkbox is active this time:

Figure 10.18 – Generating a model archive with encryption

When you click **Continue**, Xcode creates an encrypted archive this time. The steps that follow are exactly the same as the steps we learned in the *Prepare and Deploy the model* section.

However, you can also tell Xcode to encrypt the bundled model (the local copy). To do this, after generating the encryption key (as we just did), you need to click on your project, go to **Build Phases**, and open the **Compile Sources** section:

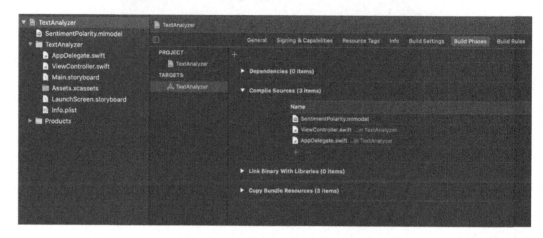

Figure 10.19 – The Build Phases tab

Now select the **SentimentPolarity.mlmodel** model and on the right side of its row, you can double-click to add a flag. Add the route to the encryption key in your project folder:

```
--encrypt "$SRCROOT/SentimentPolarity.mlmodelkey"
```

It should look like this after you have added the flag:

Figure 10.20 – Model with the encryption flag

Now if you build the app, Xcode will generate an encrypted version of the model inside your app.

You have learned how to encrypt your model locally (and how to encrypt an archive for the Apple servers). Let's see now how you can load that model at runtime. There is a new class method in ML Models named `load` that will decrypt the model for you, downloading the encryption key from the Apple servers. Check out the following example code:

```
SentimentPolarity.load { [self] result in
  switch result {
  case .success(let model):
    self.model = model
    guard let prediction = try? self.model?.prediction(input:
    wordCount) else { return }
    showResult(prediction: prediction)
  case .failure(let error):
    handleDecryptError(error)
  }
}
```

In the preceding code, the `class func load` will try to download the encryption key from the Apple servers and will decrypt the model with it, storing it in memory. We assign that decrypted model to our variable model, and it is ready to use. We also handle the failure case, displaying an error.

In this section, you learned how to generate an encryption key, how to encrypt an archived model to upload to the Apple servers and also to encrypt the local copy of it, and finally how to load and decrypt the model for the app to use.

Summary

In this chapter, you have seen how you can make use of the machine learning capabilities that iOS provides. You saw that adding a machine learning model to your app is extremely simple since you only have to drag it to Xcode and add it to your target app. You also learned how you can obtain models, and where to look to convert existing models to Core ML models. Creating a machine learning model is not simple, so it's great that Apple has made it so simple to implement machine learning by embedding trained models in your apps.

In addition to Core ML, you also learned about the Vision and Natural Language frameworks. Vision combines the power of Core ML and smart image analysis to create a compelling framework that can perform a massive amount of work on images. Convenient requests, such as facial landmark detection, text analysis, and more are available out of the box without adding any machine learning models to your app. If you do find that you need more power in the form of custom models, you now know how to use Create ML to train, export, and use your own custom trained Core ML models. You learned that Create ML makes training models simple, but you also learned that the quality of your model is drastically impacted by the quality of your training data.

Finally, you learned how to deploy your Core ML models in the cloud in order to update them without the need to update the app, and how to encrypt and decrypt them to store your models safely on the user device.

In the next chapter, you will learn how you can capture, manipulate, and use media files in your apps, including audio, photo, and video elements.

11
Adding Media to Your App

A lot of the apps that people use every day make use of media in some way. Some apps show photos and videos in a user's feed. Other apps focus on playing audio or video, while there are also apps that allow users to record media and share it with their peers. You can probably name at least a couple of very well-known apps that make use of such media in one way or the other.

Because media has such a significant presence in people's daily lives, it's good to know how you can integrate media into your own apps. iOS has excellent support for media playback and offers several different ways to create and consume different types of media. Some ways provide less flexibility but are more straightforward to implement. Others are more complex but provide significant power to you as a developer.

In this chapter, you will learn about several ways to play and record media on iOS. You will learn how to play and record video, play audio, and take pictures, and you'll even learn how to apply filters to images with Apple's Core Image framework. This chapter covers the following topics:

- Playing audio and video
- Recording video and taking pictures
- Manipulating photos with Core Image

By the end of this chapter, you will have a great foundation that you can build on to create engaging experiences for your users, allowing them to not only view content but also to create their own content in your app.

Technical requirements

The code bundle for this chapter includes two starter projects called `Captured_start` and `MediaPlayback_start`. You can find them in the code bundle repository:

`https://github.com/PacktPublishing/Mastering-iOS-14-Programming-4th-Edition`

Playing audio and video

To make playing audio and video files as simple and straightforward as can be, Apple has created the `AVFoundation` framework. This framework contains a lot of helper classes that provide very low-level control over how iOS plays audio and video files. You can use `AVFoundation` to build a rich, custom media player with as many features as you need for your purpose.

If you're looking for a simpler way to integrate media into your app, the `AVKit` framework might be what you need. `AVKit` contains several helpers that build upon the `AVFoundation` components to provide an excellent default player that supports many features, such as subtitles, AirPlay, and more.

In this section, you will learn how to implement a simple video player with `AVPlayerViewController` from the `AVKit` framework. You will also implement a more complex audio player with `AVFoundation` components that play audio in the background and display, on the lock screen, the audio track currently being played.

To follow along with the examples, you should open the `MediaPlayback_start` project in this chapter's code bundle. The starter app contains a straightforward interface with a tab bar and two pages. You will implement a video player on one page, and the audio player on the other page. The audio page comes with some predefined controls and actions that you will implement later.

Creating a simple video player

The first thing you need to do to implement a video player is to obtain a video file. You can use any video that is encoded in the h.264 format. A good sample video is the **Big Buck Bunny** sample movie that was created by the Blender Foundation. You can find this video at the following URL: http://bbb3d.renderfarming.net/download.html. If you want to use this video to practice with, make sure to download the 2D version of the video.

As stated before, you will implement the video player using AVPlayerViewController. This view controller provides a convenient wrapper around several components from AVFoundation, and also provides default video controls, so you don't have to build your entire video player from scratch, as you will do for the audio player later.

AVPlayerViewController is highly configurable, which means that you can choose whether the player supports AirPlay, shows playback controls, whether it should be full screen when a video plays, and more. For a complete list of configurable options, you can refer to Apple's AVPlayerViewController documentation.

Once you have found your test video, you should add it to the MediaPlayback project and ensure that the video is added to the app target. You can follow these steps:

1. Click on your project.
2. Click on your target.
3. Select **Build Phases**.
4. Expand **Copy Bundle Resources**.
5. Click + and select your file.

After doing this, open VideoViewController.swift and add the following line to import AVKit:

```
import AVKit
```

You should also add a property to VideoViewController to hold on to your video player instance. Add the following line to the VideoViewController class to do this:

```
let playerController = AVPlayerViewController()
```

Since `AVPlayerViewController` is a `UIViewController` subclass, you should add it to `VideoViewController` as a child view controller. Doing this will make sure that `VideoViewController` forwards any view controller life cycle events, such as `viewDidLoad()`, along with any changes in trait collections and more to the video player. To do this, add the following code to the `viewDidLoad()` method in `VideoViewController`:

```
// 1
addChild(playerController)
playerController.didMove(toParent: self)

// 2
view.addSubview(playerController.view)

let playerView = playerController.view!
playerView.translatesAutoresizingMaskIntoConstraints = false

NSLayoutConstraint
  .activate([
    playerView.widthAnchor.constraint(equalTo: view.
      widthAnchor, constant: -20),
    playerView.heightAnchor.constraint(equalTo: playerView.
      widthAnchor, multiplier: 9/16),
    playerView.centerXAnchor.constraint(equalTo: view.
      centerXAnchor),
    playerView.centerYAnchor.constraint(equalTo: view.
      centerYAnchor)
  ])
```

The previous code snippet adds the video player to the video view controller as a child view controller. When you add a view controller as a child view controller, you must always call `didMove(toParent:)` on the child controller to make sure that it knows that it has been added as a child view controller to another view controller. After adding the video player as a child view controller, the video player's view is added as a subview for the video view controller, and some constraints are set up to position the player view.

This is all you need to do to create an instance of the video player and make it appear in your view controller. The last step is to obtain a reference to your video file, create an AVPlayer that has a reference to the video file, and assign it to the player. Add the following code to do this:

```
let url = Bundle.main.url(forResource: "samplevideo",
  withExtension: "mp4")!
playerController.player = AVPlayer(url: url)
```

The preceding code looks for a video file called samplevideo.mp4 and obtains a URL for that file. It then creates an instance of AVPlayer that points to that video file and assigns it to the video player. The AVPlayer object is responsible for playing the video file. The AVPlayerViewController instance uses the AVPlayer instance to play the video and manages the actual playback of the video internally.

If you run your app after adding the player this way, you will find that the video plays perfectly well, and that you have access to all the controls you might need. This is a great demonstration of how simple it is to add basic media integration to your app. The next step is a little more complex. You will directly use an AVAudioPlayer instance to play an audio file that is controlled through several custom media controls. The player will even play audio in the background and integrate with the lock screen to show information about the current file. In other words, you will build a simple audio player that does everything a user would expect it to do.

Important note

When launching in the simulator, AVKit and large movie files can take some time to load up. Try it on a real device.

Creating an audio player

Before you can implement your audio player, you will need to obtain some .mp3 files you wish to use in your player. If you don't have any audio files on your computer, you can get some files from The Free Music Archive website, available at https://freemusicarchive.org/about, to obtain a couple of free songs that you would like to use for playback. Make sure to add them to the MediaPlayer Xcode project and ensure that they are included in the app target.

You will build the audio player using the following steps:

1. Implement the necessary controls to start and stop the player and navigate to the next and previous songs.

2. Implement the time scrubber.

3. Read the file's metadata and show it to the user.

The user interface, outlets, and actions are already set up, so make sure to familiarize yourself with the existing code before following along with the implementation of the audio player.

Implementing basic audio controls

Before you implement the audio player code, you will need to do a little bit of housekeeping. To be able to play audio, you need a list of the files that the player will play. In addition to this list, you also need to keep track of what song the user is currently playing, so you can determine the next and previous songs. Lastly, you also need to have the audio player itself. Instead of using a pre-built component, you will build your own audio player using an `AVAudioPlayer` object. `AVAudioPlayer` is perfect for implementing a simple audio player that plays a couple of local `.mp3` files. It offers some convenient helper methods to easily adjust the player's volume, seek to a specific timestamp in the song, and more.

Define the following properties in `AudioViewController.swift`:

```
let files = ["one", "two", "three"]
var currentTrack = 0
var audioPlayer: AVAudioPlayer!
```

Also, don't forget to add the import:

```
import AVKit
```

Make sure to replace the files array with the filenames that you use for your own audio files. `audioPlayer` does not have a value yet at this point. You will set up the audio player next.

Before you can play audio, you need to obtain a reference to a media file and provide this reference to an AVAudioPlayer object. Any time you want to load a new media file, you will have to create a new instance of the audio player, since you can't change the current file once a file is playing. Add the following helper method to AudioViewController to load the current track and create an AVAudioPlayer instance:

```
func loadTrack() {
    let url = Bundle.main.url(forResource: files[currentTrack],
        withExtension: "mp3")!
    audioPlayer = try! AVAudioPlayer(contentsOf: url)
    audioPlayer.delegate = self
}
```

This method reads the filename for the current track and retrieves the local URL for it. This URL is then used to create and set the audioPlayer property on AudioViewController. The view controller is also assigned as the delegate for the audio player. You won't implement any of the delegate methods just yet, but you can add the following extension to make AudioViewController conform to the AVAudioPlayerDelegate protocol to ensure your code compiles:

```
extension AudioViewController: AVAudioPlayerDelegate {
}
```

Now, let's call loadTrack() on viewDidLoad() to instantiate audioPlayer and load the first song. Add the following method to AudioViewController:

```
override func viewDidLoad() {
    super.viewDidLoad()
    loadTrack()
}
```

You will implement one of the AVAudioPlayerDelegate methods when you add support for navigating to the next and previous tracks.

Add the following two methods to the audio view controller to add support for playing and pausing the current audio file:

```
func startPlayback() {
  audioPlayer.play()
  playPause.setTitle("Pause", for: .normal)
}

func pausePlayback() {
  audioPlayer.pause()
  playPause.setTitle("Play", for: .normal)
}
```

These methods are relatively straightforward. They call the audio player's `play()` and `pause()` methods and update the button's label, so it reflects the current player state. Add the following implementation for `playPauseTapped()` so that the play and pause methods get called when the user taps the play/pause button:

```
@IBAction func playPauseTapped() {
  if audioPlayer.isPlaying {
    pausePlayback()
  } else {
    startPlayback()
  }
}
```

If you run the app now, you can tap the play/pause button to start and stop the currently playing file. Make sure your device is not in silent mode, because the audio for your app is muted when the device is in silent mode. You will learn how to fix this when you implement the ability to play audio in the background. The next step is to add support for playing the next and previous tracks. Add the following two implementations to `AudioViewController` to do this:

```
@IBAction func nextTapped() {
  currentTrack += 1
  if currentTrack >= files.count {
    currentTrack = 0
  }
  loadTrack()
```

```
    audioPlayer.play()
}


@IBAction func previousTapped() {
    currentTrack -= 1
    if currentTrack < 0 {
        currentTrack = files.count - 1
    }
    loadTrack()
    audioPlayer.play()
}
```

The preceding code adjusts the current track index, loads the new track, and immediately plays it. Note that every time the user taps on the next or previous button, a fresh audio player has to be created by calling `loadTrack()`. If you run the app now, you can play audio, pause it, and skip to the next or previous tracks.

When you allow a full song to play, it will not yet advance to the next song afterward. To implement this, you need to add an implementation for the `audioPlayerDidFinishPlaying(_:successfully:)` method from `AVAudioPlayerDelegate`. Add the following implementation to call `nextTapped()`, so the next song automatically plays when the current song finishes:

```
func audioPlayerDidFinishPlaying(_ player: AVAudioPlayer,
    successfully flag: Bool) {
    nextTapped()
}
```

Now that the first features are implemented, the next step is to implement the time scrubber that shows the current song's progress and allows the user to adjust the playhead's position.

Implementing the time scrubber

The user interface for the audio player app already contains a scrubber that is hooked up to the following three actions in the view controller:

- `sliderDragStart()`
- `sliderDragEnd()`
- `sliderChanged()`

When an audio file is playing, the scrubber should automatically update to reflect the current position in the song. However, when a user starts dragging the scrubber, it should not update its position until the user has chosen the scrubber's new position. When the user is done dragging the scrubber, it should adjust itself based on the song's progress again. Any time the value for the slider changes, the audio player should adjust the playhead, so the song's progress matches that of the scrubber.

Unfortunately, the AVAudioPlayer object does not expose any delegate methods to observe the progress of the current audio file. To update the scrubber regularly, you can implement a timer that updates the scrubber to the audio player's current position every second. Add the following property to AudioViewController, so you can hold on to the timer after you have created it:

```
var timer: Timer?
```

Also, add the following two methods to AudioViewController as a convenient way to start the timer when the user starts dragging the scrubber, or when a file starts playing, and stop it when a user stops dragging the scrubber or to preserve resources when the playback is paused:

```
func startTimer() {
    timer = Timer.scheduledTimer(withTimeInterval: 1, repeats:
        true) { [unowned self] timer in
        self.slider.value = Float(self.audioPlayer.currentTime /
            self.audioPlayer.duration)
    }
}


func stopTimer() {
    timer?.invalidate()
}
```

Add a call to startTimer() in the startPlayback() method and a call to stopTimer() in the pausePlayback() method. If you run the app after doing this, the scrubber will immediately begin updating its position when a song starts playing. However, scrubbing does not work yet. Add the following implementations for the scrubber actions to enable manual scrubbing:

```
@IBAction func sliderDragStart() {
    stopTimer()
}
```

```
@IBAction func sliderDragEnd() {
  startTimer()
}
```

```
@IBAction func sliderChanged() {
  audioPlayer.currentTime = Double(slider.value) * audioPlayer.
    duration
}
```

The preceding methods are relatively simple, but they provide a very powerful feature that immediately makes your homemade audio player feel like an audio player you might use every day. The final step for implementing the audio player's functionality is to display metadata about the current song.

Displaying song metadata

Most .mp3 files contain metadata in the form of ID3 tags. These metadata tags are used by applications such as iTunes to extract information about a song and display it to the user, as well as to categorize a music library or filter it. You can gain access to an audio file's metadata through code by loading the audio file into an AVPlayerItem object and extracting the metadata for its internal AVAsset instance. An AVAsset object contains information about a media item, such as its type, location, and more. When you load a file using an AVPlayerItem object, it will automatically create a corresponding AVAsset object for you.

A single asset can contain loads of metadata in the metadata dictionary. Luckily, Apple has captured all of the valid ID3 metadata tags in the AVMetadataIdentifier object, so once you have extracted the metadata for an AVAsset instance, you can loop over all of its metadata to filter out the data you need. The following method does this, and sets the extracted values on the titleLabel variable of AudioViewController, as shown here:

```
func showMetadataForURL(_ url: URL) {
  let mediaItem = AVPlayerItem(url: url)
  let metadata = mediaItem.asset.metadata
  var information = [String]()

  for item in metadata {
    guard let identifier = item.identifier else { continue }
    switch identifier {
```

```
      case .id3MetadataTitleDescription, .id3MetadataBand:
        information.append(item.value?.description ?? "")
      default:
        break
    }
  }

  let trackTitle = information.joined(separator: " - ")
  titleLabel.text = trackTitle
}
```

Make sure to add a call to this method from `loadTrack()`, and pass the audio file's URL that you obtain in `loadTrack()` to `showMetadataForURL(_:)`. If you run your app now, your basic functionality should be all there. The metadata should be shown correctly, the scrubber should work, and you should be able to skip songs or pause the playback.

Even though your media player seems to be pretty much done at this point, did you notice that the music pauses when you send the app to the background? To make your app feel more like a real audio player, you should implement background audio playback and make sure that the currently playing song is presented on the user's lock screen, similar to how the native music app for iOS works. This is precisely the functionality you will add next.

Playing media in the background

On iOS, playing audio in the background requires special permissions that you can enable in your app's **Capabilities** tab. If you enable the **Background Modes** capability, you can select the **Audio, AirPlay, and Picture in Picture** option to make your app eligible for playing audio in the background. The following screenshot shows the enabled capability for playing audio in the background:

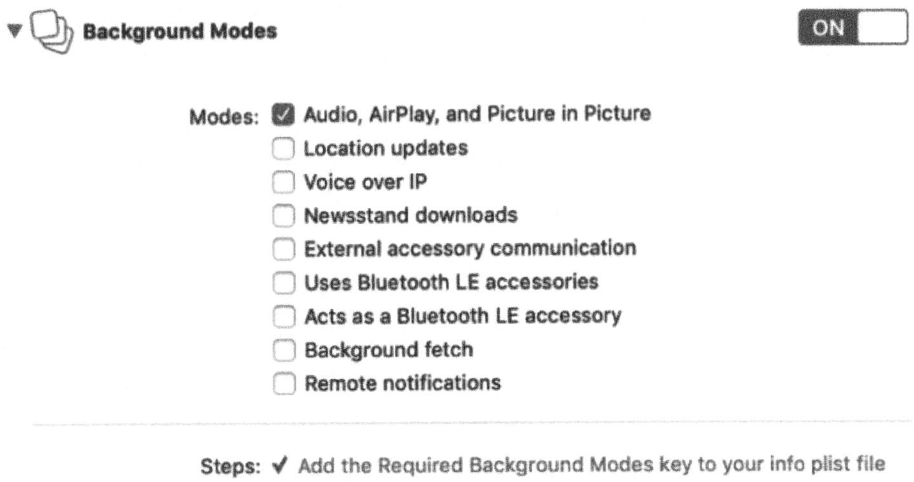

▼ 📑 **Background Modes**   `ON`

Modes: ☑ **Audio, AirPlay, and Picture in Picture**
◻ **Location updates**
◻ **Voice over IP**
◻ **Newsstand downloads**
◻ **External accessory communication**
◻ **Uses Bluetooth LE accessories**
◻ **Acts as a Bluetooth LE accessory**
◻ **Background fetch**
◻ **Remote notifications**

Steps: ✔ Add the Required Background Modes key to your info plist file

Figure 11.1 – Background Modes

If you want to add proper support for background audio playback, there are three features you need to implement:

- Set up an audio session, so audio continues playing in the background.

- Submit metadata to the "now playing" info center.

- Respond to playback actions from remote sources, such as the lock screen.

You can set up the audio session for your app with just two lines of code. When you create an audio session, iOS will treat the audio played by your app slightly differently; for instance, your songs will play even if the device is set to silent. It also makes sure that your audio is played when your app is in the background, if you have the proper capabilities set up. Add the following code to `viewDidLoad()` to set up an audio session for the app:

```
try? AVAudioSession.sharedInstance().setCategory(.playback,
  mode: .default, options: [.allowAirPlay])
try? AVAudioSession.sharedInstance().setActive(true, options:
  [])
```

The second feature to add is to supply information about the currently playing track. All information about the currently playing media file should be passed to the `MPNowPlayingInfoCenter` object. This object is part of the `MediaPlayer` framework and is responsible for showing the user information about the currently playing media file on the lock screen and in the command center. Before you pass information to the "now playing" info center, make sure to import the `MediaPlayer` framework at the top of the `AudioViewController.swift` file:

```
import MediaPlayer
```

Next, add the following line of code to `viewDidLoad()`:

```
NotificationCenter.default.addObserver(self, selector:
  #selector(updateNowPlaying), name: UIApplication.
  didEnterBackgroundNotification, object: nil)
```

In the documentation for `MPNowPlayingInfoCenter`, Apple states that you should always pass the most recent "now playing" information to the info center when the app goes to the background. To do this, the audio view controller should listen to the `UIApplication.didEnterBackgroundNotification` notification, so it can respond to the app going to the background. Add the following implementation for the `updateNowPlaying()` method to `AudioVideoController`:

```
@objc func updateNowPlaying() {
  var nowPlayingInfo = [String: Any]()
  nowPlayingInfo[MPMediaItemPropertyTitle] = titleLabel.text ??
    "untitled"
  nowPlayingInfo[MPNowPlayingInfoPropertyElapsedPlaybackTime] =
    audioPlayer.currentTime
  nowPlayingInfo[MPMediaItemPropertyPlaybackDuration] =
    audioPlayer.duration
  MPNowPlayingInfoCenter.default().nowPlayingInfo =
    nowPlayingInfo
}
```

The preceding code configures a dictionary with metadata about the currently playing file and passes it to the "now playing" info center. This method is called automatically when the app goes to the background, but you should also update the "now playing" information when a new song begins playing. Add a call to `updateNowPlaying()` in the `loadTrack()` method to make sure the "now playing" information is updated whenever a new track is loaded.

The next and final step is to respond to remote commands. When the user taps the play/pause button, next button, or previous button on the lock screen, this is sent to your app as a remote command. You should explicitly define the handlers that should be called by iOS when a remote command occurs. Add the following method to `AudioViewController` to add support for remote commands:

```swift
func configureRemoteCommands() {
  let commandCenter = MPRemoteCommandCenter.shared()

  commandCenter.playCommand.addTarget { [unowned self] event in
    guard self.audioPlayer.isPlaying == false else { return
      .commandFailed }
    self.startPlayback()
    return .success
  }

  commandCenter.pauseCommand.addTarget { [unowned self] event
    in
    guard self.audioPlayer.isPlaying else { return
      .commandFailed }
    self.pausePlayback()
    return .success
  }

  commandCenter.nextTrackCommand.addTarget { [unowned self]
    event in
    self.nextTapped()
    return .success
  }

  commandCenter.previousTrackCommand.addTarget { [unowned self]
    event in
    self.previousTapped()
    return .success
  }

  UIApplication.shared.beginReceivingRemoteControlEvents()
}
```

The preceding code obtains a reference to the remote command center and registers several handlers. It also calls `beginReceivingRemoteControlEvents()` on the application object to make sure it receives remote commands. Add a call to `configureRemoteCommands()` in `viewDidLoad()` to make sure that the app begins receiving remote commands as soon as the audio player is configured. As an exercise to practice, try implementing the commands to control the time scrubber and `+15` and `-15` from the lock screen yourself.

Try to run your app and send it to the background. You should be able to control media playback from both the control center and the lock screen. The visible metadata should correctly update when you skip to the next or previous song, and the scrubber should accurately represent the current position of playback in the song.

At this point, you have implemented a reasonably complete audio player that has pretty sophisticated behaviors. The next step in your exploration of media on iOS is to discover how you can take pictures and record video.

Recording video and taking pictures

In addition to playing existing media, you can also make apps that allow users to create their own content. In this section, you will learn how you can use a built-in component to enable users to take a picture. You will also learn how you can use a raw video feed to record a video. If you want to follow along with the samples in this section, make sure to grab the starter project for `Captured` from this chapter's code bundle.

The starter project contains a couple of view controllers and some connected outlets and actions. Note that there is a `UIViewController` extension in the project, too.

This extension includes a helper method that makes displaying an alert to the user a little bit simpler. This extension will be used to show an alert that informs the user when their photo or video is stored in the camera roll.

Since a user's camera and photo library are considered very privacy-sensitive, you need to make sure that you add the following privacy-related keys to the app's `Info.plist`:

- **Privacy - Camera Usage Description**: This property is required in order to access the camera so that you can take pictures and record video.

- **Privacy - Microphone Usage Description**: You must add this property so that your videos record audio, as well as images.

- **Privacy - Photo Library Additions Usage Description**: This property allows you to write photos to the user's photo library.

Make sure to provide a good description for the privacy keys, so the user knows why you need access to their camera, microphone, and photo library. The better your description is, the more likely the user is to allow your app to access the associated privacy-sensitive information. After adding the keys, you are ready to see how you can take a picture using the built-in `UIImagePickerController` component of UIKit.

Taking and storing a picture

When you need a user to supply an image, they can do this by either selecting an image from their photo library or by taking a picture with the camera. `UIImagePickerController` supports both ways of picking an image. In this section, you will learn how you can allow users to take an image using the camera. Changing the example to allow users to select an image from their photo library should be straightforward, as long as you remember to add the **Privacy - Photo Library Usage Description** key to `Info.plist`.

Add the following implementation for `viewDidLoad()` to the `ImageViewController` class:

```
override func viewDidLoad() {
  super.viewDidLoad()
  let imagePicker = UIImagePickerController()
  imagePicker.sourceType = .camera
  imagePicker.delegate = self
  present(imagePicker, animated: true, completion: nil)
}
```

The previous implementation creates an instance of the `UIImagePickerController` object and configures it so that it uses the camera as the image source and presents it to the user. Note that the view controller is set as a delegate for the image picker.

When the user has taken a picture, the image picker will notify its delegate about this so that it can extract the image and use it. In this case, the image should be given the `selectedImage` label in the view controller so that it can be shown in the image view, and saved when the user taps on the save button, and the `saveImage()` method is called as a result.

Add the following extension to make `ImageViewController` conform to
`UIImagePickerControllerDelegate`:

```
extension ImageViewController: UIImagePickerControllerDelegate,
  UINavigationControllerDelegate {
  func imagePickerController(_ picker: UIImagePickerController,
    didFinishPickingMediaWithInfo info:
     [UIImagePickerController.InfoKey : Any]) {
    picker.dismiss(animated: true, completion: nil)
    guard let image = info[.originalImage] as? UIImage else {
      return }
    selectedImage = image
  }
}
```

Note that this extension also makes the image view controller
conform to `UINavigationControllerDelegate`. The delegate
property on the image picker controller requires all delegates to
conform to both `UINavigationControllerDelegate` and
`UIImagePickerControllerDelegate`.

When the user has taken a picture with the camera, `imagePickerController(_:
didFinishPickingMediaWithInfo)` is called to notify the delegate about the photo
that the user took. The first thing that the preceding code does is dismiss the picker, as
it's no longer needed. The picture that the user just took is stored in the `info` dictionary
as the original image. When the image is extracted from the dictionary, it is set as
`selectedImage`.

To store the image, add the following implementation of `saveImage()`:

```
@IBAction func saveImage() {
  guard let image = selectedImage else { return }
  UIImageWriteToSavedPhotosAlbum(image, self,
    #selector(didSaveImage(_:withError:contextInfo:)), nil)
}


@objc func didSaveImage(_ image: UIImage, withError error:
  Error?, contextInfo: UnsafeRawPointer) {
  guard error == nil else { return }
  presentAlertWithTitle("Success", message: "Image was saved
    succesfully")
}
```

The preceding code calls `UIImageWriteToSavedPhotosAlbum(_:_:_:)` to store the image in the user's photo library. When the save operation completes, the `didSaveImage(_:withError:contextInfo:)` method will be called. If this method does not receive any errors, then the photo was successfully stored in the photo library and an alert is shown.

Allowing the user to take a picture by implementing `UIImagePickerController` is relatively straightforward, and it is a great way to implement a camera feature in your app without too much effort. Sometimes, you need more advanced access to the camera. In these cases, you can use `AVFoundation` to gain access to the raw video feed from the camera, as you will see next.

Recording and storing video

In the previous section, you used `AVFoundation` to build a simple audio player app. You will now use `AVFoundation` again, except instead of playing video or audio, you will now record video and store it in the user's photo library. When using `AVFoundation` to record a video feed, you do so with an `AVCaptureSession` object. A capture session is responsible for taking the input from one or more `AVCaptureDeviceInput` objects and writing it to an `AVCaptureOutput` subclass.

The following diagram shows the objects that are involved with recording media through `AVCaptureSession`:

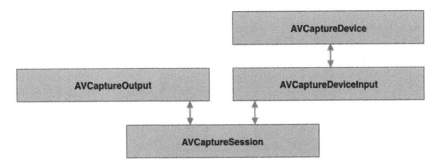

Figure 11.2 – AVCaptureSession entities

To get started on implementing the video recorder, make sure to import `AVFoundation` in `RecordVideoViewController.swift`. Also, add the following properties to the `RecordVideoViewController` class:

```
let videoCaptureSession = AVCaptureSession()
let videoOutput = AVCaptureMovieFileOutput()
var previewLayer:   AVCaptureVideoPreviewLayer?
```

Most of the preceding properties should look familiar because they were also shown in the screenshot that outlined the components that are involved with AVCaptureSession. Note that AVCaptureMovieFileOutput is a subclass of AVCaptureOutput, specialized in capturing video. The preview layer will be used to render the video feed at runtime and present it to the user so that they can see what they are capturing with the camera.

The next step is to set up the AVCaptureDevice objects for the camera and microphone and associate them with AVCaptureSession. Add the following code to the viewDidLoad() method:

```
override func viewDidLoad() {
  super.viewDidLoad()


  // 1
  guard let camera = AVCaptureDevice.default(.
      builtInWideAngleCamera, for: .video, position: .back),
    let microphone = AVCaptureDevice.default(.builtInMicrophone,
      for: .audio, position: .unspecified) else { return }


  // 2
  do {
    let cameraInput = try AVCaptureDeviceInput(device: camera)
    let microphoneInput = try AVCaptureDeviceInput(device:
      microphone)
    videoCaptureSession.addInput(cameraInput)
    videoCaptureSession.addInput(microphoneInput)
    videoCaptureSession.addOutput(videoOutput)
  } catch {
    print(error.localizedDescription)
  }
}
```

The preceding code first obtains a reference to the camera and microphone that will be used to record the video and audio. The second step is to create the AVCaptureDeviceInput objects that are associated with the camera and microphone and associate them with the capture session. The video output is also added to the video capture session. If you examine the screenshot that you saw earlier and compare it with the preceding code snippet, you will find that all four components are present in this implementation.

The next step is to provide the user with a view that shows the current camera feed so that they can see what they are recording. Add the following code to viewDidLoad() after the capture session setup code:

```
previewLayer = AVCaptureVideoPreviewLayer(session:
    videoCaptureSession)
previewLayer?.videoGravity = .resizeAspectFill
videoView.layer.addSublayer(previewLayer!)
videoCaptureSession.startRunning()
```

The preceding code sets up the preview layer and associates it with the video capture session. The preview layer will directly use the capture session to render the camera feed. The capture session is then started. This does not mean that the recording session starts; rather, only that the capture session will begin processing the data from its camera and microphone inputs.

The preview layer is added to the view at this point, but it doesn't cover the video view yet. Add the following implementation for viewDidLayoutSubviews() to RecordVideoViewController to set the preview layer's size and position, so it matches the size and position of videoView:

```
override func viewDidLayoutSubviews() {
    super.viewDidLayoutSubviews()
    previewLayer?.bounds.size = videoView.frame.size
    previewLayer?.position = CGPoint(x: videoView.frame.midX,
        y:videoView.frame.size.height / 2)
}
```

Running the app now will already show you the camera feed. However, tapping the record button doesn't work yet, because you haven't yet implemented the startStopRecording() method. Add the following implementation for this method:

```
@IBAction func startStopRecording() {
    // 1
    if videoOutput.isRecording {
        videoOutput.stopRecording()

    } else {
```

```
// 2
guard let path = FileManager.default.urls(for:
  .documentDirectory, in: .userDomainMask).first else {
  return }
let fileUrl = path.appendingPathComponent("recording.mov")


// 3
try? FileManager.default.removeItem(at: fileUrl)


// 4
videoOutput.startRecording(to: fileUrl, recordingDelegate:
  self)
  }
}
```

Let's go over the preceding snippet step by step to see what exactly is going on:

1. First, the isRecording property for the video output is checked. If a recording is currently active, the recording should be stopped.

2. If no recording is currently active, a new path is created to store the video temporarily.

3. Since the video output cannot overwrite an existing file, the FileManager object should attempt to remove any existing files at the temporary video file path.

4. The video output will start recording to the temporary file. The view controller itself is passed as a delegate to be notified when the recording has begun and is stopped.

Since RecordVideoViewController does not conform to AVCaptureFileOutputRecordingDelegate yet, you should add the following extension to add conformance to AVCaptureFileOutputRecordingDelegate:

```
extension RecordVideoViewController:
  AVCaptureFileOutputRecordingDelegate {
// 1
func fileOutput(_ output: AVCaptureFileOutput,
    didStartRecordingTo fileURL: URL, from connections:
    [AVCaptureConnection]) {
  startStopButton.setTitle("Stop Recording", for: .normal)
  }
```

```
// 2
func fileOutput(_ output: AVCaptureFileOutput,
    didFinishRecordingTo outputFileURL: URL, from connections:
    [AVCaptureConnection], error: Error?) {
  guard error == nil else { return }
  UISaveVideoAtPathToSavedPhotosAlbum(outputFileURL.path,
      self, #selector(didSaveVideo(at:withError:contextInfo:)),
      nil)
}


// 3
@objc func didSaveVideo(at path: String, withError error:
    Error?, contextInfo: UnsafeRawPointer?) {
  guard error == nil else { return }
  presentAlertWithTitle("Success", message: "Video was saved
      succesfully")
  startStopButton.setTitle("Start Recording", for: .normal)
}
}
```

The preceding extension contains three methods. The first is a delegate method, called when the video output has begun recording. When the recording has started, the title of the startStopButton button is updated to reflect the current state. The second method is also a delegate method. This method is called when the recording has completed. If no errors occur, the video is stored at the temporary location you set up earlier. UISaveVideoAtPathToSavedPhotosAlbum(_:_:_:_:) is then called, to move the video from the temporary location to the user's photo library. This method is very similar to the UIImageWriteToSavedPhotosAlbum(_:_:_:_:) method that you used to store a picture. The third and final method in the extension is called when the video is stored in the user's photo library. When the video has been successfully stored, an alert is shown, and the title of the startStopButton button is updated again.

You can now run the app and record some videos! Even though you have done a lot of manual work by implementing the video recording logic directly with AVCaptureSession, most of the hard work is done inside of the AVFoundation framework. One final media-related feature to explore is applying visual filters to images using **Core Image**. Applying filters to images is a very popular functionality in lots of apps and it can make your photo app more appealing.

Manipulating photos with Core Image

In this chapter, you have already seen that iOS has powerful capabilities for recording and playing media. In this section, you will learn how you can manipulate images with Core Image. The Core Image framework provides many different filters that you can use to process both images and videos. You will expand on the photo-taking capabilities that you implemented in the `Captured` app so that users can grayscale and crop images.

Every Core Image filter you apply to images is an instance of the `CIFilter` class. You can create instances of filters as follows:

```
let filter = CIFilter(name: "CIPhotoEffectNoir")
```

The `name` parameter in the filter's initializer is expected to be a string that refers to a specific filter. You can refer to Apple's documentation on Core Image and the Core Image Filter Reference guide to see an overview of all the filters that you can use in your apps.

Every filter has a certain set of parameters that you need to set on the `CIFilter` instance to use the filter; for instance, a grayscale filter requires you to provide an input image. Other filters might take an intensity, location, or other properties. The best way to see how you can apply a filter to an image is through an example. Add the following implementation for `applyGrayScale()` to `ImageViewController.swift` to implement a grayscale filter:

```swift
@IBAction func applyGrayScale() {
  // 1
  guard let cgImage = selectedImage?.cgImage,
  // 2
  let initialOrientation = selectedImage?.imageOrientation,
  // 3
  let filter = CIFilter(name: "CIPhotoEffectNoir") else {
    return }

  // 4
  let sourceImage = CIImage(cgImage: cgImage)
  filter.setValue(sourceImage, forKey: kCIInputImageKey)

  // 5
  let context = CIContext(options: nil)
```

```
guard let outputImage = filter.outputImage, let cgImageOut =
    context.createCGImage(outputImage, from: outputImage.
    extent) else { return }
```

```
// 6
selectedImage = UIImage(cgImage: cgImageOut, scale: 1,
    orientation: initialOrientation)
}
```

The preceding code has a lot of small, interesting details, highlighted with numbered comments. Let's go over the comments one by one to see how the grayscale filter is applied:

1. The UIImage instance that is stored in selectedImage is converted into a CGImage instance. Strictly speaking, this conversion isn't required, but it does make applying other filters to the UIImage instance later a bit easier.

2. One downside of using CGImage, instead of UIImage, is that the orientation information that is stored in the image is lost. To make sure the final image maintains its orientation, the initial orientation is stored.

3. This step creates an instance of the grayscale filter.

4. Since Core Image does not directly support CGImage instances, the CGImage instance is converted into a CIImage instance that can be used with Core Image. The CIImage instance is then assigned as the input image for the grayscale filter, by calling setValue(_:forKey:) on the filter.

5. The fifth step extracts the new image from the filter and uses a CIContext object to export the CIImage output to a CGImage instance.

6. The sixth and final step is to create a new UIImage instance, based on the CGImage output. The initial orientation is passed to the new UIImage instance to make sure it has the same orientation as the original image.

Even though there are a lot of steps involved, and you need to convert between different image types quite a bit, applying the filter is relatively simple. Most of the preceding code takes care of switching between image types, while the filter itself is set up in just a couple of lines. Try running the app now and taking a picture. The initial picture will be in full color. After you apply the grayscale filter, the image is automatically replaced with a grayscale version of the image, as shown in the following screenshot:

Figure 11.3 – Grayscale

The next filter you will implement is a crop filter. The crop filter will crop the image so that it's a square, rather than a portrait or landscape picture. The process for implementing the crop filter is mostly the same as for the grayscale filter, except for the values that need to be passed to the crop filter. Add the following implementation for `cropSquare()` to implement the crop filter:

```
@IBAction func cropSquare() {
    let context = CIContext(options: nil)


    guard let cgImage = selectedImage?.cgImage, let
        initialOrientation = selectedImage?.imageOrientation, let
        filter = CIFilter(name: "CICrop") else { return }


    let size = CGFloat(min(cgImage.width, cgImage.height))
    let center = CGPoint(x: cgImage.width / 2, y: cgImage.height
        / 2)
    let origin = CGPoint(x: center.x - size / 2, y: center.y -
        size / 2)
```

```
let cropRect = CGRect(origin: origin, size: CGSize(width:
    size, height: size))

let sourceImage = CIImage(cgImage: cgImage)
filter.setValue(sourceImage, forKey: kCIInputImageKey)
filter.setValue(CIVector(cgRect: cropRect), forKey:
    "inputRectangle")

guard let outputImage = filter.outputImage, let cgImageOut =
    context.createCGImage(outputImage, from: outputImage.
    extent) else { return }

selectedImage = UIImage(cgImage: cgImageOut, scale: 1,
    orientation: initialOrientation)
    }
}
```

The preceding code performs several calculations to figure out the best way to crop the image into a square. The CGRect instance specifies the crop coordinates and size, which are then used to create a CIVector object. This object is then passed to the filter as the value for the inputRectangle key. Apart from specifying the crop values, the process of applying the filter is identical, so the code should look familiar to you.

If you run the app now and tap the crop button, the image will be cropped, as shown in the following screenshot:

Figure 11.4 – Cropping the image

There are many more filters available in Core Image, which you can play around with to build pretty advanced filters. You can even apply multiple filters to a single image to create elaborate effects for the pictures in your apps. Because all filters work in very similar ways, it's relatively easy to apply any filter to your images once you understand how the general process of applying a filter works. You can always use the code from the preceding examples if you need a reminder about how to apply Core Image filters.

Summary

In this chapter, you have learned a lot about media in iOS. You saw how you can implement a video player with just a couple of lines of code. After that, you learned how to use `AVFoundation` directly to build an audio player that supports features such as stopping and resuming playback, skipping songs, and scrubbing forward or backward in a song. You even learned how you can keep playing audio when the app goes to the background or when the phone is set to silent mode. To apply the finishing touches to the audio player, you learned how you can use the `MediaPlayer` framework to show the currently playing file on the user's lock screen, and how to respond to control events that are sent to the app remotely.

After implementing media playback, you learned how you can build apps that help users to create media. You saw that `UIImagePickerController` provides a quick and simple interface to allow users to take a picture with the camera. You also learned how you can use `AVFoundation` and an `AVCaptureSession` object to implement a custom video recording experience. To wrap it all up, you learned about the Core Image framework, and how you can use it to apply filters to images.

In the next chapter, you will learn everything you need to know about location services and how to use Core Location in your apps. Depending on the use case of your app, handling the user location properly can be a critical task for your app to be successful. Examples are well known by now: food delivery apps, map apps, sport tracker apps, and so on.

12
Improving Apps with Location Services

All iOS devices come with a huge variety of chips and sensors that can be used to enhance the user experience. Augmented reality applications make heavy use of sensors such as the gyroscope, accelerometer, and camera. These sensors are great if you want to grab a picture or want to know how a device is moving. Other apps require different data, such as the user's GPS location at a given time. In this chapter, you will learn how to use the **Core Location** framework to do just that.

Core Location is a framework that allows developers to gain access to a user's current location, but it also allows developers to track whether a user has entered or exited a specific area, or even to monitor a user's location over time. A proper implementation of Core Location can be the core of many great features in your app, but a lousy implementation could drain a user's battery in no time.

In this chapter, you will learn about the following location-related topics:

- Requesting a user's location
- Subscribing to location changes
- Setting up geofences

By the end of the chapter, you should be able to make educated decisions about how and when you implement Core Location in your apps.

Technical requirements

The code bundle for this chapter includes a starter project called **LocationServices**. You can find it in the code bundle repository:

```
https://github.com/PacktPublishing/Mastering-iOS-14-
Programming-4th-Edition/tree/master/Chapter%2012%20-%20
Location%20Services
```

Requesting a user's location

As you can imagine, giving an application access to your exact location is quite a big deal. In the wrong hands, this data could allow people with malicious intentions to know exactly where you are at any given time and abuse this knowledge in many different ways. For this reason, it's essential that you only request a user's location if you absolutely have to. Simply using it for a small feature, or to make sure a user is in some arbitrary location before they sign up for a service, might not always be a good enough reason to ask for a user's location.

Let's see now the different ways to ask the user for permission to access their location data in iOS.

Asking for permission to access location data

When you do need access to a user's location, you have to ask permission first. Similar to how you have to add a reason for needing the camera or a user's contacts to the `Info.plist` file, you must also provide a reason for requesting location data. In the case of location data, there are two keys you can add to the `Info.plist`:

- Privacy-Location **When In Use Usage Description** (`NSLocationWhenInUseUsageDescription`)

- Privacy-Location **Always And When In Use Usage Description** (`NSLocationAlwaysAndWhenInUseUsageDescription`)

When your app asks for permission to use a user's location data, they have the option to only allow your app access to their location when the app is in use, or they can choose to allow your app to access their location all the time, even when the app is in the background. You can also configure the type of access that you want to ask yourself. If you only need the user's location when they are using the app, make sure to configure your permission request properly so the user isn't asked to provide their location to your app when it's in the background.

After adding the required keys to the `Info.plist` file in the **LocationServices** app, you will need to write some code to ask the user for permission to use their location. Before doing this, let's quickly examine the sample project's structure and content so you are aware of what information can be found where.

First, open the `Main.storyboard` file in the project. You will find a tab bar controller with two view controllers in it. Throughout this chapter, you will implement the features to populate these view controllers with appropriate data. Next, look at the `AppDelegate` implementation. The implementation here follows the **Dependency Injection** pattern that you have seen used in earlier projects, so there should not be any surprises for you here. Now, go ahead and examine the view controllers. The `GeofenceViewController` is the one you will work on first, to make the user's current location appear on the screen.

You will notice that a lot of code has already been implemented in this view controller. Examine the existing code for a bit and you'll find that all the code makes calls to empty methods in `LocationHelper.swift`. Most of your focus in this chapter will be on implementing the Core Location code required to work with a user's location data, so the UI work has already been set up. As you add code to `LocationHelper`, you'll find that the user interface for `LocationServices` comes to life bit by bit.

Now that you have a better understanding of how the LocationServices app was set up, let's see what steps are involved in asking the user for permission to use their location. Since this app will eventually track location changes in the background, you should ask the user for access to their location even when the app is in the background. To do this, add the following `viewDidAppear(_:)` code to `GeofenceViewController`:

```
locationHelper.askPermission { [weak self] status in if status
  == .authorizedAlways {
  self?.showCurrentLocation()
  } else {
    // handle the case where you don't always have access
  }
}
```

This is the first view controller the user will see, so asking the user for their location as soon as this view appears is a good idea. If it's not obvious that you will be prompting the user for their location, it's often a good idea to inform the user about why you are going to ask them for location permissions before actually showing the location access dialog. To actually make the permission dialog appear, you will need to add some code to `LocationHelper.swift`.

All location service-related requests are performed through an instance of `CLLocationManager`. The location manager is responsible for obtaining the user's GPS location, asking for permission to access the user's location, and more. When the location manager receives updates about the user's location, authorization status, or other events, it will notify its delegate. A location manager delegate should conform to the `CLLocationManagerDelegate` protocol. Note that the `LocationHelper` already conforms to `CLLocationManagerDelegate`, and that an instance of `CLLocationManager` is already created on this object. All that's left to do is assign the helper as the delegate for the location manager. Add the following line at the end of the `init()` method in `LocationHelper` to set it as the location manager delegate:

```
locationManager.delegate = self
```

Next, add the following implementation for the `askPermission(_:)` method:

```swift
func askPermission(_ completion: @escaping
  (CLAuthorizationStatus) -> Void) {
  let authorizationStatus =
    CLLocationManager.authorizationStatus()
  if authorizationStatus != .notDetermined {
    completion(authorizationStatus)
  } else {
    askPermissionCallback = completion
    locationManager.requestAlwaysAuthorization()
  }
}
```

This implementation checks whether a current authorization status exists. If it does, the completion `callback` is called with the current status. If the current status has not been determined yet, the location manager is asked to request authorization to access the user location using the `requestAlwaysAuthorization()` method. This will prompt the user for their location permissions. The reason you need to have permanent access to a user's location in this app is to ensure you can implement geofencing later in this chapter. Add the following method to the `CLLocationManagerDelegate` to retrieve the user's response to the authorization prompt:

```
func locationManager(_ manager: CLLocationManager,
    didChangeAuthorization status: CLAuthorizationStatus) {
    askPermissionCallback?(status)
    askPermissionCallback = nil
}
```

The preceding code immediately passes the user's response to the stored completion callback that was passed to `askPermission(_:)`. After calling the callback, it is set to nil to avoid accidentally calling it again. At this point, you have done all the work required to request access to a user's location. Let's see how you can retrieve a user's current location next, so you can make use of it in your apps.

Obtaining a user's location

Once your app has access to location data, you can use the location manager to begin observing a user's location, the direction in which a user is heading, and more. For now, you will focus on obtaining the user's current location. `GeofenceViewController` already contains a method, called `showCurrentLocation()`, that is responsible for asking the location helper for a current location. If you examine this method closely, you'll find that it also asks the location helper for a location name by calling `getLocationName(for:_:)` and passing the obtained location to this method. The `showCurrentLocation()` method also uses the obtained location to focus a map view on the user's location by calling `setRegion(_:animated:)` on the map view.

Since the view controller is already fully prepared to handle location updates, all you need to do is add the proper implementations for `getLatestLocation(_:)` and `getLocationName(for:_:)`. Begin by adding the following implementation for `getLatestLocation(_:)`:

```
func getLatestLocation(_ completion: @escaping (CLLocation) ->
    Void) {
    if let location = trackedLocations.last {
```

```
    completion(location)
  } else if CLLocationManager.locationServicesEnabled() {
    latestLocationObtainedCallback = completion
    locationManager.startUpdatingLocation()
  }
}
```

The preceding method first checks whether a location has already been obtained. If it has, then the latest obtained location is returned. If there is no existing location, the code checks whether location services are enabled. It's always good practice to check whether the location service you are about to use is actually available. If location services are available, the completion callback is stored in the helper, and the location manager is told to start monitoring the user's location by calling startUpdatingLocation().

Calling startUpdateLocation() will make the location observer continuously monitor the user's GPS location, and will send any relevant updates to its delegate by calling locationManager(_:didUpdateLocations:). This method will always receive one or more new locations that the manager has obtained, where the latest location will be the last item in the list of obtained locations. Add the following implementation for this method to the CLLocationManagerDelegate extension of LocationHelper:

```
func locationManager(_ manager: CLLocationManager,
  didUpdateLocations locations: [CLLocation]) {
  latestLocationObtainedCallback?(locations.last!)
  latestLocationObtainedCallback = nil
  locationManager.stopUpdatingLocation()
  trackedLocations += locations
}
```

The implementation for locationManager(_:didUpdateLocations:) is fairly straightforward: the latest location is passed to the callback, and the callback is removed to prevent subsequent location updates from triggering the callback unexpectedly. Also, the location manager is told to stop monitoring the user's location by calling stopUpdatingLocation(). Lastly, the obtained locations are stored for later use.

> **Important note**
>
> It's always good practice to make the location manager stop monitoring location updates if you won't be needing updates any time soon. Monitoring location updates has a pretty significant impact on battery life, so you shouldn't spend more time tracking a user's location than needed.

Now that you can retrieve the user's location, the last step is to also retrieve the location name by implementing `getLocationName(for:_:_)` in the location helper. Add the following implementation for this method to the location helper:

```swift
func getLocationName(for location: CLLocation, _ completion: @
    escaping (String) -> Void) {
  let geocoder = CLGeocoder()
  geocoder.reverseGeocodeLocation(location) { placemarks,
    error in
  guard error == nil else {
    completion("An error ocurred:
    \(error?.localizedDescription ?? "Unknown error")")
    return
  }

    completion(placemarks?.first?.name ?? "Unkown location")
  }
}
```

The preceding code uses `CLGeocoder` to find a placemark that corresponds with the user's current location. Note that this feature uses an internet connection, so the name lookup will only work if the user has an internet connection. Regular GPS-related features do not require internet access, so your app can monitor and track a user's location even if they don't have an active internet connection.

Try running your app now—you should be able to see the user's current location on the map, and the location name, latitude, and longitude should be displayed on the screen as well. Now that you know how to obtain a user's location, let's see how you can efficiently subscribe your app to follow changes in a user's location in order to track their position.

Subscribing to location changes

One way of subscribing to changes in a user's location has already been covered in the previous section of this chapter. When you call `startUpdatingLocation()` on a location manager, it will automatically subscribe to the user's location. This method of tracking a user's location is excellent if you need very detailed reporting on a user's location, but usually, you don't need this level of detail. More importantly, using this kind of location tracking for an extended period will drain the user's battery.

Luckily, there are better ways to monitor location changes. One way is to subscribe to locations that the user visits by calling startMonitoringVisits(). This method is used if you aren't interested in the user's detailed movement but only want to know whether the user spent an extended period in a particular area. This type of tracking of a user's location is perfect if you need a low-power way to track very rough location changes. This kind of tracking even works well if your app is running in the background, because your app will automatically be woken up or launched if a visit event occurs.

If your app is relaunched due to a location-related event, then UIApplication. LaunchOptionsKey.location will be present in the application's launch options dictionary. When it is, you are expected to create an instance of a location manager and assign it a delegate to receive the relevant location update.

If the visit monitoring is a bit too inaccurate for your purposes but you don't need continuous location tracking, you can use **significant location change tracking**. This type of tracking triggers when a user has moved a significant distance over time, providing your app with updates only when the user is truly moving. This is a lot more power efficient than making your app track the user's location even when their current location hasn't changed. Just like visit tracking, significant location changes will wake up your app or even relaunch it when a visit occurs. When an event is delivered to the app like this, you should re-enable the significant location change monitoring. Let's implement significant location changes in the LocationServices sample app to see exactly how they work.

If you look at SignificantChangesViewController, you'll note that the view controller is fully set up to begin monitoring significant location changes. The monitorSignificantChanges(_:) method, defined in the location helper, takes a callback that's called every time a significant location change occurs. Every time new location data is retrieved, the table view is reloaded to display the latest available data. Since significant location changes can wake the app up with a special key in the app's launch options, let's update AppDelegate so it can handle this scenario. Add the following code application(_:didFinishLaunchingWithOptions:) right before the return statement:

```
if launchOptions?[UIApplication.LaunchOptionsKey.location] !=
  nil

  { locationHelper.monitorSignificantChanges { _ in
    // continue monitoring
  }
}
```

Since `AppDelegate` already has a reference to the location helper, all it needs to do is re-enable significant location changes monitoring. This small change to `AppDelegate` is quite powerful because it allows your app to respond to changes in the user's location even when the app is not running. Let's implement the appropriate code in the location helper next.

Add the following implementation for `monitorSignificantLocationChanges(_:)` to `LocationHelper`:

```
func monitorSignificantChanges(_ locationHandler: @escaping
  (CLLocation) -> Void) {
  guard CLLocationManager.
    significantLocationChangeMonitoringAvailable()
      else { return }

  significantChangeReceivedCallback = locationHandler
  locationManager.startMonitoringSignificantLocationChanges()

  isTrackingSignificantLocationChanges = true
}
```

This method is very similar to the location helper methods you have seen before. When a significant location change is detected, the location manager calls `locationManager(_:didUpdateLocations:)` on its delegate. Since this method is already implemented, you should update the implementation as follows:

```
func locationManager(_ manager: CLLocationManager,
  didUpdateLocations locations: [CLLocation]) {
  latestLocationObtainedCallback?(locations.last!)
  latestLocationObtainedCallback = nil

  if isTrackingSignificantLocationChanges == false {
    locationManager.stopUpdatingLocation()
  }

  significantChangeReceivedCallback?(locations.last!)

  trackedLocations += locations
}
```

Note that the location manager is only told to stop updating the user's location when significant location change tracking is not active. When you call `stopUpdatingLocation()`, the location manager will cease to deliver any location updates to this delegate method. Also, note that `significantChangeReceivedCallback` is not removed after being calling. The reason for this is that the caller of `monitorSignificantChanges(_:)` is interested in continuous location updates, so any time this method is called, the `SignificantChangesViewController` view controller that initiated significant location change tracking should always be called.

One last thing you need to do so that your app receives significant location changes while it's not in the foreground is to set the `allowsBackgroundLocationUpdates` property to `true`. Add the following line of code to the location helper's `init()`:

```
locationManager.allowsBackgroundLocationUpdates = true
```

In addition to subscribing to significant location changes or visits, you can also respond to the user entering or leaving a certain area with geofences.

Setting up geofences

Sometimes, your app doesn't really need to know the details of the user's whereabouts. Sometimes, you're only interested in tracking whether the user has exited or left a certain area, in order to show certain content in your app or to unlock some kind of special feature. Core Location has great support for monitoring geofences. A **geofence** is a certain area that is defined using a certain GPS coordinate and a circular radius around this point. In Core Location, geofences are set up using `CLRegion` subclasses. Core Location provides two different region types that you can use:

- `CLCircularRegion`
- `CLBeaconRegion`

A `CLCircularRegion` type is used to set up a geofence, as described before. A `CLBeaconRegion` type is used with physical BLE iBeacons, and essentially provides geofencing in a very small radius, for instance, just a couple of meters. In this section, you will learn how to set up a `CLCircularRegion` type that is set up around a user's first detected location. Setting up geofencing, or region monitoring, with both types of regions is very similar so all principles for monitoring a circular region also applies to beacon regions.

If you look at the `GeofenceViewController`, you'll notice that it has a button labeled **Set Geofence**. The `@IBAction` for this button does quite a lot of the work already, but one key element is missing—it doesn't inform the location manager about the region that should be monitored. Add the following code to the end of `setGeofence()` in `GeofenceViewController`:

```
let region = CLCircularRegion(center: location.coordinate,
    radius: 30, identifier: "current-location-geofence")
    locationHelper.setGeofence(at: region, exitHandler,
    enterHandler)
```

The preceding code uses the location that was obtained from the user before and uses it to create a circular region with a radius of 30 meters. The identifier that is passed to the region should be an identifier that uniquely defines the region. If you reuse an identifier, Core Location will stop monitoring the old region with that identifier and will monitor the new region instead. For the LocationServices app this is perfect, but if you want your app to observe multiple regions, you must make sure every region has its own unique identifier.

Next, add the following implementation for `setGeofence(at:_:_:)` to the `LocationHelper`:

```
func setGeofence(at region: CLRegion, _ exitHandler: @escaping
    () -> Void, _ enterHandler: @escaping () -> Void) {
    guard CLLocationManager.isMonitoringAvailable(for:
    CLCircularRegion.self) else { return }
    geofenceExitCallback = exitHandler
    geofenceEnterCallback = enterHandler
    locationManager.startMonitoring(for: region)
}
```

The preceding method is again very similar to the other location helper methods. Let's move right on to implementing the `CLocationManagerDelegate` methods that the location manager will call:

```
func locationManager(_ manager: CLLocationManager,
    didEnterRegion region: CLRegion) {
    geofenceEnterCallback?()
}
```

```
func locationManager(_ manager: CLLocationManager,
  didExitRegion region: CLRegion) {
  geofenceExitCallback?()
}
```

The preceding two methods are part of the CLocationManagerDelegate protocol and are called when a user enters or exits a certain area. Since there's no extra work to be done by the helper, the corresponding callbacks are immediately called so the GeofenceViewController can update its interface accordingly.

Try opening the app and tapping the **Set Geofence** button. An orange circle should now appear on the map to visualize the geofence you have set up. If you exit or enter the region, the status label should update accordingly to show whether you have just entered or left the geofence. Note that it might take up to five minutes for iOS to properly register, monitor, and report updates about your geofence. Note that your user should have an active internet connection for region monitoring to work optimally.

Summary

In this chapter, you have learned several techniques to obtain and respond to a user's location. You have implemented a LocationHelper class that provided a simple interface for view controllers to use the location manager that is contained in the helper. You learned about the best practices in the area of asking the user for access to their location data, and you have learned that asking for a user's location is a pretty privacy-sensitive question that shouldn't be asked without a good reason.

You learned that there are different ways, each with different levels of detail, that you can use to track a user's location. You saw that you can subscribe to continuous changes, which has a bad impact on battery life. You also learned about subscribing to visits and significant location changes. In addition to learning about tracking a user's location, you also learned about monitoring whether a user has entered or exited a certain area by implementing geofencing. When you implement Core Location in your own apps, always make sure to keep the user's privacy in mind. If you don't really need the location data, then don't request access to it. And if you do, make sure to handle your user's location data with great care.

In the next chapter, you will learn about the Combine framework and how you can use it to enhance your apps.

13
Working with the Combine Framework

With the launch of **Combine**, Apple provided developers with a new way of handling events in their code; a functional and declarative approach, where developers can implement streams and publisher/subscriber paradigms easily, without the need for external libraries. Centralizing event processing in your apps with the help of Combine makes your code easier to understand than using other traditional methods like nested closures or callbacks all around your code.

In this chapter, you will learn about the following topics:

- Understanding the Combine framework: We will review the basic components of the framework with code samples – publishers, subscribers, subjects, and operators.

- Combining publishers, subscribers, and operators: We will build a small feature in an example app mixing all these concepts together.

- Using operators to build error-proof streams: We will use `flatMap` and `catch` to create streams that can deal properly with errors in a real-world example app.

By the end of the chapter, you should be able to use Combine in multiple parts of your own apps to produce simple, effective, and easy to understand declarative code that will help your app's code be easy to understand, extend, and maintain.

Technical requirements

The code bundle for this chapter includes two starter projects called **CombineExample_ start** and **PublishersAndSubscribers_start**. You can find them in the code bundle repository:

```
https://github.com/PacktPublishing/Mastering-iOS-14-
Programming-4th-Edition
```

Understanding the Combine framework

Apple released the Combine framework in 2019, and they defined it as a framework that provides a declarative Swift API for processing values over time. There are **publishers**, which produce those values, and **subscribers**, which consume them. These values that change over time may represent different asynchronous events.

Let's see an overview of the Publisher and Subscriber protocol definitions to understand their key concepts in the following sections.

Understanding Publisher

As mentioned before, publishers are used in Combine to produce values over time. Let's dig into the Swift protocol that defines them to understand the key concepts. The `Publisher` definition in Swift looks as follows:

```
public protocol Publisher {
    //1
    associatedtype Output


    //2
    associatedtype Failure : Error


    //3
    public func subscribe<S>(_ subscriber: S) where S :
        Subscriber, Self.Failure == S.Failure, Self.Output ==
        S.Input


}
```

Let's explain each numbered comment in more detail:

1. Every `Publisher` instance has an associated type, `Output`. This defines the type of values that the publisher will generate over time.

2. At the same time, the `Publisher` can also generate errors, and the associated type `Failure` is used to define the type of those errors. If a `Publisher` never generates errors, the `Failure` can be defined as type `Never`.

3. Finally, a `Publisher` allows `Subscriber` entities to `subscribe` to it to receive the values that are being produced over time. Note that to generate a valid subscription, the publisher's `Output` type must match the subscriber's `Input` type. In the same way, the `Failure` type of both must match too.

The following figure shows a summary of the **Publisher**:

Figure 13.1 – Publisher summary

Now that we have an initial description of the critical concepts of a publisher, let's do the same with the `Subscriber` protocol.

Understanding Subscriber

We have seen that `Publisher` entities produce values over time. Now let's see how `Subscriber` entities can consume those values. `Publisher` and `Subscriber` work closely together in Combine, so let's see their internal details. The `Subscriber` protocol in Swift looks like this:

```
public protocol Subscriber : CustomCombineIdentifierConvertible
{

    //1
    associatedtype Input

    //2
    associatedtype Failure : Error

    //3
```

```
    func receive(subscription: Subscription)


    //4
    func receive(_ input: Self.Input) -> Subscribers.Demand


    //5
    func receive(completion: Subscribers.Completion<Self.
        Failure>)
}
```

Again, let's review each numbered line:

1. A Subscriber entity is going to receive values over time. The associated type Input defines the type of those values.

2. At the same time, the Subscriber can also receive errors, and the associated type Failure is used to define the type of those errors. If a Subscriber never receives errors, the Failure can be defined as type Never.

3. This method informs the Subscriber that the subscription to the Publisher is successful and it may start requesting elements.

4. Informs the Subscriber that the Publisher has produced a new item.

5. Some subscriptions may end over time. In those scenarios, this method is called to inform the Subscriber that it will not receive any more values. It allows us to execute a completion block before finishing.

The following figure shows a summary of the **Subscriber**:

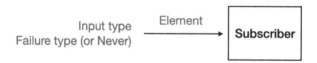

Figure 13.2 – Subscriber summary

If we put together both Publisher and Subscriber figures, we have the following schema:

Figure 13.3 – Publisher and Subscriber schemas

Notice how the output-input and the failure types of the publisher and the subscriber must be equal.

Now that we have a basic idea of what a publisher and a subscriber look like, let's see how they communicate. There are three steps, pictured in the following figure:

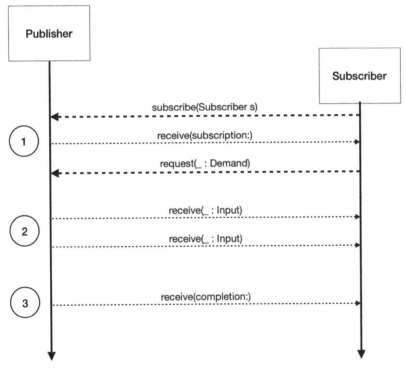

Figure 13.4 – Publisher and Subscriber communication process

The following list describes the process in more detail:

1. In the first step, the Subscriber tells the Publisher that it wants to subscribe. The Publisher sends back a subscription. The Subscriber uses that subscription to start requesting elements. The subscriber can request from N to unlimited values.

2. Now the Publisher is free to send those values over time. The Subscriber will receive those inputs.

3. In subscriptions that are not expecting unlimited values, a completion event is sent to the Subscriber, so it is aware that the subscription is over.

Now we have a basic idea of what a publisher is and what a subscriber is. We also know the steps involved in their communication. That is enough theory! Here is a practical example of a single publisher sending the values of an array to a subscriber. You can open a new Xcode playground and try the following code:

```
import Cocoa
import Combine


//1
let publisher = [1,2,3,4].publisher
//2
let subscriber = publisher.sink { element in
   print(element)
}
```

In the first comment, we create an array of integers from 1 to 4, and we use the convenience instance property publisher from the Sequence protocol to wrap it inside a new Publisher instance.

In the second comment, we use the method sink to attach a subscriber to the publisher, defining inside its completion block an action to perform over each value received over time.

If you execute this code, the output will be like this:

```
1
2
3
4
```

The initial array contained the numbers from 1 to 4, and that is what we printed. But what if we just want to print the even numbers? How can we transform the data between the producer and the subscriber? Luckily for us, Combine provides **Operators** to help us. Let's see more about them next.

Understanding Operators

An **Operator** is also a **Publisher**. It sits between a publisher and a subscriber. We say that an operator subscribes to a publisher ("upstream") and sends results to a subscriber ("downstream"). Operators can also be chained in sequence. In this section, we are going to review some operators with example code: `filter`, `map`, `reduce`, `scan`, `combineLatest`, `merge`, and `zip`.

Using filter

The `filter` operator is used to just remove values matching some condition out of the stream.

Let's see a fundamental example using the `filter` operator. Imagine that from the previous array (`[1,2,3,4]`), we only want to print the even numbers of the array. We do it as follows:

```
import Cocoa
import Combine

let publisher = [1,2,3,4].publisher
let subscriber = publisher
    .filter { $0 % 2 == 0}
    .sink { print($0) }
```

Note how the `filter` operator sits between the publisher and the subscriber, and defines a modification of the elements in a declarative way.

If you run this code, you will obtain the following result in the console:

```
2
4
```

Now let's see another example of how operators can be handy when working with Combine. Remember that the first rule of the subscriber and publisher is that the `Input` of the subscriber must be equal to the `Output` of the publisher. What happens when they are not equal? Well, operators can help us to transform the `Output` of a publisher to adapt it to the proper `Input` type of the subscriber. One of the operators that helps us is map.

Using map

The map operator helps us to apply a certain operation to every value of the stream, transforming it into a different type.

The following code uses the map operator to transform the `Output` of a publisher (`int` values) into the `Input` that our subscriber needs (`User` instances):

```
let publisher = [1,2,3,4].publisher
let subscriber = publisher
  .map { return User(id: $0) }
  .sink { print($0.description()) }
```

The map operator is transforming a stream of `Int` values `[1,2,3,4]` into a stream of `User` instances. When we use the `sink`, we can call the `description()` method of those users.

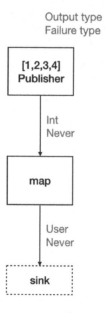

Figure 13.5 – Using map to transform outputs on the stream

The previous figure represents how map changes the **Output** type (while the **Failure** type, in this case, keeps being the same). When working with Combine, using this kind of graph (on a document or just in your mind) can be really helpful to work with the proper types at every step of the stream.

There are more operators available rather than just filter and map. Let's see other useful ones like reduce, scan, combineLatest, merge, and zip.

Using reduce

The reduce operator returns the result of combining all the values of the stream using a given operation to apply.

You can try out the following examples in an Xcode playground. Go ahead and check this example of reduce:

```
import Combine
let reduceExample = [1,2,3,4].publisher
  .reduce(1, { $0 * $1 })
  .sink(receiveValue: { print ("\($0)", terminator: " ") })
```

If you execute this code, the output in the console is as follows:

```
24
```

If you have used the regular reduce function from the Swift standard library, the reduce version from Combine should be easy to understand. It works the same but using values that come from a publisher. What reduce does is apply an operation and accumulate the result for the next value, starting with a given value. In our example, 1, { $0 * $1 }, the first param is the initial value, hence 1, and the following param is the operation to perform: multiply the current value (stored as $0) by the next incoming value ($1), and keep it for the next iteration. So, if our input is [1,2,3,4] and our starting value is 1, what reduce is doing is *1 x 1 x 2 x 3 x 4 = 24*. The next operator that we are going to explain is very similar to reduce. Let's jump into scan.

Using scan

An operator very much related to `reduce` is `scan`. The `scan` operator does exactly the same as `reduce` but it emits the result at each step. Check this code:

```
import Combine
let scanExample = [1,2,3,4].publisher
    .scan(1, { $0 * $1 })
    .sink(receiveValue: { print ("\($0)", terminator: " ") })
```

Now, executing this will result in the following output:

```
1 2 6 24
```

As you can see, it is giving us the same final result as `reduce` (**24**), but `scan` emits a value in each step, not just at the end. So, with `scan`, we get the following values over time:

- 1x1 = **1**
- 1x2 = **2**
- 2x3 = **6**
- 6x4 = **24**

These operators (`filter`, `map`, `reduce`, and `scan`) helped us to transform the values coming from another publisher. But some operators combine multiple publishers' input into one single stream output. Let's see some of them: `combineLatest`, `merge`, and `zip`.

Using combineLatest

It is a publisher that combines the latest values from two other publishers. Both publishers must have the same failure type. The downstream subscriber will receive a tuple of the most recent elements from the upstream publishers when any of them emit a new value.

Try the following code in a playground:

```
import Combine
let chars = PassthroughSubject<String, Never>()
let numbers = PassthroughSubject<Int, Never>()

let cancellable = chars.combineLatest(numbers)
    .sink { print("Result: \($0).") }

chars.send("a")
```

```
numbers.send(1)
```

```
chars.send("b")
```

```
chars.send("c")
```

```
numbers.send(2)
```

```
numbers.send(3)
```

The output on the console is as follows:

```
Result: ("a", 1).
Result: ("b", 1).
Result: ("c", 1).
Result: ("c", 2).
Result: ("c", 3).
```

Notice how we don't have any output until `("a", 1).`, which means that `combineLatest` doesn't produce any output until all the inputs send an initial value. After that, it will produce a value every time an input sends a new value, sending the latest from each of the inputs.

There are also other versions of `combineLatest` to combine three or even four inputs, instead of just two: `combineLatest3`, `combineLatest4`.

What if we only want to have the latest output of any of the input publishers (meaning just a value, not a tuple)? For those cases, we can use `merge`.

Using merge

With `merge`, we will aggregate multiple input publishers into a single stream, and the output will be just the latest value from any of them. Check out this code in a playground:

```
import Combine
let oddNumbers = PassthroughSubject<Int, Never>()
let evenNumbers = PassthroughSubject<Int, Never>()

let cancellable = oddNumbers.merge(with: evenNumbers)
    .sink { print("Result: \($0).") }
```

```
oddNumbers.send(1)
evenNumbers.send(2)
oddNumbers.send(3)
```

The output will be as follows:

```
Result: 1.
Result: 2.
Result: 3.
```

As you can see, the output is one value at a time, which differs from the tuple with all the latest values from all the inputs that we got with combineLatest.

There is another useful method to work with multiple publishers. Let's see what zip can do.

Using zip

zip is a publisher that emits a pair of elements when both input publishers have emitted a new value. Let's see how it differs from combineLatest with the same example. Execute the following code in a playground:

```
import Combine
let chars = PassthroughSubject<String, Never>()
let numbers = PassthroughSubject<Int, Never>()

let cancellable = chars.zip(numbers)
    .sink { print("Result: \($0).") }

chars.send("a")
numbers.send(1)
// combineLatest output:    (a,1)
// zip output:              (a, 1)

chars.send("b")
// combineLatest output:    (b,1)
// zip output:              nothing

chars.send("c")
// combineLatest output:    (c,1)
```

```
// zip output:                nothing

numbers.send(2)
// combineLatest output:    (c,2)
// zip output:              (b,2)

numbers.send(3)
// combineLatest output:    (c,3)
// zip output:              (c,3)
```

Check out the comments under each line, representing what combineLatest and zip will output every given time. Notice how zip doesn't send a new pair of values downstream until both of the publishers have emitted a new value. And when that happens, it will send a tuple with the oldest non-emitted values of both of them. CombineLatest will use the most recent and will emit a tuple every time one of the publishers emits a single new value (it will not wait to have both publishers emitting!). That is the main difference.

With the basics about publisher, subscriber, and operator entities explained, let's see another useful entity in Combine in the next section: **Subject**.

Understanding Subject

As per the Apple documentation:

> *"A subject is a publisher that exposes a method for outside*
> *callers to publish elements."*

The definition is pretty straightforward. Subjects are like publishers, but they have a method, send(_:), which you can use to inject new elements into their stream. A single Subject allows multiple subscribers to be connected at the same time.

There are two types of built-in subjects: CurrentValueSubject and PassthroughSubject. Let's see the differences between them.

Working with CurrentValueSubject

This is a subject that holds an initial value. It broadcasts the current value every time it changes.

When a subscriber connects to a `CurrentValueSubject`, it will receive the current value, and the next ones when it changes. This means that a `CurrentValueSubject` has state. Here is an example (you can try this code in a playground):

```
import Combine
let currentValueSubject = CurrentValueSubject<String,
  Never>("first value")
let subscriber = currentValueSubject.sink { print("received: \
  ($0)") }
currentValueSubject.send("second value")
```

If you execute this code, the output looks like this:

```
received: first value
received: second value
```

Here are the interesting bits:

- When we initialize the subject, we need to pass an initial value.

- When the subscriber subscribes, it gets the current value that is held in the subject. Note how in the console output, the subscriber has printed `first value` even though we subscribed to the subject after that value was generated.

- Every time we call `send(_:)`, the subscribers get the next value.

Now, let's see the other built-in type of subject, `PassthroughSubject`.

Working with PassthroughSubject

The main difference between `PassthroughSubject` and `CurrentValueSubject` is that `PassthroughSubject` doesn't hold any state. Check the following code (you can try it out in a playground):

```
import Combine


let passthroughSubject = PassthroughSubject<String, Never>()
passthroughSubject.send("first value")
let subscriber = passthroughSubject.sink { print("received: \
  ($0)") }
passthroughSubject.send("second value")
```

If you execute this code, here is the output:

```
received: second value
```

Notice how the subscriber is created after the first value is sent. This first value is not received, because there was no subscriber connected yet. However, the second value is displayed in the output because it was sent after the subscription was established.

We have seen the basic usage of `Publisher`, `Subscriber`, `Operator`, and `Subject`. Let's now create a bigger and more complex example to see how to apply Combine concepts to real-world apps.

Combining Publishers, Subscribers, and Operators

In this section, we are going to mix the concepts of the previous section altogether in a real-world example feature. Let's assume that we have an app that contains a newsletter, and we allow the users to subscribe to the newsletter by entering their email address, using two `UITextFields`: the **Email** and **Repeat Email** fields. Let's assume that in our business logic, we need to check that the email is correct, and we are going to do the following checks:

- Local check: We will ask users to repeat the email address twice, and both should be the same.

- Local check: The email should contain an "@".

- Local check: The email should be five characters long, at least.

- Remote check: We will also assume that we have a remote method to check in the backend that the email is unique, meaning it doesn't exist yet.

Once all these conditions match, we will enable a **Sign-Up** button in the user interface. We will use Combine to add all this business logic into an example app. Open the **CombineExample_start** project and launch it. You will see a screen where you can input an email address, and another `UITextfield` to repeat it. You will also see a **Sign-up** button, but it is always disabled (for now). Let's implement the business logic step by step to improve this. We are going to start by implementing the three local checks described in the list above. And we are going to use a handy Combine operator for this: `combineLatest`.

Open the `ViewController.swift` file. You will notice a couple of vars that are tagged with the property wrapper `@Published`:

```
@Published var initialEmail: String = ""
@Published var repeatedEmail: String = ""
```

What `@Published` is doing here is creating a Publisher from the property itself. So, every time `initialEmail` or `repeatedEmail` values change, they will get published to anyone subscribed to them. You can access the publisher of `initialEmail` by using `$initialEmail` (prefix a $ to the property name). Notice the two `IBActions` defined in the same class:

```
@IBAction func emailChanged(_ sender: UITextField) {
    initialEmail = sender.text ?? ""
}
```

```
@IBAction func repeatedEmailChanged(_ sender: UITextField) {
    repeatedEmail = sender.text ?? ""
}
```

By combining `IBAction` and `@Published`, we are creating a funnel in which every time the user types something in the `initialEmail` `UITextField`, it will get published through the `$initialEmail` publisher.

Why is this handy? Remember that according to the business logic defined above, we need to ensure that both `initialEmail` and `repeatedEmail` are equal. Now we have two publishers that will emit their value every time the user types in either of the two text fields. How can we combine those two values to compare them? The Combine framework has the perfect method for this: `CombineLatest`. Add the following vars to the `ViewController.swift` file:

```
var validatedEmail: AnyPublisher<String?, Never> {
  return Publishers
    .CombineLatest($initialEmail, $repeatedEmail) //1
    .map { (email, repeatedEmail) -> String? in   //2
      guard email == repeatedEmail, email.contains("@"), email.
          count > 5 else { return nil }
      return email
```

```
        }
        .eraseToAnyPublisher() //3
  }
var cancellable: AnyCancellable? //4
```

Let's analyze the code comment by comment:

1. First, we are using `Publishers.CombineLatest` to combine two
   different publishers into one: `$initialEmail` and `$repeatedEmail`.
   This will result in a new stream (publisher) of type `Publishers.`
   `CombineLatest<Published<String>.Publisher,`
   `Published<String>.Publisher>`. Don't let the long type scare you. It means
   "a publisher of two string publishers." The magic of `CombineLatest` is that if
   either of the two inputs changes, you will get the new value, but also the latest value
   that the other input had, which is very useful for cases like this.

2. Second, we are applying the `map` operator over the "publisher of two string
   publishers." By using `map`, we are unwrapping the underlaying published strings
   to be able to use the string themselves and return a different result after working
   with them. Here is where we apply our business rules: If both emails are equal, they
   include an "@" and they are longer than five characters long, we return the `email`.
   Otherwise, we return `nil`. So, with `map`, we are transforming a stream output type
   into a new one, to adapt it to what we need.

3. At this point, if we inspect the type of what we have, you will see this:
   `Publishers.Map<Publishers.CombineLatest<Published<String>.`
   `Publisher, Published<String>.Publisher>, String?>`. That is
   quite complex to read and use. But Combine provides us with a way to simplify
   this, because what is important is what is inside of the publisher itself, not all the
   wrappers around it. By using `eraseToAnyPublisher`, we are changing this type
   to just `AnyPublisher<String?, Never>`. This is much easier to understand
   and use (and if you want to publish it in an API, for example, it's much easier to
   digest by other developers).

4. We create a cancellable property var to use it in the following piece of code.

This flow can be represented as follows

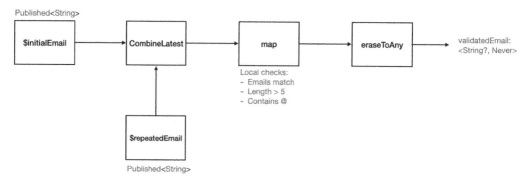

Figure 13.6 – validatedEmail stream

Now, add this line of code to the `viewDidLoad()` method:

```
cancellable = validatedEmail.sink { print($0) }
```

By calling `sink`, we are attaching a subscriber to the `validatedEmail` publisher, and we store it in our new `var` property `cancellable`. Every time we receive a new value, we will just print it into the console for testing purposes. Let's try it out! Execute the app and type any email address (in both fields) that fulfills all the conditions (for example, `abc@email.com`).

When you type valid addresses, you will see it in the console. When the addresses are not valid, you will see `nil`.

We have seen a lot of new Combine concepts packed into very little code. Before continuing with our demo project, we are going to look at a quick summary of these new concepts:

- The `@Published` property wrapper: Allows us to create a Publisher from a property variable. We can access the publisher by prefixing `$` to the name of the property. It only works on class properties, not on structs.

- `Publishers.CombineLatest`: Allows us to combine two publishers into a single one that will always push the latest value of each one when there is a change (or `nil`, if there wasn't a previous value).

- map: Allows us to transform the stream. We apply a map to a publisher with an Output type and we can transform it into a new, different Output.

- eraseToAnyPublisher: Allows us to erase complex types to work with easier AnyPublisher<Otutput, Failure> streams. This is very handy when publishing our classes as an API, for example.

After this little recap, we still have one feature pending to fulfill the list of requirements. We have implemented three local checks on the email addresses, but we still need to do the last one, which was this:

- Remote check: We will also assume that we have a remote method to check in the backend that the email is unique, meaning it doesn't exist yet.

In the ViewController.swift file, there is a dummy method named func emailAvailable(...). It just returns a completion block. This method is intended to represent a network call that returns True or False in the completion block according to whether the email already exists in the backend or not. For demo purposes, we are not going to implement the network call itself, just simulate the result.

Let's implement this feature with Combine. We are going to create a new publisher that will emit a Bool indicating whether the email that the user types exists in the backend or not, using a fake network call, emailAvailable(...). Add the following code to the ViewController.swift file:

```
var isNewEmail: AnyPublisher<Bool, Never> { //1
  return $initialEmail //2
    .debounce(for: 1, scheduler: RunLoop.main) //3
    .removeDuplicates() //4
    .flatMap { email in //5
      return Future { promise in
        self.emailAvailable(email) { available in
          promise(.success(available))
        }
      }
    }
    .eraseToAnyPublisher()
}
```

There are a lot of new concepts here, so let's go through the numbered comments one by one:

1. We are defining a new publisher, `isNewEmail`, of type `<Bool, Never>`. This publisher will help us to emit events that indicate whether the email that the user is typing exists in our database or not.

2. To fetch any new value that the user types in the email field, we start by using the published property defined earlier in the `$initialEmail` section.

3. Users can type/delete in text fields pretty fast. Our goal is to make a network call every time we receive a new value through the `$initialEmail` publisher (meaning every time the user is typing in the email field). That means that we will query the network a bit too much. The Combine `.debounce` method will help us to reduce the number of values we are processing. By using `.debounce(1...)`, we specify that from all the values that we get from `$initialEmail`, we will only process a value every `1` second. The rest of the values will be discarded. This is very helpful when working with publishers that are connected to the user interface and the network (text fields, buttons, search bars, and so on).

4. Another useful method is `removeDuplicates()`. If the user types "abc" and then deletes the "c" to quickly type the "c" back, we will make several calls. But if we use `removeDuplicates()`, we will avoid this unnecessary behavior.

5. The fifth step is a bit more complicated. This is where we perform a network call. First, we have a `.flatMap` wrapping everything. This function transforms elements from a publisher into a new type of publisher. Inside the `flatMap`, we have a `Future`. A `Future` is a publisher that eventually emits a single value and then finishes (or fails). Inside the `Future`, we have a `Promise`: A `Promise` in Combine is a `typealias` for a closure that takes a `Result`. Now let's describe the whole process again, but from inside out: The network call `emailAvailable` returns a result in the form of `promise.success(...)`. This Promise is wrapped in a Future, to become a publisher stream. That stream is a `Future<Bool, Never>` at this point. Now, we wrap everything with `flatMap`, so the upstream `initialEmail`: `Published<String>.Publisher` becomes `AnyPublisher<Bool, Never>` (with the help of `eraseToAnyPublisher` too).

Here is the full flow to generate `isNewEmail`:

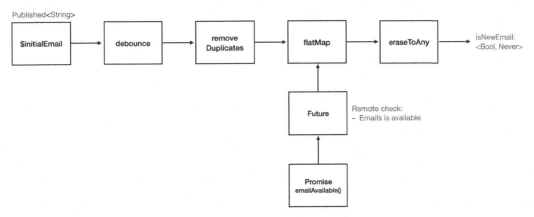

Figure 13.7 – isNewEmail stream

So, after all this chain of transformations, we have a publisher, `isNewEmail`, that will emit a `Bool` indicating whether an email address is unique or not in our backend every time (almost, except duplicates and debounced) the user types in the UI! That is pretty cool! And it's very useful for our business logic checks.

Our last step is going to be to combine the publisher of the local checks (`validatedEmail`) with the remote publisher (`isNewEmail`) to have a final output. The business logic required to enable the **Sign-up** button is that these publishers emit a valid email `String` and a `True` value, so all our conditions are met. What is the best way to combine the latest values of two different publishers and work with them? We just used it above! It is `combineLatest`. Add the following code to the `ViewController.swift` file:

```
var finalEmail: AnyPublisher<String?, Never> {
  return Publishers.CombineLatest(validatedEmail, isNewEmail).
     map { (email, isNew) -> String? in
    guard isNew else { return nil }
    return email
  }
  .eraseToAnyPublisher()
}
```

As detailed in the preceding code, we are using `CombineLatest` to work with the latest values of two different publishers. From `validatedEmail`, we get a valid email or a `nil` value otherwise. From `isNewEmail`, we get a `Bool` indicating whether the email exists in the database or not. The result of this is a new publisher, `finalEmail`, of type `<String?, Never>`. See the flow in the next figure:

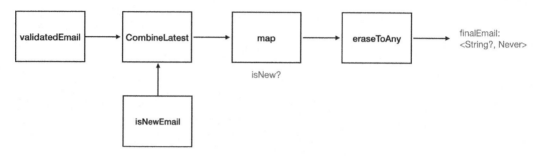

Figure 13.8 – finalEmail stream

Now, how can we enable and disable the **Sign-up** button using this new publisher? Add the following code inside the `viewDidLoad` function and let's explain it in detail:

```
signupButtonCancellable = finalEmail
  .map { $0 != nil }
  .receive(on: RunLoop.main)
  .assign(to: \.isEnabled, on: signupButton)
```

In this code, we start with the `finalEmail` publisher (`<String?, Never>`), we map over it, transforming the stream into `<Bool, Never>`, then we apply `.receive` to make sure we are executing this in the main thread (because we are handling the UI here, a `UIButton`). Finally, we assign the value inside the stream (`<Bool>`) to the `signupButton isEnabled` property! Check out the next figure, which details the steps of the stream:

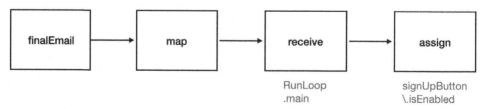

Figure 13.9 – Assigning finalEmail to signUpButton

And that is it! Execute the app, and try it yourself: If you type some email address that matches all the conditions (like abc@email.com), the **Sign-up** button will be enabled. Otherwise, it will be disabled.

In this section, we have learned about a lot of new Combine concepts and methods to combine different streams, transform outputs, modify the thread we are working on, handle user input, and so on. We used `flatMap` to transform elements of an upstream into a different type downstream. However, `flatMap` has more uses. One of them is to help streams recover from errors, with the help of `catch`. In the next section, we are going to see an example of how a stream can fail, and how to recover it using `flatMap` and `catch`.

Using Operators to build error-proof streams

For this section, go ahead and open the project in the code bundle named `PublishersAndSubscribers_start`. Take a look at the file `ViewController.swift`.

This file contains a `User` struct:

```
struct User: Codable {
  let id: String

  static var unknown: User {
    return User(id: "-1")
  }
}
```

The `User` struct is quite simple. It contains a `String` property `id`, and a `static var` named `unknown` that returns a `User` instance with `id` equal to `-1`. Apart from the `User` struct, the file contains the `ViewController` itself.

The view controller contains two methods:

- First, `postNotification()`: This just fires a notification in the Notification Center that contains a `User` instance with `id` equal to `123`. The name of the notification is `networkResult`.

- Second, `postNotificationThatFails()`: This just fires a notification in the Notification Center that contains random data that is Base-64 encoded, not a `User` instance this time. The name of the notification is `networkResult`.

We will use Combine to consume these two notifications. Both methods represent a dummy network call, whose result is being sent through the Notification Center in this way. So, think of them as the network call response that you will fetch from your backend when trying to query for some object (a user in this case) and propagate to your app with notifications.

Now, let's try to call `postNotification()` and consume the result using Combine. In the `viewDidLoad()` method, call `postNotification()`:

```
override func viewDidLoad() {
   super.viewDidLoad()
   postNotification()
}
```

Now let's create a publisher that emits values from the Notification Center and use the `cancellable` property to consume them as a subscriber. Change the `viewDidLoad()` method to this:

```
override func viewDidLoad() {
   super.viewDidLoad()

   //1
   let publisher = NotificationCenter.default.publisher(for:
      Notification.Name("networkResult"))

   //2
   cancellable = publisher.sink { item in
     print(item)
   }

   //3
   postNotification()
}
```

Let's review the comments by lines:

1.   First, we are creating a publisher that emits any value from the Notification Center that arrives under the name `networkResult`. This matches the notification name we are sending in the `postNotification()` method.

2. We are subscribing to the publisher created in the previous step, and we store the result in the `cancellable` property. We are using `sink` when creating the subscriber to define a completion block that will print to the console any value received.

3. Finally, we post a notification.

If you execute this code and you check in the console, you should see this result:

```
name = networkResult, object = Optional(<7b226964 223a2231
   3233227d>), userInfo = nil
```

This means that our stream worked! We have sent a notification, our publisher has forwarded it, and our subscriber has printed it into the console. As you can see on the console output, the notification has three properties: `name`, `object`, and `userInfo`. We want to unwrap what is inside the `object` attribute. So, let's modify our publisher with an operator to transform what our subscriber receives. Change the publisher code for this one:

```
let publisher = NotificationCenter.default.publisher(for:
   Notification.Name("networkResult"))
   .map { notification in return notification.object as! Data }
```

Execute it and check the output in the console:

```
12 bytes
```

In this code, we are mapping over the notification value and sending the `object` content as `Data`. In the console output, you can see that our subscriber is receiving those bytes of data now, instead of the full notification. Great! The next step is going to be to transform these bytes of `Data` into a `User` instance. To do that, we need to decode the data. Combine has the perfect helper method for this. Change the publisher code to this:

```
let publisher = NotificationCenter.default.publisher(for:
   Notification.Name("networkResult"))
   .map { notification in return notification.object as! Data }
   .decode(type: User.self, decoder: JSONDecoder())
```

By adding the preceding highlighted line, we are using the `Data` from the `map` operation and decoding it into a `User` instance! All in a single line. But if you try to execute now, you will get a compile error in the subscriber `sink` line saying the following:

```
Referencing instance method 'sink(receiveValue:)' on
'Publisher' requires the types' Publishers.Decode<Publishers.
Map<NotificationCenter.Publisher, JSONDecoder.Input>, User,
JSONDecoder>.Failure' (aka 'Error') and 'Never' be equivalent
```

This means: If you inspect the method sink that we are using, you will discover that it requires the `Failure` type of the publisher that is consuming to be `Never`:

```
extension Publisher where Self.Failure == Never
```

After adding the `decode` line, our publisher no longer has a `Never` type as failure, because `decode` can produce errors. So, the compiler is telling you that the types don't match anymore. We need to do something that catches any error produced by `decode` and transforms that into a `Never`-failing operation. Combine has another useful operator that can help us in this scenario: `catch`. Change the publisher code into this new block:

```
let publisher = NotificationCenter.default.publisher(for:
    Notification.Name("networkResult"))
    .map { notification in return notification.object as! Data }
    .decode(type: User.self, decoder: JSONDecoder())
    .catch {_ in
        return Just(User.unknown)
    }
```

Let's explain `catch` in more detail. `catch` will handle any error in the upstream, and instead of crashing the app, it will complete/finish the publisher that produced the error and replace it with a new publisher (that you must provide in the `return` block).

So in this scenario, if we get an error from the `decode` operation, our notification publisher will finish, and it will be replaced by `Just(User.unknown)`. `Just` is a publisher that only emits one value and then completes. Check the next figure:

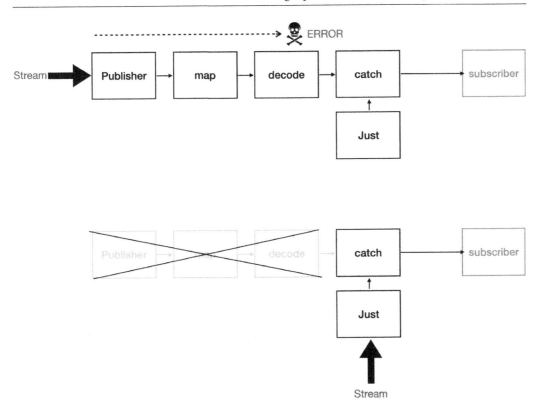

Figure 13.10 – Catch replaces the failed stream with a new one

The top part of the previous figure shows the stream when an error happens in the decode stage and catch enters into action. In the bottom part of the figure, you can see how catch drops the initial publisher and replaces it with the one defined in the catch block (a Just publisher in this case).

Let's try out what will happen if we provide a value that will produce an error in the decode stage. At the end of the viewDidLoad(), just after postNotification(), add this line:

```
postNotificationThatFails()
```

So, we are now sending two notifications, one with user data inside, and the other with a random string. The second should fail on the `decode` step. Execute the app; you will see this output:

```
User(id: "123")
User(id: "-1")
```

That is great! The first notification got decoded and transformed into a proper user. The second failed to be decoded, but our `catch` block recovered the stream with a new publisher that passed an unknown `User` struct to the receiver.

However, there is a problem with our solution. Add this line after `postNotificationThatFails()`, at the end of the `viewDidLoad()` method:

```
postNotification()
```

So now we are sending three notifications: first a regular one, then one that fails, then another regular one. Execute the app and notice the output:

```
User(id: "123")
User(id: "-1")
```

What is the issue here? The issue is that we only received two values, even though there are three notifications being sent! What is the problem then? The problem is that our `catch` block is replacing the failed stream with a `Just` publisher. As said before, a `Just` publisher only sends one value and then completes. Any value sent after the failure will be lost.

Let's improve this solution so we can keep processing values after recovering from an error with the `catch` block. Replace the `publisher` block with the following one:

```
let publisher = NotificationCenter.default.publisher(for:
    Notification.Name("networkResult"))
  .map { notification in return notification.object as! Data }
  .flatMap { data in
    return Just(data)
      .decode(type: User.self, decoder: JSONDecoder())
      .catch {_ in
        return Just(User.unknown)
      }
  }
```

In the preceding highlighted code, you can see that we have wrapped the decode and catch block in a flatMap + Just block. Check in the following figure the differences before and after the change:

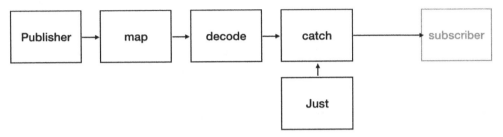

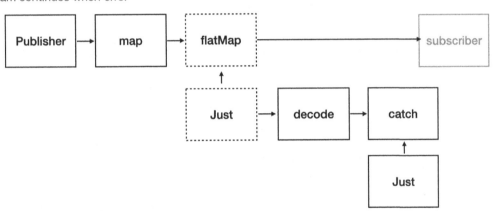

Figure 13.11 – Flow before and after flatMap

Notice in the new code how, inside the flatMap, we are now creating a new second flow for every new value with this piece of code:

```
.flatMap { data in
    return Just(data)
        .decode(type: User.self, decoder: JSONDecoder())
        .catch { _ in
            return Just(User.unknown)
        }
}
```

This is important because it means that when there is an error, and the `catch` replaces the stream with the `Just(User.unknown)` publisher, it will not replace the original stream; it will just replace the stream that we are creating for this specific element inside the `flatMap`. This means that for the next element that arrives from the Notification Center, we still have the main publisher working. Execute the app now and see the following results in the console:

```
User(id: "123")
User(id: "-1")
User(id: "123")
```

That is great! Not only are we handling the errors, we still process new elements that arrive after!

In this section, you have seen how to use `flatMap` and `catch` to make your streams error-proof. Let's wrap up the chapter now in the summary.

Summary

In this chapter, we have learned about the basics of Combine: what a publisher is, what a subscriber is, why we need operators, which ones are more useful, and how all these elements chain together to help us.

We have built two different apps to demonstrate how Combine can help in our apps, from processing user interface events, decoding, and applying business rules, to creating error-proof streams and methods to recover from operations that fail. Combine provides us with a lot of built-in functionalities that will make our code easy to read and maintain.

In the next chapter, we are going to learn about one of the new features of iOS 14: App Clips.

14
Creating an App Clip for Your App

One of the main features that iOS 14 brings to the table is App Clips. App Clips provide users with a fast new way to discover and make use of what your app has to offer. By triggering an App Clip from a QR code, a link, an NFC tag, or other mechanism, it can pop into the user's device (even without your app installed) and bring some of your app's functionality to life in a matter of seconds.

In this chapter, we are going to learn what an App Clip is, what they are used for, and what the user's journey will be like while using them. We will review the different options that users have to trigger them. We will then develop an App Clip and learn how to configure it with App Store Connect's new features. Finally, we will learn how to test them using Local Experiences. By the end of this chapter, you will be able to develop your own App Clips and bring your apps to the next level.

Let's summarize the topics of this chapter:

- Introducing App Clips
- Developing your first App Clip
- Testing your App Clip experiences

Let's get started!

Technical requirements

The code bundle for this chapter includes three starter projects called `AppClipExample_start`, `AppClipExample_configure_start`, and `AppClipExample_test`. You can find them in the code bundle repository for this book:

`https://github.com/PacktPublishing/Mastering-iOS-14-Programming-4th-Edition`

Introducing App Clips

App Clips allow users to discover an app in a fast and lightweight manner. With App Clips, a user can quickly use a feature of your app without having the app installed on their phone. An App Clip is a small set of features from your app that can be discovered and used without the user having your app installed. Users can open your App Clip by using different triggers, such as QR codes, NFC tags, links in Messages, places in Maps, and Smart Banners in websites. The App Clip will pop up on the user's home screen as an overlay called an App Clip Card. The App Clip Card describes what your App Clip does so that the user can choose to either open and use the App Clip or dismiss it. Let's look at an example of what an App Clip Card looks like:

Figure 14.1 – App Clip Card

As shown in the preceding screenshot, an App Clip Card is an overlay on the user's home screen that displays the following:

- **A header image, describing your app or the App Clip's main feature**: In this example, the header image is of someone preparing a coffee.
- **A title, describing what the App Clip does**: "Mamine Café".
- **A subtitle, describing what feature the App Clip offers**: "Order coffee in 3 taps".
- **A button, describing the action to be performed (such as open/view the App Clip)**: "View".
- **Extra info footer**: The App Clip's main app. A link is provided to the App Store so that the user can download it.

App Clips should be lightweight, brief, and complete a user's task in seconds. Let's take a look at some use cases of App Clips:

- An App Clip for ordering coffee when you pass by a coffee shop's door and tap on an NFC tag, such as the one shown in the preceding screenshot.
- An App Clip for renting an electric bike parked in the street, just by scanning its QR code. You can also use **Sign in with Apple and Apple Pay** to avoid forms and interface complexities, allowing you to rent the bike in seconds.
- An App Clip for pre-ordering from the menu of a restaurant, saving you time while you're waiting to be seated.
- An App Clip that triggers when you tap around NFC spots in an art gallery or a museum so that Augmented Reality scenes are displayed on your iPhone.

As you can see, the possibilities for App Clips are endless. Now that we have covered what an App Clip is, we are going to explain the user's journey of using an App Clip (from its invocation to when it's finally used). We will cover various invocation methods (how to make an App Clip appear) before describing the recommended guidelines for building an App Clip.

App Clip User Journey

Now, let's explore the whole App Clip process and steps in more detail, starting from when the user discovers your App Clip to when the user finishes their App Clip journey.

Let's imagine that we have an app for renting electric bikes. There are several stages involved in the App Clip process:

Figure 14.2 – App Clip process and steps

The preceding image explains the different stages of an App Clip:

1. **Invocation method**: The App Clip invocation method is how the user can trigger and open an App Clip. For our example, a user scans a QR code that's been placed on the bike with their device's camera, and the App Clip opens on their home screen. In this case, the invocation method is the QR code. We will explore these in more detail later in this chapter.

2. **User journey**: After invocation, the App Clip presents some options for the user to choose from (for example, 1-hour rental for $2 and 24-hour rental for $5). The user makes their desired selection inside the App Clip.

3. **Accounts and payment**: In our bike rental example, our App Clip needs to identify which user is renting the bike, and the user needs to pay for the service. Some App Clips will not require a registered user account nor payment to work; this step is optional.

4. **Full app recommendation**: When the rental decision for the bike has been made and the user is ready to proceed, your App Clip can recommend that the user downloads your complete app so that they can use it instead of the App Clip the next time they wish to use your service. Suggesting the entire app is an optional step, but it is recommended.

Now that we have provided an overview of the high-level steps an App Clip follows, we will take a closer look at what invocation methods are available.

App Clips Invocation Methods

We have seen that in order to display an App Clip, the user needs to invoke or discover it. Previously, we discussed that this can be done via a QR code, an NFC tag, a link in Messages, and so on. Here is a summary of the options available:

- **App Clip codes**: Each App Clip code includes a QR code and an NFC tag so that a user can scan it with their camera or tap on it.
- **NFC tags**.
- **QR codes**.
- **Safari App Banner**.
- **Links in Messages**.
- **Place cards in Maps**.
- **The Recently Used App Clips category on the new App Library on iOS 14**.

In this section, we learned what an App Clip is, what the user's journey is when they're using it, and the different invocation methods that can be used to trigger it. In the next section, we are going to build and configure an App Clip for a coffee shop.

Developing your first App Clip

In this section, we are going to start with an existing app, and we will add an App Clip to it step by step. Open the `AppClipExample_start` project in this book's code bundle. If you launch the app, you will see that we have a coffee shop app in which we can order three different types of drinks, review the order, and pay by Apple Pay or by entering our credit card details:

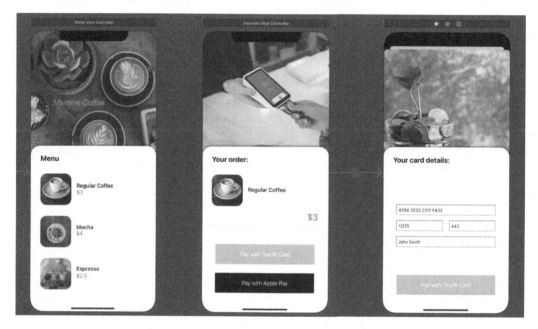

Figure 14.3 – Our app's main screens – Menu, Payment, and Credit Card controllers

Note that the purpose of this example app is to help us build the interesting part: the App Clip. Some functionalities, such as the credit card and Apple Pay payments, are not fully implemented; they just simulate this feature.

Before we jump into the App Clip process, let's take a moment to review the project's structure and its contents:

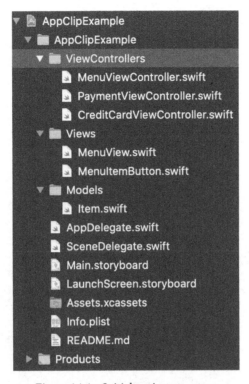

Figure 14.4 – Initial project structure

The app contains a single target named AppClipExample. Inside that target, we have three ViewControllers (MenuViewController, PaymentViewController, and CreditCardViewController) and some extra views (MenuView and MenuItemButton). It only contains a single model file named Item, which helps us with the menu products. We also have other common files, such as AppDelegate and Assets – short and simple. However, it is important to have a snapshot of this in mind because when we start adding our App Clip, this architecture will evolve.

Before we continue, ensure that you're using your own Apple Developer account settings in the project. In the AppClipExample target, do the following:

1. Select your own Development Team.

2. Change the App ID to {yourDomain}.AppClipExample.

In the next section, we'll create the App Clip for our coffee shop app. We will start by creating a new Target for the App Clip. Then, we will learn how to share code and images between our app and its App Clip (as well as how to create exceptions for when we don't want to share the exact same code). Finally, we will learn how to configure the App Clip's experiences in App Store Connect before testing it out.

Creating the App Clip's Target

In order to create an App Clip, an Xcode project needs to have a target for it. Currently, our project has a single target: `AppClipExample`. Let's proceed and create a new target for the App Clip. Follow these steps:

1. In Xcode, click on **File | New | Target**.

2. In the modal that appears, select **iOS | Application | App Clip**, as shown in the following screenshot:

Figure 14.5 – Adding an App Clip target

3. Press **Next**. Now, you can configure some of the initial values of the App Clip target.

4. Enter the name `MyAppClip`, as follows:

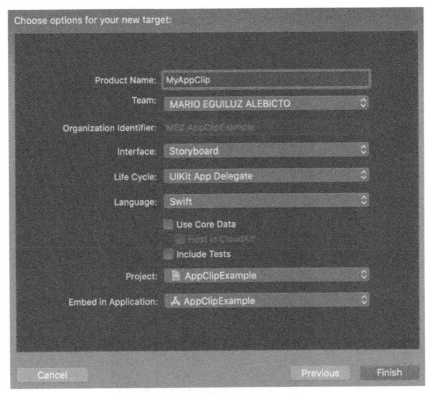

Figure 14.6 – App Clip target options

5.   When you click **Finish**, you will see a new popup:

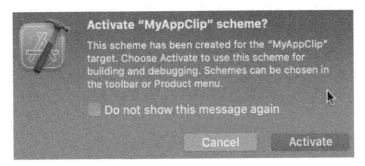

Figure 14.7 – Activating the new scheme

6. Press **Activate** so that the scheme can used for building and debugging. Now, take a look at the project structure; you'll see that a new target has been added for the App Clip:

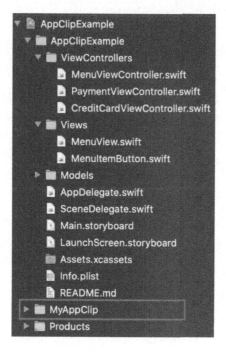

Figure 14.8 – New target for the App Clip

But this is not the only change that's been made to the project. Xcode did several things under the hood when it added the new App Clip target:

*   It created a new scheme for building and running the App Clip and its tests.

*   It added a new capability called **On Demand Install Capable** in the **App Clip Target settings | Signing & Capabilities** tab. This capability identifies the bundle as an App Clip.

*   In the same tab, you can also check how the Bundle identifier for the App Clip contains the same root as the full app's bundle identifier. So, if your app bundle identifier is `{yourDomain}.AppClipExample`, the App Clip will have `{yourDomain}.AppClipExample.Clip`. This is because an App Clip only corresponds to one parent app, so they share part of the bundle identifier.

- It also added _XCAppClipURL. If you edit the scheme of the App Clip, you will see an environment variable with that name. The default value is https://example.com. But in order to activate it, you need to activate the checkbox near the name of the variable. When activated, the App Clip will receive this URL as part of scene(_ scene: UIScene, continue userActivity: NSUserActivity) on launch so that you can test the flows that you want to trigger, depending on the URLs that are received.

Apart from this, Xcode also created a new build phase for your main app target that embeds the App Clip inside it:

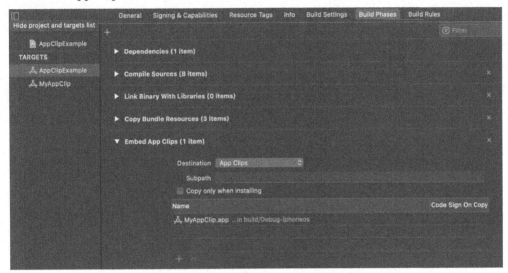

Figure 14.9 – Embed App Clip build phase

So, as you can see, even though creating the App Clip's target is relatively straightforward, there is a lot going on under the hood. Now you know all the bits. Let's launch the App Clip on the iOS simulator (remember to select the MyAppClip App Clip target when launching it). You will see a blank screen. This is fine – we still need to add some code and prepare our App Clip! We'll do this in the next section.

Sharing resources and code with the App Clip

App Clips usually need to reuse code and resources from your main app. They typically consist of some of the features that conform to the entire app. In our case, we are going to create an App Clip that shows everything in our main app, but not the credit card screen. In order to provide a fast and easy App Clip experience, we will only allow our users to view the menu, review their order, and pay with Apple Pay; we don't want them to input any credit card details inside the App Clip.

Let's consider every file and resource that we need from the main app and add them to the target of the App Clip. Let's start with the assets. Follow these steps:

1. From the project navigator, click on the `Assets.xcassets` file, and in the **Options** panel, add it to the App Clip target:

Figure 14.10 – Adding assets to the App Clip target

By doing this, our App Clip target will have access to all the images that we have in the main app. You can also create individual assets files and specify different images/resources for each target. For simplicity, in this example, we will share all of them.

If you opt to use a single `Assets` file for both the app and the App Clip, you can delete the `Assets` file inside the `MyAppClip` folder. Otherwise, you will have two `AppIcon` references (one inside each asset file), and you will get a compile error:

Figure 14.11 – Deleting the second Assets file inside MyAppClip

It is also a good practice to move the main app's `Assets` file to the top of the project and rename it `SharedAssets`. This lets other developers know that the file applies to both targets:

Figure 14.12 – SharedAssets on top of the project

Once you've made these changes, make sure you can build and compile both targets; that is, the app and the App Clip.

Now, let's include the App Clip target, as well as the code that we need. Previously, we mentioned that we want to have the same functionalities that can be found in the main app, except for the credit card screen.

2. In the project navigator, select the following files and add them to the App Clip target:

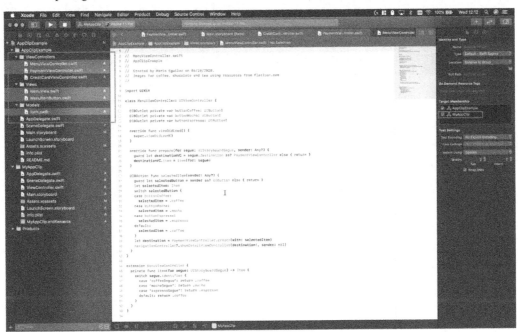

Figure 14.13 – Sharing code files with the App Clip target

Notice how we shared all the files inside the `ViewController`, `Views`, and `Model` folders, except for `CreditCardViewController`.

You have now shared all the images and code that your App Clip will need. However, you still need to reuse some content: the storyboard flow.

3.   Go ahead and open the `Main.storyboard` file in your `AppClipExample` target. Zoom out a bit and select everything except for `CreditCardViewController` (we don't want that one in our App Clip):

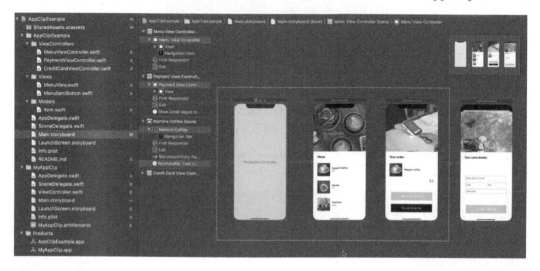

Figure 14.14 – Copying the contents of the Main.storyboard file of your App

4.   Once you've copied the elements highlighted in the previous screenshot, go ahead and paste them into the `Main.storyboard` file of your **MyAppClip** target.

5.   Now, select the **Navigation Controller** option and in the **Options** panel on the right, check the **Is Initial View Controller** option:

Figure 14.15 – Assigning the entry point for your App Clip

Now, you have enough code, resources, and flow in your App Clip to try it out.

6. Select the **MyAppClip** target and launch it. It should compile and run without any issues at this point.

However, there is a problem. If you launch the App Clip and order an item, you will notice that we are still showing the **Pay with Credit Card** button. Previously, we mentioned that we want our App Clip to just use Apple Pay in order to streamline the service, as per Apple's recommendations. In the next section, we will achieve this by learning how to conditionally use parts of our code, depending on which target is executing it, using Active Compilation Conditions.

Using Active Compilation Conditions

In the previous section, we learned how to share code and assets between our app and App Clip. This time, we need to "remove" some pieces of code when the App Clip is executing specific files. Specifically, we want to hide the **Pay with Credit Card** button from our PaymentViewController when the App Clip executes it.

To do this, we need to work with Active Compilation Conditions. Follow these steps:

1. In the **Project Navigator** window, go to **Project | MyAppClip target | Build Settings | Active Compilation Conditions**. In both **Debug** and **Release**, add `APPCLIP` to the list, as shown in the following screenshot:

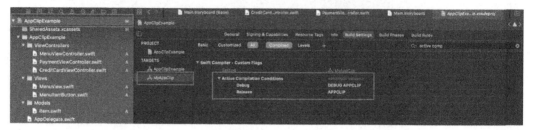

Figure 14.16 – Adding Active Compilation Conditions

2. With the `APPCLIP` flag set, go ahead and open the `PaymentViewController` file. Add the following code at the end of the `viewDidLoad()` method:

```
#if APPCLIP
    buttonPayByCard.isHidden = true
#endif
```

With this piece of code, we are telling the compiler to only add this line when we are executing the App Clip target.

3. Let's try this out. Execute the app and the App Clip and compare both screens. When the App Clip launches, you should not see the **Pay with Credit Card** button:

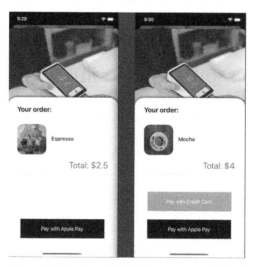

Figure 14.17 – App Clip (left) versus app (right)

As you can see, we have achieved our goal of showing different parts of the UI by using Active Compilation Conditions.

This is great! We have a perfectly configured App Clip that runs and shows the user what we wanted them to see. In the next section, we are going to jump into a critical part of this process: invoking the App Clip.

Configuring, linking, and triggering your App Clip

In this section, and with the App Clip ready to roll, we are going to learn how to configure, link, and trigger the App Clip.

Users can trigger an App Clip by using various invocations, some of which are as follows:

- Scanning an NFC tag or visual code at a physical location
- Tapping a location-based suggestion from Siri Suggestions
- Tapping a link in the Maps app
- Tapping a Smart App Banner on a website
- Tapping a link that someone shared in the Messages app (as a text message only)

To ensure these invocations work, you must configure your App Clip for link handling and also configure the App Store's Connect App Clip Experiences. We will go through this now.

> **Important Note**
> When users install an App Clip's corresponding app, the full app replaces the App Clip. Every invocation from that moment on launches the full app instead of the App Clip. As a result, your full app must handle all possible invocations and offer the App Clip's functionality.

An App Clip needs an entry point for users to be able to discover and launch it. We are going to review three topics in this section:

- Configuring link handling
- Configuring App Clip experiences
- Configuring a Smart App Banner

By the end of this section, our project will have a fully configured App Clip ready to go. Let's get started!

Configuring link handling

Our first step is to configure our web server and App Clip for link handling. You can use the project in the code bundle for this chapter named `AppClipExample_configure_start` to help with this.

If you want to be able to display your App Clip on your website, you need to perform the following steps:

1. Configure the `apple-app-site-association` file on your web server.

2. Add associated domains entitlement to your App Clip.

3. Handle `NSUserActivity` in your App Clip.

4. First, let's configure the `apple-app-site-association` file, as follows:

```
{
    "appclips" : {
      "apps" : ["<Application Identifier Prefix>.<Bundle
          Identifier>"]
    },
    ...
}
```

This file should be located in the root folder of your server. If you have set up universal links, you should have this file already. You need to add the highlighted code to it so that you can reference your App Clip. Remember to use your own Application Identifier Prefix and bundle identifier.

5. Next, let's add the associated domains entitlement. In the **Project Navigator** window, select the project and the App Clip target and go to **Signing & Capabilities**:

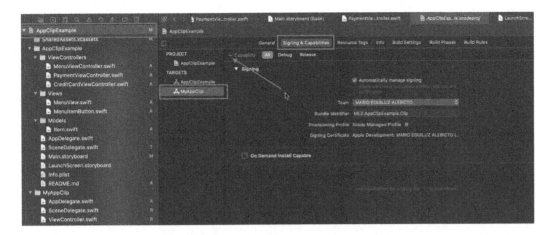

Figure 14.18 – Signing & Capabilities

6. Next, add a new associated domain, as shown in the following screenshot:

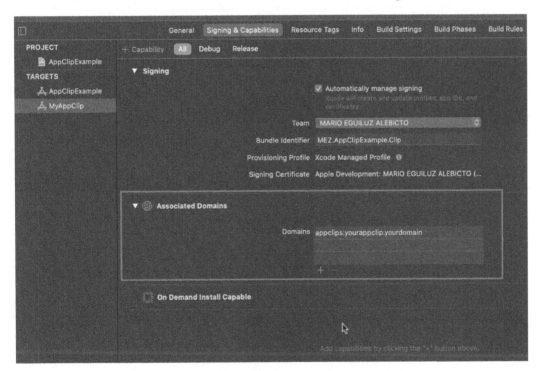

Figure 14.19 – Adding an associated domain

Now that your server and App Clip have been configured, let's handle `NSUserActivity`.

7. Go ahead and edit the App Clip scheme. Under **Run | Arguments**, check the _XCAppClipURL variable and assign it the following value: `https://myappclip.com/test?param=value`.

With this value set, let's learn how to process it.

8. Inside the **MyAppClip** target, open the `SceneDelegate.swift` file. Add the following implementations:

```swift
func scene(_ scene: UIScene, willConnectTo session:
  UISceneSession, options connectionOptions: UIScene.
  ConnectionOptions) {
  for activity in connectionOptions.userActivities {
    self.scene(scene, continue: activity)
  }
}

func scene(_ scene: UIScene, continue userActivity:
  NSUserActivity) {
  // 1
  guard
    userActivity.activityType ==
      NSUserActivityTypeBrowsingWeb,
    let url = userActivity.webpageURL,
    let components = NSURLComponents(url: url,
      resolvingAgainstBaseURL: true) else { return }
  print(url)


  //2
  guard
    let path = components.path,
    let params = components.queryItems else { return }
  print(path)
  print(params)
  // Handle your own navigation based on path and params
}
```

These two methods are handling the NSUserActivity information that your App Clip will receive when it is triggered by an URL-type element. See how, in the scene (...) method, we are checking that the activity is of the NSUserActivityTypeBrowsingWeb type and that we then examine the URL, path, and components elements. Here, you can navigate your App Clip to the correct element. If you launch the App Clip and check the console's output, you will see this:

```
https://myappclip.com/test?param=value
/test
[param=value]
```

As you can see, we are handling the test URL that has been defined in the _XCAppClipURL target environment variable and extracting the required path and components from it. When you want to handle different flows in your App Clip based on the incoming URL, you can test it like this.

If your app has been built with SwiftUI, then you can handle it like this:

```
var body: some Scene {
    WindowGroup {
        ContentView().onContinueUserActivity(
        NSUserActivityTypeBrowsingWeb) { activity in
            guard let url = activity.webpageURL else { return }
            // Navigate to proper flow based on the url
        }
    }
}
```

By defining onContinueUserActivity(NSUserActivityTypeBrowsingWeb) via ContentView, you can use the activity object that is passed and extract the incoming URL from there. By analyzing the URL, you can link to the proper part of your App Clip.

Now that we have configured our server and App Clip so that they handle links, let's continue by configuring our App Clip experiences.

Configuring our App Clip experiences

With the App Clip and your server ready to handle links, we can start configuring our App Clip experiences. App Clip experiences are defined in App Store Connect and define the App Clip Card and the links for different scenarios that you want to handle. An App Clip Card looks like this:

Figure 14.20 – App Clip Card

As shown in the preceding screenshot, the App Clip Card contains the following:

- A header image, describing your app or the App Clip's main feature: In this example we display someone preparing a coffee.

- A title, describing the App Clip name: **Mamine Cafe.**

- A subtitle, describing what feature does the App Clip offer: **Order coffee in 3 taps.**

- A button, describing the action to perform (like open-view the App Clip): **View.**

- Extra info footer: The App Clip's main app and a link to the App Store to download it.

This App Clip Card is what the device will display to the user so that they can launch your App Clip. We will configure it in App Store Connect.

Once you have created the corresponding app via the App Store Connect website and uploaded a build with the App Clip included, you will be able to configure your App Clip Experience:

Figure 14.21 – App Clip Experience configuration

As you can see, there are three main things to configure in the default App Clip Experience:

- **A header image**: Size = 3000 x 2000 px. Aspect Ratio = 3:2. Format = .png/.jpg. No transparency.

- **A copy of the subtitle**: 43 characters maximum.

- **The call to action**: Here, you can choose from Open, View, and Play.

You can also click on **Edit Advanced Experiences** to configure different triggers and flows. If you want to launch your App Clip from NFC tags or visual codes, associate your App Clip with a physical location, or create an App Clip for multiple businesses to use, then you need Advanced Experiences. First, you will need to specify the URL that will trigger the App Clip Experience:

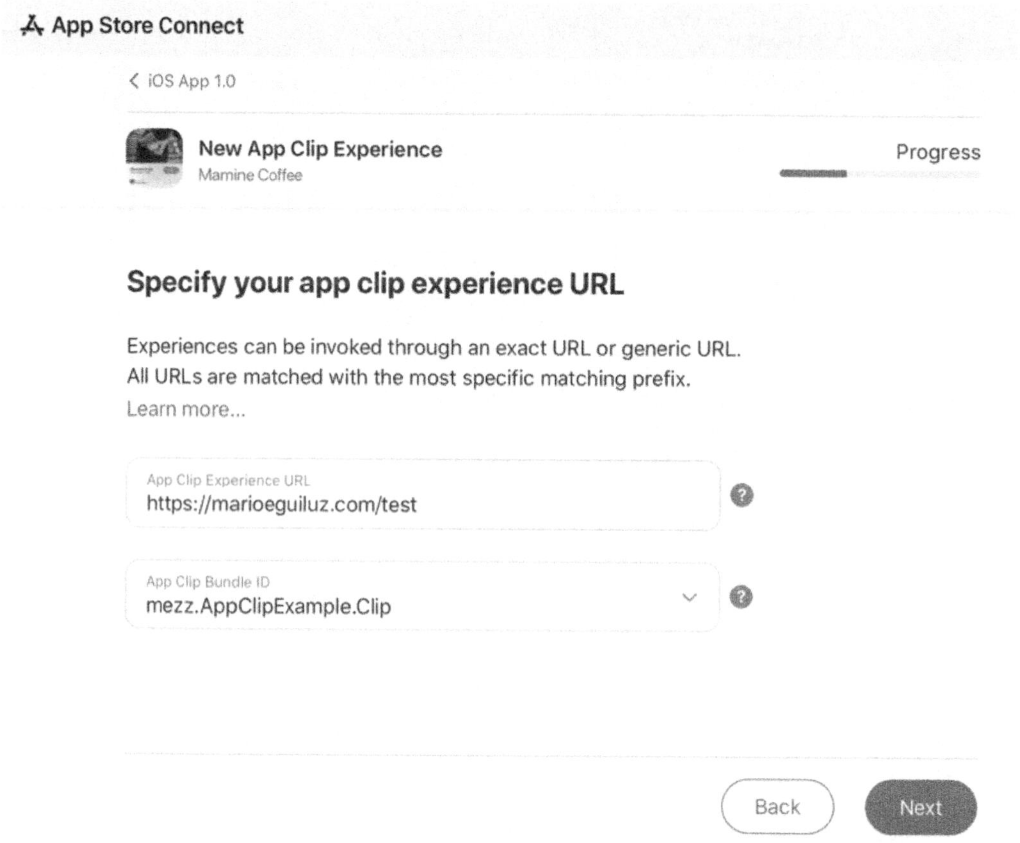

Figure 14.22 – URL configuration to invoke an App Clip Experience

After pressing **Next**, you can configure the App Clip Card:

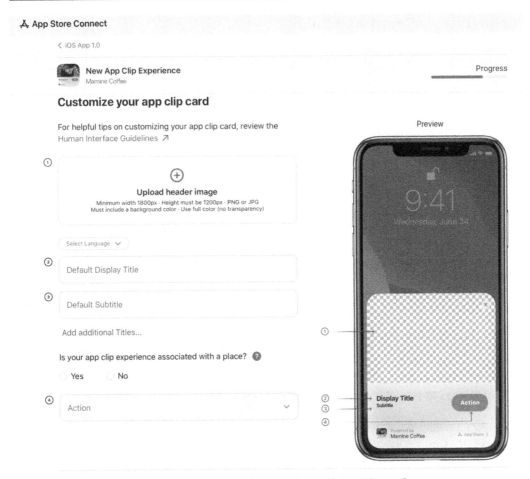

Figure 14.23 – Configuring the advanced App Clip card

At this point, you can configure the language of the card, and even specify whether the experience is triggered at a specific location.

Adding advanced App Clip Experiences allows your App to show different App Clips for different URLs. For example, is you have a coffee shop app, you can have an App Clip for showing the menu, an App Clip for ordering a coffee straight away, an App Clip for displaying your clients' points cards, and so on.

In this section, we learned how to configure an App Clip and its experiences in App Store Connect. Now, let's learn how to configure the Smart App Banner so that you can trigger a banner on your website so that users can display your app and App Clip.

Configuring a Smart App Banner

By adding a Smart App Banner to your website, you're offering your users a fast and native way to discover and launch your app. You need to add the following meta tag to your website HTML files (where you want the banner to be displayed):

```
<meta name="apple-itunes-app" content="app-id=myAppStoreID,
  app-clip-bundle-id=appClipBundleID, affiliate-
    data=myAffiliateData, app-argument=myAppArgument">
```

You need to replace the highlighted values with your own. Also, note that `app-argument` is not available when you're launching an App Clip. Remember that you should add the domain of any page that displays this banner to the app and your App Clip's Associated Domains Entitlements.

In this section, we learned how to configure link handling, App Clip Experiences, and Smart App Banners. In the next section, we'll how to test our App Clip while in development.

Testing your App Clip Experiences

Once you have finished developing and configuring your App Clip, it is time to test everything to double-check that your App Clip Experiences work as expected. There are three ways to test your App Clip Experiences:

- By debugging the invocation URL in Xcode (we have seen this throughout this chapter, when using _XCAppClipURL).

- By creating an App Clip Experience for testers in TestFlight (so that your App is ready for launch and is complete).

- By creating a local experience on a device and testing invocations from NFC or visual codes during development.

Let's dig deeper into this last point. Let's use the `AppClipExample_test` project in this book's code bundle so that we can test our App Clip Experiences on it.

One advantage of testing your App Clip Experiences while in development with Local Experiences is that you don't need to configure your associated domains, make changes to your server, or deal with TestFlight. We can do everything locally. Let's get started:

1. First, build and run your app and App Clip on any device. Then, on the device, open **Settings | Developer | Local Experiences** and select **Register Local Experience…**:

Figure 14.24 – Local Experiences setup

2. Now, you can configure the Local Experience, as shown in the following screenshot. Remember to use your own values for the app:

Figure 14.25 – Local Experience data

To launch the App Clip Card, you can use any tool that allows you to generate a QR code or NFC tag with the same URL you specified in the preceding screen (under **URL PREFIX**). Upon doing this, your App Clip Card should appear when you scan it with your device.

Important Note

The bundle ID that's defined in Local Experience must match the bundle ID of your App Clip.

The App Clip must be installed on the device.

If the camera app doesn't open the App Clip, try using the QR Code Scanner from the Control Center of iOS (if you don't have it, you can add it by going to **Settings | Control Center**).

In this section, we learned how to configure Local Experiences in order to test our App Clip Cards while they're in development. Now, let's wrap up this chapter.

Summary

In this chapter, we reviewed one of the best new features of iOS 14: App Clips. We explained what an App Clip is, what the user journey is, which features we should focus on when developing an App Clip, and which options are available for invoking them.

After learning the basics, we developed and configured our first App Clip for a coffee shop app. We refactored the project so that we could share code and resources between the app and the App Clip. We then learned how to use **Active Compilation Conditions** to trigger pieces of our code base, but only for the App Clip or the app itself, as well as how to configure our app and server for link handling.

Finally, we learned how to configure the App Clip Experiences in App Store Connect and how to test them while in development.

In the next chapter, you will learn about the Vision Framework.

15
Recognition with Vision Framework

The Vision framework has been available to developers for a few years now. Apple has been introducing better and better features for it, from text recognition to image recognition. On iOS 14, Vision comes with more improvements to text recognition and other existing functions, but it also allows developers to perform two different actions: hand and body pose recognition. The possibilities that these new features open up for developers are limitless! Just think about gym apps, yoga apps, health apps, and so on.

In this chapter, we are going to learn about the basics of the Vision framework and how to use the new advancements in text recognition. We will also learn about the new hand landmark recognition, building a demo app that can detect the tips of the four fingers and the thumb. The chapter code bundle also provides a similar example demonstrating body pose recognition. We will discuss these topics in the following sections:

- Introduction to the Vision framework
- Recognizing text in images
- Recognizing hand landmarks in real time

By the end of this chapter, you will be able to work with the Vision framework with total confidence, being able to apply the techniques explained in this chapter to implement any type of recognition that Vision provides, from the recognition of text in images to the recognition of hand and body poses in videos.

Technical requirements

The code bundle for this chapter includes a starter project called `HandDetection_start` and a couple of playground files named `Vision.playground` and `RecognitionPerformance_start.playground`. It also contains a completed example for body pose detection named `BodyPoseDetection_completed`. You can find them in the code bundle repository:

```
https://github.com/PacktPublishing/Mastering-iOS-14-
Programming-4th-Edition
```

Introduction to the Vision framework

Since the beginning of the App Store, there have been many apps that use the camera to build great functionalities using image and video recognition. Think of the bank apps that can now scan a check or a credit card so that the user doesn't need to input all the numbers. There are networking apps that can take a picture of a business card and extract the relevant information. Even the Photos app from your iPhone can detect faces in your photographs and classify them.

The Vision framework provides developers with a robust set of features to make it easier than ever to achieve these functionalities: from text and image recognition to barcode detection, face landmarks analysis, and now, with iOS 14, hand and body pose recognition.

Vision also allows the use of Core ML models to allow developers to enhance object classification and detection in their apps. Vision has been available since iOS 11 and macOS 10.13.

There are several concepts in Vision that are common to any type of detection (text detection, image detection, barcode detection, and so on), including the `VNRequest`, `VNRequestHandler`, and `VNObservation` entities:

- `VNRequest` is the task that we want to perform. For example, `VNDetectAnimalRequest` would be used to detect animals in a picture.

- `VNRequestHandler` is how we want to detect. It lets us define a completion handler where we can play around with the results and shape them in the way that we need.

- `VNObservation` encapsulates the results.

Let's look at an example that combines all these concepts and shows how Vision can easily help us to detect text inside an image. Open the playground named `Vision.playground`. This example code is grabbing an image from a specific URL and trying to extract/detect any text on it. The image being used is this one:

Figure 15.01 – Example image to extract text with Vision

If we try to extract text from this image, we should get results such as *Swift Data Structure and Algorithms*, or the name of the authors, or the description below the title. Let's review the code in the playground:

```
import Vision
```

```
let imageUrl = URL(string: "http://marioeguiluz.com/img/
    portfolio/Swift%20Data%20Structures%20and%20Algorithms%20
    Mario%20Eguiluz.jpg")!
```

```swift
// 1. Create a new image-request handler.
let requestHandler = VNImageRequestHandler(url: imageUrl,
  options: [:])


// 2. Create a new request to recognize text.
let request = VNRecognizeTextRequest { (request, error) in
  guard let observations = request.results as?
    [VNRecognizedTextObservation] else { return }

  let recognizedStrings = observations.compactMap { observation
    in

    // Return the string of the top VNRecognizedText instance.
    return observation.topCandidates(1).first?.string
  }


  // Process the recognized strings.
  print(recognizedStrings)
}


// 3. Select .accurate or .fast levels
request.recognitionLevel = .accurate


do {
  // 4. Perform the text-recognition request.
  try requestHandler.perform([request])
} catch {
  print("Unable to perform the requests: \(error).")
}
```

Let's go through the numbered comments:

1. First, we are creating a `VNImageRequestHandler` instance with a given image URL. We instantiate this handler to perform Vision requests on an image. Remember that we need to call `perform(_:)` later on to launch the analysis.

2. Now we create a `request` (`VNRecognizeTextRequest`) instance that we will perform on the `requestHandler` instance instantiated previously. You can perform multiple requests on a `requestHandler` instance. We define a block of code to be executed when the request finishes. In this block, we are extracting the observations from the request results (`VNRecognizedTextObservation` instances). These observations will contain potential outcomes for the analyzed text from the image (`VNRecognizedText` instances). We print `topCandidate` from each observation, which should be the best match according to the Vision parameters.

3. We can specify the recognition level for the request. In this example, we are using `.accurate` (the alternative is `.fast`). We will see later the results with `.fast` and when to use one or the other.

4. Finally, we are performing the request on the `requestHandler` instance to execute everything with the `perform(_:)` method.

If you execute the code, the console in the playground will display the following:

```
["Erik Azar, Mario Eguiluz", "Swift Data", "Structure and",
"Algorithms", "Master the most common algorithms and data
structures,", "and learn how to implement them efficiently
using the most", "up-to-date features of Swift", "Packt>"]
```

Those seem to be great results, right? If you recheck the image, we are extracting the correct text from it! The author names, the title (per line), the description, and more! Seems to be a great result! But have you noticed that when you execute the playground, it takes a while to finish? This is because we are using the `.accurate` option. Let's see what happens if we use `.fast` instead. Change it in the playground code:

```
// 3. Select .accurate or .fast levels
request.recognitionLevel = .fast
```

The output is as follows:

```
["Swift Data", "Structure and", "Algorithms",
"upto4atefeaturesofSwift3", "Packt>", "ErfkAz•r.
M•rb Eguluz", "ml5tertket(w4VIthMsarodats5tr&KtUre",
"learnItolpIettmeffK1WttIY5lt1fft", "LIJJ"]
```

This time, the analysis can be done faster, but as you can see, the results are far worse for what we wanted (we wanted to detect the text properly!). Why should anyone prefer speed over accuracy? Well, for some apps, speed is critical and it is fine to sacrifice some accuracy for it. Think of real-time camera-based translations or applying real-time filters to take photos. In these scenarios, you need fast processing. We will discuss this further later in the chapter.

This playground example should help you to have a grasp of the incredible potential that Vision contains. Just with a few lines of code, we were able to process and extract the text of an image with no issues or complex operations. Vision allows developers to do amazing things. Let's dive deeper into it in the following sections, starting with a more detailed look at text detection for images.

Recognizing text in images

The Vision framework has been improving its detection of text in images since its first iteration. In this section, we are going to learn some state-of-the-art techniques to obtain the best results on iOS 14.

We saw in the previous section that text detection in Vision can happen in two different ways, as defined by the value of `recognitionLevel` that we specify in the request: `.fast` and `.accurate`. Let's see the differences:

- **Fast recognition**: This uses character recognition to detect text character by character within a bounding box. It is optimized for real-time recognition and uses a smaller memory footprint than `.accurate`. It doesn't handle rotated text or different fonts as well as the `.accurate` method.

- **Accurate recognition**: This uses a neural network to detect strings and full lines, and then recognizes the words and sentences. By using a neural network and identifying words, the framework can detect or correct observations for certain characters that are difficult to extract. It takes more time than `.fast` but is more accurate (of course!). It works in the same way that our brain recognizes words. If you read the word "m0untain," your brain can extract "mountain" from it, and it knows that the 0 (zero) stands for an o. If you use `.fast`, which recognizes character by character, the 0 (zero) would still be a 0 (zero) in your results, because no context is taken into account.

In both cases, after the initial recognition phase is finished, results are passed into a traditional natural language processor for language processing, and the outcome of that is the results (observations). This whole process happens exclusively on the device.

So, when should anyone use `.fast`, you might wonder. Well, there are scenarios in which it is more convenient than `.accurate`:

- To read codes or barcodes quickly

- When user interactivity is a crucial aspect, so you want a fast response from the text detection

To demonstrate the differences between the recognition levels, let's analyze the same image using different techniques. You will also learn some useful tricks that you can apply to your projects. Follow the steps given here:

1. Go ahead and open the playground named `RecognitionPerformance_ start.playground`. The code is roughly the same as what we tried in the previous section.

    The only difference is that the image that we are using now contains a 4-digit number that represents the serial number of the book:

Figure 15.02 – Book cover with a serial number (1015) below the author names

If you pay close attention to the number font, you will see that it might be tricky for a computer to tell whether some digits are numbers or letters. This has been done on purpose. In this example, we are going to test the capabilities of Vision.

2. Go ahead and execute the playground code. The console output should look like this:

```
["Erik Azar, Mario Eguiluz", "1015", "Swift Data",
"Structure and", "Algorithms", "Master the most common
algorithms and data structures,", "and learn how to
implement them efficiently using the most", "up-to-date
features of Swift", "Packt>"]
1.9300079345703125 seconds
```

We have successfully retrieved the serial number of the book: 1015. The code is also taking a measure of how long it takes to finish the text-recognition process. In our case, it was **1.93 seconds** (this can differ from computer to computer and also between executions). Can we do better than that? Let's try out some techniques that will help us to improve this processing time while keeping the same accuracy. We are going to start with the **region of interest**.

Region of interest

Sometimes, when we are analyzing an image with Vision, we don't need to process the whole image. For example, if we are processing a specific type of form where we know in advance that the first name always goes at the top of the document, we may want to just process that area. Processing the whole form would only waste time and resources if we just need a specific area.

Let's assume that in the previous example (the book cover), the serial number that we want to extract is always in the top-left area. How can we speed up the 1.93-seconds processing time? We can do so by defining a region of interest. Defining a region of interest will tell Vision to only process that area and avoid the rest of the image. That will result in a faster processing time.

`regionOfInterest` is a `CGRect` property of `VNRequest`:

- It defines a rectangular area in which the request will be performed.

- The rectangle is normalized to the dimensions of the image, meaning that the width and height of the region of interest go from 0 to 1.

- The origin of the rectangle is in the bottom-left corner of the image, which is (0,0). The top-right corner will be (1,1).

- The default value is `{{0,0},{1,1}}`, which covers everything from the bottom-left corner (0,0) to the top-right corner, with width 1 and height 1: the whole image.

In the following figure, you can see the region of interest that we need to define to capture the serial number (**1015**):

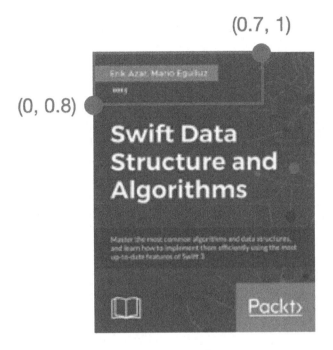

Figure 15.03 – Region of interest

Let's add that region to the code from the previous section:

1. In the `ScanPerformance_start.playground` project, add the following code just after setting `recognitionLevel` to `.accurate`:

    ```
    request.regionOfInterest = CGRect(x: 0, y: 0.8, width:
        0.7, height: 0.2)
    ```

2. Now launch the playground and check the result in the console:

    ```
    ["Erik Azar, Mario Eguiluz", "1015"]
    1.2314139604568481 seconds
    ```

There are a couple of differences when comparing these results to the previous ones:

*   We are no longer extracting that much text. Now that we are defining a region of interest, we just extract the words/digits that are contained in that area.

*   We reduced the processing time from 1.93 seconds to 1.23 seconds. That is 36% faster.

3. Let's now try to reduce the region of interest to catch just the serial number. Modify the region to the following:

```
request.regionOfInterest = CGRect(x: 0, y: 0.8, width:
    0.3, height: 0.1)
```

4. Launch the playground. Now the console output is as follows:

```
["1015"]
```
```
0.8156689405441284 seconds
```

Great! If we have to work with the results now, we don't need to do extra work to discard values that we don't need. We reduced the region of interest to pinpoint the exact string that we needed and saved some processing time.

At this point, why don't we try to use `.fast` for `recognitionLevel` instead of `.accurate`, if what we want is speed? Let's see what happens.

5. Modify this line to use `.fast`:

```
request.recognitionLevel = .fast
```

6. Save and execute. Check the console output:

```
["Iois"]
```
```
0.5968900661468506 seconds
```

You can see how this time, the processing time has been made shorter again, but the result is not accurate at all. Instead of detecting `1015`, we have wrongly obtained `Iois`.

However, there is a common way to fix this situation in scenarios where we have domain knowledge. In our case, we know that the processed characters should be numbers only. Therefore, we can adjust the output from Vision to improve the results and fix misclassifications. For example, see the following adjustments:

- The character "I" can be "1."

- The character "o" can be "0."

- The character "s" can be "5."

Let's implement this in the code:

1. At the very end of the playground file, add the following method:

```
extension Character {
    func transformToDigit() -> Character {
        let conversionTable = [
            "s": "5",
            "S": "5",
            "o": "0",
            "O": "0",
            "i": "1",
            "I": "1"
        ]
        var current = String(self)
        if let alternativeChar = conversionTable[current] {
            current = alternativeChar
        }
        return current.first!
    }
}
```

We are extending the `Character` class by adding a new method named `transformToDigit()`. This new method is going to help us to improve potential misclassifications. Note how in the method itself, we have a table of letter characters that relate to a similarly shaped number. What we are doing is just transforming those letters into the corresponding digits.

2. Let's use it now. Below the `print(recognizedStrings)` line, add the following code:

```
if let serialNumber = recognizedStrings.first {
    let serialNumberDigits = serialNumber.map {
        $0.transformToDigit() }
    print(serialNumberDigits)
}
```

We are getting the result of the Vision process; in our case, it was `"Iois"`, and for each character, we are applying to it our new `transformToDigit()` method.

3. Execute the code, and you will see the following result in the console:

```
["Iois"]
["1", "0", "1", "5"]
0.5978780269622803 seconds
```

That looks great! Note how the `"Iois"` result is now looking much better when transformed to `"1"` `"0"` `"1"` `"5"`. Also, note how the processing time didn't increase that much; this operation is relatively easy to compute.

Now let's summarize what we have done in this section and the improvements we made in each step. We started by processing a whole image and using the `.accurate` recognition level, and that took us 1.93 seconds. Then, we applied a region of interest to just process part of the image that we were interested in, reducing the processing time to 1.23 seconds. After that, we changed from `.accurate` to `.fast`. This move reduced the processing time to 0.59 seconds, but the results were incorrect. Finally, we implemented an easy algorithm to improve the results and make them as good as with the `.accurate` level. So, in the end, we got perfect results and a processing time of 0.59 seconds rather than 1.93!

In the next section, you will learn about one of the new features of iOS14, hand detection.

Recognizing hand landmarks in real time

One of the additions to Vision in iOS 14 is hand detection. This new feature to detect hands in images and video allows developers to find with great detail the positions of the wrist and the individual fingers in a video frame or photo.

In this section, we are going to explain the basics behind hand detection, and we will demonstrate how it works with a sample project. Let's start with the hand landmarks that we will be able to recognize.

Understanding hand landmarks

There are 21 landmarks that we will be able to detect in a hand:

- 4 in the thumb
- 4 in each finger (16 in total)
- 1 in the wrist

As you can see, Vision differentiates between finger and thumb. In both the finger and thumb, there are 4 points of interest. The following figure shows how these landmarks are distributed:

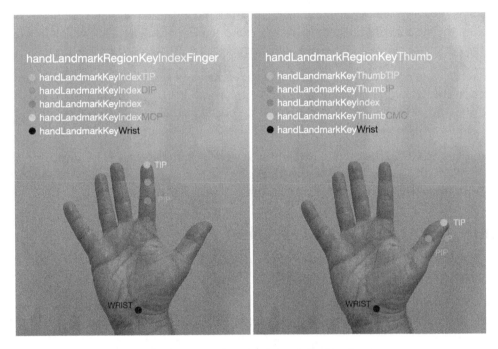

Figure 15.04 – Finger and thumb landmarks

Note how there is also a landmark in the middle of the wrist.

For the four fingers, we can access each of them individually using the following keys:

- `littleFinger`
- `middleFinger`
- `ringFinger`
- `indexFinger`

Inside each of them, we can access the four different landmarks:

- **TIP**
- **DIP**
- **PIP**
- **MCP**

Note how for the thumb, these names are slightly different (TIP, IP, PIP, and CMC). In the example code that we will build later in this section, we will demonstrate how to use these points and each of the fingers plus the thumb.

Vision is capable of detecting more than just one hand at a time. We can specify the maximum amount of hands that we want to detect. This parameter will have an impact on the performance of our detection. Use `maximumHandCount` to set the limit.

For performance and accuracy, it is also better if the hand is not near the edges of the frame, if the light conditions are good, and if the hands are perpendicular to the camera angle (so the whole hand is visible, not just the edge of it). Also, take into account that feet can be recognized as hands sometimes, so avoid mixing them.

That is enough theory; let's jump straight into a code example! We will build a demo app that will be able to detect hand landmarks using the front video camera of a phone and will display an overlay on the detected points.

Implementing hand detection

In this section, we are going to implement a demo app that will be able to detect hand landmarks using the front video camera of a phone.

The code bundle of this project contains the initial project and also the final result. Go ahead and open the project named `HandDetection_start`.

The project contains two main files: A `UIView` instance named `CameraView.swift` and a `UIViewController` instance called `CameraViewController.swift`.

The view contains helper methods to draw points on coordinates. It will serve as an overlay to draw on top of the camera feed. Just know that the `showPoints(_ points: [CGPoint], colour: UIColor)` method will allow us to draw an array of `CGPoint` structs into the overlay on top of the video camera feed.

The view controller will be the centerpiece of the example and is where we are going to implement the relevant code to perform the hand detection. Go ahead and open the `CameraViewController.swift` file. Let's examine the code skeleton that we will fill out step by step.

At the top of the file, we are defining four properties:

- **The Vision hand detection request**: `handPoseRequest`: `VNDetectHumanHandPoseRequest`. We will apply this request at the top of the video stream, to detect hand landmarks in each frame. If we detect any, we will display some points in the overlay to show them.

- **The properties to work with the front video queue, the overlay, and the video stream**: `videoDataOutputQueue`, `cameraView`, and `cameraFeedSession`.

With the `viewDidAppear` and `viewWillDisappear` methods, we are starting/ creating and stopping `AVCaptureSession` for the camera.

And finally, in the next four methods, we have four TODO comments, which we are going to implement one by one to create this app. Let's summarize the TODO tasks that we are going to perform:

- **TODO 1**: Detect one hand only.

- **TODO 2**: Create a video session.

- **TODO 3**: Perform hand detection on the video session.

- **TODO 4**: Process and display detected points.

We are going to implement these four tasks in the following subsections.

Detecting hands

Vision can do more than detect one hand at a time. The more hands we ask it to detect, the more it will impact performance. In our example, we only want to detect one hand. By setting `maximumHandCount` to 1 on the request, we will improve performance.

Let's start by adding this code below `// TODO 1`:

```
// TODO 1: Detect one hand only.
handPoseRequest.maximumHandCount = 1
```

Now, let's create a video session to capture the video stream from the front video camera of the device.

Creating a video session

For the second task, we are going to fill out the code inside the `setupAVSession()` method. Go ahead and paste the following code inside the method:

```
// TODO 2: Create video session
// 1 - Front camera as input
guard let videoDevice = AVCaptureDevice.default(.
   builtInWideAngleCamera, for: .video, position: .front) else {
   fatalError("No front camera.")
}
// 2- Capture input from the camera
guard let deviceInput = try? AVCaptureDeviceInput(device:
   videoDevice) else {
   fatalError("No video device input.")
}
```

First, we are creating a `videoDevice: AVCaptureDevice` instance by querying for the video front camera (if it exists!) with this:

```
guard let videoDevice = AVCaptureDevice.default(.
   builtInWideAngleCamera, for: .video, position: .front) else {
   fatalError("No front camera.")
}
```

Then, we use that `videoDevice` to generate a `deviceInput: AVCaptureDeviceInput` instance, which will be the video device used for the stream, with the following code:

```
guard let deviceInput = try? AVCaptureDeviceInput(device:
   videoDevice) else {
   fatalError("No video device input.")
}
```

Now add this code:

```
let session = AVCaptureSession()
session.beginConfiguration()
session.sessionPreset = AVCaptureSession.Preset.high
```

```
// Add video input to session
guard session.canAddInput(deviceInput) else {
  fatalError("Could not add video device input to the session")
}
session.addInput(deviceInput)


let dataOutput = AVCaptureVideoDataOutput()
if session.canAddOutput(dataOutput) {
  session.addOutput(dataOutput)
  // Add a video data output.
  dataOutput.alwaysDiscardsLateVideoFrames = true
  dataOutput.videoSettings = [kCVPixelBufferPixelFormatTypeKey
      as String: Int(kCVPixelFormatType_420YpCbCr8BiPlanarFull
      Range)]
  dataOutput.setSampleBufferDelegate(self, queue:
      videoDataOutputQueue)
} else {
  fatalError("Could not add video data output to the session")
}
session.commitConfiguration()
cameraFeedSession = session
```

After creating the `videoDevice` instance, we are creating a new `session`:
`AVCaptureSession` instance. With the session created, we assign `videoDevice` as the
input and create and configure an output to handle the video stream. We assign the class
itself as `dataOutput AVCaptureVideoDataOutputSampleBufferDelegate`
by calling this:

```
dataOutput.setSampleBufferDelegate(self, queue:
  videoDataOutputQueue)
```

This means that when the front video camera captures new frames, our session will handle
them and send them to our delegate method, which we are going to implement in the next
step (TODO 3).

Performing hand detection in the video session

Now that we have set up and configured a video session, it is time to handle every frame as it comes and tries to detect any hands and their landmarks! We need to implement the `captureOutput(_ output: AVCaptureOutput, didOutput sampleBuffer: CMSampleBuffer, from connection: AVCaptureConnection)` method.

Under the `// TODO 3: Perform hand detection on the video session` line, add this code:

```
var thumbTip: CGPoint?
var indexTip: CGPoint?
var ringTip: CGPoint?
var middleTip: CGPoint?
var littleTip: CGPoint?
```

We want to detect the tip of the four fingers (index, ring, middle, and little) and the thumb. So, we are creating five variables of type `CGPoint` to store their coordinates, if they are found.

Just after these new lines, add the following code:

```
let handler = VNImageRequestHandler(cmSampleBuffer:
  sampleBuffer, orientation: .up, options: [:])
do {
  try handler.perform([handPoseRequest])
  guard let observation = handPoseRequest.results?.first else {
    return
  }


    // Get observation points

} catch {
  cameraFeedSession?.stopRunning()
  fatalError(error.localizedDescription)
}
```

With this code, we are asking Vision to execute `handPoseRequest` over `sampleBuffer` (the video stream). Then, we guard (using `guard`) against the case in which we don't detect any observations (so that if there is no hand in the video frame, we just stop at this point).

But if the guard doesn't trigger, it means that we have some hand landmarks and we need to process them. Add the following code just after the // Get observation points line:

```
let thumbPoints = try observation.recognizedPoints(.thumb)
let indexFingerPoints = try observation.recognizedPoints(.
    indexFinger)
let ringFingerPoints = try observation.recognizedPoints(.
    ringFinger)
let middleFingerPoints = try observation.recognizedPoints(.
    middleFinger)
let littleFingerPoints = try observation.recognizedPoints(.
    littleFinger)


guard let littleTipPoint = littleFingerPoints[.littleTip],
  let middleTipPoint = middleFingerPoints[.middleTip], let
    ringTipPoint = ringFingerPoints[.ringTip], let indexTipPoint
    = indexFingerPoints[.indexTip], let thumbTipPoint =
    thumbPoints[.thumbTip] else {
    return
}
```

Now we are extracting from the observation any instances of recognizedPoints() that are related to the thumb and the four fingers. Note that we use try to do this operation because a result is not guaranteed. With the extracted recognized points, we later unwrap the TIP point of each finger and thumb with the guard statement.

At this point, we should have five variables with the coordinates of the TIP point of each finger plus the thumb.

Although we already have the five coordinates that we are looking for, we still need to perform an extra step. Vision coordinates are different from AVFoundation ones. Let's transform them; add the following code just after the last guard statement:

```
thumbTip = CGPoint(x: thumbTipPoint.location.x, y: 1 -
    thumbTipPoint.location.y)
indexTip = CGPoint(x: indexTipPoint.location.x, y: 1 -
    indexTipPoint.location.y)
ringTip = CGPoint(x: ringTipPoint.location.x, y: 1 -
    ringTipPoint.location.y)
```

```
middleTip = CGPoint(x: middleTipPoint.location.x, y: 1 -
  middleTipPoint.location.y)
```

```
littleTip = CGPoint(x: littleTipPoint.location.x, y: 1 -
  littleTipPoint.location.y)
```

As you can see, the x coordinate is the same in both systems, but the y coordinate is different. In Vision, the bottom-left corner is the (0,0). So, we just need to subtract the y coordinate of the Vision point to 1 to get a result on the AVFoundation system.

Great! At this point, we have the hand landmarks detection system up and running, with a result in the form of AVFoundation CGPoint coordinates. The last step is to draw those points!

Add the following code after the catch block (outside of it), just at the end of the func captureOutput (...) method:

```
DispatchQueue.main.sync {
  self.processPoints([thumbTip, indexTip, ringTip, middleTip,
    littleTip])
}
```

We are calling the processPoints (...) method inside the main thread because we want it to work on the UI, so we ensure that everything works perfectly by dispatching this work into the correct thread. Let's implement the processPoints (...) method next.

Processing and displaying detected points

After the hand landmarks have been detected inside the captureOutput (...) method, we now want to draw them into the camera overlay. Replace the empty implementation of processPoints (...) with this one:

```
func processPoints(_ fingerTips: [CGPoint?]) {
  // Convert points from AVFoundation coordinates to UIKit
    // coordinates.
  let previewLayer = cameraView.previewLayer
  let convertedPoints = fingerTips
    .compactMap {$0}
    .compactMap {previewLayer.
      layerPointConverted(fromCaptureDevicePoint: $0)}

  // Display converted points in the overlay
  cameraView.showPoints(convertedPoints, color: .red)
}
```

Remember how we are using `CGPoints` converted to `AVFoundation` coordinates? Now we want to convert those points into the `UIKit` preview layer. We are performing `map` over them, and finally, we are calling the `cameraView` helper method `showPoints` to display them.

Everything is now in place! It is time to build and run the application. You will see the selfie camera triggering, and if you point it at your hand, the tips of your fingers and thumb should be overlayed with red dots. Give it a try and you should get something like the following:

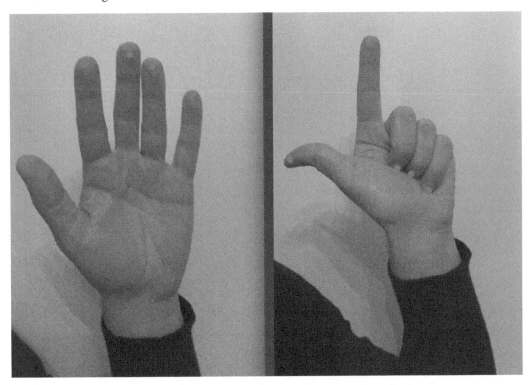

Figure 15.05 – TIP detection

However, this approach still has some issues! Try this: let the app detect your hand, and then remove the hand from the camera's view – the red dots are still on the overlay! They are not cleaned up when no hand is detected.

This has an easy fix. The reason for it is that inside the `captureOutput(...)` method, we are not always executing the `processPoints(...)` method. There are times (the `guard` statements) where we return without calling it. The solution is to wrap the `processPoints(...)` block into a `defer`, moving it to the beginning of the code, just after we define the five properties to store the coordinates of each tip. It should look like this:

```
public func captureOutput(_ output: AVCaptureOutput,
    didOutput sampleBuffer: CMSampleBuffer, from connection:
    AVCaptureConnection) {

  var thumbTip: CGPoint?
  var indexTip: CGPoint?
  var ringTip: CGPoint?
  var middleTip: CGPoint?
  var littleTip: CGPoint?

  defer {
    DispatchQueue.main.sync {
      self.processPoints([thumbTip, indexTip, ringTip,
        middleTip, littleTip])
    }
  }

  ...
}
```

The highlighted code is the part that we have wrapped into a `defer` (so it will always execute before returning the method). Execute the app again, and you will notice that when there is no hand on the screen, the red dots will not be there either! We are calling `processPoints` with empty values, so nothing is being drawn. With this last step, we have a working example of hand landmark detection up and running! Congratulations!

Body pose detection

Vision also provides body pose detection on iOS 14. Body pose detection is quite similar to hand detection, so we are not going to give a step-by-step demo of it. But the code bundle of this book contains an example app similar to the one in this section but for body pose detection. You can check out the project named `BodyPoseDetection_completed` and see the little differences that it has from the hand detection project.

In this section, we have learned about the new Vision methods to detect hand landmarks and how to detect hand landmarks using the video stream of a phone as input (instead of just detecting a hand in a static image). We also provided a similar demo that can be used for body pose detection. Let's jump into the summary to finish the chapter.

Summary

We started this chapter by learning about the basic building blocks of every Vision feature: how to use a `VNRequest` instance, its corresponding `VNRequestHandler` instances, and the resulting `VNObservation` instances.

After learning the basics, we applied them to text recognition. We compared different recognition levels by using `.fast` and `.accurate`. We also learned about regions of interest and how they can affect the performance of Vision requests. Finally, we improved our results in text recognition by applying domain knowledge, fixing potential errors and misreads from Vision.

Finally, we learned about the new hand landmarks recognition capability. But this time, we also learned how to apply Vision requests to real-time video streams. We were able to detect hand landmarks in a video feed from a device's front camera and display an overlay to show the results. This chapter also provided a similar example that could be applied to body pose recognition.

In the next chapter, we will learn about a brand new feature of iOS 14: widgets!

16

Creating Your First Widget

With iOS 14, Apple introduced WidgetKit. Users are now able to use widgets on their home screens. By displaying small amounts of useful information on the home screen, widgets provide a key functionality to users that was long-awaited. Some examples are checking stock market prices, weather or traffic conditions, the next meeting on your calendar, and so on with just a glance at the home screen. The use cases are limitless!

In this chapter, you will learn about the basic foundations of WidgetKit, as well as the key aspects of widget design and their limitations. Then, we will build a widget from scratch. Starting with a very simple, small-sized widget, we will extend its capabilities by creating new sizes, network calls, dynamic configurations, placeholder views, and much more! We will discuss all these topics in the following sections:

- Introducing widgets and WidgetKit
- Developing your first widget

By the end of this chapter, you will be able to create your own widgets to enable your apps to provide a unique new feature so that users will download your app and engage with it much more.

Technical requirements

The code bundle for this chapter includes a starter project called `CryptoWidget_1_small_start` and subsequent parts. You can find them in the code bundle repository:

```
https://github.com/PacktPublishing/Mastering-iOS-14-
Programming-4th-Edition
```

Introducing widgets and WidgetKit

In this section, we are going to learn about the basics of WidgetKit and the options and guidelines for widgets in iOS 14.

Users and developers have been requesting a particular feature for years: they all wanted to have widgets on their home screen. Widgets allow users to configure, personalize, and consume little pieces of relevant data from their home screen. They also enable developers to offer users glanceable content and create added value to their apps.

Here is a preview of what a **widget** (in this case, the Calendar and Reminders widgets) looks like on the home screen of the iPhone:

Figure 16.1 – iOS home screen with widgets

This is now possible on iOS 14 and macOS 11 and later. Developers can create widgets across iOS, iPadOS, and macOS using **WidgetKit** and the new **widget API** for SwiftUI.

Smart Stack on iOS 14 contains a set of different widgets, including ones that the user opens frequently. If the user enables **Smart Rotate**, Siri can highlight relevant widgets within custom stacks.

Widgets created on iOS 13 and earlier

Widgets created before iOS 14 can't be placed on the home screen, but they are still available on the Today view and in the macOS Notification Center.

After this intro to the new widget feature, let's see what options we have when building a widget and what the design guidelines from Apple are.

Widget options

Users can place widgets on the home screen or the Today view on iOS, the Today view on iPad, or the Notification Center on macOS.

Widgets come in three sizes: small, medium, and large. Each size should have a different purpose; a bigger version of a widget should not just be the same as the small one but with bigger font and images. The idea behind having different sizes for a widget is that the bigger the size, the more information it should contain. For example, a weather widget will provide just the current temperature in the small-sized version, but it will also include the weekly forecast in the medium-sized one.

Users can arrange widgets on different parts of their screen, and even create stacks of widgets to group them up.

In order to develop a widget, developers need to create a new extension for their app: a **widget extension**. They can configure the widget with a timeline provider. A timeline provider updates the widget information when needed.

Suppose a widget needs some configuration (for example, selecting a default city in a weather app, or multiple cities to display in a large-sized weather widget). In that case, developers should add a custom Siri intent to the widget extension. Creating a custom Siri intent automatically provides the widget with a customization interface for the user.

Widget guidelines

When creating a widget for iOS 14 or macOS 11, take into account the following design guidelines:

- Focus your widget on the main feature of your app. For example, if your app is about the stock market, your widget could display the user portfolio's total value.

- Each widget size should display a different amount of information. If your cycling tracker widget displays the current calories burned today in the small size, it can also display the week's calories per day in the medium size, and add extra info such as the number of km/miles traveled on the big size.

- Prefer dynamic information that changes during the day to fixed information; it will make your widget more appealing to the user.

- Prefer simple widgets with fewer configuration options to the opposite.

- Widgets offer tap target and detection, letting the user select and tap on them to open detailed information in the app. Small-sized widgets support a single tap target; medium- and big-sized widgets support multiple targets. Try to keep it simple.

- Support dark mode. Also consider using SF Pro as the font and SF Symbols if needed.

In this section, we learned about the new widget feature and WidgetKit. We covered the different options available and the design guidelines when building a widget. In the next section, we will start building a simple widget from scratch, and we will add more features step by step.

Developing your first widget

In this section, we will use an existing app to create a widget on top of it step by step.

The app that we will work on is a crypto ticker, in which the user can check the latest prices of different cryptocurrencies. We will create a widget that will allow users to glance at crypto prices from their home screen, so they don't have to open the app itself.

Go ahead and open the project named `CryptoWidget_start` from the code bundle of this chapter. This is the base project on top of which we will build our widget. Before jumping into the task, let's do a quick review of the base project itself.

Build and launch the project. The app displays a list of cryptocurrencies' prices:

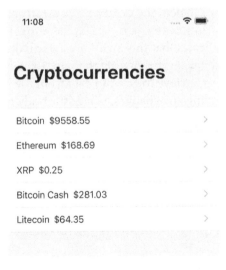

Figure 16.2 – Base app

You can also go into a detailed view of each coin, but just for demo purposes, it doesn't contain additional info. As we are going to work with an existing code base, let's highlight some key points before modifying it:

- The project is structured into three groups of files (apart from the default-generated files and app delegates): `Views`, `Model`, and `Network`.

- The `Views` folder contains the `UIView` files of the project. The views have been created using SwiftUI. SwiftUI is the recommended way to go when building widgets with WidgetKit. Don't worry if you are not familiar with SwiftUI; we will only use basic views in this project.

- Inside the `Network` folder, we have a class named `DataManager.swift`. This class contains the `getData()` method, which is responsible for fetching the crypto prices from the API of CoinMarketCap. You can create a free developer account on their website to get up-to-date prices. Otherwise, the demo app uses a demo key that gives us historical prices for the cryptos that we are using. If you create your own account, you just need to substitute the value of this key with your own key: `let apiKeyValue = "b54bcf4d-1bca-4e8e-9a24-22ff2c3d462c"`.

- The `Model` folder contains basic structs to work with the `getData()` method results: `Coin` and `CoinList`. These structs will contain information about the crypto symbols and prices from the API.

Now, let's take a look at the main view of the project, located in the `ContentView.swift` file inside the `Views` folder. The `ContentView` struct contains `@ObservedObject var dataManager = DataManager()`. The `@ObservedObject` tag indicates that this SwiftUI view will observe changes in the `dataManager` struct, and it will refresh/react to them. Remember that `dataManager` is the class that we are using to retrieve the crypto data from the network, so it makes sense that our main view is observing any changes. Check the body of `ContentView`:

```
var body: some View {
  NavigationView {
    if dataManager.loading {
      Text("Loading...")
    } else {
      CoinListView(data: dataManager.coins.data)
    }
  }
}
```

The view will display a simple `Loading...` text while `dataManager` is in the loading state, and it will display `CoinListView` when `dataManager` finishes loading and contains some data. Simple! Now, if you check the implementation of `CoinListView`. `swift`, you will see that it is a simple list displaying the information for every coin that it receives as input:

```
var body: some View {
  VStack {
    ForEach(data, id: \.symbol){ coin in
      CoinRow(coin: coin)
    }
  }
}
```

Nothing too fancy for now! We have, so far, `dataManager`, which calls `getData()` to fetch coin information from an API, and `ContentView`, which displays `Loading...` text while the data is being called, and displays a list with coin details when the coin's information has been retrieved. Everything was done with a few classes and a few lines of code… that is the power of SwiftUI! Now that we have a clear view of the base project, let's jump into creating a widget extension to start building our awesome crypto coin widget!

Creating a widget extension

The first step to add a widget to an app is to create a widget extension. Creating a widget extension will provide us with a default implementation of the widget protocol, which will help us to get the basic pieces ready.

Before creating the extension, let's review the parts of a widget extension displayed in the following diagram:

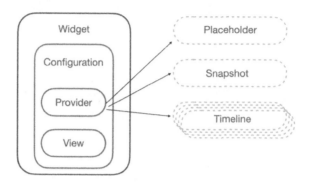

Figure 16.3 – Widget building blocks

As you can see in the preceding diagram, the following are descriptions of the building blocks of a widget extension:

- If the widget is configurable by the user, it will need a custom Siri intent configuration definition. For example, a widget that displays stocks can ask the user for a configuration to choose what stocks to display.

- A provider is needed that will provide the data to display on the widget. The provider can generate placeholder data (that is, show when the user is browsing the widget gallery or loading), a timeline (to represent data over time), and a snapshot (the units that compose a timeline).

- A SwiftUI view to display the data is needed.

When creating a widget target, Xcode will autogenerate placeholders for all these classes. Let's do it now; follow these steps:

1. In the project named CryptoWidget_start, go to **File** | **New** | **Target** | **Widget Extension**.

2. You can use CryptoWidgetExtension as the product name and check the **Include Configuration Intent** option:

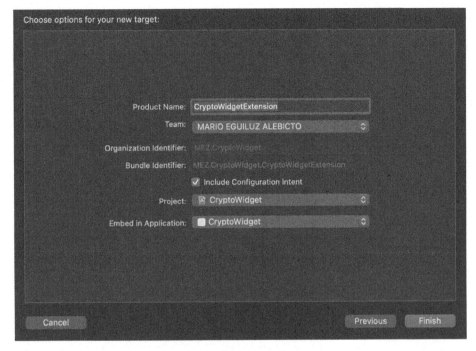

Figure 16.4 – Widget extension options

3. Click **Activate** on the following popup.

If you have followed the preceding steps, your project should now contain a new target with the following folder structure:

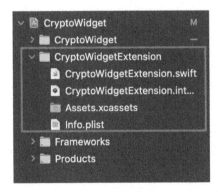

Figure 16.5 – Widget target structure

When creating the widget extension, Xcode has autogenerated two important files: `CryptoWidgetExtension.swift` and `CryptoWidgetExtension.intentdefinition`. Let's focus for now on `CryptoWidgetExtension.swift`. Open it and let's take a look. Check the following piece of code:

```swift
@main
struct CryptoWidgetExtension: Widget {
    let kind: String = "CryptoWidgetExtension"

    var body: some WidgetConfiguration {
        IntentConfiguration(kind: kind, intent:
          ConfigurationIntent.self, provider: Provider()) {
            entry in
            CryptoWidgetExtensionEntryView(entry: entry)
        }
        .configurationDisplayName("My Widget")
        .description("This is an example widget.")
    }
}
```

As you can see, and as discussed before, we have the basic building pieces of the widget:

- An intent configuration, to allow the user to configure the widget, named `IntentConfiguration`

- A provider to provide data to the widget: `Provider()`

- A view to display the data: `CryptoWidgetExtensionEntryView`

The `CryptoWidgetExtension` struct is tagged as `@main`, meaning that is the entry point of the widget. The body is formed of `IntentConfiguration` and `CryptoWidgetExtensionEntryView`, which receives an `entry` instance as input.

In the same file, we also have the autogenerated definitions for the required methods of `Provider` (`placeholder()`, `getSnapshot()`, and `getTimeline()`):

- The `placeholder(...)` method will provide the widget with the initial view the first time the widget is rendered. The placeholder will give the user a general idea of what the widget will look like.

- The `getSnapshot(...in context...)` method will provide the widget with a value (entry) to display when the widget needs to be shown in transient situations. The `isPreview` property from `context` indicates that the widget is being shown in the widget gallery. In those cases, the snapshot has to be fast: those scenarios may require the developer to use dummy data and avoid network calls to return the snapshot as fast as possible.

- The `getTimeline(...)` method will provide the widget with an array of values to display over the current time (and optionally in the future).

There is another important modifier that we will use later. Just after `.description("This is an example widget.")`, add the following line:

```
.supportedFamilies([.systemSmall])
```

This is where we configure the different sizes available for this widget. Later on in the chapter, we will add the medium-sized type.

Now, let's take a look at another part of the code. At the end of the file, you will find the `Preview` section:

```
struct CryptoWidgetExtension_Previews: PreviewProvider {
    static var previews: some View {
        CryptoWidgetExtensionEntryView(entry: SimpleEntry(date:
            Date(), configuration: ConfigurationIntent()))
            .previewContext(WidgetPreviewContext(family:
                .systemSmall))
    }
}
```

This part of the code will allow us to display a preview with SwiftUI of what our widget will look like while developing it. If you launch the preview, you will see that right now, it just displays the time (go to **Editor | Canvas** on the top menu of Xcode if you don't see the preview tab):

Figure 16.6 – Editor canvas preview

That is great! We can code and see the final results in real time. Let's analyze a bit how we are getting this kind of widget view with the time on it. See how we are using `CryptoWidgetExtensionEntryView` as the main view of the preview?

```
CryptoWidgetExtensionEntryView(entry: SimpleEntry(date: Date(),
   configuration: ConfigurationIntent()))
   .previewContext(WidgetPreviewContext(family: .systemSmall))
```

This view is receiving `SimpleEntry` (with just the date) and a plain, empty `ConfigurationIntent`.

Then, we are applying a modifier to the view by creating `previewContext` and assigning `WidgetPreviewContext` as `.systemSmall`. By doing this, we are rendering the view inside the preview of a small widget!

What is `CryptoWidgetExtensionEntryView` doing with `SimpleEntry`? Let's check the implementation:

```
struct CryptoWidgetExtensionEntryView : View {
    var entry: Provider.Entry


    var body: some View {
        Text(entry.date, style: .time)
    }
}
```

Well, it is just displaying text with the date! So, in summary, the preview is doing the following:

- Using `SimpleEntry` as the data input for the widget
- Using `CryptoWidgetExtensionEntryView` as the main view to display that data entry
- Using the `WidgetPreviewContext` modifier to use a small widget as the canvas for the preview

With all these concepts in mind, it is time to start creating our own widget. Let's modify the preceding structs to display the value of Bitcoin instead of a simple date.

First, if we want to display a coin's value (Bitcoin, for example) in the widget, we need an entry to contain that information. Let's add an array of `Coin` to the properties of the `SimpleEntry` struct:

```
struct SimpleEntry: TimelineEntry {
    let date: Date
    let configuration: ConfigurationIntent
    let coins: [Coin]
}
```

By storing the `coins` property, the entry can deliver this information to the widget's view later on. If you try to build the project, you will get an error like this:

```
Cannot find type 'Coin' in scope
```

This happens because the `Coin` file is only part of the main app target. We need to select `Coin` and all the other files under the `Views`, `Network`, and `Model` folders and add them to the widget's target:

Figure 16.7 – Sharing files from the main app to the widget target

After adding the files of the previous screenshot to the widget target, you will get new, different errors when compiling. The main reason for all these errors is that you have added a new property to `Coin`, and now there are parts in the `Provider` struct where we are initializing a `Coin` instance without that new property. To fix it, we will add some dummy data (for now) into the `Provider` implementation to pass it as the coins when creating any `SimpleEntry` instance inside `Provider`. Later on, we will use real data from the API instead of that dummy one.

Add the following code inside the `Provider` struct. Its first line will appear as follows:

```
struct Provider: IntentTimelineProvider {
    let coins = [Coin(id: 1, name: "Bitcoin", symbol: "BTC",
        quote: Quote(USD: QuoteData(price: 20000))), Coin(id:
        1, name: "Litecoin", symbol: "LTC", quote: Quote(USD:
        QuoteData(price: 200)))]
//...
```

We are creating some fake data to generate a `Coin` array, containing some values for Bitcoin and Litecoin. Now, we can use this `coins` value to inject it into the three places in which we are creating `SimpleEntry` inside the `Provider` class:

- First, we inject it inside the `placeholder(...)` method:

```
SimpleEntry(date: Date(), configuration:
    ConfigurationIntent(), coins: coins)
```

- Then, we inject it inside the `getSnapshot(...)` method:

```
let entry = SimpleEntry(date: Date(), configuration:
    configuration, coins: coins)
```

- We then inject it inside the `getTimeline(...)` method:

```
let entry = SimpleEntry(date: entryDate, configuration:
    configuration, coins: coins)
```

Finally, you may have the exact same problem inside the `CryptoWidgetExtension_Previews` struct. The `previews` property is using `SimpleEntry` to display it in the widget. You need to add the `coins` property again. Just use this code:

```
CryptoWidgetExtensionEntryView(entry: SimpleEntry(date: Date(),
    configuration: ConfigurationIntent(), coins: [Coin(id:
    1, name: "Bitcoin", symbol: "BTC", quote: Quote(USD:
    QuoteData(price: 20000))), Coin(id: 1, name: "Litecoin",
    symbol: "LTC", quote: Quote(USD: QuoteData(price: 200)))]))
```

```
        .previewContext(WidgetPreviewContext(family:
            .systemSmall))
```

Great! The project should compile properly now. Try to render the preview to see what happens. Oops! You should still see the date/time in the little widget and no coin values! Why? We are passing the coin values into the entry to the widget, but the view of the widget is not using it yet. Check the current implementation:

```
struct CryptoWidgetExtensionEntryView : View {
    var entry: Provider.Entry

    var body: some View {
        Text(entry.date, style: .time)
    }
}
```

We have `entry` with coins information inside, but we are only displaying the date. We need to modify the view to show the new information! In the main app, we have a view that, given a coin, displays its name and price. Let's use it. Change the `CryptoWidgetExtensionEntryView` implementation for this (changes are highlighted):

```
struct CryptoWidgetExtensionEntryView : View {
    var entry: Provider.Entry

    var body: some View {
        CoinDetail(coin: entry.coins[0])
    }
}
```

Now, build and refresh the preview. Great! You should see the price and name of Bitcoin on the widget, as in the following screenshot:

Figure 16.8 – Widget showing the Bitcoin price

If you want to try it in the simulator, just launch the widget target. Remember that you should have launched (at least once) the main app first.

In this section, we learned how to add a widget extension to an app. Then, we explored the main components and the relationship between them: the provider, the entries, the view of the widget, and the preview system of SwiftUI. Finally, we modified all these components to adapt them to our needs and created our first small widget. In the next section, we will learn how to add a placeholder preview and how to add a medium-sized widget too!

Implementing multiple-size widgets

In the previous section, we added a widget target to a project and created the widget's first view, the small-sized one. Let's do some modifications now in order to develop a medium-sized widget, and also a placeholder preview for the widget.

If you didn't follow along with the previous section, you can use the project named `CryptoWidget_1_small_widget`. Let's start by adding a placeholder preview to the project. When rendering your widget for the first time, WidgetKit will render it as a placeholder. In order to render data, it will ask the provider for an entry using the following method:

```
func placeholder(in context: Context) -> SimpleEntry
```

But in order to be able to see how it would appear while we develop it, we can create a preview of it using SwiftUI. Go ahead and add the following struct to the `CryptoWidgetExtension.swift` file:

```
struct PlaceholderView : View {
    let coins = [Coin(id: 1, name: "Bitcoin", symbol: "BTC",
        quote: Quote(USD: QuoteData(price: 20000))), Coin(id:
        1, name: "Litecoin", symbol: "LTC", quote: Quote(USD:
        QuoteData(price: 200)))]

    var body: some View {
        CryptoWidgetExtensionEntryView(entry: SimpleEntry(date:
            Date(), configuration: ConfigurationIntent(), coins:
            coins)).redacted(reason: .placeholder)
    }
}
```

See how we are using the main widget view (`CryptoWidgetExtensionEntryView`) as the placeholder view, and we are feeding it with dummy coins data? However, the interesting part is the highlighted part: `.redacted(reason: .placeholder)`. Now that we have created a placeholder view with dummy data, let's create a preview of it and check what the effect of the `redacted` modifier is.

Remove the implementation of `CryptoWidgetExtension_Previews` and add this new one, with the modified code highlighted as follows:

```swift
struct CryptoWidgetExtension_Previews: PreviewProvider {
    static var previews: some View {
        Group {
            CryptoWidgetExtensionEntryView(entry: SimpleEntry(date:
            Date(), configuration: ConfigurationIntent(), coins:
            [Coin(id: 1, name: "Bitcoin", symbol: "BTC", quote:
            Quote(USD: QuoteData(price: 20000))), Coin(id:
            1, name: "Litecoin", symbol: "LTC", quote:
            Quote(USD: QuoteData(price: 200)))]))
                .previewContext(WidgetPreviewContext(family:
                .systemSmall))
            PlaceholderView()
                .previewContext(WidgetPreviewContext(family:
                .systemSmall))
        }
    }
}
```

First, we are encapsulating the previous `CryptoWidgetExtensionEntryView` view inside `Group`. This is because now we want to display a group of previews, `CryptoWidgetExtensionEntryView`, and the new `Placeholder`.

Then, we are adding the newly created `Placeholder` view, and applying to it a `previewContext` of a small widget, like before. Compile and resume the preview render; you should see the following:

Figure 16.9 – Placeholder view with a redacted modifier

Do you now see the effect of `.redacted(reason: .placeholder)`? SwiftUI is replacing labels with placeholder views of them. It is straightforward to create a placeholder view of your widgets like this!

Currently, we have a small-sized widget and a preview of it. Let's start creating a medium-sized version of it. Bigger widgets should use the extra available space to provide users with added value. Your medium- or big-sized widget should not be a simple, bigger-sized version of the small one. In our case, we are displaying the price of Bitcoin in a small size. Now, in the medium size, we will display the value of multiple cryptocurrencies at once. The user will get a bigger picture of the market with just a glance!

In the previous section, we configured `supportedFamilies` to allow the small size of the widget. We need to add the medium size too. You will find it in the `CryptoWidgetExtension` struct. Add `.systemMedium` to `supportedFamilies`, so the configuration line should look like this:

```
.supportedFamilies([.systemSmall, .systemMedium])
```

Let's now create a preview of the medium-sized widget. Go ahead and add a new `Group` below the existing one in `CryptoWidgetExtension_Previews`. Add the following code just where the existing `Group{ ... }` finishes (so you should have one group after the other):

```
Group {
    CryptoWidgetExtensionEntryView(entry: SimpleEntry(date:
    Date(), configuration: ConfigurationIntent(), coins:
    [Coin(id: 1, name: "Bitcoin", symbol: "BTC", quote:
    Quote(USD: QuoteData(price: 20000))), Coin(id: 1, name:
    "Litecoin", symbol: "LTC", quote: Quote(USD:
    QuoteData(price: 200))), Coin(id: 1, name: "Ethereum",
    symbol: "ETH", quote: Quote(USD: QuoteData(price:
    1200)))]))
    .previewContext(WidgetPreviewContext(family:
    .systemMedium))
    PlaceholderView()
    .previewContext(WidgetPreviewContext(family:
    .systemMedium))
}
```

See how this new group of views is the same as the existing one, with the only difference being in the highlighted code? We are now displaying the widget and its placeholder inside a `systemMedium` preview. If you resume the render, you should see these two new previews (apart from the previous small-sized ones):

Figure 16.10 – Medium-sized widget and placeholder

You can imagine how, for a user, this result would be very disappointing. We are displaying the exact same information as in the small widget but taking up more space on their home screen (which is very valuable to them!). Let's improve this by changing the layout of our `CryptoWidgetExtensionEntryView` when the system is displaying a medium-sized version. We can make use of the extra space to display more than just one coin at a time. Remove the implementation of `CryptoWidgetExtensionEntryView` and use the following one:

```swift
struct CryptoWidgetExtensionEntryView : View {
  var entry: Provider.Entry
  //1
  @Environment(\.widgetFamily) var family
  //2
  @ViewBuilder
  var body: some View {
    switch family {
    //3
    case .systemSmall where entry.coins.count > 0:
      CoinDetail(coin: entry.coins[0])
    //4
    case .systemMedium where entry.coins.count > 0:
      HStack(alignment: .center) {
        Spacer()
        CoinDetail(coin: entry.coins.first!)
        Spacer()
        CoinListView(data: entry.coins)
        Spacer()
      }
    //5
    default:
      PlaceholderView()
    }
  }
}
```

Let's discuss the numbered comments in the code:

1. We are using the `@Environment(\.widgetFamily)` variable, which allows us to know which widget family is being used. Based on that info, we can use different layouts for different sizes.

2. The view has to declare its body with `@ViewBuilder` because the type of view it uses varies.

3. We use the `family` (`widgetFamily`) property to switch over it and provide different views for different widget sizes. For the small-sized widget, we keep using the `CoinDetail` view as before.

4. For the medium-sized widget, we use a combination of views that let us display the details of a coin and a list of other coins by its side. In this way, we add more value and use the space available to provide extra info to the user.

5. Finally, we use `Placeholder` for the `default` case of the switch.

Now you can resume the preview to see the changes. The medium-sized group should look like this:

Figure 16.11 – Medium-sized widget

Great! We now have a different widget for the medium-sized family that provides some extra value to the user! We still have one important task ahead. The data that we are displaying in both the small and medium sizes is just dummy data. Also, we are not letting the user choose which coin they want to display in the small-sized widget; we are forcing it to display Bitcoin, and they may not be interested in that one.

In the next section, we will learn how to provide the widget with a dynamic configuration (so the user can configure options for the widget) and how to display real data.

Providing the widget with data and configuration

Up to this point, we have a widget with various sizes and a placeholder view that is displaying dummy data about cryptocurrencies. In this section, we will swap that dummy data with real data coming from an API, and we will also let the user configure some options to personalize the widget even more.

If you didn't follow along with the previous section, you can use the project named `CryptoWidget_2_medium_widget`.

Let's start by providing the widget with real data. The entity that is providing the entries (and therefore the data) to the widget view is `Provider`. Somehow, we need `Provider` to be aware of our data source and serve incoming data to the views. In our main app, the struct responsible for providing data is `DataManager`. Go ahead and add the following property to the `Provider` struct, in the `CryptoWidgetExtension.swift` file:

```
@ObservedObject var dataManager = DataManager()
```

We are adding an instance of `DataManager` to the widget's `Provider`. Note that we are marking this property with the `@ObservedObject` tag. If you haven't used it in SwiftUI before, whenever an observable property wrapped with this tag changes, it invalidates any view that depends on it.

Every time that `DataManager` changes, the views that depend on it will invalidate and refresh to reflect those changes. Now, we can delete the dummy data from `Provider` and use the data manager instead. Remove this line:

```
let coins = [Coin(id: 1, name: "Bitcoin", symbol: "BTC",
  quote: Quote(USD: QuoteData(price: 20000))), Coin(id: 1, name:
   "Litecoin", symbol: "LTC", quote: Quote(USD: QuoteData(price:
   200)))]
```

If you build the project, you will get three compile errors—one in each provider's method, where we were using the `coins` property that we just deleted. Go ahead and use the `dataManager.coins.data` property instead of the deleted coins one. This property from `dataManager` contains the real data retrieved from the API.

Now, launch the main app, remove the previous widget from the device, and add it again to the home screen. You should see something like this:

Figure 16.12 – Widget gallery

That is excellent news! This is no longer dummy data; we have up to five coins in the list with real values (remember that these values will not be up to date if you are using the sandbox endpoint, as discussed at the beginning of the chapter).

Now we have real values showing in the widget. The final step is going to be to improve the small-sized widget a little bit. Currently, the small-sized widget shows the price of Bitcoin. But the user may be interested in other cryptocurrencies. We will use a configuration intent to allow the user to input configuration values and make our widgets more dynamic.

At the beginning of the chapter, when we added the widget extension to the main app, we selected the **Include Configuration Intent** option. This option generated a file called `CryptoWidgetExtension.intentdefinition` inside the widget extension folder. This is a Siri intent definition file, where we can configure the options that our widget will accept as user input. Let's configure the intent definition for our specific case. We want the user to be able to select a coin from a predefined list of coin names, to display the price of that coin in the small-sized widget.

Let's start by creating an enum with the following values: BTC, LTC, and ETH:

1. Click on the `CryptoWidgetExtension.intentdefinition` file. In the **Parameters** section, add a new parameter by clicking on the + button. Call it `coinSelect` and change the type to **Add Enum**.

2. This action will take you forward to creating a new enum. Call the enum `Coin Select` and add the following values:

    Case: ltc: **Index**: 1. **Display Name**: LTC

    Case: eth: **Index**: 2. **Display Name**: ETH

    Case: btc: **Index**: 3. **Display Name**: BTC

    It should look like this:

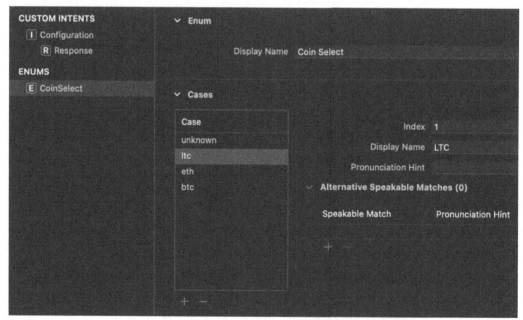

Figure 16.13 – Coin Select enum configuration

3. Now go back to the **Configuration** section of the intent. You can uncheck the **Siri can ask for value when run** option. Make sure that the other options are set as in the following screenshot:

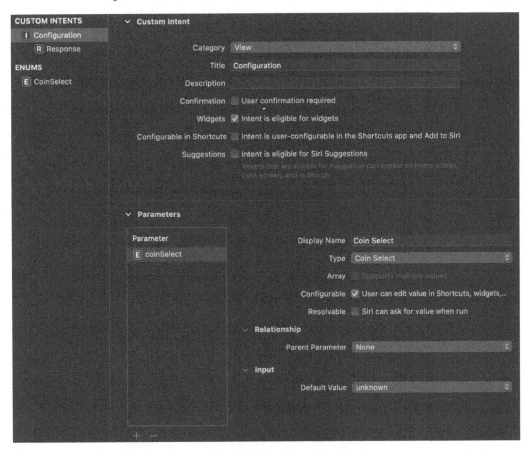

Figure 16.14 – Custom Intent configuration

With the custom intent configured like this and the enum created to display some list values, we are ready to use this intent in our widget.

4. Go back to the `CryptoWidgetExtension.swift` file and check the `SimpleEntry` definition. Inside each entry, we have access to the `configuration` property (which is an instance of the `ConfigurationIntent` that we just configured). This means that we have access to the custom intent values every time we access an entry.

Now, in `CryptoWidgetExtensionEntryView`, we have an `entry` available (of course! It is the data that we want to display). Therefore, we have access to the configuration intent inside it. Let's make use of it then! We are going to modify the `.systemSmall` switch case to use the configuration intent information and display different coins, instead of just displaying Bitcoin.

5. Go ahead and locate the following code:

```
case .systemSmall where entry.coins.count > 0:
    CoinDetail(coin: entry.coins[0])
```

6. Replace it with this new one:

```
case .systemSmall where entry.coins.count > 0:
  switch entry.configuration.coinSelect {
  case .btc:
    CoinDetail(coin: entry.coins.filter { $0.symbol ==
      "BTC" }.first!)
  case .ltc:
    CoinDetail(coin: entry.coins.filter { $0.symbol ==
      "LTC" }.first!)
  case .eth:
    CoinDetail(coin: entry.coins.filter { $0.symbol ==
      "ETH" }.first!)
  default:
    CoinDetail(coin: entry.coins.filter { $0.symbol ==
      "BTC" }.first!)
  }
```

In this new code, we use the information inside the custom Siri intent (`entry.configuration.coinselect`) to know which coin from the enum the user selected. Based on that, we are displaying a specific coin in the small-sized widget.

Try to build the project. You may get a compile error. This error happens because the widget doesn't yet know about the custom Siri intent type (even though Xcode generated it for us). This error may be fixed in future versions of Xcode. If you have an error, check the following:

7. Go to the main app settings and, under the **General** tab, add the `ConfigurationIntent` intent under the **Supported Intents** section, as in the following screenshot:

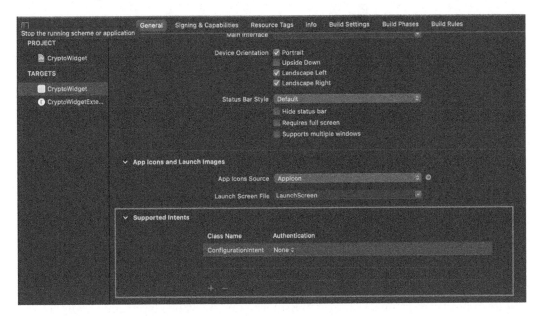

Figure 16.15 – Adding your intent to the Supported Intents section

8. Build the project again, and the compile errors should be gone.

9. If you still have any errors, try the following:

a) Compile and run the target of the main app.

b) Run the target of the widget. Delete the widget from the simulator and add it again (the small-sized one).

10. Now, if you long-press over the small-sized widget on the device (or simulator), you should be able to see the **Edit Widget** option. It will display your new custom intent, as in the following screenshot:

Figure 16.16 – Widget configuration options

11. Try selecting **ETH** or **LTC**. Then, your widget will reload and display that coin! This is great; we now have a configurable crypto widget.

In this section, we learned how to make a widget configurable using a Siri intent, so the user is able to select values and edit the widget from the home screen.

Now, there is another topic that we haven't discussed yet. In the `Provider` struct, we learned that the `getTimeline(...)` method will provide the widget with an array of values to display over time, to refresh the information being displayed and stay up to date. But we didn't discuss how we control when the widget is actually refreshing, or even whether we are in control of it. We are going to learn about this in the next section.

Refreshing the widget's data

Keeping widgets up to date consumes system resources and can require significant battery usage. For this reason, the system will limit the number of updates that each widget can perform during the day in order to save battery life.

With this idea in mind, we have to understand that we don't have full control over our widget's refresh time and frequency, and that widgets are not always active. We are able to give the system some hints about when would be ideal for our widget to refresh, but ultimately, the system will decide it.

The system uses a budget to distribute reloads over time. That budget is affected by the following factors:

- How many times has the widget been displayed to the user?
- When was the last time the widget was reloaded?
- Is the widget's main app active?

The allocated budget for a widget lasts 24 hours. A widget that a user visits a lot can get up to 70 refreshes per day, meaning it can update once every 15 minutes or so.

You can help WidgetKit estimate the best budget for your widget by providing as much information as you can in your widget's `Timeline` method. Some examples are as follows:

- A cooking widget that follows a recipe can schedule different steps in the timeline to show the cooking steps at certain points in time: preheat the oven for 15 minutes, cook for 30 minutes, let it rest for 10 minutes, and so on. That would result in a timeline with entries separated over time at specific minutes (15 – 30 – 10). WidgetKit will try to refresh your widget at those points in time, to display the proper entries.
- For a widget to remind users to drink water every 2 hours, you may produce a timeline to remind users about drinking a glass of water every 2 hours. But you can also be more efficient and avoid any refreshes during nighttime when the user is sleeping. That will produce a more efficient timeline and save some budget that WidgetKit can use to refresh your widget more often when it is really needed.

Now, in our specific example of the crypto ticker widget, let's modify the timeline to ask WidgetKit to refresh our widget every 5 minutes (a very aggressive request!). But we know cryptocurrencies are very volatile and for this example, we want to refresh the price as much as possible. Follow these steps:

1. Go ahead and open the project named `CryptoWidget_4_timeline` from the code bundle of this chapter. First, let's create a new method inside `DataManager` that allows us to fetch the latest crypto data with a completion block.

2. Add the following method to the struct:

```
func refresh(completionHandler: @escaping (CoinList) ->
   Void) {
   guard let url = URL(string: apiUrl) else { return }
   var request = URLRequest(url: url)
   request.setValue(apiKeyValue, forHTTPHeaderField:
```

```
apiKeyHeader)


URLSession.shared.dataTask(with: request){ (data, _, _)
   in
  print("Update coins")
  guard let data = data else { return }
  let coins = try! JSONDecoder().decode(CoinList.self,
     from: data)
  DispatchQueue.main.async {
    print(coins)
    self.coins = coins
    self.loading = false


    completionHandler(coins)
  }
}.resume()
}
```

See how the method is similar to getData(), but this one is not private and it also returns coins inside a completion handler for us to use on demand.

3. Next, go to the file called CryptoWidgetExtension.swift and modify the getTimeline(...) method inside the Provider struct to contain the following implementation instead:

```
func getTimeline(for configuration: ConfigurationIntent,
  in context: Context, completion: @escaping
  (Timeline<Entry>) -> ()) {
  print("New Timeline \(Date())")
  dataManager.refresh { (coins) in
    let currentDate = Date()
    let futureDate = Calendar.current.date(byAdding:
      .minute, value: 15, to: currentDate)!
    let timeline = Timeline(entries: [SimpleEntry(date:
      Date(), configuration: configuration, coins:
      coins.data)], policy: .after(futureDate))
    completion(timeline)
  }
}
```

Let's see what is happening in the method:

1. First, we are using the new method that we created, `refresh(...)`, to get the latest values of the crypto coins.

2. Once we have the coins ready in the completion handler, we are creating a future date that is 15 minutes into the future.

3. Then, we create `Timeline` with a `SimpleEntry` that contains the latest values for `coins`, and a refresh policy. The refresh policy is set to create a new timeline after 15 minutes have passed (`futureDate`). Usually, 15 minutes is the minimum time needed for WidgetKit to update your widget again. If you try lower values, you may not get any results.

   So, to wrap this method up, when WidgetKit requests a timeline from us, we are calling our API to get the latest crypto values, then we wrap them in an entry ready for the widget views to be displayed, and we establish a refresh policy of "after 15 minutes have passed."

4. Now try deleting the app and the widget from the simulator or your device. Install both the app and the extension and add a small widget to the home screen. The moment you add the widget, you should see in the logs the first statement of the timeline method, similar to this:

```
New Timeline 2021-01-23 20:51:51 +0000
```

   Then, after 15 minutes, you should see it appearing again. The refresh policy has kicked in, and we have provided a refreshed version with the latest values again:

```
New Timeline 2021-01-23 21:06:52 +0000
```

Great! We know now how to refresh our widgets! Just a last note: there are more refresh policies other than `.after`. Here are the options:

- `TimelineReloadPolicy.after(Date)`: A new timeline will be generated after the specific date has passed.

- `TimelineReloadPolicy.atEnd`: A new timeline will be generated after the last entry of the current timeline passes.

- `TimelineReloadPolicy.never`: The widget's app will be responsible for letting WidgetKit know when the next timeline is ready.

In this section, we learned the basics of how WidgetKit decides when to refresh your widgets, and how we can provide timelines and refresh policies so that the system has a better idea of when we want our widgets to be updated. Now, let's wrap up the chapter with a summary.

Summary

We started the chapter by learning about the basics of widgets and WidgetKit. We learned about the general guidelines, the basic options, and their purpose. After that intro, we jumped straight into developing our first widget. We started by adding a small-sized widget to an existing app.

Then, we added a placeholder view to the widget so that it gives the user a good idea of what the widget would look like the first time it loads. After that, we created a bigger, medium-sized widget version that is able to display much more information and provide more value than the small-sized widget.

Finally, we learned how to make the widget configurable by the user with the help of Siri custom intents. By using a custom intent, users are able to provide certain configuration values to the widget to personalize the experience.

In this chapter, you learned how to create widgets and make the most out of WidgetKit. In the next chapter, we will learn about ARKit, the augmented reality framework from Apple.

17
Using Augmented Reality

One of the major features that Apple shipped as part of iOS 11 was **ARKit**. ARKit enables developers to create amazing **Augmented Reality (AR)** experiences with only a minimal amount of code. Apple has continuously worked on improving ARKit, resulting in the release of ARKit 2 at WWDC 2018, ARKit 3 at WWDC 2019, and ARKit 4 at WWDC 2020.

In this chapter, you will learn what ARKit is, how it works, what you can do with it, and how you can implement an AR art gallery that uses several ARKit features, such as image tracking. We will also learn about some basic concepts from SpriteKit and SceneKit.

This chapter covers the following topics:

- Understanding ARKit
- Using ARKit Quick Look
- Exploring SpriteKit
- Exploring SceneKit
- Implementing an AR gallery

By the end of this chapter, you will be able to integrate ARKit into your apps and implement your own ARKit experiences.

Understanding ARKit

In this section, we will learn about **Augmented Reality (AR)** and ARKit. Augmented Reality (AR) is a topic that has captured the interest of app developers and designers for a long time now. Implementing an excellent AR experience had not been easy though, and many applications haven't lived up to the hype. Small details such as lighting and detecting walls, floors, and other objects have always been extremely complicated to implement and getting these details wrong has a negative impact on the quality of an AR experience.

Augmented reality apps usually have at least some of the following features:

- They show a camera view.
- Content is shown as an overlay in the camera view.
- Content responds appropriately to the device's movement.
- Content is attached to a specific location in the world.

Even though this list of features is simple, they aren't all trivial to implement. An AR experience relies heavily on reading the motion sensors from the device, as well as using image analysis to determine exactly how a user is moving and to learn what a 3D map of the world should look like.

ARKit is Apple's way of giving developers the power to create great AR experiences. ARKit takes care of all the motion and image analysis to make sure you can focus on designing and implementing great content rather than getting slowed down by the intricate details involved in building an AR app.

Unfortunately, ARKit comes with a hefty hardware requirement for the devices that can run ARKit apps. Only devices with Apple's A9 chip or newer can run ARKit. This means that any device older than the iPhone 6s or the first iPad Pro cannot run ARKit apps.

In the following sections, we will start by understanding how ARKit renders content on the device and how it tracks the physical environment around it in order to deliver the best AR experience.

Understanding how ARKit renders content

ARKit itself only takes care of the massive calculations related to keeping track of the physical world the user is in. To render content in an ARKit app, you must use one of the following three rendering tools:

- SpriteKit
- SceneKit
- Metal

Later in this chapter, you will have a quick look at SpriteKit and SceneKit, and you will ultimately implement your AR gallery using SceneKit. If you already have experience with any of the available rendering techniques, you should feel right at home when using ARKit.

Implementing ARKit in your app is not limited to manually rendering the contents you want to show in AR. In iOS 12, Apple has added a feature called **ARKit Quick Look**. You can implement a special view controller in your app that takes care of placing a 3D model you supply in a scene. This is ideal if you're implementing a feature that allows users to preview products or other objects in the real world.

Understanding how ARKit tracks the physical environment

To understand how ARKit renders content, it's essential that you understand how ARKit makes sense of the physical environment a user is in. When you implement an AR experience, you use an ARKit session. An ARKit session is represented by an instance of ARSession. Every ARSession uses an instance of ARSessionConfiguration to describe the tracking that it should do in the environment. The following diagram depicts the relationship between all objects involved in an ARKit session:

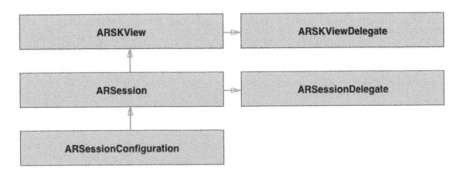

Figure 17.1 – ARKit session components

The preceding diagram shows how the session configuration is passed to the session. The session is then passed to a view that is responsible for rendering the scene. If you use SpriteKit to render the scene, the view is an instance of ARSKView. When you use SceneKit, this would be an instance of ARSCNView. Both the view and session have a delegate that will be informed about certain events that can occur during an ARKit session. You will learn more about these delegates later when you implement your AR gallery.

There are several different tracking options that you can configure on a session. One of the most basic tracking configurations is `AROrientationTrackingConfiguration`. This configuration only tracks the device's orientation, so not the user's movement in the environment. This kind of tracking monitors the device using three degrees of freedom. To be more specific, this tracking tracks the device's *x*, *y*, and *z* orientation. This kind of tracking is perfect if you're implementing something such as a 3D video where the user's movements can be ignored.

A more complex tracking configuration is `ARWorldTrackingConfiguration`, also known as **world tracking**. This type of configuration tracks the user's movements as well as the device's orientation. This means that a user can walk around an AR object to see it from all different sides. World tracking uses the device's motion sensors to determine the user's movements and the device's orientation. This is very accurate for short and small movements, but not accurate enough to track movements over long periods of time and distances. To make sure the AR experience remains as precise as possible, world tracking also performs some advanced computer vision tasks to analyze the camera feed to determine the user's location in an environment.

In addition to tracking the user's movements, world tracking also uses computer vision to make sense of the environment that the AR session exists in. By detecting certain points of interest in the camera feed, world tracking can compare and analyze the position of these points in relation to the user's motion to determine the distances and sizes of objects. This technique also allows world tracking to detect walls and floors, for instance.

The world tracking configuration stores everything it learns about the environment in an `ARWorldMap`. This map contains all `ARAnchor` instances that represent different objects and points of interest that exist in the session.

There are several other special tracking types that you can use in your app. For instance, you can use `ARFaceTrackingConfiguration` on devices with a **TrueDepth** camera to track a user's face. This kind of tracking is perfect if you want to recreate Apple's Animoji feature that was added to the iPhone X and newer in iOS 12.

You can also configure your session so it automatically detects certain objects or images in a scene. To implement this, you can use `ARObjectScanningConfiguration` to scan for specific items or `ARImageTrackingConfiguration` to identify still images.

In this section, you have learned the basics of AR and ARKit, how ARKit renders content on the device, and how it tracks the physical environment around it. Before you get your hands dirty with implementing an ARKit session, let's explore the new **ARKit Quick Look** feature to see how simple it is for you to allow users of your app to preview items in AR.

Using ARKit Quick Look

In this section, we will learn about ARKit Quick Look, a feature from Apple that allows users to preview virtual 3D or AR models with the camera of their device.

One of the great benefits that AR brings to end users is that it is now possible to preview certain objects in the real world. For instance, when you buy a new sofa, you might want to see what it looks like in the real world. Of course, it was possible to implement features such as this in iOS 11 using ARKit, and many developers have, but it wasn't as easy as it could be.

iOS users can preview content using a feature called **Quick Look**. Quick Look can be used to preview certain types of content without having to launch any specific applications. This is convenient for users because they can quickly determine whether a particular document is the document they are looking for by previewing it in Quick Look.

In iOS 12, Apple added the **USDZ** file format to the content types that can be previewed using Quick Look. Apple's USDZ format is a 3D file format based on Pixar's USD format that is used to represent 3D objects. Using Quick Look for 3D models is not just available in apps; ARKit Quick Look can also be integrated on the web. Developers can use a special HTML tag on their web pages to link to a USDZ and Safari will display the model in an ARKit Quick Look view controller.

Before you implement your AR gallery, it's a good idea to get a feel for how AR works on iOS by implementing the ARKit Quick Look view controller to show one of the models that Apple provides at `https://developer.apple.com/arkit/gallery/`. To download a model you like, all you need to do is navigate to this page on your Mac and click on an image. The USDZ file should start downloading automatically.

> TIP
> Navigate to the ARKit gallery on a device that supports ARKit and tap on one of the models to see what ARKit Quick Look in Safari looks like.

In this section, we explained what Quick Look is. Now let's use it inside our own app in the next section.

Implementing the ARKit Quick Look view controller

After obtaining a USDZ file from Apple's gallery, also make sure to capture the image that belongs to this file. Taking a screenshot of the model should be fine for testing purposes. Make sure to prepare your image in the different required sizes by scaling your screenshot up to two and three times the size of your screenshot.

Create a new project in Xcode and pick a name for your project. The sample project in this book's code bundle is called `ARQuickLook`. Add your prepared image to the `Assets.xcassets` file. Also, drag your USDZ file into Xcode and make sure to add it to the app target by checking your app's checkbox when importing the file:

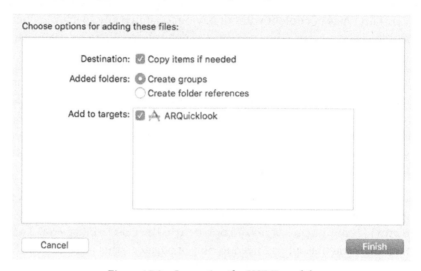

Figure 17.2 – Importing the USDZ model

Next, open the storyboard file and drag an image view to the view controller. Add the proper constraints to the image so it's centered in the view controller and give it a width and height of 200 points. Make sure to check the **User Interaction Enabled** checkbox in **Attributes Inspector** and set your model image as the image for the image view.

After doing this, open `ViewController.swift`, add `@IBOutlet` for the image view, and connect the image in the storyboard to this outlet. If the details regarding outlets are a little bit fuzzy right now, refer to the sample project in the code bundle for a refresher. The image view in the sample project uses an outlet called `guitarImage`.

The next steps to implement Quick Look for the USDZ model are to add a tap gesture recognizer to the image view and then trigger the Quick Look view controller when a user taps on the image.

Quick Look uses delegation to object one or more items that it should preview from a data source. It also uses a delegate to obtain the source view from which the Quick Look preview should animate. This flow applies to all kinds of files that you can preview using Quick Look.

To begin implementing Quick Look, you must import the `QuickLook` framework. Add the following `import` statement to the top of `ViewController.swift`:

```
import QuickLook
```

Next, set up the tap-gesture recognizer for the image by adding the following code to `viewDidLoad()`:

```
let tapGesture = UITapGestureRecognizer(target: self,
    action: #selector(presentQuicklook))
guitarImage.addGestureRecognizer(tapGesture)
```

The next step is to implement `presentQuicklook()`. This method will create a Quick Look view controller, set the delegate and data source, and then present the Quick Look view controller to the user. Add the following implementation for this method to the `ViewController` class:

```
@objc func presentQuicklook() {
    let previewViewController = QLPreviewController()
    previewViewController.dataSource = self
    previewViewController.delegate = self
    present(previewViewController, animated: true,
        completion: nil)
}
```

This implementation should not contain any surprises for you. `QLPreviewController` is a `UIViewController` subclass that is responsible for displaying the content it receives from its data source. It is presented in the same way you would present any other view controller, by calling `present(_:animated:completion:)`.

The final step is to implement the data source and delegates. Add the following extensions to `ViewController.swift`:

```
extension ViewController: QLPreviewControllerDelegate {
    func previewController(_ controller: QLPreviewController,
        transitionViewFor item: QLPreviewItem) -> UIView? {
        return guitarImage
```

```
    }
}

extension ViewController: QLPreviewControllerDataSource {
  func numberOfPreviewItems(in controller:
    QLPreviewController) -> Int {
    return 1
  }

  func previewController(_ controller: QLPreviewController,
    previewItemAt index: Int) -> QLPreviewItem {
    let fileUrl = Bundle.main.url(forResource:
      "stratocaster", withExtension: "usdz")!
    return fileUrl as QLPreviewItem
  }
}
```

The first extension you added makes `ViewController` conform to `QLPreviewControllerDelegate`. When the preview controller is about to present the 3D model, it wants to know which view is the source for the transition that is about to happen. It's recommended to return the view that acts as a preview for the Quick Look action from this method. In this case, the preview is the image of the 3D model.

The second extension acts as the Quick Look data source. When you implement Quick Look for ARKit, you can only return a single item. So, when the preview controller asks for the number of items in the preview, you should always return 1. The second method in the data source provides the item that should be previewed in the preview controller. All you need to do here is obtain the file URL for the item you wish to preview. In the sample app, the Stratocaster model from Apple's gallery is used. If your model has a different name, make sure to use the correct filename.

After obtaining the URL that points to the image in the app bundle, it should be returned to the preview controller as a `QLPreviewItem` instance. Luckily, URL instances can be converted to `QLPreviewItem` instances automatically.

If you run your app now, you can tap on your image of the 3D model to begin previewing it. You can preview the image on its own, or you can choose to preview it in AR. If you tap this option, the preview controller will tell you to move your device around.

To make a mapping of the world around you, ARKit requires some samples of the environment. When you move your device around, make sure to not just tilt it, but physically move it. Doing this will help ARKit discover trackable features in your surroundings.

Once ARKit has enough data about your surroundings, you can place the 3D model in the environment, scale it by pinching, rotate it, and move it around in the space. Note that the model is placed on a flat surface such as a table or the floor automatically rather than awkwardly floating around:

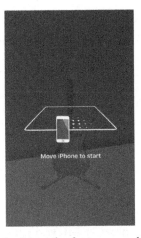

Figure 17.3 – Move the device around the scene

Also note that ARKit applies very realistic lighting to your object. The visual data that ARKit gathers about the environment is used to create a lighting map that is applied to the 3D model to make it properly blend in with the context in which the object was placed:

Figure 17.4 – AR model placed in the real world

While playing around with ARKit like this is a lot of fun, it's even more fun to create your own AR experiences. Since ARKit supports several rendering techniques, such as SpriteKit and SceneKit, the next two sections will spend a little bit of time explaining the very basics of SpriteKit and SceneKit. You won't learn how to build complete games or worlds with these frameworks. Instead, you will learn just enough to get you started with implementing either rendering engine in an ARKit app.

Exploring SpriteKit

In this section, we are going to explore **SpriteKit**. SpriteKit is mostly used by developers to build two-dimensional games. SpriteKit has been around for quite some time already, and it has helped developers to create many successful games over the years. SpriteKit contains a full-blown physics simulation engine, and it can render many sprites at a time. A **sprite** represents a graphic in a game. A sprite could be an image for the player, but also a coin, an enemy, or even the floor that the player walks on. When sprites are mentioned in the context of SpriteKit, it is meant to refer to one of the nodes that are visible on the screen.

Because SpriteKit has a built-in physics engine, it can detect collisions between objects, apply forces to them, and more. This is pretty similar to what UIKit Dynamics is capable of.

To render content, SpriteKit uses scenes. These scenes can be considered levels or major building parts of a game. In the context of AR, you will find that you typically only need a single scene. A SpriteKit scene is responsible for updating the position and state of the scene. As a developer, you can hook into the rendering of frames through the `update(_:)` method of `SKScene`. This method is called every time SpriteKit is about to render a new frame for your game or ARKit scene. It is essential that this method's execution time is as short as possible, as slow implementation of the `update(_:)` method will cause frames to drop, which is considered bad. You should always aim to maintain a steady 60 frames per second. This means that the `update(_:)` method should always perform its work in less than 1/60th of a second.

To begin exploring SpriteKit, create a new project in Xcode and choose the **Game** template. Pick SpriteKit as the underlying game technology and give the project a name, for instance, `SpriteKitDefault`, as shown in the following screenshot:

Figure 17.5 – Creating a SpriteKit project

When Xcode generates this project for you, you should notice some new files that you haven't seen before:

- `GameScene.sks`
- `Actions.sks`

These two files are to SpriteKit games what storyboards are to regular apps. You can use these to set up all the nodes for your game scene or to set up reusable actions that you can attach to your nodes. We will not get into these files now as they are pretty specific to game development.

If you build and run the sample project that Xcode provides, you can tap the screen to make new sprite nodes appear on the screen. Each node performs a little animation before it disappears. This isn't very special in itself, but it does contain a lot of valuable information. For instance, it shows you how to add something to a scene and how to animate it. Let's see exactly how this project is set up so you can apply this knowledge if you wish to build an AR experience with SpriteKit at some point.

Creating a SpriteKit scene

SpriteKit games use a special type of view to render their contents. This special view is always an instance or subclass of `SKView`. If you want to use SpriteKit with ARKit, you should use `ARSKView` instead because that view implements some special AR-related behavior, such as rendering the camera feed.

The view itself usually doesn't do much work regarding managing the games or its child views. Instead, the `SKScene` that contains the view is responsible for doing this work. This is similar to how you usually work with view controllers in other apps.

When you have created a scene, you can tell an `SKView` to present the scene. From this moment on, your game is running. In the sample code for the game project you created earlier, the following lines take care of loading and presenting the scene:

```
if let scene = SKScene(fileNamed: "GameScene") {
    scene.scaleMode = .aspectFill
    view.presentScene(scene)
}
```

When you create your scenes, you can choose whether you want to use `.sks` files or create scenes programmatically.

When you open the `GameScene.swift` file that Xcode created for you, most of the code should be pretty self-explanatory. When the scene is added to a view, a couple of `SKNode` instances are created and configured. The most interesting lines of code in this file are the following:

```
spinnyNode.run(SKAction.repeatForever(SKAction.rotate(byAng
    le: CGFloat(Double.pi), duration: 1)))
spinnyNode.run(SKAction.sequence([SKAction.wait(forDuration
    : 0.5), SKAction.fadeOut(withDuration: 0.5),
    SKAction.removeFromParent()]))
```

These lines set up an animation sequence for the spinning squares that get added when you tap the screen. In SpriteKit, actions are the preferred way to set up animations. You can group, chain, and combine actions to achieve pretty complicated effects. This is one of the many powerful tools that SpriteKit has to offer.

If you examine the code a little bit more, you'll find that copies of `spinnyNode` are created every time the user taps on the screen, moves their finger, or lifts their finger. Each interaction produces a slightly different copy of `spinnyNode`, so you can determine why `spinnyNode` was added to the scene by looking at its appearance.

Study this code, play around with it, and try to make sure that you grasp what it does. You don't have to become a SpriteKit expert by any means, but in this section, we have reviewed the basics of it so you can start using it. Let's have a look at how SceneKit works to prepare and implement your AR gallery.

Exploring SceneKit

If you're looking for a game framework that has excellent support for 3D games, SceneKit is a great candidate. SceneKit is Apple's framework for creating 3D games, and it is structured very similarly to how SpriteKit is set up.

Of course, SceneKit is entirely different from SpriteKit because it's used for 3D games rather than 2D games. Because of this, SceneKit also has very different ways of creating views and positioning them onscreen. For instance, when you want to create a simple object and place it on the screen, you will see terms such as geometry and materials. These terms should be familiar to game programmers, but if you're an AR enthusiast, you will probably have to get used to the terminology.

This section will walk you through setting up a straightforward SceneKit scene that closely resembles a part of the AR gallery you will implement later. This should provide you with enough information to begin experimenting with SceneKit.

Creating a basic SceneKit scene

To practice your SceneKit knowledge, create a new project and instead of choosing the **Game** template, pick the **Single View Application** template. Of course, you are free to explore the default project Xcode creates for you when you choose the **Game** template with SceneKit, but it's not terribly useful for the AR gallery.

After creating your project, open the main storyboard and look for a SceneKit view. Drag this view into the view controller. You should notice that the view you just added to the view controller has replaced the default view entirely. Because of this, the `view` property on `ViewController` will not be a regular `UIView`; it will be an instance of `SCNView` instead. This is the view that will be used to render the SceneKit scene in.

Add the following code to `viewDidLoad()` in `ViewController.swift` to cast the `view` property from `UIView` to `SCNView`:

```
guard let sceneView = self.view as? SCNView
   else { return }
```

Now, remember to add `import SceneKit` to the top so that `SCNView` compiles.

Similar to how SpriteKit works, SceneKit uses a scene to render its nodes in. Create an instance of SCNScene right after guard in viewDidLoad(), as shown:

```
let scene = SCNScene()
sceneView.scene = scene
sceneView.allowsCameraControl = true
sceneView.showsStatistics = true
sceneView.backgroundColor = UIColor.black
```

The preceding code creates a simple scene that will be used to render all elements in. In addition to creating the scene, several debugging features are enabled to monitor the performance of the scene. Also, note that the allowsCameraControl property on the scene view is set to true. This will allow users to move a virtual camera around so they can explore the scene by swiping around in it.

Every SceneKit scene is viewed as if you're looking at it through a camera. You will need to add this camera to the scene yourself, and you must set it up appropriately for your purpose. The fact that SceneKit uses a camera is very convenient because the camera that you are going to set up in a second is replaced by the actual camera of a device when the scene is run with ARKit.

Add the following lines of code to viewDidLoad() to create and configure the camera:

```
let cameraNode = SCNNode()
cameraNode.camera = SCNCamera()
cameraNode.position = SCNVector3(x: 0, y: 0, z: 15)
scene.rootNode.addChildNode(cameraNode)
```

Setting up a basic camera isn't very complicated. All you need is an SCNNode to add the camera to and an SCNCamera that will be used to view your scene through. Note that the camera is positioned using an SCNVector3 object. All nodes in a SceneKit scene use this object to express their positions in 3D space.

In addition to using a simulated camera, SceneKit also simulates real lighting conditions. When you run your scene with ARKit, the lighting conditions will be automatically managed by ARKit, making your objects look as if they truly are part of the environment. When you create a plain scene, however, you will need to add the lights yourself. Add the following lines of code to implement some ambient lighting:

```
let ambientLightNode = SCNNode()
ambientLightNode.light = SCNLight()
ambientLightNode.light!.type = .ambient
```

```
ambientLightNode.light!.color = UIColor.orange
scene.rootNode.addChildNode(ambientLightNode)
```

You can add different types of lights to a SceneKit scene. You can use ambient light as this sample does, but you can also add directional lights that focus on a particular direction, spotlight, or light points that light in all directions.

Now that you have lighting and a camera in place, you can add an object to the scene. You can use several pre-made shapes, also known as geometries, in your scene. Alternatively, you could import an entire 3D model in your scene. If you take a look at the default SceneKit app that Xcode generates if you create a new project with the **Game** template, you can see that it imports a 3D model of an airplane.

In the AR gallery you will build later, the artwork is augmented with digital information signs that are attached to the piece of art they belong to. To practice building such a sign, you will add a rectangular shape, or plane, to your SceneKit scene and place some text on top of it.

Add the following code to create a simple white plane, a node that renders the plane, and add it to the scene:

```
let plane = SCNPlane(width: 15, height: 10)
plane.firstMaterial?.diffuse.contents = UIColor.white
plane.firstMaterial?.isDoubleSided = true
plane.cornerRadius = 0.3


let planeNode = SCNNode(geometry: plane)
planeNode.position = SCNVector3(x: 0, y: 0, z: -15)
scene.rootNode.addChildNode(planeNode)
```

If you were to build and run your app now, you would see a white square that is positioned in front of the camera. By swiping on the scene, you can make the camera move around the plane to view it from all possible sides. Note that the plane appears to be quite large even though it was only set to be 15 wide and 10 high. You might have guessed that these numbers represent points on the screen, just like in other apps. In SceneKit, there is no concept of points. All values for size and distance must be specified in meters. This means that everything you do is done relative to other objects or their real-world sizes. Using real sizes is essential when you take your SceneKit knowledge to ARKit.

To add some text to the plane you just created, use the following code:

```
let text = SCNText(string: "Hello, world!", extrusionDepth:
  0)
text.font = UIFont.systemFont(ofSize: 2.3)
text.isWrapped = true
text.containerFrame = CGRect(x: -6.5, y: -4, width: 13,
  height: 8)
text.firstMaterial?.diffuse.contents = UIColor.red
let textNode = SCNNode(geometry: text)
planeNode.addChildNode(textNode)
```

The preceding code creates a text geometry. Since all values in SceneKit are in meters, the text size will be a lot smaller than you would probably expect. To make sure the text is positioned properly in the plane, text wrapping is enabled, and a `containerFrame` is used to specify the bounds for the text. Since the origin for the text field will be in the center of the plane it is displayed on, the x and y positions are offset negatively from the center to make sure the text appears in the correct place. You can try to play around with this frame to see what happens. After configuring the text, it is added to a node, and the node is added to the plane node.

If you run your app now, you can see the **Hello, World!** text rendered on the white plane you created before. This sample is an excellent taste of what you're going to create next. Let's dive straight into building your AR gallery!

Implementing an Augmented Reality gallery

Creating an excellent AR experience has been made a lot simpler with the great features that exist in ARKit. However, there are still several things to keep in mind if you want to build an AR experience that users will love.

Certain conditions, such as lighting, the environment, and even what the user is doing, can have an impact on the AR experience. In this section, you will implement an AR gallery, and you will discover firsthand how ARKit is both amazingly awesome and sometimes a little bit fragile.

First, you'll set up a session in ARKit so you can implement image tracking to discover certain predefined images in the world, and you'll show some text above the found picture. Then, you'll implement another feature that allows users to place art from a gallery in the app in their own room.

If you want to follow along with the steps to implement the ARKit gallery, make sure to grab the ARGallery_start project from the book's code bundle. Before you move on to implementing the AR gallery, explore the starter project for a little bit. The user interface that is prepared contains an instance of ARSCNView; this is the view that will be used to render the AR experience. A collection view has been added in preparation for the user adding their own images to the gallery, and a view for error messages has been added to inform the user about certain things that might be wrong.

You'll find that the project is quite basic so far. All the existing code does is set up the collection view, and some code was added to handle errors during the AR session. Let's implement image tracking, shall we?

Adding image tracking

When you add image tracking to your ARKit app, it will continuously scan the environment for images that match the ones you added to your app. This feature is great if you want users to look for specific images in their environment so you can provide more information about them or as part of a scavenger hunt. But more elaborate implementations might exist as part of a textbook or magazine where scanning a particular page would cause the whole page to come alive as part of a unique experience.

Before you can implement the image tracking experience, you must prepare some images for your users to find in the app. Once the content is ready, you're ready to build the AR experience itself.

Preparing images for tracking

Adding images to your app that are eligible for image tracking is relatively straightforward. The most important part is that you pay close attention to the images you add to your app. It's up to you to make sure that the images you add are high-quality and well-saturated. ARKit will scan for special features in an image to try to match it, so it's important that your image has enough details, contrast, and colors. An image of a smooth gradient might look like a recognizable image to you, but it could be tough for ARKit to detect.

To add images to your project, go to the `Assets.xcassets` folder, click the + icon in the bottom-left corner, and select **New AR Resource Group**, as shown in the following screenshot:

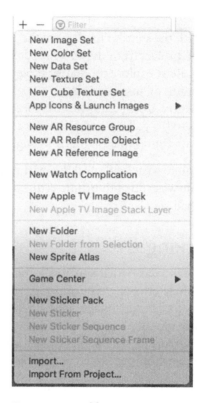

Figure 17.6 – Adding an AR resource

After adding a new resource group, you can drag images into the folder that was created. Each resource group will be loaded and monitored by ARKit all at once, so make sure you don't add too many images to a single resource group because that could negatively impact the performance of your app. Apple recommends you add up to about 25 images to a single resource group.

After you add an image to a resource group, Xcode will analyze the images and warn you if it thinks something is wrong with your image. Usually, Xcode will inform you as soon as you add a new image because ARKit requires the physical size of the image you want to detect to be known. So, if you're going to detect a specific painting or a page in a magazine, you must add the dimensions for these resources in centimeters as they exist in the real world.

The start project from the code bundle comes with a couple of prepared images that you can explore to see some examples of the kinds of images that you could use in your own apps.

> **Tip**
>
> If you want to have some content of your own, take photos of artwork or pictures that you have around the house or office. You can use the Measure app in iOS to measure the physical dimensions of the pictures and add them to your AR gallery project. Make sure that your pictures are well-saturated and free of any glare or reflections.

Once you have found and added some excellent content to use in your AR gallery, it's time to build the experience itself.

Building the image tracking experience

To implement image tracking, you will set up an ARSession that uses ARWorldTrackingConfiguration to detect images and track a user's movement through the environment. When one of the images you have prepared is discovered in the scene, an SCNPlane will be added above the picture with a short description of the picture itself.

Because ARKit uses the camera, your app must explicitly provide a reason for accessing the camera, so the user understands why your app needs permission to use their camera. Add the NSCameraUsageDescription key to the Info.plist file and add a short bit of text about why the gallery needs access to the camera.

If you open ViewController.swift, you will find a property called artDescriptions. Make sure to update this dictionary with the names of the images you added to the resource group and add a short description for each image.

Next, update viewDidLoad() so ViewController is set as the delegate for both ARSCNView and ARSession. Add the following lines of code to do this:

```
arKitScene.delegate = self
arKitScene.session.delegate = self
```

The scene delegate and session delegate are very similar. The session delegate provides very fine-grained control of the content that is displayed in the scene, and you'll usually use this protocol extensively if you build your own rendering. Since the AR gallery is rendered using SceneKit, the only reason to adopt ARSessionDelegate is to respond to changes in the session's tracking state.

All of the interesting methods that you should adopt are part of ARSCNViewDelegate. This delegate is used to respond to specific events, for instance, when new features are discovered in the scene or when new content has been added.

Currently, your AR gallery doesn't do much. You must configure the ARSession that is part of the scene to begin using ARKit. The best moment to set this all up is right before the view controller becomes visible. Therefore, you should do all of the remaining setup in viewWillAppear(_:). Add the following implementation for this method to ViewController:

```
override func viewWillAppear(_ animated: Bool) {
  super.viewWillAppear(animated)
  // 1
  let imageSet = ARReferenceImage.referenceImages(
    inGroupNamed: "Art", bundle: Bundle.main)!

  // 2
  let configuration = ARWorldTrackingConfiguration()
  configuration.planeDetection = [.vertical, .horizontal]
  configuration.detectionImages = imageSet

  // 3
  arKitScene.session.run(configuration, options: [])
}
```

The code is explained as follows:

1. The first step in this method is to read the reference image from the app bundle. These are the images you added to Assets.xcassets.

2. Next, ARWorldTrackingConfiguration is created, and it's configured to track both horizontal and vertical planes, as well as the reference images.

3. Lastly, the configuration is passed to the session's run(_:options:) method.

If you run your app now, you should already be prompted for camera usage, and you should see the error-handling working. Try covering the camera with your hand, which should make an error message appear.

Keeping an AR session alive if a view isn't visible anymore is quite wasteful, so it's a good idea to pause the session if the app is closed or if the view controller that contains the AR scene becomes invisible. Add the following method to `ViewController` to achieve this:

```
override func viewWillDisappear(_ animated: Bool) {
    super.viewWillDisappear(animated)
    arKitScene.session.pause()
}
```

In the current setup, the AR session detects your images, but it does nothing to visualize this. When one of the images you added is identified, `ARSCNViewDelegate` is notified of this. To be specific, the `renderer(_:didAdd:for:)` method is called on the scene delegate when a new `SCNNode` is added to the view. For instance, when the AR session discovers a flat surface, it adds a node for `ARPlaneAnchor`, or when it detects one of the images you're tracking, a node for `ARImageAnchor` is added. Since this method can be called for different reasons, it's essential that you add logic to differentiate between the various reasons that could cause a new `SCNNode` to be added to the scene.

Because the AR gallery will implement several other features that could trigger the addition of a new node, you should separate the different actions you want to take for each different type of anchor into specialized methods. Add the following method to `ARSCNViewDelegate` to add the information plane next to a detected image:

```
func placeImageInfo(withNode node: SCNNode, for anchor:
    ARImageAnchor) {
    let referenceImage = anchor.referenceImage
    // 1
    let infoPlane = SCNPlane(width: 15, height: 10)
    infoPlane.firstMaterial?.diffuse.contents = UIColor.white
    infoPlane.firstMaterial?.transparency = 0.5
    infoPlane.cornerRadius = 0.5
    // 2
    let infoNode = SCNNode(geometry: infoPlane)
    infoNode.localTranslate(by: SCNVector3(0, 10, -
        referenceImage.physicalSize.height / 2 + 0.5))
    infoNode.eulerAngles.x = -.pi / 4
    // 3
    let textGeometry = SCNText(string:
    artDescriptions[referenceImage.name ?? "flowers"],
```

```
    extrusionDepth: 0.2)
  textGeometry.firstMaterial?.diffuse.contents =
    UIColor.red
  textGeometry.font = UIFont.systemFont(ofSize: 1.3)
  textGeometry.isWrapped = true
  textGeometry.containerFrame = CGRect(x: -6.5, y: -4,
    width: 13, height: 8)
  let textNode = SCNNode(geometry: textGeometry)
  // 4
  node.addChildNode(infoNode)
  infoNode.addChildNode(textNode)
}
```

The preceding code should look somewhat familiar to you. First, an instance of
SCNPlane is created. Then, this plane is added to SCNNode. This node is translated
slightly to position it above the detected image. This translation uses SCNVector3 so
it can be translated into three dimensions. The node is also rotated a little bit to create
a nice-looking effect.

Next, add the following implementation for renderer(_:didAdd:for:):

```
func renderer(_ renderer: SCNSceneRenderer, didAdd node:
  SCNNode, for anchor: ARAnchor) {
  if let imageAnchor = anchor as? ARImageAnchor {
    placeImageInfo(withNode: node, for: imageAnchor)
  }
}
```

This method checks whether the anchor that was discovered is an image anchor; if it is,
placeImageInfo(withNode:for:) is called to display the information sign.

Go ahead and run your app now! When you find one of the images that you added to
your resource group, an information box should appear on top of it, as shown in the
following screenshot:

Figure 17.7 – AR box on top of the image

Pretty awesome, right? Let's take it one step further and allow users to position some of the pictures from the collection view wherever they want in the scene.

Placing your own content in 3D space

To spice up the AR gallery a little bit, it would be great to be able to add some new artwork to the environment. Using ARKit, doing this becomes relatively simple. There are a couple of gotchas to take into account when implementing a feature such as this, but overall, Apple did a great job making ARKit an accessible platform to work with for developers.

When a user taps on one of the images in the collection view at the bottom of the screen, the image they tapped should be added to the environment. If possible, the image should be attached to one of the walls surrounding the user. If this isn't possible, the image should still be added, except it will float in the middle of the space.

To build this feature, you should implement `collectionView(_:didSelectItemAt:)` since this method is called when a user taps on one of the items in a collection view. When this method is called, the code should take the current position of the user in the environment and then insert a new `ARAnchor` that corresponds to the location where the new item should be added.

Also, to detect nearby vertical planes, such as walls, some hit testing should be done to see whether a vertical plane exists in front of the user. Add the following implementation of collectionView(_:didSelectItemAt:):

```swift
func collectionView(_ collectionView: UICollectionView,
    didSelectItemAt indexPath: IndexPath) {
  //1
  guard let camera =
    arKitScene.session.currentFrame?.camera
    else { return }
  //2
  let hitTestResult = arKitScene.hitTest(CGPoint(x: 0.5, y:
    0.5), types: [.existingPlane])
  let firstVerticalPlane = hitTestResult.first(where: {
    result in
    guard let planeAnchor = result.anchor as? ARPlaneAnchor
      else { return false }

    return planeAnchor.alignment == .vertical
  })
  //3
  var translation = matrix_identity_float4x4
  translation.columns.3.z = -
    Float(firstVerticalPlane?.distance ?? -1)
  let cameraTransform = camera.transform
  let rotation = matrix_float4x4(cameraAdjustmentMatrix)
  let transform = matrix_multiply(cameraTransform,
    matrix_multiply(translation, rotation))

  //4
  let anchor = ARAnchor(transform: transform)
  imageNodes[anchor.identifier] = UIImage(named:
    images[indexPath.row])!
  arKitScene.session.add(anchor: anchor)

  storeWorldMap()
}
```

Even though there are only four steps in this snippet, a lot is going on. Let's review it:

1. First, the camera is grabbed from the current frame in the AR session so it can be used later to determine the user's location in the scene.

2. Next, a hit test is performed to see whether any planes were already detected in the scene. Since this hit test will return both vertical and horizontal planes, the results are filtered to find the very first vertical plane that was found in the hit test.

3. Since the location of every ARAnchor is represented as a transformation from the world origin, the third step is to determine the transformation that should be applied to position the new artwork in the correct place. The world origin is the place where the AR session first became active. After creating a default translation, the z value for the translation is adjusted, so the object is added either in front of the user or against the nearest vertical plane. Next, the current position of the user is retrieved through the camera. The rotation for the camera will have to be adjusted in the next steps because the camera does not follow the device's orientation. This means that the camera will always assume that the x axis runs across the length of the device, starting at the top and moving downward toward the home indicator area. A computed property to determine how the rotation should be adjusted is already added to the AR gallery starter project.

4. After setting up the correct transformation properties for the anchor, an instance of ARAnchor is created. The unique identifier and image that the user tapped are then stored in the imageNodes dictionary so the image can be added to the scene after the new anchor is registered on the scene.

To add the image to the scene, you should implement a helper method that will be called from rendered(_:didAdd:for:), similar to the helper method you added to show the information card for the image tracking feature. Add the following code to ViewController to implement this helper:

```
func placeCustomImage(_ image: UIImage, withNode node:
  SCNNode) {
  let plane = SCNPlane(width: image.size.width / 1000,
    height: image.size.height / 1000)
  plane.firstMaterial?.diffuse.contents = image

  node.addChildNode(SCNNode(geometry: plane))
}
```

To make it easier to see whether an appropriate vertical plane exists, you can implement a helper method that visualizes the planes that the AR session discovers. Add the following code to the `ViewController` class to implement this helper:

```
func vizualise(_ node: SCNNode, for planeAnchor:
  ARPlaneAnchor) {
  let infoPlane = SCNPlane(width:
   CGFloat(planeAnchor.extent.x), height:
     CGFloat(planeAnchor.extent.z))
  infoPlane.firstMaterial?.diffuse.contents =
    UIColor.orange
  infoPlane.firstMaterial?.transparency = 0.5
  infoPlane.cornerRadius = 0.2

  let infoNode = SCNNode(geometry: infoPlane)
  infoNode.eulerAngles.x = -.pi / 2

  node.addChildNode(infoNode)
}
```

The previous method takes a node and anchor to create a new `SCNPlane`, which is added to the exact position where the new plane anchor was discovered.

The final step in implementing this feature is to call the helper methods when needed. Update the implementation for `renderer(_:didAdd:for:)` as follows:

```
func renderer(_ renderer: SCNSceneRenderer, didAdd node:
  SCNNode, for anchor: ARAnchor) {
  if let imageAnchor = anchor as? ARImageAnchor {
    placeImageInfo(withNode: node, for: imageAnchor)
  } else if let customImage = imageNodes[anchor.identifier]
  {
    placeCustomImage(customImage, withNode: node)
  } else if let planeAnchor = anchor as? ARPlaneAnchor {
    vizualise(node, for: planeAnchor)
  }
}
```

If you run your app now, you should see orange squares appear in areas where ARKit detected a flat surface. Note that ARKit needs textures and visual markers to work well. If you try to detect a solid white wall, it's unlikely that ARKit will properly recognize the wall due to a lack of textures. However, a brick wall or a wall that has wallpaper with some graphics on it should work well for this purpose.

The following screenshot shows an example where an image is attached to a wall, together with the plane indicator:

Figure 17.8 – Adding an image to an AR plane

This wraps up the implementation of your own personal AR gallery. There is still much to learn about the things you can do with AR, so make sure to keep on experimenting and learning so you can create amazing experiences for your users.

Summary

In this chapter, you learned a lot. You gained some insight into what AR is, the basic workings of AR, and what you can do with it. Then you learned about the components that make up an excellent AR experience, and you implemented your first small AR experience by adopting Quick Look in an app to preview AR content in a real AR session.

Then you explored different ways to render content in an AR scene. You took a quick look at SpriteKit and SceneKit and learned that SpriteKit is Apple's 2D game development framework. You also learned that SceneKit is Apple's 3D game framework, which makes it extremely well-suited for usage in an AR app.

Then you implemented an AR gallery that uses image tracking and plane detection and allows users to add their own content to their gallery. In the process of doing this, you saw that it's not always easy to get ARKit to work well. Bad lighting and other factors can make AR experiences less than ideal.

In the next chapter, you will create a macOS app with Catalyst.

18
Creating a macOS app with Catalyst

At WWDC 2019, Apple introduced Mac Catalyst to developers worldwide. With Mac Catalyst, developers could bring iPad apps into Mac quite easily. Catalyst allows iPad apps to be ported to Mac without much effort. This brings a whole new audience (Mac users) to iPad apps and expands the possibilities of the macOS ecosystem.

In this chapter, we are going to review the basics of Mac Catalyst. We will explore the new features introduced at WWDC 2020, and we will turn an iPad app into a Mac app using Catalyst. We will put into practice the two different ways to do this using Catalyst: **Scale Interface to Match iPad** and the new **Optimize Interface for Mac** option. We will compare the differences between them and the pros and cons of both approaches.

In this chapter, we're going to cover the following main topics:

- Discovering Mac Catalyst
- Exploring new Mac Catalyst features
- Building your first Mac Catalyst app

By the end of this chapter, you will be able to migrate your iPad apps to macOS and grow the audience and possibilities of your app within the Mac ecosystem.

Technical requirements

The code bundle for this chapter includes a starter project called `todo_start` and its completed version. You can find them in the code bundle repository:

`https://github.com/PacktPublishing/Mastering-iOS-14-Programming-4th-Edition`

Discovering Mac Catalyst

Mac Catalyst helps developers to bring their iPad apps into Mac. Native Mac apps can share code with iPad apps, creating a unified ecosystem for users and developers.

With Mac Catalyst, developers can adapt touch gestures and controls from the iPad to mouse and keyboard controls in the Mac app counterpart.

When Apple added support on Mac Catalyst for UIKit on Mac, it took a huge step forward in terms of compatibility between the iPad and Mac. Apps that use SwiftUI instead had the advantage of becoming Universal apps and therefore they adapt even better on both systems.

Once an app has made the initial transition from iPad to iPad + Mac with the help of Mac Catalyst, the result is very promising. There is one codebase to serve both platforms. By having just one codebase, companies can reduce the amount of time and effort needed to develop, maintain, and fix features in the app (for both systems).

There are also some drawbacks with Mac Catalyst. Not every iOS framework is supported right now. Apple is adding more and more every year. Also, some third-party libraries may not be supported, and it is the developer's responsibility to exclude them from the Mac system and look for an alternative.

Another drawback of Mac Catalyst is that some apps that go from iPad to Mac can feel a bit out of context. I refer to some apps that make use of a heavy iOS look-and-feel and are ported to Mac as is. Some elements of the UI differ a lot in both systems (checkboxes, popups, placement of the buttons, and so on). Some apps may require some extra work to adapt the UI from the iPad to the Mac style, but not every company or team has the resources, time, or intention to do so.

In order to help with this issue, Mac Catalyst has a new feature called **Optimize Interface for Mac**. Instead of the former **Scale Interface to Match iPad** option, Mac Catalyst allows this new feature that transforms some UIKit controls into more Mac-styled ones automatically.

In this section, we have learned about the basics of Mac Catalyst. Let's discuss the new improvement showcased during WWDC 2020 for Mac Catalyst in the next section.

Exploring new Mac Catalyst features

During WWDC 2020, Apple showcased the new **Optimize Interface for Mac** method. When we port an iPad app to Mac using this method, it brings some significant differences from the previous method, **Scale Interface to Match iPad**. The differences are as follows:

1. Content is rendered 1:1. With **Scale Interface**, the views are scaled to 77% of their original sizes on Mac. This could cause problems in some views with **AutoLayout** rules that break or that simply change the overall shape of your UI. Now, with 1:1 rendering, the iPad app and the Mac app will keep the same dimensions and sizes. This increases the text quality a lot by not scaling it down on Mac; the text looks better and easier to read on your app.

2. macOS controls for UIKit counterparts. With the new **Optimize Interface for Mac** option, Catalyst uses Mac-style controls instead of the UIKit ones from your iPad app. By doing so, the UI of the app in Mac looks much more familiar to Mac users.

3. Similar to the previous point, macOS font spacing and standard macOS spacing are used in the Mac Catalyst app instead of those defined on the iPad version (which is different).

4. Much more iOS frameworks have been made available to Mac with Catalyst. Examples include `AVFoundation`, `NotificationCenter`, `ReplayKit`, `StoreKit`, `MessageUI`, and tons more.

5. Added support for physical keyboard events on iOS. Now they are available on Mac Catalyst on Mac. Games can benefit from this.

6. The focus engine from tvOS is available now.

7. `.selectionFollowsFocus` from `tableViews` and `collectionViews` is now available.

8. Now we can hide the cursor on Mac when needed.

9. There are a new color wheel and color picker.

10. `UISplitViewController` now supports three columns.

11. `SFSymbols` are fully supported.

12. Mac Catalyst's new extensions such as the Photo Editing extension are now available.

13. Widgets from WidgetKit are also available from iPad to Mac thanks to Catalyst.

14. Users can enjoy universal purchases (buying items on iPad and using them on the Mac app too).

15. New toolbar styles.

Later in the chapter, when building an app with both methods, you will be able to see these differences, and you will be applying the necessary fixes and steps to avoid them in your apps.

In this section, we have learned about the new features launched in 2020 for Mac Catalyst. Now, let's start building our first Mac Catalyst app in the next section!

Building your first Mac Catalyst app

In this section, we are going to start working with a simple iPad to-do app, and we will transform it into a macOS app using two different techniques. The base app is very basic (you can't even add new to-do elements to it!) but it illustrates what kinds of errors, UI modifications, and methods you need to go through when going from iPad to Mac.

We will follow these steps:

1.   First, we will explore the iPad app itself to understand its essential elements and components.

2.   Then, we will use the first method to make it compatible with macOS: **Scale Interface to Match iPad**.

3.   Finally, we will use the new method, **Optimize Interface for Mac**. We will compare the results with the **Scale Interface** method to match the iPad method, so you will learn when to use one or another, depending on your app.

Let's start by exploring our iPad to-do app!

Exploring the iPad app

In this section, we are going to take a quick look at the base app and its components to be able to modify them while understanding what we are doing.

You can find the code in the code bundle of this book. The project name is `todo_start`. Go ahead and open the project. Build and run it. You should see something like this in the iPad simulator in landscape mode:

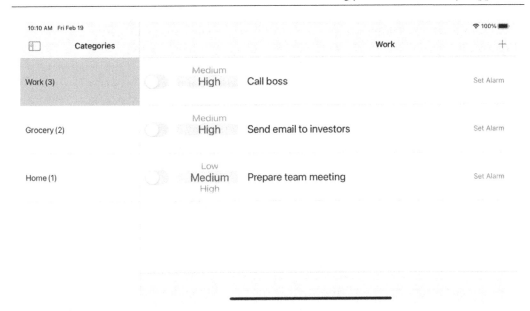

Figure 18.1 – To-do app landscape mode

If you are familiar with iPad apps, you will already be able to tell from these screenshots that the main component of this iPad app is `SplitViewController`. `SplitViewController` typically has two or three columns (`UIViewController` instances) inside it. In our case, we have two: a side menu on the left and a detail panel on the right (in landscape mode). In portrait mode, the side menu becomes a popover menu, and the detail panel is the main view.

Let's quickly check out the project structure and highlight the most important files in it:

- The `MasterViewController.swift` file contains `MasterViewController`, which is the side menu of `SplitViewController`. It has a table view with its corresponding table view cells (`CategoryTableViewCell`).

- The `DetailViewController.swift` file contains `DetailViewController`, which is the detail view of `SplitViewController`. It has a table view, with its corresponding table view cells (`EntryTableViewCell`).

- The `Datasource.swift` file contains the `Datasource` of the project, which will feed the view controllers with the to-do list using the `load() -> [Category]` method. It also contains the models of our to-do project. The to-do list is built using categories (such as work, grocery, or home), and entries inside those categories (such as "call my boss"). The `Datasource.swift` file contains structs representing these models: `Category`, `Entry`, and `Priority`. In a real-world app, you would separate these models into their own file/directory, but for simplicity, we are keeping them within the `Datasource` itself.

So, to summarize the components of the app, the side menu (`MasterViewController`) displays a list of to-do categories in the form of a table (`Category` and `CategoryTableViewCell` instances). When selecting one category, the detail view (`DetailViewController`) displays a table with different to-do entries (`Entry` and `EntryTableViewCell` instances). All the data is provided by `Datasource`.

The entries of the to-do in each category are represented by cells that contain different information in each to-do (`EntryTableViewCell`):

Figure 18.2 – Entry cell

These table view cells contain the following:

- One `UISwitch` to represent whether the to-do is pending or complete.
- One `UIPickerView` to represent the priority of the task (**High**, **Medium**, or **Low**).
- One `UILabel` to describe the task.
- One `UIButton` to set an alarm in the task.

There is also an additional button in the top-right corner:

Figure 18.3 – Add to-do button

This button represents the action that will allow the user to add a new entry to the to-do list.

There is no functionality at all except for displaying the elements themselves right now, but you will understand later in the chapter why each of these elements is there. An easy and simple app, right? Let's start the transformation process from iPad to Mac now!

Scaling your iPad app for Mac

In this section, we are going to transform the iPad app into a Mac-compatible app using the Mac Catalyst **Scale Interface to Match iPad** method. This was the first way introduced by Apple to transform iPad apps into Mac apps easily.

Open the project from the current section and go to the project navigator. In the **Deployment Info** section, check the **Mac** checkbox and press **Enable** in the popup:

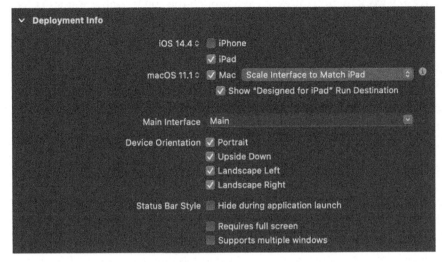

Figure 18.4 – Enabling Mac support

Make sure that the option is set to **Scale Interface to Match iPad**.

Now, build and run the app using Mac as the target device. You should see the following UI:

Figure 18.5 – The Mac version of the to-do app

That was extremely easy! It is true that our example app is very simple and straightforward. But with a simple click, it is already compatible and "usable" on Mac. We didn't have any work to do! However, even though the app is usable, it doesn't have the Mac style. Let's list some elements that differ from a traditional Mac app:

- Mac apps don't use toolbars to contain actions such as the + symbol. The actions are usually located in the bottom-right corner.
- Buttons such as **Set Alarm** don't look like Mac buttons.
- Mac apps don't use this kind of Picker that much.
- Mac apps use checkboxes instead of switches.
- The views have been scaled to 77% of the original ones. That can break some constraints in your code, and you may need to review parts of the UI.

The more complex UI your app has on the iPad, the less "Mac" it will feel using this method. But we can't complain too much; we just made it compatible with one click!

This first iteration is always recommended as the first step to port your iPad app to Mac. Now that we have a Mac app, we are going to work on improving the UI to give it a more Mac look-and-feel. To do so, we will use the new method created by Apple: **Optimize Interface for Mac**. This method has its pros and cons, and we will see them in the next section.

Optimizing your iPad app for Mac

In this section, we are going to use the **Optimize Interface for Mac** option on the iPad app and we will learn how to adapt the result to suit the expected Mac-style interface on our app.

In the project navigator, in the **Deployment Info** section, go ahead and change the Mac option to **Optimize Interface for Mac**:

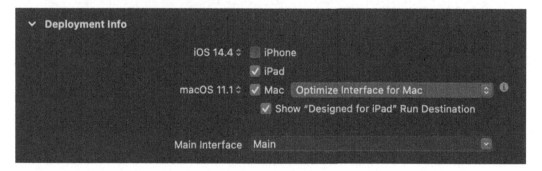

Figure 18.6 – Using Optimize Interface for Mac

After selecting this option, change the target to Mac and launch the app. You should get a crash saying the following:

```
[General] UIPickerView is not supported when running Catalyst
apps in the Mac idiom.
```

We didn't have any problem when we used the **Scale Interface** option in the previous section. However, when using **Optimize Interface**, we are applying bigger and deeper changes in the transformation of our app into a Mac one. And things can get tricker. This error is displayed in the console because some UIKit elements are not available in Catalyst when using the **Optimize Interface** option. In such cases, we should provide an alternative component, hide the component for Mac, or adapt other solutions. We can't use UIPickerView instances as displayed in this example. One solution could be to use SwiftUI's Picker (which is available under **Optimize Interface** as ComboBox).

We are going to learn now how to use or not use specific components in our app, depending on the device that is running it. We are going to install this UIPickerView on iPad, but we will remove it from the Mac version (to make it compile for now). We will achieve this by using storyboard variations.

Storyboard variations can help us to install or uninstall specific components in our view controllers based on certain parameters, such as the device, the width of the screen, the height, and the gamut.

Let's uninstall UIPickerView from the cell when the app runs on a Mac. Follow these steps:

1. Open the Main.storyboard file and go to **Detail View Controller**. Select the **entry** cell prototype:

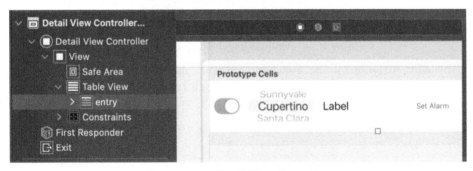

Figure 18.7 – Detail View Controller

2. Now, select the `UIPickerView` of the cell, and in its **Attributes Inspector** window, add a variation on the **Installed** section by clicking on the + sign:

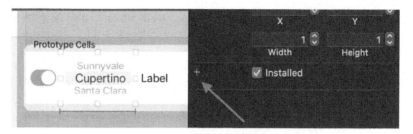

Figure 18.8 – Adding an Installed variation

3. In the popup that shows up, select **Mac** from the **Idiom** selector:

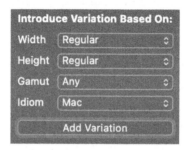

Figure 18.9 – Adding a Mac idiom variation

4. Now, you want to uncheck the new variation so that this component will not be installed in the Mac idiom:

Figure 18.10 – Uninstalling the Mac idiom variation

Great! By using variations in the storyboard, you are able to specify when to install certain components based on the device that is running it and other factors! Now try launching the app again, using Mac as the target. This time, the app should not crash and you will get the following screen:

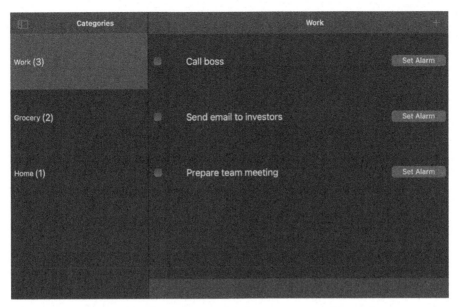

Figure 18.11 – First optimization for the Mac version of the to-do app

Great! We managed to use storyboard variations to adapt the Mac version of our app. Ideally, you should now find an alternative to this `UIPickerView` that works on Mac (SwiftUI's Picker is an example). That will be homework for you!

You can see in the preceding screenshot that there are still some issues that are common when translating an iPad app to Mac using the **Optimize Interface** option:

- In the **Categories** table cells, the word font size is different from the number font size. In our iPad app, the font size was the same. Take a closer look at the font size of **Work (3)** as an example.

- Mac apps don't use buttons such as + in the toolbar. The most common place for such actions is the bottom-right corner of the window.

Let's work on these two issues next. Open the `Main.storyboard` file and check the font used in the labels of the **Root View Controller** table:

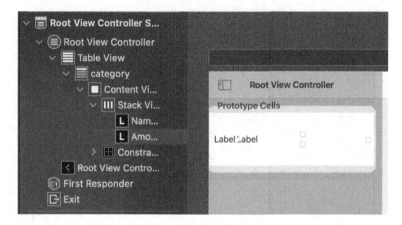

Figure 18.12 – Root View Controller cell labels

If you take a look at the font size used in these two labels, it is not the same. The first label is using the **Body** font. The second label is using the **System - 17.0** font. But then why do they look the same in **Scale Interface to Match iPad**? The reason is that in that option, the views are scaled down to 77% of the original size, and both fonts look the same. But in **Optimize Interface for Mac**, views are kept 1:1 in ratio and the predefined text styles adapt to the view content size. So, if you are going to use an iPad app in Mac with **Optimize Interface**, the best way to tackle fonts is to use these predefined styles all around your app. You will not have to tweak them later depending on the device.

In order to fix the problem, change the **System – 17.0** font to the **Body** font in the label attribute inspector:

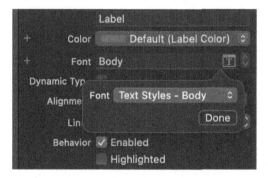

Figure 18.13 – Using Text Styles

Now run the app on the Mac target:

Figure 18.14 – New font style results on the Mac

As displayed in the previous screenshot, the font sizes of both **Work** and **(3)** are now the same. If you execute the app on an iPad, they will also be the same. We don't have any difference anymore.

With this fix in place, it is time for us to hide the toolbar on `DetailViewController`. Mac apps don't use toolbars to display a single action as we are doing right now:

Figure 18.15 – Toolbar with a right-side action button

We learned how to show/hide elements using storyboard variations, but for this toolbar, we are going to do it programmatically. The component will still be installed, but we will hide it on Mac. Open the `DetailViewController` file and change the `viewWillAppear` method implementation for this one:

```
override func viewWillAppear(_ animated: Bool) {
  super.viewWillAppear(animated)

  if traitCollection.userInterfaceIdiom == .mac {
    navigationController?.setToolbarHidden(true, animated:
      false)
  } else {
    navigationItem.rightBarButtonItem =
      UIBarButtonItem(barButtonSystemItem: .add, target: self,
        action: #selector(createTapped))
    navigationController?.setToolbarHidden(false, animated:
      animated)
  }
}
```

Review the highlighted code. We are able to detect in which device we are launching the app by using the `userInterfaceIdiom` property of `traitCollection`. When it is `.mac`, we hide the toolbar, and only add the right-side + button when we are on another device (such as an iPad).

If you build and execute the app on the Mac target, the + button is gone. Great! But now we cannot create new to-do items! We have lost access to this button for Mac. We need to adapt this scenario in a different way.

Traditionally, for a Mac interface, the **Create** action will be in the bottom-right corner of the window. Let's add it now. Open the `Main.storyboard` file. Select the table view of **Detail View Controller**:

Figure 18.16 – Detail View Controller table view

Now we are going to make space at the bottom of the controller for a new button, but only on Mac. Follow these steps:

1. Go into the size inspector of **Table View** of **Detail View Controller**.

2. Edit the constraint that attaches the bottom of the table view with the bottom of the controller, **Edit the Align Bottom with Safe Area**, and give it a constant of `-60`:

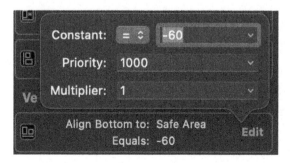

Figure 18.17 – Editing the table view bottom constraint

3. Now add a new `UIButton` in the space between the table and the bottom of the view controller. Set **Create** as the button title. Add the four constraints displayed in the following screenshot:

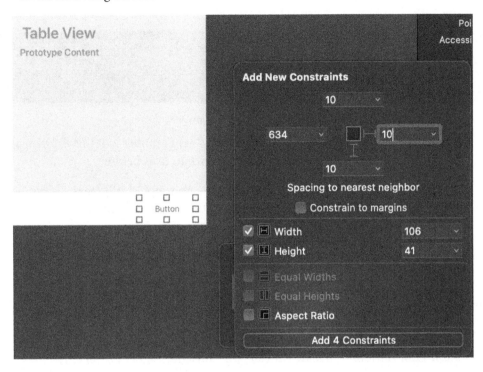

Figure 18.18 – Adding a new button

4. Now add a **Vertical Spacing** constraint from the table view to the new **Create** button that you just added (you can hold *Ctrl* + drag from the table to the button).

5. We want to add a variation to the button. We want the button to be installed only for Mac idioms. So, go ahead and add a variation for Mac and uncheck the default one (as we did previously in this chapter for `UIPickerView`). By doing this, the button will only be visible on Mac devices:

Figure 18.19 – Installing the new button only in Mac

6. If you did it properly, the button should disappear in the storyboard if you are using an iPad as the preview device. You can change the device to **Mac** with **Mac Idiom** (*not Mac with iPad Idiom!*) and it will be shown again (you can do this in the bottom options of the storyboard window):

Figure 18.20 – Device preview selection

7. Finally, we need to again edit the constraint of item number 2 of this list. You added a -60 constant to it. Now we want to put it back to 0, as before.

Now go ahead and execute the app on an iPad target. You should still see the + symbol in the top-right corner and not see the new **Create** button at the bottom. Execute it now on a Mac target. You should get the following error on the console:

```
[LayoutConstraints] Unable to simultaneously satisfy
constraints.
```

This is because we added two different constraints that are not able to co-exist:

- **TableView.Bottom** to **Safe Area.Bottom** with constant 0
- **TableView.Bottom** to **Create Button** with constant 9

In fact, we need both constants, but one is for iPad devices and the other only applies to Mac. Go ahead and change the priority of one of them to 250:

Figure 18.21 – Changing the constraint priority

With this, we can keep both constraints, but they will not be exclusive to each other. When the Mac button is not installed, that constraint will not take effect and the other one will apply (attaching the table view bottom to the bottom of the safe area). Go ahead and execute the app using a Mac target:

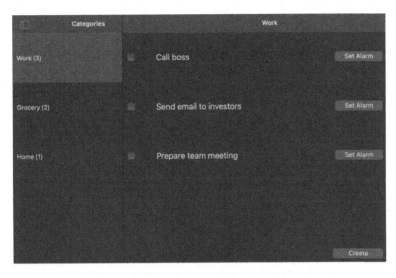

Figure 18.22 – Mac app final version

That looks great! Now we have two different variations of the UI, one for iPad and another one more adapted to Mac standards. Compare it now with the previous iPad-looking version for Mac that **Scale Interface to Match iPad** provided us:

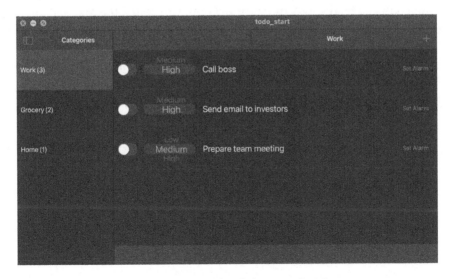

Figure 18.23 – Initial scaled version for Mac

As you can see, it is quite different! The new version feels more Mac-native. The buttons, toolbar, controls placement, and overall scale of the elements feel much better for the Mac version. It requires a bit more work, but the results are worth the effort. You can always do an initial port of your iPad app to Mac with **Scale Interface to Match iPad**, and then work on **Optimize Interface for Mac** later on!

In this section, we started with a simple to-do iPad app. We used Mac Catalyst to port it to the Mac. First, we used the **Scale Interface to Match iPad** option, making the app available on Mac with one click. But then, we wanted to improve the UI to feel more aligned with the Mac standards, so we used the new **Optimize Interface for Mac** option. This option is not as straightforward as the scaling one, and we had to adapt certain sizes, remove some UI controls that are not available on the Mac, and create different variations specifically for the Mac. But the results are looking great!

Let's now wrap up the chapter with a summary.

Summary

We started the chapter with a brief Mac Catalyst introduction. We explained how Apple has provided developers with an easy way to port iPad apps into Mac apps with Mac Catalyst, and all the benefits that this new feature provides.

Then, we discussed the most recent improvements and changes on Mac Catalyst presented in 2020. Among those new features, we mentioned the implications of **Optimize Interface for Mac**, and how it can enhance your iPad apps to become great Mac apps.

Finally, and taking an iPad app as the starting point, we created the Mac version using both Mac Catalyst methods: **Scale Interface to Match iPad** and **Optimize Interface for Mac**. We showcased their pros and cons, and we applied the most common fixes and improvements that you will find yourself using with these two methods. By comparing them with the same app, you have got an understanding of the main differences between them and when to apply one or the other.

In the next chapter, we will learn how and when to test your code.

19
Ensuring App Quality with Tests

In all of the chapters so far, the main focus has been code that ran as part of an app. The apps you have worked on are small and can easily be tested manually. However, this approach doesn't scale well if your apps become larger. This approach also doesn't scale if you want to verify lots of different user input, lots of screens, convoluted logic, or even if you're going to run tests on many different devices.

Xcode comes with built-in testing tools. These tools allow you to write tests so you can make sure that all of the business logic for your app works as expected. More importantly, you can test that your user interface functions and behaves as intended in many different automated scenarios.

Many developers tend to shy away from testing and postpone it until the end of the project, or don't do it at all. The reason for this is that it's often pretty hard to figure out how to write proper tests. This is especially true if you're just starting out with testing. Lots of developers feel like large parts of the logic their tests validate are so obvious that writing tests for that logic just feels silly. When testing is not approached correctly, it can be more of a burden than a relief by being high-maintenance and not testing the essential areas of code.

This chapter serves as an introduction to writing both logic and user interface tests using Xcode and its built-in tools. By the end of this chapter, you should be able to set up a robust suite of tests and understand how you can make use of the tools provided by Xcode to write better code that is testable and reliable. This chapter covers the following topics:

- Testing logic with XCTest
- Optimizing code for testability
- Testing the user interface with XCUITest

Testing logic with XCTest

This section is going to help you to discover the testing capabilities on iOS with XCTest. Even if you haven't written any tests before, you might have thoughts or ideas about it. To start testing code, you don't need to have a computer science degree or spend days studying the absolute best way to test your code. In fact, the chances are that you're already testing your code and you don't even know it.

So, what does it mean to test your code? That's what this section aims to make clear. First, you will read about the different types of tests you can write. Then, you'll learn what XCTest is and how you can set up a test suite for an app. Finally, you'll learn how to optimally test some actual code and how code can be refactored to make it more testable.

Understanding what it means to test code

When you test your code, you're essentially making sure that certain input produces the desired output. A very basic example of a test would be to make sure that calling a method that increments its input by a given value produces the output you expect.

Any time you launch your application and perform any action within your app, you are testing some part of your code. Any time you print something to the console to verify that the expected value is printed, you are also testing your code. Once you think about testing this way, a concept that might have sounded hard before actually does not seem as complicated as you may have thought. So, if just by using your app, you are indeed testing it already, then, what should you write tests for? Let's see how to determine when to write a test for your code.

Determining which tests to write

When you start testing, it's often hard to decide what logic you want to test and what logic you don't want to test. Reasons for this could include certain logic being too trivial, too hard, or just not important enough to test. This statement implies that you do not have to test absolutely every line of code in your app, and that is intentional. Sometimes it's simply not reasonable to write tests for a certain part of your code. For instance, you don't have to test that UIKit behaves as it should; it's Apple's job to make sure that the frameworks they ship are bug-free.

Determining what to test is important, and the longer you defer deciding whether you will add tests for a particular piece of logic, the harder it will be to write tests for it. A simple rule of thumb is that you don't need to test Apple's frameworks. It's safe to assume that Apple makes sure that any code they ship is tested and if it contains bugs, there's not much you can do to fix it anyway. Moreover, you don't want your tests to fail where Apple's tests should have failed.

What you should at least test is the *call site* of your methods, structs, and classes. You can think of the call site as the methods that other objects use to perform tasks. It's a good practice to make anything that's not used by the call site of your objects private, meaning that outside code can't access that part of the code. We'll cover more on this later when you learn more about refactoring code to make it more testable.

You should also test code that you might consider too trivial to write tests for. These parts of your code are likely to receive the *too trivial* treatment in other parts of the development process too. This usually causes you and your coworkers to pay less and less attention to this trivial piece of code, and before you know it, a bug gets introduced that might not be spotted until the app is in the App Store. Writing trivial tests for trivial code takes very little time and saves you from minor oversights that could lead to massive complications.

A few simple guidelines that you should follow when you write tests are the following:

- **Test trivial code**: This usually requires minimal effort.
- **Test the call site of your objects**: These tests will ensure that your public APIs are consistent and work as expected.
- **Don't test Apple's frameworks or any other dependencies**: Doing this is the responsibility of the framework vendor.

Once you've determined what you should test, it's time to start writing the actual tests. However, if you've heard about testing before, you might have heard of terms such as integration tests, unit tests, sanity tests, and a couple of others. The next segment explains a couple of the most important and well-known types of testing.

Choosing the correct test type

When you write tests, it's often a good idea to ask yourself what kind of test you're writing. The kind of test you want to write will typically guide you toward the way your test should be structured and scoped. Having tests that are well-scoped, structured, and focused will ensure that you're building a stable test suite that properly tests your code without unintended side-effects that influence the quality of your test. Now let's dive into the following types of tests: unit tests and integration tests.

Unit tests

Probably the most well-known type of test is the unit test. A lot of people call any other test they write a **unit test**, which is probably why this is such a well-known term for testing. Another reason for unit tests being so popular is that it's a very sensible test type.

A unit test is intended to make sure that an isolated object works as expected. This isolated object will usually be a class or struct, but it could just as well be a standalone method. It's important that unit tests do not rely on any other test or object. It's perfectly fine to set up an environment that has all the preconditions you need for your unit test, but none of this setup should be accidental. For instance, you shouldn't accidentally test other objects or depend on the order in which your tests are executed.

When you write a unit test, it's not uncommon to create instances of models that are stored in an array to represent a dummy database or fake REST APIs. Creating such a list of dummy data is done to ensure that a unit test does not fail due to external factors such as a network error. If your test should depend on certain external factors, you are probably writing an **integration test**.

Integration tests

An integration test ensures that a certain part of your code can integrate with other components of the system. Similar to unit tests, an integration test should never rely on other tests. This is important for any test you write. Whenever a test depends on certain preconditions, they must be set up within the test itself. If your test does depend on other tests, this dependency might not be obvious at first, but it can make your tests fail in weird and unexpected ways.

Because no test can depend on another test, integration tests require a little more setup than unit tests. For example, you might want to set up an API helper, fetch some data from the API, and feed it into a database. A test such as this verifies that the API helper can cooperate with the database layer. Both layers should have their separate unit tests to ensure they work in isolation while the integration test ensures that the database and API can work together. There are many other types of tests that you can write or learn about, but for now, integration tests and unit tests provide an excellent starting point.

Isolating tests

Assumptions are a considerable risk when you're testing. Any time you assume anything about the environment you're testing in, your test is not reliable. If you're just getting into writing tests, it's tempting to make assumptions such as *I'm testing on the simulator and my test user is always logged in so my tests can be written under the assumption that a logged-in user exists.* This assumption makes a lot of sense to a lot of people, but what if one of your tests logs the current user out?

When this happens, a lot of your tests will fail due to assumptions that you made about the test environment. More importantly, these tests might fail even if the code they're testing works flawlessly.

As mentioned before, tests should test a single thing in your app. They should rely on as little outside code as possible, and they should be properly focused. A typical pattern that people use to structure their tests and improve reliability is the 3-As or AAA approach. The name of this pattern is short for Arrange, Act, and Assert. The following is an explanation of each *A*.

Arrange

The arrange step is all about preparation. Make sure a logged-in user exists, populate the (in-memory) database, and create instances of your fake API or other helpers. You essentially arrange everything to be in place for your testing environment. Note that this step should not involve too much setup. If you find yourself writing a lot of code in the arrange step, your test might be too broad. Or the code you're testing relies on too many other pieces of code. You can't always avoid this, but if it happens, make sure you consider refactoring your code and test to keep the quality on par with what you're trying to achieve.

Act

In the act step, you set everything for your test in motion. You call methods on the object you're testing, you feed it data, and you manipulate it. This is where you take your code for a proverbial spin. Don't perform too many actions in succession though; too many actions will lead to problems during the next step, assert.

Assert

The final A in the 3-As approach is assert. During the assert step, you make sure that the state of the object you're testing is as you'd expect. Act and assert can be used multiple times in a single test. For instance, you might want to assert that doing something once places the object in a particular state and that doing it again places the object in another state. Or possibly that the state stays the same. Just as with the other two steps, if you're asserting a lot of things, or if you're acting and asserting over and over again in a test, the chances are that your test is too broad. This can't always be avoided, but long tests with a lot of acting and asserting are often an indication of testing too much at once.

Reading about testing can be quite dull, and it tends to get abstract quickly, so let's leave the theory for now. You will set up a test suite for an existing project in Xcode and start writing some tests, so all of the information you've taken in so far becomes a bit more tangible.

Setting up a test suite with XCTest

In this section, you'll work on a test suite for a new app: **MovieTrivia**. You'll find the basic setup for this project in this book's code bundle. If you open the project, there are some view controllers, an `Info.plist` file, and all the other files you would normally expect to find in a project. There's also a JSON file in the project named `TriviaQuestions.json`. This file contains a couple of dummy questions that you can load by uncommenting a bit of code in `LoadTriviaViewController.swift`.

By default, `LoadTriviaViewController.swift` attempts to load questions from a non-existing web server. This is intentional, to demonstrate how one would normally set up a project like this. Since you don't have a web server at your disposal right now, you can swap out the dummy networking code for the JSON file to test this app.

Before you write tests or perform any optimization, you must add a test target to the project. You add a test target in the same way you added extensions before. The only difference is that you select a different type of target. When adding a test target, you should pick the **iOS Unit Testing Bundle** template. The following screenshot shows the correct template you should select:

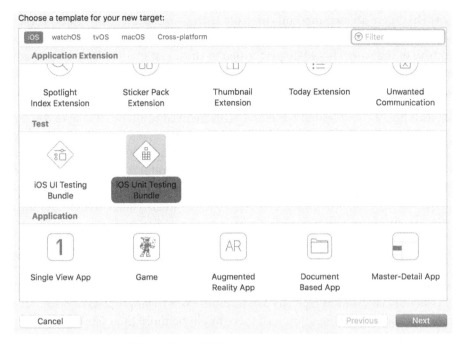

Figure 19.1 – Adding a unit testing target

After adding the target, Xcode adds a new folder to your project. If you choose the default name for the test target, it's called `MovieTriviaTests`. You should add all the tests you write for this project to the test target.

If you think about when you used files in multiple targets with extensions, you might expect that you would need to add all of the files you want to write tests for to both of the targets. Fortunately, this isn't the case. When you write tests, you can import the entire app as a testable target, enabling you to write tests for all of the code in the app target.

If you look inside the `MovieTriviaTests` folder that Xcode created when you added the unit test target, you'll find a single file called `MovieTriviaTests.swift`. This file contains a couple of hints about what tests should look like for your test suite. First of all, note that the test class inherits from `XCTestCase`. All of your test classes should inherit from this `XCTestCase` so they can be identified as a test.

One of the methods you'll find in the test template is the `setUp()` method. This method is executed before every test in the file and helps you to fulfill the first stage of the AAA pattern in testing: Arrange. You use this method to ensure that all of the preconditions for your test are met. You could make sure that your user is logged in or that your database is populated with test data. Of course, the depth of your setup in this method depends on the unit of code for which you're writing a test.

Also, note that there are two methods prefixed with `test` in the `test` class. These methods are executed as tests, and they are expected to perform the act and assert steps. The majority of the work should be performed in these test methods. Do note that it's often better to have multiple short test methods rather than a single test method that tests everything. The larger the methods, the harder it will be to maintain and debug your tests.

Finally, you'll find a `tearDown()` method. This method is intended to give you an opportunity to clean up after yourself. When you have inserted dummy data into your database, it's often desirable to remove this data when your tests have been completed. This will ensure a clean slate for the next test that runs, and it minimizes the chances of your first test accidentally influencing the second test that runs. As mentioned before, tests should never depend on other tests. This means that you also don't want to pollute other tests by leaving traces of previous tests.

Note that `setUp()` and `tearDown()` should be specific to the unit you're testing. This means that you can't put all of your tests in a single class. Separating tests into several classes is a good thing. You should create a test class for every unit of code that you're testing. One test class should typically not test more than a single class or struct in your app. If you're writing an integration test, there might be more than one class involved in the test, but you should still make sure that you're only testing a single thing, which is the integration between the classes involved in the integration you're testing.

Now that you have a test suite in place, let's see how you can write tests for the existing code in the **MovieTrivia** app and how the app can be refactored to be tested appropriately.

Optimizing code for testability

Now that the project has a test target, it's time to start adding some tests to it. Before you add tests, you should determine what to test. Take some time to look at the app and the code and try to think of things to test. Assume that the app is finished and that the trivia questions are loaded from a server.

Some of the things you might have thought of to test are the following:

- Making sure that we can display the data we load from the network
- Testing that selecting the correct answer triggers the expected code
- Testing that choosing a wrong answer triggers the expected code
- Ensuring that the first question is displayed after we show the last one
- Testing that the question index increments

If you came up with most of the tests on this list, good job. You've successfully identified a lot of good test cases. But how do you test these cases? The project has been made hard to test intentionally, but let's see what tests can be written without refactoring the app right away.

Remove the test class that Xcode has generated for you and create a new one called `LoadQuestionsTest`. Use the following bit of boilerplate code in this file's implementation as a starting point for the tests:

```
import XCTest
@testable import MovieTrivia

typealias JSON = [String: Any]

class LoadQuestionsTest: XCTestCase {

    override func setUp() {
        super.setUp()
    }

    func testLoadQuestions() {

    }
}
```

Note the `@testable` import `MovieTrivia` line at the top of the file. This line imports the entire app target so you can access it in your tests. Before you implement the test body for `testLoadQuestions`, it's wise to think about what this method should test. If you look at the code in the app target, the trivia questions are loaded in the `viewDidAppear(_:)` method of `LoadTriviaViewController`. Once the questions are loaded, the app moves on to the next screen. An important detail is that the `triviaJSON` property on `LoadTriviaViewController` is set once the questions are loaded.

Based on this information, you could write a test that creates an instance of LoadTriviaViewController, makes it appear, so the questions will load, and then waits until triviaJSON has a value to verify that the questions were successfully loaded. Writing a test that fits this description would involve many moving parts, way more than you should be comfortable with. MovieTrivia uses storyboards, so to obtain an instance of LoadTriviaViewController, the storyboard would have to be involved. This means that any changes or mistakes in the user interface would cause the logic test that checks whether data is loaded to fail. This is not desirable because this test should only verify whether it's possible to load data, not whether the user interface updates once the load completes.

This is a great moment to start refactoring some code and make it more testable. The first piece of code that should be revamped for testability is the question-loading code.

Introducing the question loader

To make MovieTrivia more testable, you should create a special helper that can load questions. The helper will go to the network and fetch the questions. Once the data is loaded, a callback is called to notify the object that initiated the request about the loaded questions. Because you already know that you're going to write tests for the new helper, you should think of a way to make sure that the helper works with both an offline and an online implementation, so the tests don't have to depend on an internet connection to work.

Because tests should rely on as few outside factors as possible, removing the networking layer from this test would be great. This means that the helper needs to be split into two parts. One part is the helper itself. The other part would be a data fetcher. The data fetcher should conform to a protocol that defines the interface that a data fetcher must have, so you can choose to inject either an online or offline fetcher into the helper.

If the preceding explanation seems a little bit abstract and confusing to you, that's OK. The following code samples will show you the process of separating the different helpers step by step. Add a new Swift file to the application target and call it QuestionsLoader. swift. Then add the following implementation to it:

```
typealias JSON = [String: Any]
typealias QuestionsLoadedCallback = (JSON) -> Void

struct QuestionsLoader {
  func loadQuestions(callback: @escaping
    QuestionsLoadedCallback) {
    guard let url = URL(string:
```

```
        "http://questions.movietrivia.json")
      else { return }

    URLSession.shared.dataTask(with: url) { data, response,
      error in guard let data = data, let jsonObject = try?
      JSONSerialization.jsonObject(with: data, options:
        []), let json = jsonObject as? JSON
      else { return }

      callback(json)
    }
  }
}
```

This struct defines a method to load questions with a callback. This is already nice and a lot more testable than before. You can now isolate the question loader and test it separated from the rest of the app. A test for the helper in its current state would look like the test shown in the following code snippet:

```
func testLoadQuestions() {
  let questionsLoader = QuestionsLoader()
  let questionsLoadedExpectation = expectation(description:
    "Expected the questions to be loaded")
  questionsLoader.loadQuestions { _ in
    questionsLoadedExpectation.fulfill()
  }
  waitForExpectations(timeout: 5, handler: nil)
}
```

The preceding test creates an instance of `QuestionLoader` and sets up an expectation. An expectation is used when you expect something to happen in your test eventually. Since `QuestionLoader` loads its questions asynchronously, you can't expect the questions to be loaded by the time this test method is done executing. The callback that's called when the questions are loaded is used to fulfill the expectation in this test. To make sure that the test waits for the expectation to be fulfilled, `waitForExpectations(timeout:handler:)` is called after `loadQuestions(callback:)`. If the expectation isn't fulfilled within the 5-second timeout that is specified, the test fails.

Examine this test closely; you should be able to see all of the As (Arrange, Act, Assert) that you read about earlier. The first A, arrange, is where the loader and expectation are created. The second A, act, is when `loadQuestions(callback:)` is called. The final A, assert, is inside the callback. This test doesn't validate whether the data passed to the callback is valid, but you'll get to that later.

Separating the loader into its own object is great but it still has one problem. There is no way to configure whether it loads data from a local file or the network. In a production environment, the question loader would load data from the network, which would make the test for the question loader depend on the network as well.

This isn't ideal because a test that depends on the network might fail for reasons you can't control.

This can be improved by utilizing some protocol-oriented programming and the dependency-injection pattern. This means that you should define a protocol that defines the public API for a networking layer. Then you should implement a networking object in the app target that conforms to the protocol. `QuestionsLoader` should have a property that holds anything that conforms to the networking protocol. The test target should have its own object that conforms to the networking protocol so you can use that object to provide `QuestionsLoader` with mock data.

By setting the test up like this, you can take the entire networking logic out of the equation and arrange tests in such a way that the networking doesn't matter. The mock networking layer will respond with valid, reliable responses that can be used as test input.

Mocking API responses

It's common practice to mock API responses when you're testing. In this segment, you will implement the mock API that was described before to improve the quality and reliability of the `MovieTrivia` test suite. Follow these steps to create a mock response to test your API:

1. First, let's define the networking protocol. Create a new file in the app target and name it `TriviaAPIProviding`:

```
typealias QuestionsFetchedCallback = (JSON) -> Void


protocol TriviaAPIProviding {
    func loadTriviaQuestions(callback: @escaping
    QuestionsFetchedCallback)
}
```

The protocol only requires a single method. If you want to expand this app later, everything related to the Trivia API must be added to the protocol to make sure that you can create both an online version of your app and an offline version for your tests.

2. Next, create a file named `TriviaAPI` and add the following implementation to it:

```
struct TriviaAPI: TriviaAPIProviding {

    func loadTriviaQuestions(callback: @escaping
      QuestionsFetchedCallback) {
      guard let url = URL(string:
        "http://questions.movietrivia.json")
        else { return }

      URLSession.shared.dataTask(with: url) { data,
        response, error in guard let data = data, let
          jsonObject = try? JSONSerialization.jsonObject(
            with: data, options: []), let json =
              jsonObject as? JSON
          else { return }

        callback(json)
      }
    }
}
```

3. Lastly, update the `QuestionsLoader` struct with the following implementation:

```
struct QuestionsLoader {
    let apiProvider: TriviaAPIProviding

    func loadQuestions(callback: @escaping
      QuestionsLoadedCallback) {
      apiProvider.loadTriviaQuestions(callback:
        callback)
    }
}
```

The question loader now has an `apiProvider` that it uses to load questions. Currently, it delegates any load call over to its API provider, but you'll update this code soon to make sure that it converts the raw JSON data that the API returns to question models.

4. Update the `viewDidAppear(_:)` method of `LoadTriviaViewController` as shown in the following code snippet. This implementation uses the loader struct instead of directly loading the data inside the view controller:

```
override func viewDidAppear(_ animated: Bool) {
  super.viewDidAppear(animated)

  let apiProvider = TriviaAPI()
  let questionsLoader = QuestionsLoader(apiProvider:
    apiProvider)
  questionsLoader.loadQuestions { [weak self] json in
    self?.triviaJSON = json
    self?.performSegue(withIdentifier:
      "TriviaLoadedSegue", sender: self)
  }
}
```

The preceding code is not only more testable but also a lot cleaner. The next step is to create the mock API in the test target so you can use it to provide the question loader with data.

The JSON file in the app target should be removed from the app target and added to the test target. You can leave it in the app folder but make sure to update the `Target Membership` so the JSON file is only available in the test target.

5. Now add a new Swift file named `MockTriviaAPI` to the test target and add the following code to it:

```
@testable import MovieTrivia

struct MockTriviaAPI: TriviaAPIProviding {
  func loadTriviaQuestions(callback: @escaping
    QuestionsFetchedCallback) {
    guard let filename = Bundle(for:
      LoadQuestionsTest.self).path(forResource:
```

```
            "TriviaQuestions", ofType: "json"), let
            triviaString = try? String(contentsOfFile:
            filename), let triviaData = triviaString.data(
            using: .utf8), let jsonObject = try?
            JSONSerialization.jsonObject(with: triviaData,
             options: []), let triviaJSON = jsonObject
              as? JSON
        else { return }


        callback(triviaJSON)
    }
 }
```

This code fetches the locally stored JSON file from the test bundle. To determine the location of the JSON file, one of the test classes is used to retrieve the current bundle. This is not the absolute best way to retrieve a bundle because it relies on an external factor to exist in the test target. However, structs can't be used to look up the current bundle. Luckily, the compiler will throw an error if the class that is used to determine the bundle is removed so the compiler would quickly error and the mistake can be fixed. After loading the file, the callback is called, and the request has been successfully handled.

6. Now update the test in `LoadQuestionsTest` so it uses the mock API as follows:

```
func testLoadQuestions() {
   let mockApi = MockTriviaAPI()
   let questionsLoader = QuestionsLoader(apiProvider:
     mockApi)
   let questionsLoadedExpectation =
    expectation(description: "Expected the questions
      to be loaded")
   questionsLoader.loadQuestions { _ in
     questionsLoadedExpectation.fulfill()
   }
   waitForExpectations(timeout: 5, handler: nil)
}
```

Let's summarize what we have done here: We have defined our API as a protocol. By doing that and with dependency injection, we are now capable of creating a mock class to test the API. As long as our mock class conforms to that protocol, we can inject it anywhere we need the API.

A lot of apps have way more complex interactions than the one you're testing now. When you get to implementing more complex scenarios, the main ideas about how to architect your app and tests remain the same, regardless of application complexity.

Protocols can be used to define a common interface for certain objects. Combining this with dependency-injection as you did for QuestionsLoader helps to isolate the pieces of your code that you're testing, and it enables you to swap out pieces of code to make sure that you don't rely on external factors if you don't have to.

So far, the test suite is not particularly useful. The only thing that's tested at this point is whether QuestionsLoader passes requests on to the TriviaAPIProviding object and whether the callbacks are called as expected. Even though this technically qualifies as a test, it's much better also to test whether the loader object can convert the loaded data into question objects that the app can display.

Testing whether QuestionsLoader can convert JSON into a Question model is a test that's a lot more interesting than just testing whether the callback is called. A refactor such as this might make you wonder whether you should add a new test or modify the existing test.

If you choose to add a new test, your test suite will cover a simple case where you only test that the callback is called and a more complex case that ensures the loader can convert JSON data to models. When you update the existing test, you end up with a test that validates two things. It will make sure that the callback is called but also that the data is converted to models.

While the implications for both choices are similar, the second-choice sort of assumes that the callback will be called. You always want to limit your assumptions when writing tests and there's no harm in adding more tests when you add more features. However, if the callback does not get called, none of the tests will work. So, in this case, you can work with a single test that makes sure the callback is called and that the loader returns the expected models.

The test you should end up with will have a single expectation and multiple assertions. Writing the test like this makes sure that the expectation of the callback is fulfilled when the callback is called, and at the same time you can use assertions to ensure that the data that's passed to the callback is valid and correct.

By making `QuestionsLoader` create instances of a `Question` model rather than using it to return a dictionary of JSON data, it not only makes the test more interesting but also improves the app code by making it a lot cleaner. Right now, the app uses a dictionary of JSON data to display questions. If the JSON changes, you would have to update the view controller's code. If the app grows, you might be using the JSON data in multiple places, making the process of updating quite painful and error-prone. This is why it's a much better idea to use the `Codable` protocol to convert raw API responses to `Question` models. Using `Codable` objects means you can get rid of the JSON dictionaries in the view controllers, which is a vast improvement.

Using models for consistency

Adding a question model to `MovieTrivia` involves quite a bit of refactoring. First, you must define the `Question` model. Let's create and make use of our models instead of using JSON structs around the code. Follow these steps:

1. Create a new Swift file named `Question` and add the following implementation to it:

    ```swift
    struct Question: Codable {
        let title: String
        let answerA: String
        let answerB: String
        let answerC: String
        let correctAnswer: Int
    }
    ```

    The `Question` struct conforms to the `Codable` protocol.

2. Since the dummy JSON data contains a list of questions, you'll want to define a `Codable` object that contains the response as well:

    ```swift
    struct QuestionsFetchResponse: Codable {
        let questions: [Question]
    }
    ```

    Now that the `Question` model and the response container are in place, a couple of changes must be made to the existing code.

3. Modify the `typealias` in the `TriviaAPIProviding` protocol as follows:

    ```swift
    typealias QuestionsFetchedCallback = (Data) -> Void
    ```

4. Next, update the implementation of the `TriviaAPI` for the `URLSession` callback in `loadTriviaQuestions(callback:)` as follows:

```
URLSession.shared.dataTask(with: url) { data,
  response, error in guard let data = data
  else { return }
  callback(data)
}
```

5. Also, update `MockTriviaApi` so it executes its callback with data instead of a JSON dictionary:

```
func loadTriviaQuestions(callback: @escaping
QuestionsFetchedCallback) {
  guard let filename = Bundle(for:
   LoadQuestionsTest.self).path(forResource:
   "TriviaQuestions", ofType: "json"), let
    triviaString = try? String(contentsOfFile:
    filename), let triviaData = triviaString.data(
      using: .utf8)
  else { return }
  callback(triviaData)
}
```

6. Update the `QuestionsLoadedCallback` typealias in `QuestionsLoader` to the following definition:

```
typealias QuestionsLoadedCallback = ([Question]) -> Void
```

7. And lastly, update the implementation for `loadQuestions(callback:)` as follows:

```
func loadQuestions(callback: @escaping
  QuestionsLoadedCallback) {
    apiProvider.loadTriviaQuestions { data in
    let decoder = JSONDecoder()
    decoder.keyDecodingStrategy = .convertFromSnakeCase
    guard let questionsResponse = try?
    decoder.decode(QuestionsFetchResponse.self,
      from: data)
```

```
      else { return }
    callback(questionsResponse.questions)
    }
  }
```

This wraps up the changes for the API. However, there still is some refactoring to be done in the view controllers.

8. Rename the `triviaJSON` property on `LoadTriviaViewController` to the following:

```
var questions: [Question]?
```

Make sure you replace all occurrences of `triviaJSON` with the new `questions` array. Also, make sure you change the following line in `prepare(for:sender:)`:

```
questionViewController.triviaJSON = triviaJSON
```

9. Change the preceding line to this:

```
questionViewController.questions = questions
```

10. In `QuestionViewController`, change the type of `questions` to `[Question]` and remove the `triviaJSON` property.

At this point, you can clear all of the JSON-related code from the guards in this class. You should be able to do this on your own since the compiler should guide you with errors. If you get stuck, look at the finished project in the code bundle.

By now, you should be able to run the tests, and they should pass. To run your tests, click the **Product** menu item and select **Test**. Alternatively, press *Cmd + U* to run your tests. The tests run fine, but currently, the test doesn't test whether all of the questions in the JSON data got converted to `Question` models. To make sure this conversion worked, you can load the JSON file in the test, count the number of questions in the JSON file, and assert that it matches the number of questions in the callback.

Update the `testLoadQuestions()` method as shown in the following code snippet:

```
func testLoadQuestions() {
  let apiProvider = MockTriviaAPI()
  let questionsLoader = QuestionsLoader(apiProvider:
    apiProvider)
  let questionsLoadedExpectation = expectation(
```

```
    description: "Expected the questions to be loaded")
questionsLoader.loadQuestions { questions in
    guard let filename = Bundle(for: LoadQuestionsTest.self).
path(forResource: "TriviaQuestions", ofType: "json"),
      let triviaString = try? String(contentsOfFile:
        filename),
      let triviaData = triviaString.data(using: .utf8),
      let jsonObject = try?
        JSONSerialization.jsonObject(with: triviaData,
          options: []),
      let triviaJSON = jsonObject as? JSON,
      let jsonQuestions = triviaJSON["questions"]
        as? [JSON]
    else { return }


    XCTAssert(questions.count > 0, "More than 0 questions
      should be passed to the callback")
    XCTAssert(jsonQuestions.count == questions.count,
      "Number of questions in json must match the number
        of questions in the callback.")
    questionsLoadedExpectation.fulfill()
  }
  waitForExpectations(timeout: 5, handler: nil)
}
```

This test loads the dummy JSON file and uses XCTAssert to make sure that more than
zero questions were passed to the callback and that the number of questions in the JSON
file matches the number of questions that were loaded.

XCTAssert takes a Boolean expression and a description. If the assertion fails, the
description is shown. Adding good descriptions will help you to quickly figure out
which assertion in your test has made your test fail.

This new version of the load-questions test is a small addition to the test suite but has
vast consequences. By improving the test suite, you have improved the quality of the
app because you can now prove that the question loader correctly transforms JSON
into model objects. By adding model objects, you have improved the code in the view
controllers as well. Instead of reading raw JSON, you are now reading properties from
a model. And lastly, these changes have made your view controllers a lot cleaner.

In this section, you have learned how to create and use your own data models through your code. By doing so, your code is more consistent and easier to test (and maintain).

One more metric that has improved by refactoring your code is the amount of code that is covered by the test suite. You can measure the percentage of code your test suite covers with Xcode's built-in code coverage tracking. You'll learn how to use this tool next.

Gaining insights through code coverage

Code coverage is a tool in Xcode that is used to gain insights into how much of your code you are testing with your test suite. It tells you exactly which parts of your code were executed during a test and which parts of your code were not. This is extremely useful because you can take focused action based on the information provided by code coverage.

Follow these steps to enable the code coverage functionality:

1. To enable **Code Coverage**, open the scheme editor through the (**Product | Scheme**) menu:

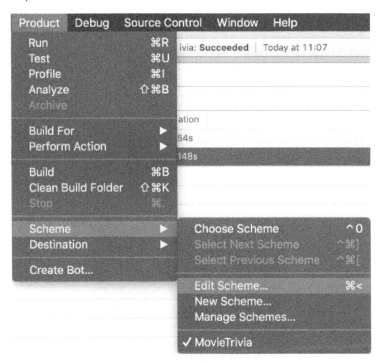

Figure 19.2 – Editing scheme

2. Select **Test action** and make sure the **Gather coverage** checkbox on the **Options** tab is checked:

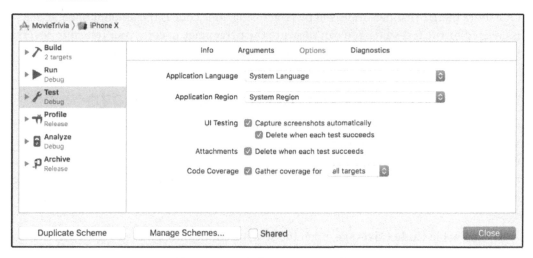

Figure 19.3 – Gather coverage option

> **Tip**
> You can also press *Command* + < to open the scheme editor quickly.

3. After doing this, close the scheme editor and run your tests.

    This time, Xcode will monitor which parts of your code were executed during this test, and which parts weren't. This information can give you some good insights into which parts of your code could use some more testing.

4. To see the coverage data, open the **Report navigator** in the left sidebar in Xcode. The rightmost icon in this sidebar represents the report navigator:

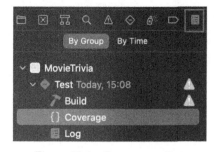

Figure 19.4 – Coverage option

There are several reports listed under your app name. If you select the **Coverage** report, the coverage report will open in the editor area in Xcode. You can see all the files in your app and the percentage of code in the file that's covered by your tests. The following screenshot shows coverage for the **MovieTrivia** app:

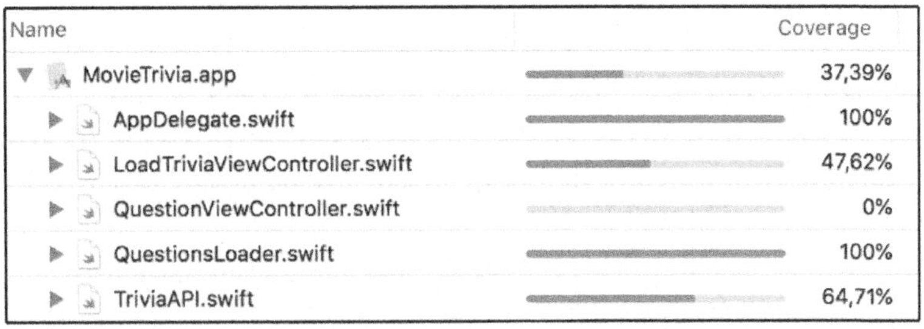

Name		Coverage
▼ 🅰 MovieTrivia.app	▬▬▬▬▬	37,39%
▶ 📄 AppDelegate.swift	▬▬▬▬▬▬▬	100%
▶ 📄 LoadTriviaViewController.swift	▬▬▬▬	47,62%
▶ 📄 QuestionViewController.swift		0%
▶ 📄 QuestionsLoader.swift	▬▬▬▬▬▬▬	100%
▶ 📄 TriviaAPI.swift	▬▬▬▬▬	64,71%

Figure 19.5 – Coverage details

The more a bar is filled, the more lines of code in that file or method were executed during your test. You'll notice that the `AppDelegate.swift` file is covered under the tests even though you haven't written any tests for it. The reason this happens is that the app must launch during the test to act as a host for the test suite. This means that parts of the code in `AppDelegate.swift` are actually executed during the test, and therefore Xcode considers it covered in the tests.

You can see which methods for a specific file were executed by clicking on the triangle next to the class name. This enables you to see exactly which parts of a file are tested and which parts aren't.

One last feature of code coverage that's worth mentioning is inline code coverage. Inline code coverage will show you how often a specific block of code has been executed during testing. This will give you code coverage insights right next to your code, without having to navigate to the report navigator. To enable this feature, open up your Xcode preferences and navigate to the **Text Editing** tab. Check the **Show iteration counts** checkbox at the bottom of the tab. If you open a file now, you'll see the iteration count for your code on the right side of the editor window.

The following screenshot shows the iteration count for the `loadQuestions(callback:)` method:

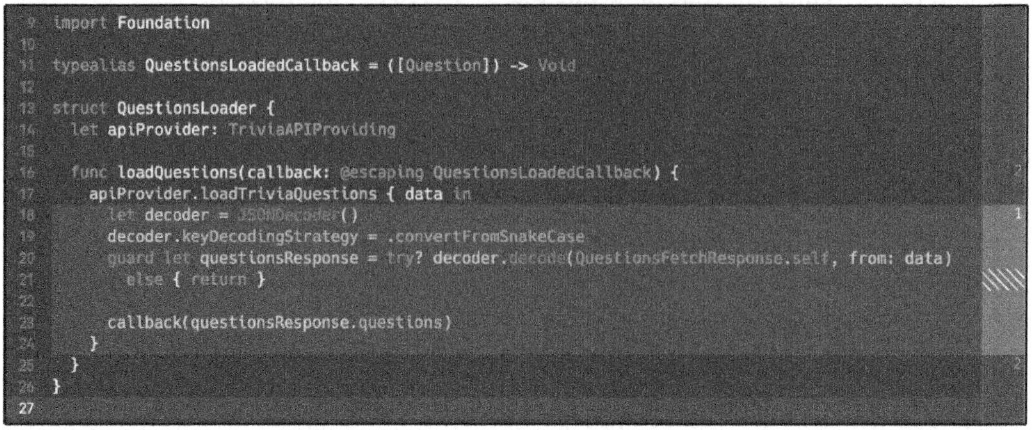

```
9   import Foundation
10
11  typealias QuestionsLoadedCallback = ([Question]) -> Void
12
13  struct QuestionsLoader {
14      let apiProvider: TriviaAPIProviding
15
16      func loadQuestions(callback: @escaping QuestionsLoadedCallback) {
17          apiProvider.loadTriviaQuestions { data in
18              let decoder = JSONDecoder()
19              decoder.keyDecodingStrategy = .convertFromSnakeCase
20              guard let questionsResponse = try? decoder.decode(QuestionsFetchResponse.self, from: data)
21                  else { return }
22
23              callback(questionsResponse.questions)
24          }
25      }
26  }
27
```

Figure 19.6 – Show iteration counts

Even though code coverage is a great tool for gaining insights into your tests, you shouldn't let it influence you too much. Regularly check the code coverage for your app and look for methods that are untested and are either easy to write tests for or should be tested because they contain important logic. Code coverage is also great for discovering parts of your code that should be tested but are hard to test because they're nested deep inside a view controller or are otherwise hard to reach.

You should always aim for as much code coverage as possible, but don't push yourself to reach 100%. Doing this will make you jump through all kinds of hoops, and you'll invest way more time in testing than you should. Not all paths in your code have to be tested. However, don't shy away from doing some refactoring. Proper testing helps you to avoid bugs and to structure your code better. Code coverage is just one extra tool in your tool belt to help identify which parts of your code could benefit from some tests.

If you look at the current state of the coverage in the **MovieTrivia** app, we're doing quite well. Most of the logic in the app is tested. The only parts that are not tested thoroughly are the view controllers. Testing view controllers and navigation flows with XCTest can be quite hard and tedious. Luckily, there is one last testing tool that we'll discuss in this chapter: XCUITest.

Testing the user interface with XCUITest

We have learned how to test your code and the logic behind it. In this section, we are going to learn how to test the UI of your app with **XCUITest**.

Knowing that most of your app logic is covered with tests is great. What's not so great, however, is adding your view controllers to your logic test. Luckily, you can use XCUITest to easily record and write tests that focus on the user interface of an app. XCUITest uses the accessibility features in iOS to gain access to the user interface of your app. This means that implementing user interface tests forces you to put at least a little bit of effort into accessibility for your applications. The better your app's accessibility is, the easier it will be to write UI Tests for.

XCUITest has two great features that we'll look at in greater detail. First of all, UI tests help you to enhance the accessibility of your apps. Secondly, it's easy to get started with UI testing because Xcode can record your tests while you navigate through your app. This can significantly benefit the amount of code that is covered by your test suite since code coverage also takes UI tests into account.

Before we start recording our first UI test, let's have a quick look at accessibility.

Making your app accessible to your tests

One of the lesser thoughts about features in iOS is accessibility. The design teams at Apple work hard to ensure that iOS is accessible for everybody. This includes blind people and people with other disabilities that could somehow affect the user's ability to operate their iOS device.

Just looking at the accessibility settings in the iOS Settings app makes it evident that this is a subject that Apple invests a lot of time in. If you're working on an app, Apple expects you to put in the same kind of effort. Doing this will be rewarded by more app downloads and if you're lucky, even a couple of great reviews. In their talk on iOS accessibility from WWDC 2015, Apple even mentioned that implementing accessibility features can be helpful if you ever want to be featured in the *App Store*. Only the best apps get featured by Apple, and if your app is accessible to all people, that significantly boosts your app's quality.

A common myth surrounding accessibility is that it's hard to implement or that it takes a lot of time. Some people even go so far as to say that it looks ugly or gets in the way of beautiful design. None of this is entirely correct. Sure, making your app accessible requires some effort, but the UIKit framework is very helpful when it comes to accessibility. Using standard components and keeping your users in mind while you design your app will make sure that your app is both accessible and looks good.

So, how does accessibility work on iOS? And how can we make sure our app is accessible? A fun way to experiment with this is to turn on **VoiceOver** on your device. Follow these steps to enable it:

1. To enable **VoiceOver**, go to the **Accessibility** menu. You'll find several vision-related accessibility settings. **VoiceOver** should be the topmost one.

2. To quickly enable and disable **VoiceOver**, scroll all the way to the bottom of the settings page and select **VoiceOver** as your accessibility shortcut:

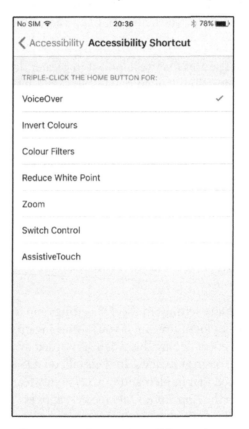

Figure 19.7 – Device Accessibility options

This will allow you to toggle **VoiceOver** off and on by triple-clicking the home button or side button, depending on your device.

3. After enabling this, run the **MovieTrivia** app on your device and triple-click your home button or the side button to enable **VoiceOver**.

4. Swipe around and try to use the app.

This is how a person with a visual handicap would use your app. You won't get past the loading screen because the dummy questions aren't loaded, but you should find the splash screen to be pretty accessible, especially considering no special work had to be done to achieve this. UIKit uses great default settings to make sure your app will be accessible by default.

You can set your own accessibility information through the **Identity Inspector** in Interface Builder. You can add custom labels, hints, identifiers, and traits to your interface to aid accessibility and, coincidentally, your UI tests. The following screenshot shows the **Accessibility** panel:

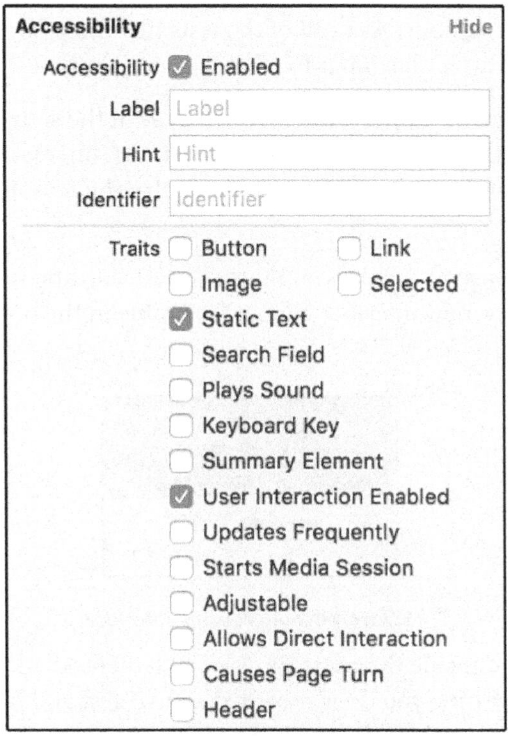

Figure 19.8 – Accessibility options

For most UIKit interface elements, you won't have to touch these settings yourself. UIKit will make sure that your objects have sensible defaults that automatically make your app accessible. Now that you have a little bit of background information about accessibility, let's have a look at testing the app's (accessible) UI.

Recording UI tests

Before you can record UI tests, you must add a UI testing target to the project. Follow the same steps as before to add a new testing target but pick the iOS UI Testing Bundle this time around. If you look inside the newly created group in your project, the structure of your UI tests looks very similar to the structure of unit tests.

One significant difference between UI test targets and unit test targets is that your UI tests do not have access to any code that's inside your app. A UI test can only test the interface of your app and make assertions based on that.

If you open the `MovieTriviaUITest.swift` file, you'll notice the `setUpWithError()` and `tearDown()` methods. Also, all of the tests that must be executed are methods with the `test` prefix. This is all similar to what you've already seen for `XCUITest`.

One big difference is that the app is launched explicitly in the setup stage. This is because the UI test target is essentially just a different app that can interact with your main app's interface. This limitation is very interesting, and it's also the reason why it's important to make your app accessible.

To start recording a UI test in Xcode, you must start a recording session. If you're editing code in a UI test target, a new interface element is visible in the bottom-left corner of your code editor area:

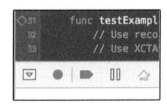

Figure 19.9 – Recording interface

Place your typing cursor inside the `testExample()` method and click the red dot. Your app is launched and anything you do is recorded as a UI test and played back when you run your tests. If you tap on the label and the activity indicator on the loading screen, Xcode produces the following Swift code in the testing method:

```
let app = XCUIApplication()
app.staticTexts["Loading trivia questions..."].tap()
app.activityIndicators["In progress"].tap()
```

The UI test you recorded is a set of instructions that are sent to the app. In this sample, the test looks for a certain element in the app's UI and calls `tap()` on it. This test doesn't do a lot, so it's not particularly useful. To make the test more useful, we should let the app know that it should run in a special test mode so it can load questions from the JSON file instead of trying to load it from the network. To do this, you can send launch arguments to the app. Launch arguments can be used by the app to enable or disable certain functionalities. You can think of them as variables that are sent to the app when it launches.

Passing launch arguments to your app

To switch the loading of questions from the network to a local file for testing, you can pass your app a launch argument. This launch argument is then read by the app to make sure it loads questions from the JSON file, as you did before in the unit tests, rather than attempting to load trivia questions from the server.

To prepare for the launch argument and loading the JSON file, make sure you add it to the test target, the app target, and the UI test target. You won't need it in the UI test target just yet, but you will later, so you might as well add it to the UI test target while you're at it.

In order to pass launch arguments to the app, the `setUpWithError()` method in the UI test class should be modified:

```
override func setupWithError() {
  continueAfterFailure = false
  let app = XCUIApplication()
  app.launchArguments.append("isUITesting")
  app.launch()
}
```

The `XCUIApplication` instance that represents the app has a `launchArguments` property, which is an array of strings. You can add strings to this array before launching the app. These strings can then be extracting inside of the app. Modify the `loadTriviaQuestions(callback:)` method in `TriviaAPI.swift` as shown in the following code snippet:

```
func loadTriviaQuestions(callback: @escaping
  QuestionsFetchedCallback) {
  if ProcessInfo.processInfo.arguments.contains(
    "isUITesting") {
    loadQuestionsFromFile(callback: callback)
```

```
    return
  }

  // existing implementation...
}
```

The preceding code should be inserted above the existing implementation of this method. The snippet checks whether we're UI testing by reading the app's launch arguments. If the UI testing argument is present, we call the `loadQuestionsFromFile(callback:)` method to load the questions from the JSON file instead of loading it from the network.

Note that it's not ideal to perform checks such as the preceding one in your production code. It's often better to wrap a configuration such as this in a struct that can be modified easily. You can then use this struct throughout your app instead of directly accessing process info throughout your app. An example of such a configuration could look like this:

```
struct AppConfig {
  var isUITesting: Bool {
    ProcessInfo.processInfo.arguments.contains(
    "isUITesting") }
}
```

We won't use this configuration class in this app since it's not needed for an app this small. But for your own apps, you might want to implement a configuration object regardless of app size since it leads to more maintainable code in the long run.

If you build the app right now, you should get a compiler error because `loadQuestionsFromFile(callback:)` is not implemented in the API class yet. Add the following implementation for this method:

```
func loadQuestionsFromFile(callback: @escaping
  QuestionsFetchedCallback) {
  guard let filename = Bundle.main.path(forResource:
    "TriviaQuestions", ofType: "json"), let triviaString =
      try? String(contentsOfFile: filename), let triviaData =
        triviaString.data(using: .utf8)
  else { return }
  callback(triviaData)
}
```

It's very similar to the question-loading method in the unit tests; the only difference is that it uses a different way to obtain the bundle from which the questions are loaded.

If you run your UI tests now, they will fail. The reason for this is that when the test framework starts looking for the elements it tapped before, they don't exist. This results in a test failure because the test can't tap elements that don't exist.

The test should be adjusted a bit because tapping a loader isn't very useful anyway. It's a lot more useful to make sure that buttons can be tapped and whether the UI updates accordingly. To do this, you can write a UI test that waits for the question and buttons to appear, taps them, and checks whether the UI has updated accordingly. The dummy data will be loaded in this test as well to verify that the correct question is shown and the buttons behave as they should.

Making sure the UI updates as expected

You're going to write two tests to make sure that the trivia game works as expected. The first test will test that the question and the answer buttons appear and that they have the correct labels. The second test will make sure that the answers can be tapped and that the UI updates accordingly.

Instead of recording the tests, you'll write them manually. Writing tests manually gives you a bit more control and allows you to do much more than just tapping on elements. Before you do this, you should open the `Main.storyboard` file and give accessibility identifiers to the UI elements. Follow these steps to create a UI test manually:

1. Select the question title and give `UILabel` an identifier of `QuestionTitle`.

2. Select each of the answers and give them the `AnswerA`, `AnswerB`, and `AnswerC` identifiers, respectively.

3. Also, give the next button an accessibility identifier of `NextQuestion`. The following screenshot shows what the question title should look like:

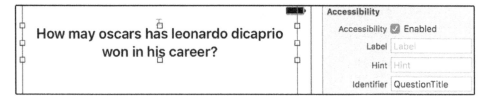

Figure 19.10 – Accessibility identifiers

4. Remove the existing UI test, called `testExample()`, from the
    `MovieTriviaUITests` class and add the one shown in the following
    code snippet:

```swift
func testQuestionAppears() {
  let app = XCUIApplication()

  // 1
  let buttonIdentifiers = ["AnswerA", "AnswerB",
    "AnswerC"]
  for identifier in buttonIdentifiers {
    let button = app.buttons.matching(identifier:
      identifier).element
    // 2
    let predicate = NSPredicate(format: "exists ==
      true")
    _ = expectation(for: predicate, evaluatedWith:
      button, handler: nil)
  }

  let questionTitle = app.staticTexts.matching(
    identifier: "QuestionTitle").element
  let predicate = NSPredicate(format: "exists ==
    true")
  _ = expectation(for: predicate, evaluatedWith:
    questionTitle, handler: nil)

  // 3
  waitForExpectations(timeout: 5, handler: nil)
}
```

- Each element is selected through its accessibility identifier. You can do this because
  the `XCUIApplication` instance we create provides easy access to the UI elements.

- Next, a predicate is created that is used to check whether each element exists, and
  an expectation is created. This expectation will continuously evaluate whether the
  predicate is true and once it is, the predicate will be fulfilled automatically.

- Lastly, the UI test will wait for all expectations to be fulfilled.

To make sure the questions are loaded correctly, you should load the JSON file as you did before.

5. Add the following property to the test so you have a place to store the trivia questions:

```
typealias JSON = [String: Any]
var questions: [JSON]?
```

6. Next, add the following code to the top of the setUp() method before launching the app:

```
guard let filename = Bundle(for:
  MovieTriviaUITests.self).path(forResource:
    "TriviaQuestions", ofType: "json"),
  let triviaString = try? String(contentsOfFile:
    filename), let triviaData = triviaString.data(
      using: .utf8),
  let jsonObject = try? JSONSerialization.jsonObject(
    with: triviaData, options: []),
  let triviaJSON = jsonObject as? JSON,
  let jsonQuestions = triviaJSON["questions"] as? [JSON]
    else { return }
questions = jsonQuestions
```

This code should look familiar to you because it's similar to the code you already used to load JSON. To make sure that the correct question is displayed, update the test method as shown here:

```
func testQuestionAppears() {
  // existing implementation...
waitForExpectations(timeout: 5, handler: nil)
  guard let question = questions?.first else {
    fatalError("Can't continue testing without
      question data...")
  }
  validateQuestionIsDisplayed(question)
}
```

The preceding code calls validateQuestionIsDisplayed(_:), but this method is not implemented yet.

7. Add the following implementation:

```
func validateQuestionIsDisplayed(_ question: JSON) {
  let app = XCUIApplication()
  let questionTitle = app.staticTexts.matching(
    identifier: "QuestionTitle").element

  guard let title = question["title"] as? String, let
    answerA = question["answer_a"] as? String, let
      answerB = question["answer_b"] as? String, let
        answerC = question["answer_c"] as? String
        else { fatalError("Can't continue testing without
          question data...") }

  XCTAssert(questionTitle.label == title, "Expected
    question title to match json data")

  let buttonA = app.buttons.matching(identifier:
    "AnswerA").element
  XCTAssert(buttonA.label == answerA, "Expected
    AnswerA title to match json data")

  let buttonB = app.buttons.matching(identifier:
    "AnswerB").element
  XCTAssert(buttonB.label == answerB, "Expected
    AnswerB title to match json data")

  let buttonC = app.buttons.matching(identifier:
    "AnswerC").element
  XCTAssert(buttonC.label == answerC, "Expected
    AnswerC title to match json data")
}
```

This code is run after checking that the UI elements exist because it's run after waiting for the expectations we created. The first question is extracted from the JSON data, and all of the relevant labels are then compared to the question data using a reusable method that validates whether a specific question is currently shown.

The second test you should add is intended to check whether the game UI responds as expected. After loading a question, the test will tap on the wrong answers and then makes sure the UI doesn't show the button to go to the next question. Then, the correct answer will be selected, and the test will attempt to navigate to the next question. And of course, the test will then validate that the next question is shown:

```
func testAnswerValidation() {
  let app = XCUIApplication()
  let button = app.buttons.matching(identifier:
    "AnswerA").element
  let predicate = NSPredicate(format: "exists == true")
  _ = expectation(for: predicate, evaluatedWith: button,
    handler: nil)
  waitForExpectations(timeout: 5, handler: nil)

  let nextQuestionButton = app.buttons.matching(identifier:
    "NextQuestion").element
  guard let question = questions?.first, let correctAnswer
    = question["correct_answer"] as? Int else {
    fatalError("Can't continue testing without question
      data...")
  }

  let buttonIdentifiers = ["AnswerA", "AnswerB", "AnswerC"]
  for (i, identifier) in buttonIdentifiers.enumerated() {
    guard i != correctAnswer else { continue }
    app.buttons.matching(identifier:identifier)
      .element.tap()
    XCTAssert(nextQuestionButton.exists == false, "Next
      question button should be hidden")
  }

  app.buttons.matching(identifier: buttonIdentifiers[
    correctAnswer]).element.tap()
  XCTAssert(nextQuestionButton.exists == true, "Next
    question button should be visible")
```

```
nextQuestionButton.tap()

guard let nextQuestion = questions?[1] else {
fatalError("Can't continue testing without question
  data...") }
validateQuestionIsDisplayed(nextQuestion)
XCTAssert(nextQuestionButton.exists == false, "Next
  question button should be hidden")
}
```

The preceding code shows the entire test that validates that the UI responds appropriately to correct and incorrect answers. Tests such as these are quite verbose, but they save you a lot of manual testing.

When you test your UI like this, you can rest assured that your app will at least be somewhat accessible. The beauty in this is that both UI testing and accessibility can significantly improve your app quality and each actively aids the other.

Testing your UI is mostly a matter of looking for elements in the UI, checking their state or availability, and making assertions based on that. In the two tests you have written for **MovieTrivia**, we've combined expectations and assertions to test both existing UI elements and elements that might not be on screen yet. Note that your UI tests will always attempt to wait for any animations to complete before the next command is executed. This will make sure that you don't have to write asynchronous expectations for any new UI that is added to the screen with an animation.

Summary

Congratulations! You've made it to the end of this lengthy, information-packed chapter. You should know enough about testing and accessibility right now to begin exploring testing in greater depth than we have in this chapter.

No matter how small or big your app, writing automated tests will ensure that your app is of a high quality. More importantly, instead of assuming that something works because it worked before, your automated tests will guarantee that it works because your tests won't pass if you've broken your code.

In this chapter, you have learned the fundamentals about XCTest: when to write tests, which type of tests to write (unit and integration), and how to isolate tests following the Arrange-Act-Assert pattern. You also learned about code coverage and how to measure how much of your code is being tested. Finally, you learned about XCUITest and how it can help you to test parts of your UI.

You also learned that writing testable code sometimes requires you to refactor large portions of code. More often than not, these refactoring sessions leave your code in a much better state than before. Code that is easy to test is often cleaner and more robust than code that is hard to test.

Now that you know how to cover your app with tests, in the next chapter, we'll look at how you can submit your app to the App Store.

20
Submitting Your App to the App Store

Possibly the most exciting part of the development cycle is getting your app into the hands of some real users. The first step in doing so is usually to send out a beta version of your app so you can get feedback and gather some data about how your app is performing before you submit it to the App Store and release your app to the world. Once you're satisfied with the results of your beta test, you must submit your app to Apple so they can review it before your app is released to the App Store.

In this chapter, you'll learn all about packing up your app and submitting it to Apple's App Store Connect portal. Using App Store Connect, you can start beta testing your app, and you can also submit it to Apple for review. App Store Connect is also used to manage your app's App Store description, keywords, promotional images, and more. This chapter will show you how to fill out all the information for your app correctly. You will go through the following steps in this chapter:

- Adding your application to App Store Connect
- Packaging and uploading your app for beta testing
- Preparing your app for launch

These steps closely resemble the process you'll go through when you're ready to launch your app. Let's get right to it, shall we?

Adding your application to App Store Connect

The first thing you're going to want to do when you're ready to release your app is to register your app with App Store Connect. In this section, we are going to learn how to configure a new app in App Store Connect. To access **App Store Connect**, you must be enrolled in the Apple Developer program. You can do this through Apple's Developer portal at `https://developer.apple.com`. After purchasing your membership, you can log in to your App Store Connect account on `https://appstoreconnect.apple.com` using your Apple ID.

After logging in to your App Store Connect account, you are presented with a screen that has a few icons on it:

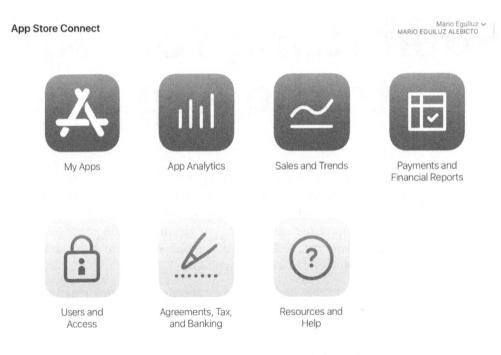

Figure 20.1 – App Store Connect dashboard

This screen is your portal to manage your App Store presence. From here, you can manage test users, track your app's downloads, monitor app usage, and more. But most importantly, it's where you create, upload, and publish your apps to Apple's beta distribution program, called **TestFlight**, and once you're done beta testing, to the App Store. Go ahead and peek around a bit; there won't be much to see yet, but it's good to familiarize yourself with the App Store Connect portal.

Let's create a new app in the App Store Connect portal. Follow these steps:

1. The first step in getting your app out to your users is to navigate to the **My Apps** section. This section is where you'll find all the apps you have created and where you can add new apps. To add a new app, click the + icon in the top left and click **New App**:

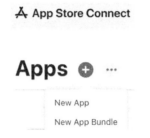

Figure 20.2 – Creating a New App

2. After clicking this, you're presented with a window in which you can fill out all the necessary information about your app. This is where you pick your app's name, select the platform on which it will be released, and a few more properties:

Figure 20.3 – New App parameters

The **Bundle ID** field is a drop-down menu that contains all of the app IDs that you have registered for your team in Apple's Developer portal. If you've been developing with the free-tier developer account up until the last minute, or you haven't used any special features such as push notifications or App Groups, it's possible that your app's Bundle ID is not in the drop-down menu.

If this is the case, you can manually register your Bundle ID in the Developer portal. Follow these steps:

1. Navigate to `https://developer.apple.com/` in your browser.

2. Click the **Account** menu item. You can use the **Account** page to manage certificates, Bundle IDs, devices, and more. A lot of this is automatically taken care of by Xcode, but you'll occasionally find yourself in this portal. For example, let's look at how to manually register your app's Bundle ID:

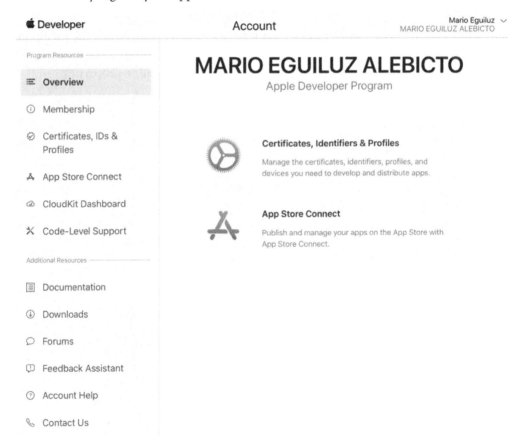

Figure 20.4 – Apple Developer Account dashboard

3. To register your Bundle ID, click on the **Certificates, IDs & Profiles** item on the left-hand side of the page.

4. On the **Certificates, Identifiers & Profiles** page, click **Identifiers** in the menu on the left-hand side. This will present you with a list of currently registered apps. Near the **Identifiers** heading at the top of the list, there's a blue + icon. Click this, then select **App IDs** and the **App** to add a new ID to your profile:

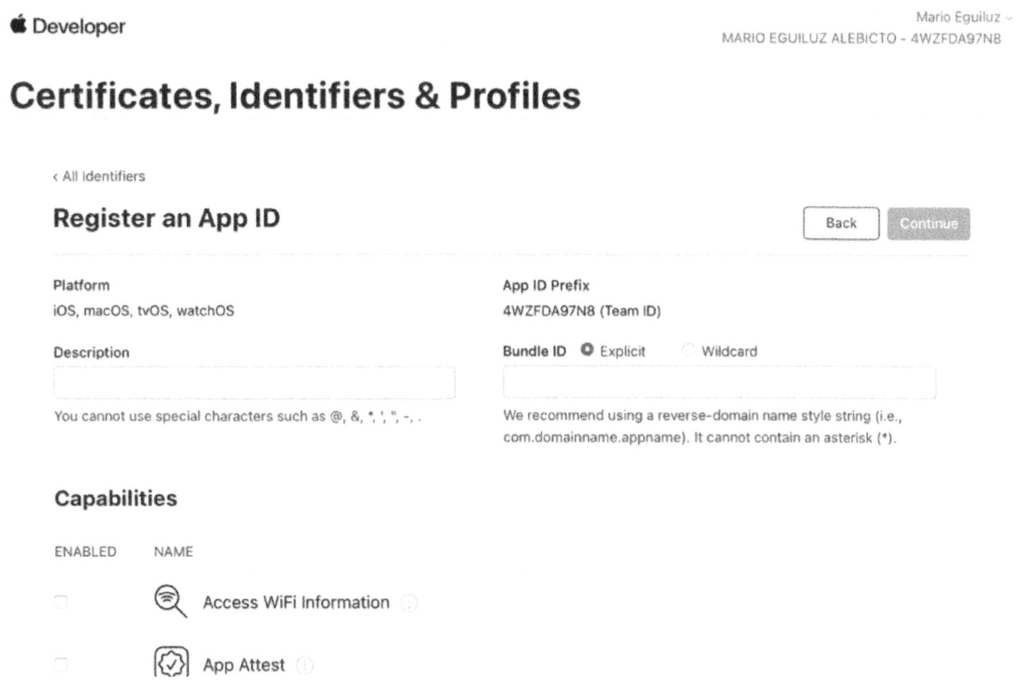

Figure 20.5 – Certifcates, Identifiers & Profiles

To add your Bundle ID, all you need to do is fill in the form fields. You'll want to use a descriptive name for your app name. It can be the same as the name you have set for your app in Xcode, but it can also be a different name; it doesn't have to match.

Make sure to select the **Explicit App ID** field and copy the Bundle ID from your Xcode project. It's important that you perfectly match this. If you don't do this, you'll run into issues later because your app can't be identified if the Bundle ID is incorrect.

Once you've done this, you can save your new ID. You don't have to select any capabilities since Xcode will automatically manage this for you when you enable or disable them in the **Capabilities** tab.

After manually registering your Bundle ID, you should be able to move back to App Store Connect, add a new app, and select your app's Bundle ID. After you've done this and you've created your app in the App Store Connect portal, have a look around in your app's settings. There are a lot of form fields that you can fill in. The first screen you'll see is the **App Information** screen. This is where you fill out the information about your app, assign it a localized name that appears in the App Store, and assign categories to your app:

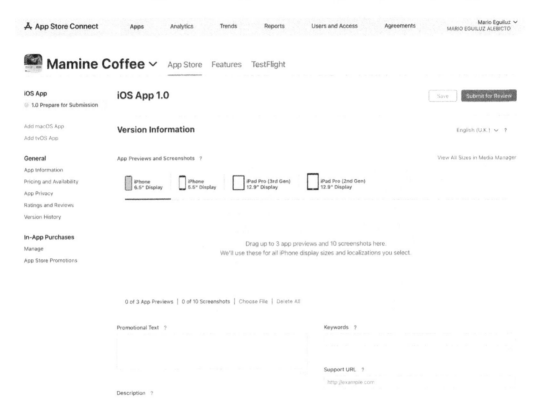

Figure 20.6 – App dashboard screen

Next, there's the **Pricing and Availability** screen. This is where you decide in which countries your app can be downloaded and also how much it costs. Lastly, there is the **Prepare for Submission** menu item.

Whenever you add a new version of your app, you should fill out the form fields on this screen, and there are quite a lot of them. The **Prepare for Submission** form is used to provide screenshots, keywords, a description for your app, privacy policies, and more. Go ahead and have a look at what's in there. Luckily, everything you have to fill in is pretty straightforward.

In this section, we have learned how to register a new app in App Store Connect and the process to generate a new Bundle ID. Once you have registered your app on App Store Connect, you can upload your app. To do this, you use Xcode to package up your app and send it off to App Store Connect. Let's see this in the next section.

Packaging and uploading your app for beta testing

To send your app out to beta testers and eventually real users, you must first archive your app using Xcode. Archiving your app will package up all contents, code, and assets. Follow these steps to archive your app:

1. Select **Generic iOS Device** from the list of devices your app runs on in Xcode:

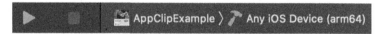

Figure 20.7 – Archiving the app

2. With this build device selected, select **Product | Archive** from the top menu in Xcode. When you do this, a build will start that's a lot slower than usual. That's because Xcode is building your app in release mode so it is optimized and can run on any device.

3. Once the archive is created, Xcode will automatically open the organizer panel for you. In this panel, you get an overview of all the apps and archives that you have created:

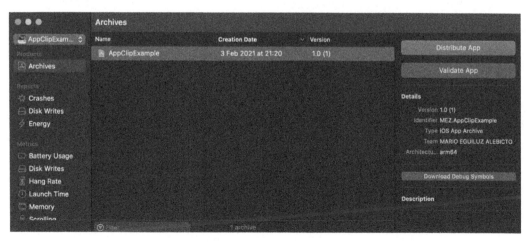

Figure 20.8 – Archive files

Before you archive your app, you should make sure that your app is ready for release. This means that you must add all of the required app icon assets to the `Images.xcassets` resource. If your app icon set is incomplete, your app will be rejected when you try to upload it to App Store Connect, and you'll have to generate your archive all over again.

4. When you're ready to upload your build to App Store Connect to send it to your beta testers and eventually your users through the App Store, you should select your latest build and click the **Upload to App Store** button. A popup will appear to guide you through a couple of settings. You should use the default settings most of the time and click **Next**. Finally, your app will be verified based on metadata and uploaded to App Store Connect. If there are errors in your archive, such as missing assets or unsigned code, you'll learn about it through error messages in the upload popup window.

    When your upload succeeds, you'll also be notified through the popup.

Once you've uploaded your build, you can go to the activity panel for your app in App Store Connect. You can see the builds uploaded under the **TestFlight** tab. If you have just uploaded a build, its status will be **Processing**. Sometimes this step takes a while, but usually no longer than a couple of hours:

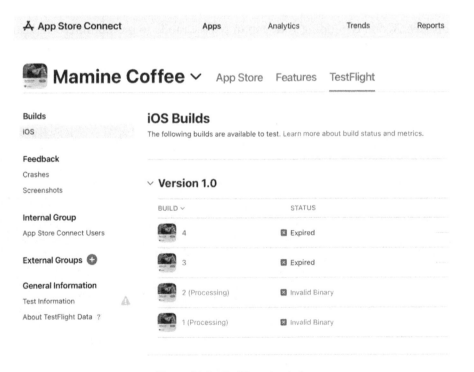

Figure 20.9 – Builds uploaded

While the app is processing, you can start to prepare your **TestFlight** settings. To do so, follow these steps:

1. Select the **TestFlight** menu item and fill in the **Test Information** form. If you're rolling out your beta test internationally, you might want to provide information in multiple languages, but you don't have to.

2. Next, select the **Internal Testing** menu item in the sidebar on the right. In this panel, you can select users that are added to your account for beta testing. This type of testing is often the first type of testing you do, and it's mostly intended for testing apps internally with members of your team or with close friends and family. You can add more internal users to your account through the **Users and Roles** section in App Store Connect.

3. Once your app is processed, you'll receive an email, and you can select which version of your app should be used for internal testing:

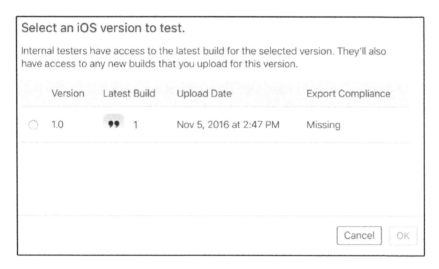

Figure 20.10 – Selecting the app version to test

Once you've added testers and you've selected a build to test, you can click the **Start Testing** button to send out a beta invite to your selected testers. They will receive an email that enables them to download your app through the **TestFlight** app for iOS.

4. Once your internal testers are happy with your app, you can select some external beta testers for your app. **External testers** are typically people who aren't in your team or organization, such as existing users of your app or a selection of people from your app's target audience.

Setting up an external beta test is done identically to how you set up the internal test. You can even use the same build that you used for internal testing for external testing. However, external tests typically require a quick review by Apple before invites can be sent out. These reviews don't take long and passing the beta test review does not mean you'll also pass the App Store review.

This is all you need to know about setting up a beta test through **TestFlight**. When you're happy with the results of your beta test and your app has passed the real-world test, it's time for you to prepare to release your app into the wild through the App Store.

Preparing your app for launch

Moving from beta testing to releasing your app does not require much effort. You use the same version of your app as you've already exported and tested with your users. To be able to submit your app for review by Apple, you have to add more information about your app, and you should set up your App Store presence. Follow these steps:

1. The first thing you should do is create a couple of screenshots of your app. You will add these screenshots to your App Store page, so they should look as good as possible because potential users will use screenshots to determine whether they want to buy or download your app. The simplest way to create screenshots is to take them on a 5.5-inch iPhone and a 12.9-inch iPad.

    You can provide screenshots for every type of device that exists, but you must at least provide them for a 5.5-inch iPhone and a 12.9-inch iPad. You can use the **Media Manager** feature in App Store Connect to upload the large-sized media and have it scaled down for smaller devices:

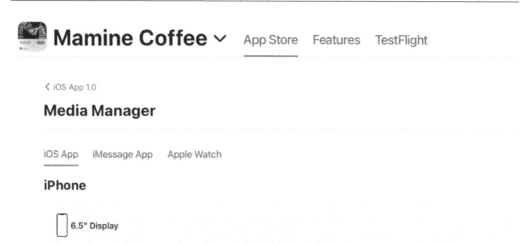

Figure 20.11 – Media Manager

2. After submitting screenshots, you should also fill out a description and keywords for your application. Make sure that your app description is clear, concise, and convincing. You should always try to use as many keywords as you can. Apple uses your keywords to determine whether your app matches search queries from users.

    Try to come up with synonyms or words you would look for when you'd search for an app that does what your app does.

    If your app features an iMessage or Apple Watch app, you should upload screenshots for these apps as well. You can't provide separate keywords or descriptions for these extensions, but they will have their own image galleries in the App Store.

3. The next step in the submission form is to select your app binary and provide some general information about the app and the person responsible for publishing the app. Usually, you'll want to choose the version of the app you've been beta testing up to the point of release.

4. Lastly, you must provide some information to Apple about how your app should be reviewed. If your app requires a demo account, provide the credentials to the reviewer. If your app has been rejected before due to something being unclear, it's usually a good idea to clarify the past misunderstanding in the notes section. This has proven to help for some apps, resulting in accepted reviews at the first try rather than being rejected and providing explanations afterward. When everything is filled out, hit the **Save** button to store all of the information you just entered. Then, if you're satisfied with everything and ready to take the final leap toward releasing your app, press **Submit for Review** to initiate the review process.

Getting your app reviewed by Apple can take from just a single day to a couple of days or even longer. Once you have submitted your app, it's important that you patiently wait until you hear from Apple. Sending them queries about reviewing your app faster or asking them about the current status often yields no results, so there's no point in trying to push Apple for a review.

> **Information**
>
> If you do need to get your app reviewed and released fast and you have a legitimate reason, you can always apply for expedited review. If Apple agrees that a faster review will benefit not just you but also your users, your app could be reviewed in a matter of hours. Note that you should not abuse this. The more often you apply for an expedited review, the less likely Apple is to grant you an exception. Expedited reviews should only be requested in exceptional cases.

Well, time to get some cocoa, coffee, tea, or whatever you prefer to drink. You can now sit back for a while and wait while Apple reviews your app so you can release it to the App Store. Let's wrap up the chapter with a summary.

Summary

This final chapter covered preparing to release your app. You learned how to archive and export your app. You saw how to upload it to App Store Connect and how to distribute your app as a beta release. To wrap everything up, you saw how to submit your app for review by Apple to release it to the App Store. Releasing an app is exciting; you don't know how well your app will perform or whether people will enjoy using it. A good beta test will help a lot, you'll be able to spot bugs and usability issues, but there's nothing like having your app in the hands of actual users.

Most developers invest a lot of time and effort into building their apps, and you are one of them. You picked up this book and went from an iOS enthusiast to an iOS master who knows exactly how to build great apps that make use of iOS' newest and greatest features. When you're ready to launch your own app on the App Store, you'll learn how exciting and nerve-racking it can be to wait for Apple to review and hopefully approve your app. Maybe you get rejected on your first try; that's possible. Don't worry too much about it; even the biggest names get rejected sometimes, and often fixing the reason for the rejection isn't too complicated. Do make sure to read the App Store review guidelines before you submit; these guidelines give a pretty good indication about what you can and can't do in your apps.

Since this is the last chapter in this book, I would like to sincerely thank you for picking up this book and using it as one of the stepping stones toward becoming a master of iOS programming. I hope to have left you with the skills required to venture out on your own, read Apple's documentation, and build amazing applications. Thanks again, and if you've created something cool using this book, please feel free to reach out to me. I would love to see your application.

`Packt.com`

Subscribe to our online digital library for full access to over 7,000 books and videos, as well as industry leading tools to help you plan your personal development and advance your career. For more information, please visit our website.

Why subscribe?

- Spend less time learning and more time coding with practical eBooks and Videos from over 4,000 industry professionals

- Improve your learning with Skill Plans built especially for you

- Get a free eBook or video every month

- Fully searchable for easy access to vital information

- Copy and paste, print, and bookmark content

Did you know that Packt offers eBook versions of every book published, with PDF and ePub files available? You can upgrade to the eBook version at `packt.com` and as a print book customer, you are entitled to a discount on the eBook copy. Get in touch with us at `customercare@packtpub.com` for more details.

At `www.packt.com`, you can also read a collection of free technical articles, sign up for a range of free newsletters, and receive exclusive discounts and offers on Packt books and eBooks.

Other Books You May Enjoy

If you enjoyed this book, you may be interested in these other books by Packt:

iOS 14 Programming for Beginners - Fifth Edition

Ahmad Sahar

ISBN: 978-1-80020-974-9

- Get to grips with the fundamentals of Xcode 12 and Swift 5.3, the building blocks of iOS development

- Understand how to prototype an app using storyboards

- Discover the Model-View-Controller design pattern and how to implement the desired functionality within an app

- Implement the latest iOS features, such as widgets and App Clips

- Convert an existing iPad app into an Apple Silicon Mac app

- Design, deploy, and test your iOS applications with design patterns and best practices

SwiftUI Cookbook

Giordano Scalzo , Edgar Nzokwe

ISBN: 978-1-83898-186-0

- Explore various layout presentations in SwiftUI such as HStack, VStack, LazyHStack, and LazyVGrid
- Create a cross-platform app for iOS, macOS, and watchOS
- Get up to speed with drawings in SwiftUI using built-in shapes, custom paths, and polygons
- Discover modern animation and transition techniques in SwiftUI
- Add user authentication using Firebase and Sign in with Apple
- Handle data requests in your app using Core Data
- Solve the most common SwiftUI problems, such as integrating a MapKit map, unit testing, snapshot testing, and previewing layouts

Packt is searching for authors like you

If you're interested in becoming an author for Packt, please visit `authors. packtpub.com` and apply today. We have worked with thousands of developers and tech professionals, just like you, to help them share their insight with the global tech community. You can make a general application, apply for a specific hot topic that we are recruiting an author for, or submit your own idea.

Leave a review - let other readers know what you think

Please share your thoughts on this book with others by leaving a review on the site that you bought it from. If you purchased the book from Amazon, please leave us an honest review on this book's Amazon page. This is vital so that other potential readers can see and use your unbiased opinion to make purchasing decisions, we can understand what our customers think about our products, and our authors can see your feedback on the title that they have worked with Packt to create. It will only take a few minutes of your time, but is valuable to other potential customers, our authors, and Packt. Thank you!

Index

Symbols

3D space
  content, placing in 449-453

A

act 477
action segues 104
Active Compilation Conditions
  using 355-357
adaptive colors 34-36
animations
  interacting, with pan gesture
    recognizer 129-132
  progress, controlling 125-129
  vibrancy, adding to 132-134
API responses
  mocking 484-489
app
  packaging and uploading, for
    beta testing 517-519
  preparing, for launch 520-522
App Clip Experiences
  testing 366-369

App Clips
  about 2, 3
  Active Compilation Conditions,
    using 355-357
  configuring 357
  deploying 346, 347
  experiences, configuring 362-365
  guidelines 5
  installing 342, 343
  invocation methods 4, 345
  link handling, configuring 358-361
  linking 357
  process, stages 4
  resources and code, sharing
    with 351-355
  Smart App Banner, configuring 366
  stages 344
  target, creating 348-351
  triggering 357
  use cases 3
  user journey 3, 4, 343-345
application
  adding, to App Store Connect 512-516
App Store Connect
  application, adding to 512-516

App Transport Security (ATS) 235
ARKit
  about 428
  physical environment, tracking
    with 429, 430
  renders content 428, 429
ARKit 4, for iOS 14 and iPadOS
  features 8
ARKit Quick Look
  about 429
  using 431
  view controller, implementing 432-436
arrange 477
assert 478
asset catalog, for Dark Mode
  custom adaptive colors, using 44-49
  custom adaptive images, using 51
associated types
  protocols, improving 176-179
audio
  playing 272
audio player
  audio controls, implementing 276-279
  creating 275, 276
  media, playing in background 282-286
  song metadata, displaying 281, 282
  time scrubber, implementing 279, 280
Augmented Reality (AR) 428
Augmented Reality gallery
  content, placing in 3D space 449-453
  images, preparing for tracking 443-445
  image tracking, adding 443
  image tracking experience,
    building 445-449
  implementing 442, 443

B

beta testing
  app, packaging and uploading
    for 517-519

C

code
  optimizing, for testability 480-482
code coverage 493-496
code testing 474
collectionViewContentSize
  implementing 91
Combine framework
  about 312
  Operators 317
  Publisher 312, 313
  Subject 323
  Subscriber 313-317
combineLatest operator
  using 320, 321
Core Data
  about 183
  adding, to application 186-189
  data, filtering with predicates 204, 205
  data persistence 195, 196
  data, reading with simple
    fetch request 201-204
  persistence code, refactoring 199, 200
  reacting, to database changes 206
  stack 184-186
Core Data, database changes
  NSFetchedResultsController,
    implementing 206-212

Core Data model
  creating 189-191
  entities, using 193-195
  persisting 196-199
  relationships, defining 192, 193
Core Data objects
  updating, with fetched data 225, 226
Core Image
  used, for manipulating photos 294-298
CoreML
  about 240-242
  models, obtaining 242, 243
  models, using 243-247
Core ML API
  using, to retrieve collections
    of models 257-259
CoreML, combining with computer vision
  about 247
  image classifier, implementing 248-251
  Vision framework 247, 248
Core ML Model Deployment 9
Core ML models
  encrypting 265-269
  encryption 9, 10
CreateML
  used, for training models 252
  used, for training Natural
    Language model 252-255
  used, for training Vision model 255, 256
custom modal presentation transition
  implementing 139-146
custom UICollectionViewLayout
  implementing 90
custom UITableViewCell override 74-76

D

Dark Mode
  about 26
  accessibility in 55
  appearance, specifying for
    ViewControllers 55
  appearance, specifying for views 55
  appearance, specifying for windows 55
  changes, handling programatically
    with trait collection 53, 54
  core developer, concepts of 28, 29
  exploring 52
  from, inside Xcode 29-33
  need for 26, 27
  views, working with in 33
  using, with SwiftUI 52, 53
  working, with asset catalog for 44
Dark Mode, views
  adaptive colors 34-36
  programmatic approach, using 42-44
  semantic colors 37-41
data persistence 195, 196
default behavior
  protocols, extending 173-176
dependency injection 188
dynamism
  adding, with UIKit Dynamics 134-139

E

enums 157
error-proof streams
  building, with Operators 333-339
external testers 519

F

Failure type 319
fetched data
    Core Data objects, updating
        with 225, 226
fetch logic
    implementing 227-231
filter operator
    using 317, 318
Float16 24

G

generics
    flexibility, adding 180-182
geofences
    setting up 308-310
GET request 218

H

hand detection implementation
    about 384, 385
    detected points, displaying 390-393
    detected points, processing 390-393
    performing, in video session 388-390
    TODO tasks 385
    video session, creating 386, 387
hand landmarks
    about 382-384
    recognizing, in real time 382
    types 383
HTTP protocol 218

I

Identity Inspector 499
ImageAnalyzer 248
images
    preparing, for tracking 443-445
image tracking
    adding 443
image tracking experience
    building 445-449
integration test 476
iOS app
    accessibility, making 497-499
iPad app
    exploring 458-460
    optimizing, for Mac 462-472
    transforming, to macOS 460-462
iPad app, files
    Datasource.swift file 459
    DetailViewController.swift file 459
    MasterViewController.swift file 459
isolating test 477

J

JSON
    in Swift 222-225

L

launch argument
    passing, to app 501, 502
layoutAttributesForElements(in*)
    implementing 91, 92
layoutAttributesForItem(at*)
    implementing 92

layouts, creating with UIStackView
   about 107
   labels, containing in stack view 108-111
logic testing
   with XCTest 474

M

Mac Catalyst
   discovering 456
   drawback 456
   feature, exploring 457
Mac Catalyst app
   building 458
   iPad app, exploring 458-460
   iPad app, optimizing for Mac 462-472
   iPad app, transforming to
      macOS 460-462
machine learning
   about 240, 241
   improvements 9
machine learning model collections 9
manual segues
   about 104
   creating 106, 107
map operator
   using 318, 319
merge operator
   using 321, 322
Model Deployment
   used, for updating models remotely 256
models
   collections, retrieving with
      Core ML API 257-259
   deploying 259-265
      preparing 259-265
      training, with CreateML 252
      updating, remotely with Model
         Deployment 256
movie cell
   rating, adding to 234
movie object
   updating, with popularity
      rating 231, 232
movie ratings
   changes, observing to 236, 237
MovieTrivia app 478
multiple animations
   working with 120-122
multiple-size widgets
   implementing 410-416
multiple threads
   visualizing 233, 234
MustC application 190

N

Natural Language model
   training, with CreateML 252-255
navigation, implementing with segues
   about 102
   details view, creating 103
neural network 241
NSFetchedResultsController
   implementing 206-212
NSManagedObjectContext
   persisting code, refactoring 214, 215
   using, for multiple instances 212-214

O

Operators
about 317
combineLatest, using 320, 321
combining, with Publishers 325-333
combining, with Subscribers 325-333
filter, using 317, 318
map, using 318, 319
merge, using 321, 322
reduce, using 319
scan, using 320
used, for building error-proof
    streams 333-339
zip, using 322, 323
Optimize Interface for Mac 456
Output type 319

P

pan gesture recognizer
interacting with 129-132
persistent store coordinator 186
photos
manipulating, with Core Image 294-298
pictures
capturing 286-289
storing 287-289
POST request 218
predicates
used, for filtering data 204, 205
protocols
defining 166-169
extending, with default
    behavior 173-176
implementing 166

improving, with associated
    types 176-179
traits, checking instead of types 169-173
Publishers
about 312, 313
combining, with Operators 325-333
combining, with Subscribers 325-333

Q

question loader 482, 484
question model
using, for consistency 489-492

R

rating
adding, to movie cell 234
reduce operator
using 319
reference types
need for 162, 163
versus value types 158
working with 150-153
reference types, versus value types
usage 159-161
region of interest 378-381

S

scan operator
using 320
SceneKit
exploring 439
scene, creating 439-442

segues
  about 104-106
  implementing 104-106
  navigation, implementing with 102
semantic colors 37-41
shouldInvalidateLayout
    (forBoundsChange*)
  implementing 92
Smart App Banner
  configuring 366
Smart Rotate 397
Smart Stack 6, 397
sprite 436
SpriteKit
  exploring 436, 437
  scene, creating 438, 439
structs 155, 156
Subject
  about 323
  CurrentValueSubject, working 323, 324
  PassthroughSubject, working 324
Subscribers
  about 313-317
  combining, with Operators 325-333
  combining, with Publishers 325-333
support vector machine 241
Swift
  types 150
  types, differentiating 158
  working, with reference types 150-153
  working, with value types 153, 155
Swift 5.2
  about 11
  callable values, of user-defined
    nominal types 12, 13
  improved diagnostics 15, 16

key path expressions, as functions 11, 12
lazy filtering order, is now
    reversed 14, 15
subscripts, declaring as default
    arguments 13, 14
Swift 5.3
  about 16
  enum cases, as protocol witnesses 23
  Float16 24
  implicit self in escaping closures,
    availability increasing when reference
    cycles are unlikely to occur 20, 21
  multi-pattern catch clauses 16-18
  multiple trailing closures 18
  refine didSet semantics 23
  synthesized comparable conformance,
    for enum types 19, 20
  type-based program entry
    points - @main 21
  where clauses, using on contextually
    generic declarations 22
SwiftUI
  custom cell, creating equivalent 98, 99
  Dark Mode, using with 52, 53
  list, building 96, 97
  lists, working with 93
SwiftUI project
  creating 94, 95

T

targeted deployments 9
tests
  determining, to write 475
  guidelines 475
test suite
  setting up, with XCTest 478, 479

test type
  selecting 476
TextAnalyzerCloud 257
threading 234
TrueDepth 430

U

UICollectionView
  cell selection 93
  collection view, setting up 80-84
  custom layout, assigning to
    collection view 92, 93
  exploring 89
  working with 79
UICollectionViewDelegateFlowLayout
  layout, implementing with 85-88
UICollectionViewDelegateFlowLayout,
    methods
  footer and header, sizing 89
  section and spacing 89
  size of an item (cell) 88
UIKit Dynamics
  dynamism, adding with 134-139
UIStackView
  layouts, creating with 107
UITableView
  cell selection, in table views 78, 79
  contacts data, fetching 64-67
  delegations 69, 70
  exploring 76
  prepping, to display contacts 67-69
  project, setting up 60-63
  protocol 69, 70
  reuse identifiers, 77
  table views, prefetching 77
  working with 60

UITableView protocols
  conforming to 71-74
UI tests
  recording 500, 501
UIView
  appearance, specifying for 55
UIView.animate
  using 118-120
UIViewController
  appearance, specifying for 55
UIViewPropertyAnimator
  refactoring with 122-124
  using 118-120
unit test 476
URLSession
  basics 219-222
  data, fetching from web 218
user interface (UI)
  testing, with XCUITest 497
  updating 503-508
user location
  obtaining 303-305
  permission, for accessing
    location data 300-303
  requesting 300
  subscribing, to changes 305-308
user privacy
  improving 10

V

value types
  need for 163
  versus reference types 158
  working with 153-155
video
  playing 272
  recording 286-293

storing 289-293
video player
creating 273-275
view controllers
data loading, updating 112
data, passing between 111
model, passing to details page 112, 113
outlets, updating 113, 114
view controller transitions
customizing 139
custom modal presentation transition,
implementing 139-146
view model
creating 114, 115
Vision framework 247, 248, 372-376
Vision framework, features
hand landmarks, recognizing
in real time 382
region of interest 378-381
text, recognizing in images 376, 377
Vision framework, text detection ways
accurate recognition 376
fast recognition 376
Vision model
training, with CreateML 255, 256

W

widget
about 396
data, refreshing 422-426
developing 399-401

extension, creating 401-409
guidelines 398
options 398
providing, with data and
configuration 416-422
widget API 397
widget extension 7, 398
WidgetKit
about 6, 396, 397
guidelines 7, 8
options 7
window
appearance, specifying for 55
world tracking 430

X

Xcode
Dark Mode, from inside 29-33
XCTest
used, for setting up test suite 478-480
used, for testing logic 474
XCUITest
about 497
used, for testing user interface (UI) 497

Z

zip operator
using 322, 323

Made in the USA
Monee, IL
12 August 2021